WORKING LIVES

'This book will be a valuable addition for students and scholars of twentieth-century working lives and will undoubtedly be cited as a key text. It is a sensitive, balanced and richly informed survey.' – **Sheila Blackburn,** *University of Liverpool*

'A comprehensive, thoroughly researched text, that makes excellent use of oral history transcripts.' – **Alan Booth,** *University of Exeter*

In the wake of economic depression, employment and equality in the workplace have never been more important. In this accessible study, Arthur McIvor investigates meanings of work and how, why and to what degree working lives have been transformed in Britain since the Second World War. The book presents a range of research data and primary material, including oral testimonies, letting the workers speak for themselves and express what work signifies to them.

Covering key themes such as gender, race, class, disability and health, it is an ideal resource for students of History, Social Sciences, Human Resource Management and Business Studies, and anyone with an interest in the history of work.

Also by Arthur McIvor

A HISTORY OF WORK IN BRITAIN, 1880–1950
ORGANISED CAPITAL
LETHAL WORK: A History of the Asbestos Tragedy in Scotland
(*with Ronnie Johnston*)
MINERS' LUNG: A History of Dust Disease in British Coal Mining
(*with Ronnie Johnston*)

Working Lives
Work in Britain since 1945

ARTHUR MCIVOR

First published 2013 by
PALGRAVE MACMILLAN

Palgrave Macmillan in the UK is an imprint of Macmillan Publishers Limited, registered in England, company number 785998, of Houndmills, Basingstoke, Hampshire RG21 6XS.

Palgrave Macmillan in the US is a division of St Martin's Press LLC, 175 Fifth Avenue, New York, NY 10010.

Palgrave Macmillan is the global academic imprint of the above companies and has companies and representatives throughout the world.

Palgrave® and Macmillan® are registered trademarks in the United States, the United Kingdom, Europe and other countries

ISBN 978–1–4039–8766–2 hardback
ISBN 978–1–4039–8767–9 paperback

This book is printed on paper suitable for recycling and made from fully managed and sustained forest sources. Logging, pulping and manufacturing processes are expected to conform to the environmental regulations of the country of origin.

A catalogue record for this book is available from the British Library.

A catalog record for this book is available from the Library of Congress.

Contents

List of Tables

Acknowledgements

In the process of researching and writing this book I have been assisted by many people who I would like to thank. My most important debt is to all those workers who have agreed to be interviewed and whose stories permeate and enliven this account. Oral history is a wonderful field in which to work and I have been blessed by narrators who have contributed by sharing their personal memories in a series of projects on the history of work since 1945. Many of these work-life testimonies are archived in the Scottish Oral History Centre (SOHC) at the University of Strathclyde and referenced in the text and the bibliography. And colleagues in the SOHC and the History Department (now the School of Humanities) at the University of Strathclyde have been enormously supportive over the years and I want to thank each and every one of them. All those involved in interviewing on SOHC history of work projects should be singled out for special thanks: Ronnie Johnston, David Walker, Andrew Perchard, Angela Bartie, Susan Morrison, Hilary Young and our lost but always remembered dear friend Neil Rafeek. Andrew Perchard and David Walker also read the whole manuscript and provided much constructive critical feedback, so I want to especially thank them for their perceptive insights and assistance, which is very much appreciated. Other colleagues who I'd like to thank who read part of the manuscript, engaged with some of the issues and/or assisted with leads, ideas and references are Anne Borsay, Joe Melling, Chris Sellers, Susan Morrison, Lynn Abrams, Callum Brown, Tim Strangleman, Kathleen Ryall, Angela Turner, Juliette Pattinson, Emma Reilly, Geoff Tweedale and Steve High. I have especially benefitted from working closely with David Walker on our AHRC-funded *Glasgow Working Lives* oral history project (2010–11) and subsequently in the SOHC, and would like to record my appreciation of David's brilliant interviewing, unstinting support, good humour and lively critical engagement with many of the ideas and issues explored in this book. I also owe an enormous debt to all the postgraduate and undergraduate students at the University of Strathclyde who have explored aspects of the social and cultural history of work in my honours special subject class, my Masters course modules on work and the body and all those I've been privileged to supervise as research Masters and PhD students over the past couple of decades.

I also want to thank all the archivists and curators who have assisted with my search for oral testimonies, autobiographies and other relevant source material and provided permission to use material. They include Dave Welsh, Stefan Dickers and Chris Coates in relation to the TUC-sponsored *Britain at Work*: *Voices from the Workplace*, *1945–1995* oral history project (these interview transcripts were accessed in 2012 and the url address is provided in the bibliography, rather than at every extract in the text), Christine Wall and Linda Clarke (building workers' stories), Ian MacDougall and Hamish Fraser (Scottish Working People's History Trust), Terry Brotherstone, Hugo Manson, Rob Perks, Carole McCallum, Martin Bellamy, Sian Reynolds and Toby Butler.

The author and publishers wish to thank the following for permission to reproduce copyright material: the Health and Safety Executive and the Office for National Statistics for statistical data licensed under the Open Government Licence v.1.0; the Trades Union Congress, TUC Library Collections (j.goddard@londonmet.ac.uk), for material in oral interview transcripts from the *Britain at Work: Voices from the Workplace, 1945–1995* project accessed at http://www.unionhistory.info/britainatwork/resources/audio.php; Taylor & Francis Books (UK) for material on p. 276, from John Burnett, *Idle Hands: The Experience of Unemployment, 1790–1990*, Routledge (1994); Palgrave Macmillan for material on p. 160, from B.R. Mitchell, *International Historical Statistics: Europe, 1750–1993*, 4th edn, Palgrave Macmillan (1988); Wiley for material on p. 40 and pp. 43–78 from George S. Bain and Richard Price, *Profiles of Union Growth*, Blackwell (1980); Cambridge University Press for material on p. 292 from Duncan Gallie, 'The Labour Force', in A. H. Halsey and J. Webb (eds) *Twentieth Century British Social Trends*, Palgrave Macmillan (2000); Institute for Social and Economic Research, University of Essex for material from British Household Panel Survey, 1991, on p. 49 from Helen Barnes, *Working for a Living? Employment, Benefits and the Living Standards of Disabled People*, Policy Press (2000); and material on p. 105 from K. Hinds, and L. Jarvis, 'The Gender Gap' in R. Jowell *et al.* (eds) *British Social Attitudes: The 17*th *Report. Focusing on Diversity*, Sage Publications (2000). Every effort has been made to trace rights holders, but if any have been inadvertently overlooked the publishers would be pleased to make the necessary arrangements at the first opportunity.

Welcome financial assistance has also been provided from a number of sources, which has been greatly appreciated, including the Arts and Humanities Research Council, the Wellcome Trust and the British Academy. The University of Strathclyde has provided a really supportive research environment over the years, including research leave to finish this book and major investment in the oral history work of the SOHC. Amongst individuals who I'd like to highlight for thanks in this respect are my colleagues Richard Finlay, Jim Mills and David Goldie. I'm also most grateful to my publishers, Palgrave, and their Humanities team – Jenna Steventon, Jenni Burnell and Felicity Noble – for their encouragement, advice, support and patience through the long gestation of this book. I'd also like to thank the three anonymous Palgrave academic referees who provided really excellent critical feedback on the first submitted typescript. Any errors, of course, are my responsibility alone.

Most important of all I want to record my thanks and appreciation to my former research collaborator and friend Ronnie Johnston, who took early retirement in December 2010. Ronnie and I worked together for more than a decade on a series of occupational health history research projects. Discussions with Ronnie over the years have helped shape this book and I deeply appreciate his contribution, support, enthusiasm and his friendship.

On a personal note, I have also benefitted enormously from the support, love and encouragement of my partner Margot and my sons Kieran and Tom. They have provided inspiration and contributed in so many ways, not least keeping me going through rough times when I've been flagging. This book is dedicated to them. Can't thank them enough.

ARTHUR MCIVOR

Abbreviations

AHRC	Arts and Humanities Research Council
ASLEF	Associated Society of Locomotive Engineers and Firemen
BME	Black and Minority Ethnic
CAA	Clydeside Action on Asbestos
CBI	Confederation of British Industries
CRE	Commission for Racial Equality
DDA	Disability Discrimination Act
DHSS	Department of Health and Social Security
DPEA	Disabled Persons (Employment) Act
ESDS	Economic and Social Data Service
EU	European Union
EVWS	European Voluntary Workers Scheme
FEA	Fair Employment Agency
GMB	General, Municipal, Boilermakers and Allied Trade Union
HSE	Health and Safety Executive
HSWA	Health and Safety at Work Act
ILO	International Labour Office
IRR	Institute of Race Relations
MSD	Muscular-Skeletal Disorder
NALGO	National Association of Local Government Officers
NCB	National Coal Board
NHS	National Health Service
NUR	National Union of Railwaymen
NUTGW	National Union of Tailors and Garment Workers
PEP	Political and Economic Planning
RIDDOR	Reporting of Injuries, Diseases and Dangerous Occurences Regulations
RRA	Race Relations Act
RSI	Repetitive Strain Injury
SMR	Standardized Mortality Rate
SOHC	Scottish Oral History Centre

SPAID Society for the Prevention of Asbestosis and Industrial
       Diseases
STUC   Scottish Trades Union Congress
SWPHT Scottish Working People's History Trust
TB   Tuberculosis
TGWU   Transport and General Workers' Union
TUC   Trades Union Congress
UCATT Union of Construction, Allied Trades and Technicians

Introduction

Work occupies a central part of our lives and has multiple meanings for those engaged in it. For many, it provides a purposeful and fulfilling activity to fill time and a focus to one's life, a vehicle to express oneself, a method of earning a living and, in many cases, supporting a family. It can be a source of lasting social relationships, of politicization, of joy and stress as well as numbing alienation. It provides 'intrinsic' and 'extrinsic' rewards, whilst it can both enhance health and destroy it. Work has been profoundly important in people's lives in the past and continues to be so in the present. This book explores the mutating nature and meaning of work in Britain since the Second World War, engaging with key (and often contested) debates, setting contemporary issues within their historical context and examining policy responses. Continuity and change in employment since 1945 is the core theme. However, my approach to the subject matter is somewhat unconventional. My aim here is to provide a refocused history pivoting on the personal narratives of workers themselves and how work identities and the meaning of work are articulated, perceived and signified by those who experienced it directly. The book thus draws heavily on autobiographies and oral testimonies, amongst a wide range of primary and secondary source material, to engage with the literature and the historiographies of work, and to offer some re-interpretation of the meaning of working lives and the connotations and impact of work. Undeniably, work meant different things to different people. At the core of the argument here is that work has changed in complex and sometimes contradictory ways and that work identities, forged in prevailing economic and material circumstances, were fundamentally shaped by gender, disability and race.

A lot has changed in Britain since the 1940s in a period of remarkable economic, social and cultural transformation. What has not come to pass, however, is the 'leisure society' that some visionary pre-Second World War thinkers – including John Maynard Keynes – predicted.

Time in employment has not contracted to 15 or so hours a week and been replaced by more recreation, nor has a revolution in work precipitated the abolition of poverty or disappearance of wealth and income inequalities. Lives remain dominated and defined by work. Nonetheless, the way that we do our work has altered profoundly in so many ways in less than a normal lifetime since the Second World War. This book investigates how, why and to what degree working lives have been transformed – focusing on paid employment over the past seventy years. This is a period when the pace of change has been particularly rapid, when employment and working lives fundamentally altered as the British economy evolved from one aligned on manual labour to a service-based, knowledge-oriented and computer-centred economy where non-manual labour dominated. We now mostly process information and provide services, rather than manufacture goods. Around 90% of all employed women and 70% of all employed men currently (2010 figures) work in the service (or tertiary) sector – that is in occupations that do not produce tangible goods, but provide a 'service' for other people, such as insurance, banking, distribution and transport.

Other key changes have been the influx of black and ethnic minority labour, the deregulation of markets from the 1980s and the shift from the pattern of 'standard' full-time secure work over a lifetime, to 'non-standard' and more flexible and profoundly insecure forms of work – part-time working and temporary contracts, with more career changes and greater risk of under-employment and unemployment. This has been linked to the notion of a 'risk society' (Beck, 1992), where labour market insecurity is the norm. But how have these changes been experienced and what did they signify for workers? Was work becoming incrementally degraded, even dehumanized (as some have argued)? Or did such changes represent amelioration, emancipation and upward social mobility? Who were the beneficiaries and who lost out as Britain's mixed capitalist economy adapted and morphed in the second half of the twentieth century? The changing relationship of women to the labour market as larger numbers entered paid employment (swelling the number of dual-income families and household earnings) has also been a key development, and along with this traditional notions of femininity and masculinity have been challenged. What did this mean for working women and men? Has there been a convergence over time in what employment signified for male and female workers?

The state also came to play a key role in working lives, with the extension of regulation deep into the workplace and the labour market during the Second World War and extended and sustained in the thirty years thereafter. This marked a clear discontinuity from the Depression era of the 1930s. In turn this was reversed from the 1980s with the revival of neo-liberal economic policies, deregulation, privatization and the shifting power balance from labour to capital. Globalization was a key force that contributed to shaping these changes. How did such transformations affect working lives? How did they impact on different groups, refracted through class, race and gender? In this wider context, the nature of authority, control and power in the workplace has also mutated as British capitalism responded to competition and labour pressures in an increasingly globalized marketplace. How did workers feel this and how did they respond? One impact was the growth – up to the mid–late 1970s – and the subsequent decline of trade unionism within the workplace and British society. What did trade unionism signify to workers? The trade unions were key players in representing and protecting employees and in the struggle with management and employers to maintain and extend wages, challenge inequalities and guard the dignity of working lives. However, they could also be sectional and exclusionist, racist and sexist in their policies. They operated within a system of production characterized by exploitation and deep inequalities in opportunities and rewards. Within this power struggle, the post-war period saw a concerted assault on inequality and unfairness in the workplace and the labour market, firstly in relation to gender, then race and latterly disability and age. The outcomes were mixed and the product of a combination of progressive forces, but included equal pay, race and disability legislation, the minimum wage and the Equality Act, 2010 – which attempted to streamline and coordinate the regulation of all unequal treatment, including on the basis of sexuality, race, gender and disability.

This book does not claim to cover all the territory, or provide a comprehensive critical review of labour sociology and work theory. There are many researchers much more competent to do this and a wide body of excellent scholarship to choose from (and the bibliography provides some guidance to this). Theories of work have been debated in a voluminous literature and scholars such as Strangleman and Warren, Watson, Grint, Noon and Blyton and provide excellent evaluations of labour sociology. Indeed, one of the difficulties for the contemporary historian is the sheer volume of source material (and I apologize to the reader if I have missed referring to your research in this field). In the place of comprehensive coverage, this book tries to take a fresh approach, providing both a synthesis and a re-focused interpretation of changing working lives since 1945 based around the personal and individual. As such, this book pivots around discourse and experience, embodiment and the emotional experience of work. This reflects a shift in the literature over the past two decades or so to a focus upon the personal and on everyday lives, upon beliefs and lived experience. Hence the book title, *Working Lives*.

My aim is to engage with historiographies in the field and explore what it *felt* like to be a worker in this period and to what extent the meaning and experience of work changed over time. What did work *signify* to those 'blue collar' workers such as coal miners, car workers, clothing and textile workers engaged in an economy centred on manufacturing at mid-twentieth century and the non-manual 'knowledge workers' that dominate in the early twenty-first century? How have the radical changes in the second half of the twentieth century affected the essence of work and its extrinsic and intrinsic meaning? What have the changes meant for citizenship and dignity at work? I have tried to elucidate such issues by a strong concentration in this account upon the *personal* experiences of workers. This book draws upon a number of oral history archives and oral history based studies, such as the interviews with London workers in the TUC-sponsored *Britain at Work* project – as well as my own interviewing fieldwork with Ronnie Johnston (and other colleagues) in coal mining and the 'heavy' industries and my fruitful collaboration with David Walker (and Glasgow Museums) in the AHRC-funded *Glasgow Working Lives* oral history project (see the bibliography). Employment is examined, where possible, through the lens of such personal accounts and memories, in as an inclusive way as possible, weaving the experience of men and women, young and old, black and ethnic minorities and the disabled into the narrative. As such, this book aims to make a contribution to the growing literature on the history of everyday lives. As a social historian, I also hope that it provides some useful historical context for the contemporary sociology of work, hence providing a bridge of sorts between the present and the recent past. This addresses one of the recurring criticisms in the sociological literature relating to how current debates about the trajectory of work in Britain and the developed world are distorted by a lack of historical perspective.

Whilst based on a wide range of primary and secondary sources, this book explicitly integrates evidence from work-life oral testimonies. It has been impossible to do full justice to the rich seam of such personal evidence, but none the less I have tried to weave workers' own narratives into this account as far as possible. Oral history methodology has much potential in the study of work, but memory evidence requires sensitive and careful treatment. Several points relating to this might be briefly made here. Firstly, oral history interviews are both interpretive and informative. Reflecting back in work-life interviews workers are genuinely trying to recall their experience but at the same time are selecting, sieving and ordering memories, struggling to interpret meaning and make sense of the lives they have lived. Hence oral historians have developed the concepts of 'composure' and 'discomposure' to describe states of mind and the nature of memory narrative construction in the interview encounter (see, for example, Summerfield, 1998; Thomson, 1994). My approach here is influenced by the ideas of the Italian oral historian Alessandro Portelli and his assertion that what narrators say is significant and full of meaning even if it is untrue or misremembered, whilst metaphors, anecdotes and repetitions in oral testimonies and autobiographies have significance (Portelli, 1991, 51; Portelli, 2011). Secondly, intersubjectivity comes into play in such interviews. Oral historians have identified that narrators respond to and are influenced by the class, gender, age, ethnicity and other characteristics of their interviewers (see, for example, Pattinson, 2007). Memories can also be 'contaminated' – shaped and influenced by public discourses – the circulating media, books, films and the like – something that has been referred to as the 'cultural circuit' (Thomson, 1994). Thirdly, as linguists have shown, oral testimonies are constructed according to certain rules and conventions, and different types of narrative are discernible. For example, an 'activist' work narrative was characterized by the juxtaposition of employers as villains and workers (and invariably their trade unions) as the heroes of the story in a struggle against inequality and exploitation (see, for example, McIvor in Abrams and Brown, 2010, pp. 103–30). Memory theory has also advanced significantly in recent years, and, if anything, has confirmed the basic reliability of long-term memory and validated the veracity of oral history as a methodology (Abrams, 2010, pp. 78–105). Almost all types of primary sources are subjective to some degree and oral history theorists have done much over recent years to advance our understanding of the dynamics involved in the process of testimony gathering. This has significantly enhanced the value of oral history methodology, which has become more sophisticated. The contention here is that autobiographical and oral evidence deserves to be utilized more widely in the study of work. For those readers interested in but perhaps unfamiliar with oral history, I would recommend Paul Thompson's seminal text, *The Voice of the Past*, as an introduction, followed perhaps by Lynn Abrams stimulating *Oral History Theory* and Robert Perks and Alistair Thomson's comprehensive edited collection, *The Oral History Reader*.

This book is organized thematically. Chapter 1 investigates the changes in the labour force from 1945 to the present, drawing upon a range of sources, including the decennial census and the Labour Force Surveys. It seeks to delineate what people worked at, reflect on the nature of labour market segregation and inequalities and identify and discuss some of the key changes over time. Chapter 2 explores the meaning of work and work identities, engaging with the literature in this area and drawing upon a wide range of personal accounts of workers – including oral history interviews – to discuss work identities. It is argued here that the work ethic has been somewhat misunderstood, that it has mutated, rather than atrophied, and that it is premature, as some scholars do, to talk of the 'collapse' or 'death' of work. Chapter 3 focuses upon the gendering of work, the domination of men in the mid-twentieth century workplace, examines the changing sexual division of labour, the evolving relationship of women with the labour market and the campaign for gender equality in the workplace. It addresses a relatively neglected area in the literature by exploring the way that work forged masculinities and how male identities were expressed in the workplace. Chapter 4 investigates race, ethnicity and work, using a range of personal accounts to reconstruct the experience of migrant labour, black and ethnic minority workers in the postwar British workplace, the attitudes of 'host' white workers and their trade unions. It aims to understand the extent and limits of the postwar colour bar and the prevalence of prejudice and discrimination, as well as the campaign for racial equality in the workplace.

Work was experienced and felt through the senses, the mind and the body. Chapter 5 focuses on the body in the workplace, investigating how employment impacted upon health and well-being, in both positive and negative ways. I draw widely upon oral testimony again here to explore such interactions. The discussion ranges from the fatigue, injuries and chronic occupational diseases associated with the manual labour that dominated in the 1950s, to the modern-day overwork culture and epidemic of work-related stress. These work-body encounters could have serious ramifications for people causing trauma, disability and inability to work which led to profound changes in identity and lifestyle. Chapter 6 investigates the patterns of power, representation, resistance and industrial relations in post-war British employment, focusing on the role played by trade unions in the workplace and their responses to employers, management and the state. Workers are perceived here as active agents capable of resisting and mediating managerial exploitation, though their capacities were intimately affected by wider economic, social and cultural changes. Amongst the latter were the challenges of globalization, economic recession, rising unemployment from the 1970s and the erosion of traditional working class solidarities as the economy shifted from manufacturing to non-manual employment. The final chapter briefly examines the experience of losing work. What it felt like and what it meant to be unemployed elucidates what work signified in the contemporary period. Again, the emphasis here is upon exploration of personal narratives, with the lived experience of unemployment and responses to retirement featuring prominently.

An historical approach with a focus on personal narratives enables the emotional history of work to take centre stage, facilitating exploration of subjective identities and enabling changes over time to be put into perspective. What is argued in this book is that changes in the nature of work are more complex than vivid prognostications about the deterioration and degradation of human labour, enslavement to an 'overwork culture' and the emergence of a diluted 'instrumental' attitude to work would have us believe. Contradictory processes have been at play here. To be sure, employment has been transformed and there have been clear degenerative tendencies since the Second World War inherent within a competitive, largely free market system that continued to prioritize the exploitation of workers' bodies over and above their health and well-being. Deskilling and growing insecurity in the labour market have made many working lives less meaningful and more precarious. Capitalism exploits an unequal power relationship and can grind workers down. However, changes in how work is experienced at an emotional and physical level suggest that there has been amelioration, liberation and a degree of 'upgrading' – not least in relation to the position of women in the labour market. Whilst workers may have had their room for manoeuvre restricted, they were still agents in this, capable of negotiating, shaping, resisting and mediating the worst excesses of exploitative capitalism. The state has also played an important, though shifting, regulatory role. Change over time has been complex and multi-faceted, rather than following one clear trajectory. Despite recent reversals associated with political change, economic recession and an increasingly globalized market, sustained improvement has occurred since the Second World War in relation to real earnings (which doubled between 1955 and 1990), health and safety, and dignity, rights and citizenship in the workplace. The recent growth of non-standard, part-time, temporary and more insecure forms of work, however, suggests a *polarization* of experience. Working lives are being divided into a privileged group with high earnings and rewarding jobs and a marginalized, low paid and insecure segment. Inequalities have persisted and been recast around work enrichment and work deprivation.

This complex matrix of amelioration and degeneration is reflected in the personal discourses of workers, which constitute a barometer of continuity and change, a lens through which we can view work and its meanings. These evocative narratives inform us about everyday working lives and teach us of the need for constant vigilance, organization and resistance to threats upon hard-won workers' rights to a dignified and fulfilling working life. This is particularly the case just now as pressures upon workers mount in a context of globalization, the debt crisis, government austerity measures and the deepening economic recession afflicting modern Britain following the financial collapse of 2008.

1

Employment Patterns and Inequalities

Historians, sociologists and other commentators on work disagree over the extent, pace and patterning of change, arguing over the degree to which work has been transformed since 1945 and what this means for the future of work. This chapter looks more closely at the data and at changing employment patterns, divisions within the labour market and the nature of work – delineating and exploring the changing occupational profile of Britain since the Second World War. Inequalities, advantages and disadvantages are considered within what is a deeply segmented labour market, divided by social class, gender, race and disability. The data explored is drawn from a range of sources, including the decennial population Census and the Office for National Statistics (Labour Force Surveys). It indicates a series of quite fundamental changes in working lives, with the sharp decline in manufacturing and mining, the transition to a service-sector and knowledge-based economy, the information technology revolution associated with computers and the web, and the marked change in the gendering of work as an increasing proportion of women entered the paid, formal economy.

The transformation of employment

In 1951, according to the decennial Census, there were a little over 20 million people in paid employment in Britain, with about 88% of eligible men (over the school leaving age of 15 and under the retirement age) and 33% of eligible women engaged in the formal economy in waged labour. This indicates the fundamentally gendered nature of work in Britain in the middle of the twentieth century and the quite different relationship that men and women had with paid employment. Most men's engagement with the labour market was continuous; most women's discontinuous. The dominant pattern for women around 1950 was school to paid employment, to unpaid domestic work within the home on marriage, then, frequently back in to paid employment, mostly on a part-time basis and often with a series of job changes. Many others *worked* in the household but like most adult women evaded being officially recorded by the state bureaucracy as such, including those who worked in the informal 'cash-in-hand' economy. The undervaluation of women's economic contribution by society was evident in that only work for the market was recorded in the decennial Census and not unpaid domestic work in the home (Edgell, 2006, p. 154). Another flaw in the Census was its failure to record formal and informal voluntary work.

People started work earlier, worked longer hours, had less holidays and men invariably continued in employment for a substantially longer period in 1950 than they do today. All but the privileged minority entered full-time employment as soon as they were eligible to leave school at 15 (raised from 14 in 1947). A significant change had occurred by the 2000s with a considerable hike in the average age of starting work, the consequence of the raising of the school leaving age to 16 in 1973 and the massive expansion in access to further and higher education from the 1960s. In 2009, 82% of 16–18 year olds were still in full-time education or training and only 8.3% in employment, whilst around 35% of 18–21 year olds were attending further and higher education. With this and a trend towards earlier retirement for men (both voluntary and compulsory) the average employment life span of male workers in the UK labour force had contracted several years by the 2000s. Before the Second World War around half of all men over 65 were employed, whereas by 1980 the figure was down to just 12% (Parker, 1982, p. 11). 95% of men aged 55–9 and 88% of men aged 60–64 were economically active in 1951. By 2000 this was down to 75% and 50% respectively (Duncan, 2003, p. 102). With reduced weekly working hours (falling on average from around 44 hours in 1950 to around 38 in 1992 and further to 36 in 2011) and increased holidays, men in the early twenty-first century spent substantially less time in paid work *over their life spans* compared to the immediate post-war generation.

For women the experience was quite the opposite, with participation in paid work increasing substantially over the period from
1945 and rising average paid working hours. Dual earning families
increased sharply. And, as Bunting (2004) has shown, the work time
trends for all workers changed from the mid–late 1990s, with a sharp
increase in the numbers working excessively long hours. This was
linked to the shift from hourly paid work to salaried work, resulting in a growing gulf between the theoretically contracted hours and
actual hours worked (as, for example, in higher education). So, comparatively speaking, the UK remained a long-working time nation
and a distinctively work-oriented one (for example in comparison to
France). The averages, however, disguise a polarization between a
segment of employees working very long hours (almost 20% worked
more than 60 hours in 2002) and those working few or none (Bunting,
2004, p. 9). One of the most contentious debates in the field just now
is how we can achieve a better work–life balance and deal with an
'overwork culture' where companies condone the practice of employees putting in excessive hours and not taking up holiday entitlements
(Bunting, 2004, pp. 9–10). This raises questions about the meaning
of work. Did these fundamental changes in the ways in which men
and women interact with the labour market impact upon the significance of work in people's lives? Were the effects different for men
and women (Johnston and Zaidi, 2007, p. 114)? These issues will be
explored further in the next chapter.

The changing shape of Britain's labour force in the decades following the Second World War is charted in Tables 1.1 (men) and 1.2
(women) below.

At a very fundamental level, Tables 1.1 and 1.2 show the way the
economy was being restructured, indicating the sharp contraction in
the primary (agriculture and extraction) and secondary (manufacturing) sectors and the concomitant expansion in the tertiary (or service)
sector jobs. New technologies were creating new jobs, new skills and
new roles and this fuelled a significant rise in real incomes, contributing to the surge in living standards from the early 1950s. At the
same time, however, other jobs were being destroyed – with a particularly marked contraction in mining, agriculture, manufacturing and
unskilled manual jobs. Well over a million jobs were shed in engineering and metal manufacturing between 1951 and 1991, whilst jobs in
textiles and clothing fell from 1.85 million to 438,000 over the same
period (Law, 1994, p. 92). Employment in underground coal mining

Table 1.1 Economically active male population by major industrial groups, UK, 1951–1991 (in thousands)

	Agriculture Forestry Fishing	Extractive Industry	Manufacturing	Construction	Commerce & Finance	Transport & communications	Services	Others occupied
1951	1025	847	6153	1390	1838	1517	2806	73
1971	643	256	6121	1476	2391	1811	2910	276
1991	450	201	3810	1640	4250	1209	3334	–

Source: B.R. Mitchell, International Historical Statistics: Europe, 1750–1993 (4th ed. 1988), 160.

Table 1.2 Economically active female population by major industrial groups, UK, 1951–1991 (in thousands)

	Agriculture Forestry Fishing	Extractive Industry	Manufacturing	Construction	Commerce & Finance	Transport & communications	Services	Others occupied
1951	117	14	2654	41	1322	217	2560	36
1971	97	5	1505	182	3561	453	3128	375
1991	119	22	1587	165	4339	337	5141	–

Source: B.R. Mitchell, International Historical Statistics: Europe, 1750–1993 (4th ed. 1988), 160.

fell from over 700,000 in 1950 to just 10,000 or so in a handful of pits by 2000. This has been interpreted on the one hand as 'creative destruction' necessary for economic growth; and on the other as a disaster that wiped out whole communities. In total, almost 4 million jobs were lost in manufacturing and a further 1.3 million in mining, agriculture, forestry and fishing in the second half of the twentieth century, whilst the services, professions, commerce and finance sectors grew by a staggering 8.5 million. Blue collar manual jobs still dominated in 1951, with 64% of all workers defined as manual. By the end of the century that figure had shrunk back to around a third of the workforce. By the 2000s around 70% of all those employed in the UK were in the service industries and only one in five in manufacturing. Big growth areas were the public sector services such as education, local and central government and medical and welfare services. Jobs in education rose from 530,000 to 2.7 million, whilst employment in the health, medical and social services rose from 647,000 to 3.9 million between 1951 and 2011. Financial and leisure services jobs also grew rapidly.

One important immediate post-war change was to create a mixed economy with the nationalization of significant swathes of industry (including coal mining) and the creation of the National Health Service (NHS). By the early 1950s almost 27% of all employees were in the public sector. This peaked at almost 7 million public sector workers in 1980, before falling back sharply in the 1980s and 1990s – to 5.5 million by 2003, totalling some 18% of the total labour force (Newell, 2007, p. 46). This was principally the consequence of Conservative government public sector spending cuts and the privatization of the utilities – gas, electricity, water. Further contraction of the public sector took place after the market collapse of 2008–9 and the change of government (to a Tory/Liberal coalition) in 2010.

Economic and labour market restructuring intensified from the late twentieth century, with further shrinkage of the manufacturing sector and growth of the tertiary sector, as the *Labour Force Survey* data gathered by the Office for National Statistics indicates. The latter data was compiled from the mid-1990s and does not readily synchronize with the decennial Census data (Tables 1.1 and 1.2), so long-term time series are difficult to construct. Nonetheless, the key changes are discernible. On the growth side, perhaps the most important change was the expansion of the managerial, technical and professional occupations ('knowledge workers'). In 1951, 17.1% of the total workforce was located in these higher echelons of the UK labour force, whereas by 2010, a staggering 44.2% of the total UK labour force had professional, technical and managerial jobs (see Table 1.5 on p. 25). As Gallie has shown, this was part of a fundamental change in that the new service sector jobs predominantly entailed interacting with people rather than with raw materials and physical products (Gallie, 2000, pp. 282–3). Now, in the early 2010s, the tertiary (or services) sector employs around 80% of the total workforce.

This kind of data, in conjunction with other evidence, has provided the empirical grist to the mill for what has become known as the 'upskilling' thesis (Gallie, 2000, p. 290). This posits that the net effect of labour market developments in the second half of the twentieth century was improved quality of work – more job satisfaction, more job control and more interest, discretion and autonomy at work. This interpretation is almost diametrically opposed to the Marxist-inspired concept of deskilling – or the *degradation* of work – a thesis associated most prominently with the American Marxist sociologist Harry Braverman who wrote a seminal text, *Labor and Monopoly Capital* in 1974. The sharp decline of skilled manual work provides some support for this case – craft apprenticeships (the traditional training route into skilled manual labour) in the UK fell from 389,000 in 1964 to just 87,000 in 1990 (Sanderson in Crafts et al., 2007, p. 284). At its extreme this thesis claims that work within free market capitalist societies (both manual and non-manual) is intrinsically alienating and dehumanizing – exemplified by the monotony of the motor car flow production track and the call centre. Other theorists, however, argue that the labour market data suggests something more complex, with some claiming more *diversity* across a spectrum of experience and others that a *polarization* of work is happening. The latter 'hourglass economy' thesis is associated with the expansion of what have been termed 'McJobs' – or 'lousy' jobs – at the bottom of the employment hierarchy and 'iMacJobs' – or 'lovely' jobs at the top (Goos and Manning, 2007). This is a useful way of conceptualizing what are very complex, diverse and contradictory ameliorative and degenerative processes occurring in labour markets and the nature of work in contemporary Britain.

What has been happening in Britain has mirrored changes in other developed economies. Twenty years ago Reich argued that the US Census failed to adequately describe the key transitions in the types of work being done. He posited that most employees could be divided into three groups: 'routine production services, in-person services and symbolic-analytic services' (Reich, 1992, p. 174). The

Table 1.3 Labour force by industrial sector, 2010 (expressed as a percentage of total employed)

	Total	Male	Female
Agriculture, Forestry & Fishing	1.2	1.7	0.6
Energy & Water	1.6	2.5	0.7
Manufacturing	9.8	14.2	4.9
Construction	7.7	13.0	1.8
Distribution	13.8	13.5	14.2
Transport	5.1	7.7	2.1
Accommodation & Food	4.8	4.2	5.5
Information & Communications	3.5	4.6	2.2
Banking, Finance & Insurance	5.1	4.9	5.4
Professional & Scientific	6.5	7.1	5.8
Administration & Support	4.6	4.6	4.5
Public Administration	6.7	6.5	7.0
Education	10.7	5.7	16.4
Health	13.3	5.2	22.5
Other	5.4	4.6	6.4
Total employed	28745000	15291000	13454000

Source: Adapted from data from the Office for National Statistics, *Labour Force Survey*. Licensed under the Open Government Licence v.1.0. Figures are for first quarter, 2010.

first group were mostly blue collar routine production jobs (which were in sharp decline), but included were the 'foot-soldiers' of the IT revolution in information processing. 'In-person services' comprised a growing group of service sector workers in 'person-to-person' roles (including sales workers, secretaries, waiters and health care workers) involving what has become termed as 'emotional' labour. Perhaps the fastest growing group of workers were those in 'symbolic-analytic services' – such as engineers, scientists, consultants, designers, executives, investment bankers, managers, planners, researchers, editors, producers and the like. These are the knowledge creators and users in the modern economy, frequently graduates, who, Reich argues, 'solve, identify and broker problems by manipulating symbols... data, words, oral and visual representations' (Reich, 1992, pp. 177–8).

Table 1.3 provides a snapshot of the UK's employment profile in 2010. Whilst this indicates the fundamental restructuring of the labour market that has taken place with the shift from manual to non-manual work since the Second World War, it also shows the persistent gendering of the labour force, with marked differences in the proportion of

male and female employees in a number of sectors, including manufacturing, transport, construction, education and health. This issue
will be explored further later in this chapter.

Getting work and getting on: the role of social class

To provide the necessary skills for this new service sector, knowledge-based and IT-driven economy, access to higher education was
expanded massively in the second half of the twentieth century. In
the 1950s only around 5% of the eligible population of young people
entered university and there was a wide gender gap in the participation rate as well as the sorts of degree courses undertaken (McKibbin,
1998, pp. 258–9; Brown et al., 2004). Fifty years later 36% of eligible
18–19 year olds were undertaking undergraduate degree programmes,
with a roughly equal participation rate by gender (Scott et al., 2008,
p. 9).

There is considerable debate about the meaning of social class
and the extent to which class patterned people's lives, including their
employment, work, education, leisure and health (see, for example,
Glass, 1954; Reid, 1989; Savage, 1999; Payne, 2000). Undoubtedly,
however, as McKibbin and Kynaston's work has shown, at mid-twentieth century Britain was a deeply class-ridden society. Those in the
working class constituted almost three-quarters of the population
(McKibbin, 1998, p. 106) and Britain had a well-defined and growing
middle class. And most people had a deep sense of their class identity. The industrial conurbations of the country, such as Clydeside,
Merseyside and Tyneside, together with the coal mining villages, were
amongst the most proletarianized. Whilst the kind of job a person
did was not entirely dependent upon the social class into which she
or he was born, nonetheless social class and family influences were
major determinants (and probably the most important). In 1950, the
extent of intergenerational social mobility across from the working
classes to the middle classes and the elites was low. This, indeed, was
the main finding of the most extensive survey on social mobility conducted to date by Glass and colleagues (Glass, 1954). Glass called it
a 'closed circuit'. So the highest status and best paid jobs at the top of
the employment hierarchy were almost exclusively filled by the sons
of the existing elites and middle classes. This was the case for business, law, medicine, the civil service, architecture, management and
science. Even mobility *within* the working class was limited at mid-
twentieth century. As the Polish political economist (and specialist on

working-class life in Britain) Ferdinand Zweig noted in his 1952 study, *The British Worker:*

> In the main industries like engineering or shipbuilding, or building or printing, the rule is: 'once a labourer always a labourer'. Sometimes, however, he gets a job as a semi-skilled man or on a machine. The upgrading of the labourer to the position of a craftsman, even if he takes an interest in the job and wants to study it properly, is rare. (Zweig, 1952a, p. 27)

The lower professions and clerical work were predominantly (though not exclusively) populated by the middle classes, including such occupations as nursing, librarianship, school teaching and secretarial work. As the seminal studies of Lockwood and Goldthorpe demonstrated, clerical workers in the 1950s and 1960s usually regarded themselves as 'middle class' and frequently distanced themselves from the working class(es). The latter tended to express their disdain for the former and vice versa: 'the relationship between clerk and manual worker lends itself readily to hostility and resentment on both sides' (Lockwood, 1958, p. 207). This came through in some of the literary and filmic representations of the 1950s – for example in Sillitoe's classic novel *Saturday Night and Sunday Morning* and the Peter Sellers comedy movie, *I'm All Right Jack*. Crompton has made the point that 'clerks were nevertheless regarded as occupying a different class situation from that of manual workers' despite both being wage earners (Crompton, 1994, p. 102). Clerks were generally more aspirational, career-oriented and more individualistic, tending to oppose trade unions (at least in the private sector) and collective industrial action. Salaried 'staff' occupations frequently came with a range of perks and privileges (such as pensions and holidays with pay) and tended to be better paid and more secure than routine semi-skilled and unskilled manual jobs.

At the root of labour market advantage and disadvantage were the cultural capital and material resources of families and the education system. Indeed the social investigation group *Mass Observation* found in a survey in 1948 that education was central to how people defined themselves as 'middle class'. One *Mass Observer* noted: 'I consider that I belong to the middle class of society. It is so because I have had a Grammar School education' (Kynaston, 2009, p. 146). For many and perhaps most youths in the working classes school education meant little and they left as soon as they could, partly because of the economic pressure within families to contribute (see Willis, 1977). In working-class communities almost 90% of 15–16 year olds in the 1950s were in paid employment and only 0.3% of secondary modern school leavers went on to any full-time further education (Sanderson, 2007, p. 279). One survey in 1956 found no male ex-secondary modern pupils in professional jobs, compared to 36% of male ex-grammar school pupils (Sanderson, 2007, p. 280).

At mid-twentieth century, the UK education system was deeply divisive and despite some reform continued to offer distinct advantages in employment opportunities to those born into higher social classes. The independent or public schools were dominated by the elites who could afford to pay the fees, whilst the grammar schools grossly over-represented the middle classes. Most of the top businessmen and most powerful within society were ex-public school – indeed two-thirds of all those high earners in excess of £1,000 income a year in the mid-1950s had been to public school (McKibbin, 1998, p. 238). The 1944 Education Act (establishing free compulsory schooling in a three tier system of technical, secondary modern and grammar schools from age 5 to 15: raised to 16 in 1973) provided the potential for change, but it was to be a further decade or so before the first generation benefited from this. Still only one in forty entrants to public schools were from working-class backgrounds in the 1970s (Ashton, 1988, p. 416). The offspring of professionals and businessmen were six times more likely to pass their eleven plus exam and gain entry to grammar schools than working-class children (Kynaston, 2009, p. 147). In her survey of working-class cultures up to 1960 Bourke has commented: 'Legislative intervention into the education of working-class children raised expectations which were then thwarted' (Bourke, 1994, p. 109). Universities also remained socially exclusive – the privilege of the elites. There were only 90,000 full-time students at University in England and Wales in 1950. Twenty years later only 3% of men and 1% of women of working age in Britain had a degree (Kondylis and Wadsworth, 2007, p. 89). This continued to stifle intergenerational upward mobility. Even in the 1960s and 1970s middle-class boys were four times more likely than working-class boys to have a better status occupation than their fathers (McKibbin, 1998, p. 268). In an important study in 1977, Willis demonstrated that there continued to be strong social, economic and cultural forces operating to ensure working-class school pupils and youths were voluntarily (and usually enthusiastically) attracted to manual jobs. To some degree this was also tied up with prevailing notions of masculinity – with clerical and other service sector jobs defined as unmanly and effeminate and hence unattractive to working-class lads (Willis, 1977, pp. 103–4; 148–51; and see Chapter 3). Whilst critical of Willis (whose work he describes as 'misleading'), Furlong's work on Scotland in the late 1980s/early 1990s also demonstrated the persistence of social class as a determinant of job choices:

> Young people still follow highly stratified routes into the labour market... class inequalities show no evidence of decline... There are still clear and predictable routes from school to work in which those who are advantaged in social and educational terms come to enter the most prestigious and well-paid segments of the labour market. (Furlong, 1992, pp. 12, 152)

People also continued to subscribe to a strong sense of class (consistently defining themselves in these terms) and to *believe* social class affected opportunities, as the *British Social Attitudes* surveys demonstrated. The 1984 survey reported that 70% of the sample believed opportunities were influenced by social class, whilst in the 1992 survey this number had increased to 74% (Airey, 1984, p. 130; Young, 1992, p. 179). Not surprisingly, perhaps, 'manual workers have a sharper sense of class disadvantage than do non-manual workers' and, the 1992 *British Social Attitudes* survey concluded, there remained, 'the bedrock belief that Britain is still a class-bound society in which a person's social origins are one of the primary determinants of his or her opportunities' (Young, 1992, pp. 179, 180). This may have been particularly so in the most proletarianized industrial heartlands of the North, Wales and Scotland (on the latter, for example, see Foster, 1998).

Class inequalities in life opportunities and employment patterns therefore persisted. Reid has mapped these in a comprehensive study in the mid-1980s. Class divisions continued to be apparent in income, property, health, education and work. Those in the lowest social class had unemployment rates in the mid-1980s around five times higher than professionals and managers. Professionals had incomes that were two and a half times on average the income of unskilled manual workers and the latter were about half as likely as professionals to be members of an employers' pension scheme (Reid, 1989, p. 111; Hannah, 1986, p. 127). Crucially, perhaps, education continued to be patterned by social class and this, in turn, influenced job opportunities. In the mid-1980s, for example, 81% of those in the top social class 1 had a higher education and only 2% had no qualifications, compared to 1% with higher education and 83% with no qualifications in the lowest social class 6 (Reid, 1989, p. 278).

Two important and related changes occurred in the half century from the 1950s. As observed already, the age of entry into the workplace rose, with the minimum school leaving age rising to 16 and a greater proportion of youths entering university – rising from 5% to around 35% of school leavers between 1960 and 2010 (Sanderson, 2007, p. 289). Secondly, the class and gender dimensions to educational attainment became blurred as pro-active policies were pursued to encourage wider participation and open access to further and higher education. The economic constraints on working-class families were alleviated by rising real wages and by state-funded higher education grants and free tuition fees (in most local education authorities from 1945 and in all from the Education Act 1962). This changed later in the century with the introduction of student loans (in 1990) and tuition fees from 1998. Whilst social class certainly did not disappear as a structural determinant of education and employment opportunities, Britain by the 2000s had moved significantly towards eroding class and gender bias in education, hence facilitating wider occupational choice, fairness and upward social mobility. This can be seen especially in the intergenerational shift across the manual/non-manual divide for those born after 1950. One measurement of the degree and pace of change can be found in the educational element of the Human Development Index (HDI) – which also takes income and life expectancy into account. As Crafts has shown, the educational component of the UK's HDI (which records the *quantity* of education, not quality) improved only slowly by some 25% or so between 1900 and 1950 whereas between 1950 and 2001 the index doubled (Crafts et al., 2007, p. 27).

The gendering of the labour force

If class patterned opportunities in the post-Second World War labour market, so too did gender. In the middle of the twentieth century, men dominated *paid* employment. Women always worked, of course, though the dominant pattern before the Second World War was for entry into full-time paid work as a teenager for a number of years then upon marriage or childbirth the paid job was left and thereafter work mainly took place in the home, in unpaid activity associated with family and home-making (perhaps supplemented with some part-time casual earnings). The designation 'housewife' rather than house or home 'worker' defined this as a *subordinate* activity in what was a deeply patriarchal society where the 'breadwinner' role was associated strongly with the male. Whilst there were signs of change – evident in the rising rate of married women's participation in paid work in the 1930s and 1940s – still the traditional sexual division of labour prevailed in the middle of the twentieth century. According to the 1951 Census the economic activity rate of women was two percentage points *below* that of 1911. Despite the emancipating effects of the Second World War when women flooded into war work to replace men called up and the heavy demand for female labour in the immediate post-war years, only one in five married women were in full-time paid employment in 1951.

What was already evident, though, was a marked difference in attitude and behaviour across the generations, with younger women increasingly breaking the mould. Whilst just 8% of married women over 55 were in paid employment in 1951, this figure rose to 37% for married women under 25 years of age (Gallie, 2000, pp. 291–3). There were also significant divergences in patterns across the UK, reflecting economic differences in job opportunities and cultural differences across nations and regions. Textile manufacturing towns, such as Blackburn and Dundee, traditionally had very high proportions of married women in paid employment, whilst the distinctively patriarchal culture of Scotland and Wales continued to be reflected in the lowest UK rates of married women in paid employment. The spectrum ranged from married women constituting 33% of the total female labour force in Scotland and Wales in 1952, to 51% in the West Midlands (Hammond, 1968, Table 2.1.3). Poorer educational opportunities for women, however, continued to act as a drag anchor on prospects. As late as the 1960s, only one in 600 working-class girls leaving school entered university (Dennis et al., 1969, p. 9).

Where women were in paid employment at this time, moreover, they tended to be clustered into a fairly narrow range of subordinate, lower paid 'feminized' occupations in a highly gender-segregated labour market. In 1951, 86% of all female employees were in occupations dominated by women and this only changed slightly by 1971 to 84% (Roberts, 1995, p. 119). Women were particularly over-represented in clerical and shop work in the 1950s, whereas few women were to be found in the traditional 'heavy' manual industries (a 'dangerous work taboo' existed, paralleling the 'combat taboo' of wartime) where men dominated, nor in the higher professions, administrative, supervisory and managerial jobs. In one survey covering 1959–66 almost 40% of all girls aged 15–17 were recorded as entering clerical work, whilst only 6.6% entered apprenticeships. For boys in the same age range, 37% entered apprenticeships and 10% clerical jobs (Hammond, 1968, Table 2.1.9). Vertical segregation by gender characterized the labour market and almost everywhere women found themselves occupying the bottom rungs of the ladder. As Lockwood noted of clerical workers in his 1958 study: 'One of the major features of the modern office – the employment of women in routine clerical jobs – has meant increased chances for male clerks because few women starting at the lower grades either choose, or are chosen for, promotion' (Lockwood, 1958, p. 68).

Whilst most of the traditional skilled and dangerous manual workplaces remained no-go areas for women (see, for example, Clarke and Wall, 2009, on the building trade), the second half of the twentieth century, nonetheless, witnessed a marked transformation with the rapidly increasing penetration of women into the formal, paid economy and their upward mobility in terms of occupational status. (Thane, 1994, pp. 395–410). The surge in mass female labour market participation and the growth of dual income households were key drivers in improving living standards from the 1950s. Whereas women constituted 31% of the total labour force in 1951 (some 6.9 million of a total labour force of 22.5 million), by 2010 the distribution had altered to 53% men: 47% women. This was pushed along by technological change (the information technology revolution), second wave feminism, the opening up of higher education to women, changing societal attitudes (it became acceptable that women no longer needed to leave work on becoming married) and smaller families with the widespread diffusion of birth control with the contraceptive pill from the 1960s. Increasing access to higher education, providing the transferable skills necessary for participation in the growing knowledge-based economy, was a key factor. In 2000, four times as many women were in higher education courses than in the early 1970s (Hinds and Jarvis, 2000, p. 101). By the end of the 2000s more women were qualifying with university degrees than men. The pivotal change was the markedly increased rate of entry of married women into formal paid employment, with more than half of all married women in paid employment by 1991 (and over 70% in the married 35–54 age group – see Crompton, 1997, pp. 25–9 and Table 1.4 below). Almost the same proportion of married as unmarried women were in paid employment by the mid-2000s (64% to 62% – Scott et al., 2008, p. 9). Starting with professionals, the trend was towards an earlier return to the labour market after childbirth.

Women gained access to a much wider range of jobs in the second half of the twentieth century and witnessed significant upward occupational mobility. Hakim's work has shown how gender segregation

Table 1.4: Women in the labour force, 1951–2010

	As a % of total labour force	% of married women in paid employment
1951	29.5	21.7
1971	36.5	42.0
1991	42.7	53.1
2010	46.7	72.0*

*Includes co-habiting mothers.

Sources: 1951–1991: Gallie, 2000, p. 292; 2010: adapted from data from the Census and the Office for National Statistics, Labour Force Survey. Licensed under the Open Government Licence v.1.0.

in the labour market had eroded markedly by the turn of the century with the growth of what she calls 'egalitarian' and 'integrated occupations' and a marked rise in better status jobs and earnings. Nonetheless, there remained a notable gender gap in opportunities and job status (as well as earnings) in the 2000s and wide differences between the younger women with experiences increasingly similar to men and the older, poorer educated generation of female employees whom Walby has asserted 'built their life trajectories around patterns of private patriarchy' (Walby, 1997, p. 2). As Hakim argued in 1998: 'occupational segregation has become an enduring feature of the labour market which is likely to continue well into the twenty-first century, long after equal opportunities policies have achieved their full impact' (Hakim, 1998, p. 236). In large part this is connected with the dogged persistence of the idea within British society that men are the *primary* earners, responsible for the family, whilst women remain the *secondary* earners working to provide a supplementary income. Hakim comments: 'In the majority of cases, women's involvement in market work is different in volume, nature and pattern from men's lifetime full-time permanent employment histories' (Hakim, 1998, p. 249).

The proliferation of part-time jobs, dominated by women, facilitated this process and this also became a characteristic feature of the post-war labour market and the sexual division of labour in the UK. Female part-time workers increased by two million between the 1951 and 1971 Censuses (Roberts, 1995, p. 122). This fitted in with prevailing notions of femininity, enabling married mothers to combine their family responsibilities with earning. This also did not significantly threaten masculinity because part-time work could be deemed to represent 'extra' income, supplementing the main 'breadwinner' wage (see Chapter 3). The 1950 Factories (Evening Employment) Order was significant, relaxing the long-standing abolition of female employment on nightshift by permitting an early evening shift up to 10pm. This 'twilight shift' became very popular with working-class women. By the mid-1980s, out of a total female labour force of 9.5 million, 4.1 million women (around 45%) were working part time. At the same point only 7% of male workers were in part-time employment (Roberts, 1995, p. 120). In the early twenty-first century, women were six times more likely than men to be working part time. They were also more likely to be living in poverty, whilst men were twice as likely as women to be in a professional occupation (Hinds and Jarvis, 2000, pp. 101–2). Some occupations continued to be virtual no-go areas for women. Almost no women were miners, and only small numbers made it into construction work, iron and steel, shipbuilding and heavy engineering. On the other hand, nursing and the domestic caring professions continued to be dominated by women. In 1991, only 2,931 of 56,260 childcare jobs were held by men whilst women outnumbered men by almost six to one in cleaning and housekeeping jobs (Crompton, 1997, p. 80).

This is important and brings us back to the issue of continuity in the gendered experience of work. Horrell has calculated that in the average family in 2000, the father contributed 68% of paid work time and the mother 28% over the course of working lifetimes (Horrell, 2007, p. 117). The corollary of this is that women still provide the vast bulk of domestic (household) labour and childcare. As Connolly and Gregory argue in their survey of women and work since 1970: 'It is clear that equality of outcomes in the labour market has not been achieved' (Connolly and Gregory, 2007, p. 143). Table 1.5 below gives an indication of the situation prevailing in 2010.

What stands out from this contemporary data is both the degree of change towards a more egalitarian workplace *and* the extent to which a sexual division of labour still persists and characterizes the labour market. Vertical segregation prevails. Women continue to be markedly under-represented in the higher status managerial and top professional jobs, as well as the self-employed, own business owners and the supervisory grades. In 2010–11, a government inquiry found only 8% of company board members were female. Men also continue to dominate the skilled trades and the plant and machine operating jobs. Where female workers remain disproportionately represented are in

Table 1.5 Labour force by occupation and gender, 2010 (%)

	Total	Male	Female
Managers and Senior Officials	15.4	18.7	11.7
Professional Occupations	14.0	14.8	13.0
Associate Professional and Technical	14.8	13.7	16.0
Administration and Secretarial	11.3	4.6	18.8
Skilled Trades	10.6	18.2	1.9
Personal Services	8.8	2.7	15.8
Sales and Customer Services	7.5	4.8	10.5
Process, Plant and Machine Operatives	6.7	11.1	1.7
Elementary Occupations*	11.1	11.4	10.7

*Elementary occupations are defined as 'simple and routine tasks which mainly require the use of hand-held tools and often some physical effort'. They consist primarily of labouring and other relatively low skilled jobs, such as cleaning and street selling.

Source: Adapted from data from the Office for National Statistics, *Labour Force Survey*. Licensed under the Open Government Licence v.1.0. Figures are for first quarter, 2010.

clerical and secretarial jobs, in sales and in personal services and in the intermediate and semi-skilled occupations. What this meant for the *subjective* experience of work will be returned to and explored in more depth later (see Chapter 3).

Race, ethnicity and the labour market

Apart from social class, locality and gender, another important division within the post-Second World War labour market was the one based on race and ethnicity. Measuring the racial and ethnic patterning of employment historically is not so easy, however, as the decennial Census did not record ethnicity consistently and the *Labour Force Survey* (which did record ethnicity) only began in 1979 (Baines, 2007, pp. 330–1). However, there were a number of studies of race, ethnicity and employment in the post-war years that provide clear evidence of a deeply divided labour force in the second half of the twentieth century, with a relatively privileged white majority (including white migrants) and a discriminated and subordinated black immigrant minority.

Peter Wright's survey in the 1960s for the Institute for Race Relations (IRR) based on questionnaires sent to a sample of firms indicated disproportionate clustering of ethnic minorities in the lowest, least skilled jobs and that apprenticeships for black school leavers were extremely rare (Wright, 1968, p. 219). 24% of white British workers in Wright's sample (and 9% of white immigrants) were in skilled jobs compared to just 2% of black immigrant workers; whilst the corresponding figures for unskilled jobs were 10% for white British workers (21% for white immigrants) and 58% for black immigrant workers. Wright reflected:

> Within the present immigration situation there are the seeds of a future race problem in British industry; a situation in which coloured workers will become the 'second class citizens' of the industrial world, confined to certain industries which the white workers prefer to avoid, confined to the least desirable jobs within these industries and socially segregated from the remainder of the labour force (Wright, 1968, p. 221)

Deakin's study, *Colour, Citizenship and British Society* (1969) focused on two key centres of black migrant employment – London and the West Midlands – and confirmed the extent of racial segregation. In the West Midlands in 1966, for example, only 2% of West Indian workers were professionals, managers, foremen or self-employed, compared to 20% within the total population (Deakin, 1969, p. 73). At the other end of the employment hierarchy, 23% of West Indian migrants and 40% of Asian migrants were in unskilled labouring jobs, compared to 8% average for the total population of the West Midlands. In London, Asian-born men and women were relatively well represented in non-manual service sector jobs and West Indian women in nursing, though they were clustered towards the bottom end of the employment hierarchy. West Indian male migrants, in contrast, were heavily over-represented in manual labouring jobs, with markedly less penetration into non-manual work in either London or the West Midlands (Deakin, 1969, pp. 73–9). Unemployment levels were also consistently higher and promotion prospects weaker for most black and ethnic minority workers, whilst the 1971 Census confirmed the persisting clustering of black and ethnic minority workers in the lower echelons of the labour market (Runnymede Trust and the Radical Statistics Group, 1981, pp. 96–108).

That said, it is also important to recognize that the UK's immigrant (overseas-born) population, which reached a total of 4.8 million in 2001 (rising from around 4% of the population in 1951 to around 8% of the population by the 2001 Census) was heterogeneous.

Table 1.6 Economic activity by ethnic group (men and women), 2010 (%)

	Economic activity rate	Unemployment rate
All origins	78.3	8.0
White	79.6	7.5
All ethnic minorities	68.3	12.7
Indian	76.5	6.8
Pakistani	56.9	18.9
Bangladeshi	54.0	16.5
Black Caribbean	80.2	15.4
Black African	68.6	15.3
Chinese	63.7	7.8
Other ethnic groups	64.4	13.6

Source: Adapted from data from the Office for National Statistics, *Labour Force Survey*. Licensed under the Open Government Licence v.1.0.

It included a white migrant segment (comprising the Irish, Poles, Italians and others, including white Indians), black ethnic minorities, refugees and asylum-seekers. Whilst race continues to influence labour market participation and ethnic minorities remain amongst the most vulnerable workers, a wide range of experience prevails, both within and across different race and ethnic groups, in economic activity and unemployment rates. As Table 1.6 indicates, Pakistanis, Bangladeshis, black Caribbeans and black Africans continue to face serious disadvantages in the labour market. The lived experience of work for migrants, black and ethnic minority workers is explored in more detail in Chapter 4.

Disability and the labour market

The post-war labour market also disadvantaged one other significant group within British society – disabled people. How we define 'disabled' is contested and has changed over time with an increasing recognition that disability is 'socially produced' and that the term covers a wide and diverse range of experience (Barnes and Mercer, 2003, pp. 1–13). Medical models – defining disability as 'personal tragedy' – have thus given way to social models where 'disability is a product of the physical configuration of the built environment, and is bolstered by prevailing social norms, values and beliefs' (Blakemore and Drake, 1996, p. 138). Disabilities – or loss of function – range from those with physical and sensory impairments (including the blind and deaf) through to those with a disabling disease or condition, such as polio or chronic bronchitis, and cognitive or mental illness.

In the nineteenth and early twentieth centuries industrialization and Fordist work regimes, combined with the growing influence of eugenics, led to a progressive exclusion of disabled people from the labour market and reliance upon family care and institutionalization through the auspices of the Poor Law (Topliss, 1979; Oliver, 1990, pp, 25–9; Barnes and Mercer, 2003, pp. 24–5). Work experience – or 'work therapy' – was achieved through sheltered and segregated workshops run by local authorities, mental asylums and institutions like the Royal National Institute for the Blind. At the same time, the ranks of disabled people were swelled by those impaired by the rising tide of occupation-related injuries (for example in mining) and incapacitating diseases – such as those affecting the respiratory system caused by inhaling dust and fumes at work (Johnston and McIvor, 2000; McIvor and Johnston, 2007). The carnage of the First World War and the Second World War further added to the number of disabled people in the UK. Anderson's recent monograph has shown how medical advances and improved rehabilitation services developed during the wars increased survival rates and swelled the numbers of disabled people actively looking for work (Anderson, 2011).

As Borsay's seminal study of disability and social policy has shown, disabled people were amongst the 'marginalised' groups extensively recruited during the Second World War to help fill the demand for labour in the stretched wartime industries (Borsay, 2005, pp. 133–4; see also Humphries and Gordon, 1992, pp. 129–36). Some 310,000 persons with disabilities flooded into employment or training during hostilities, encouraged by the government, not least through propaganda newsreels like *Blind Farmer Carries On* (Pathé 1942) and newspaper headlines like: 'Cripples Can do Vital War Work' (Humphries and Gordon,1992, pp. 132–5). Len Tasker, who had polio, reflected on his wartime experience:

> I tried for a job at a factory. I went up there, so pleased at the thought that I would be doing some proper work for myself as well as for the war effort. Anyway they gave me the job. I was rate-fixing clerk in this big factory and... I never looked back from there on. The war certainly opened up doors for me as a disabled person. I think it opened up opportunities for people with disabilities generally. I would never have been given the chance to do that job if it hadn't been for them looking for extra workers

in the war but as it happened I did really well in the job and got promoted. (cited in Humphries and Gordon, 1992, p. 131)

We know little about the experience of disabled people in wartime as they remain poorly researched compared to other groups (such as women; servicemen and the Home Guard). What Humphries and Gordon's oral history suggests is that disabled women found the going rather harder than men because of favouritism by labour exchanges in placing men in wartime jobs (Humphries and Gordon, 1992, pp. 132–3).

The Disabled Persons (Employment) Act (DPEA) of 1944 represented a 'reward' of sorts in recognition of this participation, as well as that of disabled combatants – thus identifying the latter as a special category of 'deserving poor'. It was designed to protect and extend such gains after the war, recognizing the important implications for full citizenship that paid employment implied (Borsay, 2005, pp. 134–5). In effect, this established for the first time the right of disabled people to employment and hence to maintain economic independence (Oliver, 1990, pp. 88–9). However, not all disabled people were treated equally. Turner (2010) has argued that the DPEA 1944 was geared much more towards those with physical impairments than those with mental health and learning disabilities. In cities like Glasgow, community care and a plethora of voluntary agencies developed to fill the welfare void for those with learning disabilities (Turner, 2010, pp. 102–76).

The DPEA (1944) had three main elements: it established training and rehabilitation centres to assess ability and provide some work experience; it ostensibly forced a quota system upon employers, with companies employing more than 20 required to engage 3% disabled people; and the 1944 Act extended segregated or 'sheltered' employment for those with severe disabilities for whom competition in the open market was deemed impossible (Gooding, 1994, p. 29; Clarke, 1951, pp. 156–7). The latter were provided by a non-profit making company (Remploy) or local authority workshops. The 1944 Act also established the Disabled Persons Register for Employment (administered by the Department of Employment; later the Department for Work and Pensions) – providing those who so registered with a 'green card'. The DPEA (1944) had symbolic importance and combined with the very high demand for labour and a positive policy on the part of the new nationalized industries may well have contributed to a significant shift in the integration of disabled people into the labour market in the decade or so after the Second World War, compared to the 1930s. Joan Simeon Clarke's study, *Disabled Citizens* (1951) recognized the quota was having a positive effect, though one unexpected outcome was the identification and registration of existing disabled employees to make up the 'quota':

> Employers have sought eagerly among their existing employees to find those with 'eligible' disabilities; these were quickly sent to register so that the firm did not have to take on other registered disabled persons whose infirmity might be really a handicap. (Clarke, 1951, p. 157)

Some such workers felt disadvantaged by this policy, finding difficulty with moving jobs with their 'green card' status and being passed over for subsequent promotion (Topliss, 1979, p. 50). According to Zweig's 1952 classification, disabled people were amongst the 'bottom layer' of his hierarchy of 'grades of labour', situated in the lowest paid, most insecure jobs. His examples were of physically disabled men drifting in and out of employment, unable to attain a permanent post and living on the poverty line (Zweig, 1952a, pp. 23–5). Whilst there was significant evasion of the statutory quota requirements by employers, nonetheless, some 60% of workplaces employing over 20 were reported to be complying with the 3% quota in 1961 (Borsay, 2005, p.136).

The public sector were amongst the better employers regarding employment of disabled workers. British Rail and the National Coal Board were amongst those public corporations that at least initially took their obligations towards the rehabilitation and employment of disabled people seriously (McIvor and Johnston, 2007; Kirk, 2008, p. 48). Coal mining communities were particularly blighted by disability because of the high rates of injury and persistence of a range of chronic disabling diseases – particularly those associated with dust inhalation such as pneumoconiosis, bronchitis and emphysema (see Chapter 5). Dismissal of disabled workers from the pits in the 1930s and 1940s and the limited availability of other jobs locally created massive hardship, especially in South Wales where respiratory disability was most acute (Francis and Smith, 1980, p. 439). Unemployment rates for registered disabled people seeking work in the coalfields were estimated at between 50–60% in the mid/late 1940s (McIvor and Johnston, 2007, pp. 282–3). From 1948 the newly created NCB reversed the industry's sacking policy for pneumoconiotics and thereafter routinely found jobs for many disabled employees, albeit usually away from the highest paid work at the coal face. Lighter work underground or on the surface was invariably done by disabled and older miners in the 1950s. Whilst the total employment figures for disabled people in the industry are not known, by 1960 we do know that the NCB was employing over 20,000 with respiratory disabilities alone (McIvor and Johnston, 2007, p. 149). This relatively progressive employment programme was facilitated by the prevailing labour shortage, the sympathetic support of mineworkers, the National Union of Mineworkers and, crucially, by the pioneering work of the Coal Industry Social Welfare Organization in this period in rehabilitating disabled miners – reported to be the most advanced service of its kind in the world in the 1950s (McIvor and Johnston, 2007, pp. 293–4).

There was less success, however, in creating employment opportunities for disabled people in mining districts beyond the coal industry itself. Post-war promises of government-funded specially equipped factories (Grenfell factories) for disabled people provided a few hundred jobs in the coalfields by the early 1950s, but overall were a failure (McIvor and Johnston, 2007, pp. 181–2). Moreover, even within the coal mines the prevailing situation for the employed disabled person was invariably a sharp reduction in earnings, especially when a shift from face work to working on the surface was involved, combined with diminution in the intrinsic rewards of such work. Disabled miners felt this acutely, as a loss of status, dignity, emasculation and stigma. These issues relating to embodiment and emotion are returned to and explored in more depth in Chapter 5.

With the sharp decline in manufacturing sector jobs the position worsened in the 1960s and 1970s and over the long term the 1944 DPEA (amended in 1958) proved to be pretty ineffective, being poorly regulated and widely evaded. Many companies struggled to fill quotas. The chemical giant ICI, for example, tried to pressure one worker in 1963:

> I mean they wanted me to go in as disabled because I'd had a broken leg in a motorbike accident and I said 'no, I'm no going disabled' 'cos they're obviously trying to make their figures look good...they've got to employ so many disabled guys and I said 'no' I says 'if I dinnae stick this job' I says 'I can get a disabled sticker easy' I says 'but I cannae get rid o' it easy' I says 'so I'm no willing tae go' and he said 'well' the usual ICI tactic 'we might no be able to employ you' I said 'well, that's up tae you but I'm no going disabled. (Interview by David Walker, 25 November 2005, SOHCA/022/ANON)

Exemption permits were issued routinely to employers whilst enforcement of the 1944 Act quotas was weak. There were only nine pros-
ecutions up to 1978, by which point only a little over one-third of all
companies employing over 20 complied with the 3% quota (Borsay,
2005, p. 136). A decade or so later 80% of companies employing over
20 were failing to employ the minimum 3% (Blakemore and Drake,
1996, p. 142). Provision in the sheltered workshops provided by chari-
ties and local authorities was also limited and inadequate, with the
needs of those with mental impairments and learning difficulties particularly neglected (Borsay, 2005, pp. 136–7; Turner, 2010, pp. 258–80;
311–15). The main provider, Remploy, only employed around 7,500 by
1970 in 85 factories – and by that point was making heavy financial
losses (Morris and Butler, 1972, p. 58). Reflecting on the impact of
social policy for disabled people by the mid-1990s, Blakemore and
Drake concluded: 'If the legislation as a whole was intended to provide disabled people with a route to employment then it has failed
signally' (Blakemore and Drake, 1996, p. 144).

   The failure reflected a lack of will on the part of the government,
politicians and the labour movement to bring about fundamental
change. In part it also reflected the fragmentation and weakness in
this period of disability pressure groups and the exclusion of disabled people from political decision-making (Oliver, 1990, p. 105;
Blakemore and Drake, 1996, p. 138). The outcome of this failure in
state policy was, as Borsay has argued, that 'employees as well as
employers discriminated against disabled people with impunity in the
immediate post-war period' (Borsay, 2005, p. 137; see also Humphries
and Gordon, 1992, pp. 136–9). Disabled persons were widely treated
as 'second class citizens', stigmatized by the prevailing public perception of disabled people as incapacitated and 'useless' (Barnes
and Mercer, 2003, p. 9). In fact, despite the obstacles, there did continue to be a significant level of engagement in economic activity by
disabled people, though on very difficult and unequal terms. In the
early 1970s there were around 700,000 registered disabled people in
employment (around one-third of all disabled people of working age)
– though unemployment rates at this point amongst disabled people
seeking work were four to five times higher than the national average
(Morris and Butler, 1972, pp. 55–6). Disabled people were clearly an
oppressed minority whose experience mirrored racial discrimination
with high levels of unemployment, insecurity, downgrading of skills,
ghettoization into unskilled manual jobs and very low pay (Borsay,

2005, p. 138; Blakemore and Drake, 1996, pp. 138–9). One disabled Second World War pensioner commented on his experience in 1970:

> When it comes to seeking some light part-time employment to supplement my income this is no joke. To tell any employer in this area that you are a registered disabled person is like signing your own death certificate. In January 1970, owing to my disability, I had to go into hospital for a general check-up, with promises galore from my employer of my job always being safe... I had not been in hospital for five days when my wife received by post my insurance cards and tax form. I had been dismissed – not even a letter giving me a week's notice or any pay. (Cited in Morris and Butler, 1972, p. 53)

Walker's investigation of disabled young people in 1976–7 for the Warnock Committee (based on a survey of 500 18 year olds) provided detailed evidence of inequalities and discrimination in the labour market. 'Handicapped young people', Walker concluded, 'are a severely disadvantaged minority':

> They had access to a very narrow range of jobs at a very low level of skill; these jobs were often repetitive, unrewarding and carried out in poor conditions. Furthermore these jobs were the most insecure... the proportion of handicapped young people who were underemployed since leaving school was five times that of the non-handicapped. (Walker, 1982, p. 178)

In a period when office jobs were growing rapidly it was found that disabled people were five times less likely that non-disabled people to have clerical jobs (Walker, 1982, p. 180). Not surprisingly levels of intrinsic job satisfaction amongst the sample of 18-year-old disabled people were found to be extremely low (Walker, 1982, p. 181). Surveys in the early 1990s indicated that the key problem was still with persistent *exclusion* from work (Barnes, 2000, pp. 55–8). Access remained a on-going problem. Difficulties with wheelchair entry on public transport and into and within workplaces added to a long list of access issues (Watson and Woods, 2005). There was also a marked gendering of experience for disabled people (see Table 1.7 below) – particularly evident in the exclusion of men from caring roles and virtual monopolization of such roles by disabled women – a pattern which closely matched that of non-disabled people.

And disabled people were severely undervalued in the labour market. Average earnings of disabled workers in the1970s were well below half the average earnings of all employed (Borsay, 2005, p. 138) and

Table 1.7 Labour market status by gender and disability, 1991 (%)

	Non-disabled men	Disabled men	Non-disabled women	Disabled women
Employed	64.0	36.8	64.2	38.4
Self-employed	14.7	6.9	4.5	5.4
Unemployed	10.0	6.9	4.4	3.6
Retired	3.3	6.9	1.6	2.7
Long-term sick		0.7	34.5	0.5
Family care	0.3	0.0	19.9	22.2
Student		6.1	6.9	4.0
Other	0.9	1.1	1.0	0.9

Source: British Household Panel Survey, 1991, cited in Barnes, 2000, p. 49. Copyright © Institute for Social and Economic Research.

the gap remained wide for male workers in the 1990s (Barnes, 2000, p. 54). Moreover, disabled people were also excluded from most of the intrinsic rewards of work. This effective oppression resulted in a perpetuation of dependency, exclusion, deprivation and relative poverty (Townsend, 1979) as well as the loss of respect and self-esteem which went along with this discrimination and humiliation in the labour market. Borsay has concluded that state legislation was patently ineffective in the second half of the twentieth century in integrating disabled people into the labour market or of relieving their traditional reliance upon manual labour and segregated workshops (Borsay, 2005, p. 139). Turner's important study of post-war Glasgow has shown how continuity characterized the experience of those with learning disabilities, arguing: 'oral testimonies and local sources, therefore, have shown how the lives of people with learning disabilities were often static, unaffected by wider changes in macro social policy' (Turner, 2010, p. 315). Poorer qualifications and the persistence of segregated schooling contributed to these difficulties. In the 1990s disabled people were twice as likely as non-disabled people to have no qualifications at all (Barnes and Mercer, 2003, p. 45; see also Turner, 2010, pp. 218–34). This was compounded by the persistence of prejudicial attitudes, lack of understanding and the failure of employers to redesign and adapt their labour processes and access to workplaces to take disabilities into account (Oliver, 1990, pp. 87–8). The outcome for a significant proportion of disabled people was poverty. By the standard definition of poverty (households with lower than 50% of the national average income), 26.3% of disabled persons were in poverty against 14.4% of non-disabled individuals in 1991 (Barnes, 2000, pp. 74–5).

Some commentators have argued that the coming of the post-industrial economy, with its emphasis on service sector 'brain work', information technology and computer technologies and the shift back to smaller scale production and home work will facilitate inclusion of disabled people and radically increase opportunities (e.g. Finkelsteih, 1980; Barnes and Mercer, 2003, p. 33; Stanley and Regan, 2003, pp. 20–1). Others, however, are more sceptical, suggesting that older disabled people will be disadvantaged, as well as those with mental illness and learning difficulties in the new economy (e.g. Sapey, 2000). As Barnes and Mercer argue: 'the consequences of the new informational economy seem far from clear, offering both an enabling and a disabling potential, and likely to divide disabled people in new ways' (Barnes and Mercer, 2003, p. 33). Certainly at the end of the twentieth century the exclusion of disabled people was still evident with less than 50% of disabled people classified as economically active (compared to a labour force average of over 80%) and talk of 'a missing million' from the labour force (Stanley and Regan, 2003 p. i; Barnes, 2000, p. 51). As with non-disabled people, however, these averages mask considerable differences in employment opportunities across the country. A study in 2002 found employment rates of disabled persons ranged from 70–85% in more prosperous areas of the country to as low as 30–40% in Wales, Northern Ireland and Scotland and only 25–30% in some of the big northern cities (Manchester, Liverpool and Glasgow). Unemployment rates continued to be much higher for those with mental health disabilities than those with physical and sensory impairments. In 2000, of those defined as having long-term mental health disabilities only 18% were in employment, compared to 52% of those with physical and sensory impairments (Boardman, 2003, p. 328). The Equal Opportunities Commission continued to identify wide differences in economic opportunities between those with and without disabilities through the 2000s. The activity of disabled people in the labour market continued to be characterized by horizontal and vertical segregation, with the clustering of disabled people in the lowest paid, least skilled and lowest status occupations (Barnes and Mercer, 2003, p. 47; Blakemore and Drake, 1996, p. 138).

Relatively effective anti-discriminatory legislation did not come until the Disability Discrimination Act (DDA) of 1995 – fully twenty years after equivalent legislation on gender and racial inequality. This legislation began to address the ways that society disabled those with impairments by segregating, restricting, disadvantaging and excluding them from the labour market. The DDA (1995) imposed a duty on employers to make 'reasonable adjustments to the workplace and employment arrangements' and not to discriminate on the grounds of disability (Thornton, 2005, p. 65). It was followed by greater government funding for schemes to get more disabled people into work and support those already working, including the 'Access to Work' and 'New Deal for Disabled People' initiatives (Barnes, 2000, p. 40). It was also strengthened by European Union Directives in the 2000s. It will take some time, however, before the full impact of these changes upon the employability of disabled people, access to jobs and earnings will be seen. What is evident is that an increasing number within society are now defining themselves as 'disabled' compared to a generation ago (especially in relation to mental health) and a rising number are gaining access to employment – in 2002 there were 3.5 million disabled people in paid work. However, discrimination has persisted, evident in the continuing wide discrepancy in the employment and economic inactivity rates between disabled people and non-disabled people. A 2003 report on disability and work for the Institute for Public Policy Research found that disabled people were still twice as likely as non-disabled people to have no qualifications and 'disabled people themselves suffer social isolation, reduced independence and worsening health and well-being as a result of being out of work (Stanley and Regan, 2003, pp. 1, 17; Boardman, p. 328). Referring to the DDA 1995, Thornton argued in 2005:

> There is no hard evidence that the New Deal for Disabled People provides better results, in terms of getting jobs or sustaining employment, for people who take part in it compared with those who do not. (Thornton, 2005, p. 71)

In 2009–10, 26% of all adults in Britain were disabled as defined by the Disability Discrimination Act, 1995 (Life Opportunities Survey, 2009–10, Interim Results, p. 59). However, the disabled only constituted 14.4% of total employees in 2011 (*Labour Force Survey*, Office for National Statistics). Prejudice and discrimination against disabled people remains deeply rooted within the labour market in Britain in the early twenty-first century and as a consequence the relationship between disability and poverty has doggedly persisted.

First experiences: children in the labour market

Child labour had not disappeared entirely from the post-war British labour market, though the raising of the school leaving age and campaigns against the worst excesses of child labour did result in its diminishing extent and significance. Child labour was further regulated after World War One through national legislation (Employment of Women, Young Persons and Children Act, 1920; Children and Young Persons Act, 1933 – 1937 in Scotland) and in local authority byelaws – notably through the child labour permit and licensing systems (see Pettitt, 1998, pp. 138–9). Nonetheless, the child regulations were routinely flouted. During the Depression in the 1930s and in the immediate post-war years some form of paid work before leaving school remained the norm for working-class kids and the exploitation of child and youth workers was widespread. Bill Sirs recalled how he started work as a part-time newspaper boy and a butcher's boy around aged 11 in the early 1930s and had to live at his grandmothers to ensure his father's public assistance payments were not cut off. He left school at 14 hoping to get an apprenticeship, but failed and ended up as an errand boy then a young labourer in a timber yard. He commented in his autobiography in 1985: 'Employers can no longer exploit young men as I was exploited then earning only 9s 10d a week for doing the same work as the men in the yards...the yard's owner lived in a massive mansion overlooking the park' (Sirs, 1985, p. 47). Here is how a Glaswegian born in 1947 described his job as a milk boy for the Co-operative Dairy in the early 1960s:

> Then I was in school...em...between about 12 and 15 I did that. The dairy opened about half 6 so you had to be round there to load up your crates of milk on this sort of metal cart and away you went. You would be finished for about twenty past...half past 7 in fact so much so I used to come back and have a half hour in bed. As I say, that sort of kept you fit and it got you some money which your mum would give you a couple of bob off it to go to the pictures. (Gerard Coyle, interviewed by David Walker, M74 Project SOHC/023/02)

The permit and licensing system was poorly enforced and widespread illegal child labour was exposed in a study by E. Davies for the DHSS in 1972. This report argued such work had a substantial detrimental impact upon educational performance and pupils attitudes towards schooling. It contributed to a tightening of the legislation with the passage of the Employment of Children Act (1973). Other research

showed significant changes after Second World War in the patterning of child labour in that increasing numbers of children from affluent middle-class households were taking work to earn extra money to
spend on consumer items such as records and clothes (Cunningham,
1995; Lavalette, 1998, pp. 35–6).

Serious empirical work into child labour in the UK only really
occurred in the 1990s, however, prompted in part by growing interest
in and regulation of child labour by the European Union (EU) and
the International Labour Office (ILO) and the concerns of groups
like Child Poverty Action Group. Child labour was 'rediscovered'
and empirical research across Europe indicated its wide prevalence
and resurgence in the last two decades of the twentieth century.
Rahikainen has located this within the search by capital for more flexible, cheaper and malleable labour, facilitated by the deregulation of
labour markets across developed European economies (Rahikainen,
2004, pp. 209–11). One report by the Department of Employment in
1995 found more than half of all those aged 13–18 in the UK were
in some form of employment, whilst a further 30% of 12 year olds
and 20% of 11 year old had jobs (Hobbs et al., 1996, p. 8). Whilst a
wide range of experience existed, on average children who did work
were employed 8 hours a week and frequently this work took place in
illegal periods – on weekdays before 7am and after 7pm, for example
in milk and newspapers deliveries and shop working (Hobbs et al.,
1996, pp. 17–18; see also McKechnie et al., 2000). Poverty appears to
be a significant factor in prompting child employment, but, since the
Second World War at least, not the only cause. Growing consumerism
played its part. Lavalette has made the point that levels of child working were comparatively high in Britain at the end of the twentieth
century and that the UK was out of line with European and international conventions – for example in refusing to sign the International
Labour Organization's minimum working age (15 years) conventions
(Lavalette, 1998, pp. 36–8).

Retirement

When employment ended was also changing in the post-war period.
The notion of retirement, or voluntary withdrawal, from paid employment is a relatively recent development, starting with the meagre state
pension introduced in 1908 by Lloyd George for those who reached
70 (average life expectancy at this time was under 50). By the Second
World War official state retirement ages (and pension payment) had

come down to 65 for men and 60 for women. Historically, men with-
drew from employment when their declining health necessitated this.
Increasingly, however, in the post-war years occupational and state
pension schemes defined a set date and the trend was towards earlier
retirement. The 1931 Census recorded almost half of all men over
65 still in employment. In 1951 it was down to 30% and in 1981 just
10% (Hannah, 1986, pp. 122–3). A substantial proportion of male
workers aged 55–65 were also increasingly exiting (by choice or force)
from full-time employment. By 1987, the economic activity rate of
men aged 55–64 was down to just 67% (Johnston, 1989, p. 352). This
coincided with what one scholar of retirement argued was a shift from
'discouraged' to 'encouraged retirement' (Parker, 1982, pp. 29–30).
Interpretations differ on the causes of this shift that drew men out of
the labour market earlier. Some scholars such as Johnston lean more
towards supply side factors, arguing that withdrawal from the labour
market has been influenced by personal choice, rising living standards
(real wages doubled between 1955–1990) and the wider availability of
occupational pensions (Johnston, 1989, pp. 62–71; see also Hannah,
1986). Others argue a strong case for reduced demand as the main
cause, positing that older workers became less attractive to employers
because they were less productive or an obstruction to reorganization
(Phillipson, 1998; Hannah, 1986). Those over 55 were disproportionately targeted for redundancy in the economic recession of the 1980s
and found it difficult to re-enter the overstocked labour market thereafter, swelling the ranks of the unemployed (see Chapter 7).

The addition of anti-ageism to the equal opportunities agenda was
one factor that led to change in the early twenty-first century, combined
with the sharply rising life expectancy which substantially length-
ened the average post-retirement period. Demographic change has
impacted on the sustainability of the state and private pension funds,
exacerbated by the financial crisis of 2008 and subsequent stock market collapse. The outcome was a policy shift towards the standardiza-
tion of the state pension age for men and women, increases in pension
contributions from salaries and an incremental rise in the point at
which the state pension could be claimed from age 65 (the state pension age will rise to 66 by 2020 and there are currently plans to raise
it further in subsequent years to 67 and 68), whilst workers' rights to
choose their exit point from employment have been enhanced at law.
Although some implications of this policy change were opposed by
many trade unions, this went some way to addressing the campaign
by retirement activists such as Parker (1982) that older citizens should

have the right to choose and those with a strong attachment to work or an economic incentive (or both) should have the opportunity to continue working or at least negotiate their exit point from working life gradually. The outcomes are likely to be a reversal of the post-war trend of earlier disengagement from employment, more flexible and varied incremental transitions from work to full retirement and a lengthening period in the labour market.

Increasing insecurity: flexible, part-time and non-standard work

One of the other fundamental changes in the UK labour market since the Second World War has been the decline of full-time and lifetime 'standard' work and the rise of 'non-standard' or 'flexible' jobs, including part-time work (by one common definition, under 30 hours a week), temporary contract work and self-employment. Researchers have termed this 'a retreat from permanent employment' (Kirkpatrick and Hoque, 2006). That is not to suggest that non-standard work forms did not exist before – indeed they may well have been under-represented in the decennial Census and more prevalent historically than some labour sociologists have indicated. For example, homeworking and subcontracting in the building trade have long historical antecedents.

Nonetheless, the evidence does point clearly towards a decline of the classic 'Fordist' standardized work contract characterized by full-time working in a 'job for life' in the final two decades of the twentieth century. In the late 1990s, around 20% of British workers had no written contract of employment, whilst in the region of a third of all UK jobs by the 2000s were of a non-standard, part-time, temporary, flexible type (Edgell, 2006, p. 148; Russell, 1998, p. 82). This shift to non-permanent contracts was common across Europe, but the UK was amongst the most advanced down this path by the end of the twentieth century (Russell, 1998). Some prominent theorists such as Beck (1992), and Cassells (1997) have argued that this ushered in a transformation in work, providing the potential for an improved work–life balance, whilst also being characterized by more risk, insecurity and individualization. What is evident is that these forms of work were particularly prevalent within female labour markets. As previously noted, by 2000 almost half of the entire female workforce were employed part-time (Gallie, 2000, p. 297). From the 1980s recession, however, non-standard forms of work were also growing amongst male workers, with 5.3% of all working men on part-time contracts in 1990, growing to 8.5% by 1999 (Noon and Blyton, 2002, p. 37) and to 14.2% by 2011. Total numbers working part-time have continued to grow and hit an all time high in 2010 when 7.82 million were working part-time, a little over 27% of the entire workforce – including over a million who said they wanted but could not get full-time work.

Self-employment also proliferated, markedly from the 1980s, stimulated by the economic downturn and government incentives during the 'enterprise culture' of the Thatcher era. By the 2000s, one in ten British workers were self-employed. Whilst on the one hand such work frequently involved more autonomy and independence, on the other such jobs involved less security, no access to a range of state benefits (such as unemployment benefit, holiday or sick pay) and longer working hours, frequently without any contract. The construction sector would be a classic example and, more recently, direct selling of products like double glazing and fitted kitchens. Other types of non-standard work were homeworking, temporary working and informal, or 'cash-in-hand', work in the 'black economy'. Whilst clearly widespread, the latter has proven difficult to measure. People now also move jobs frequently. The average length of service with one employer has fallen – to the extent that in 2011 almost half (48.4%) of all UK employees have been employed on contracts of five years or less (*Labour Force Survey*, Office of National Statistics).

The economic recession and the 'enterprise culture' of the 1980s and 1990s undoubtedly pushed such developments along. Employers and managers sought to reduce costs and overheads and seek competitive advantage by moving labour from permanent to temporary contracts, outsourcing through subcontractors, switching to homeworking and using temporary employment agencies to acquire labour. Whilst some workers may have welcomed the independence and the opportunity such changes offered to adjust the work–life balance, the prevailing characteristics of this growing non-standard labour force are lack of upward mobility, lower earnings, diminished state benefits, higher risk, vulnerability and insecurity. One commentator has termed this 'flexploitation' (Gray, 2004). On balance, such 'flexible' working benefited business to a greater extent than the workers and constitutes a marked retrogressive deterioration in the quality of work in the late twentieth and early twenty-first centuries (see Bunting, 2004). Such changes were intimately connected to wider issues of globalization, the resurgence of 'new right' and neo-liberal market ideologies, the rolling back of the state – the defining issue of

Thatcherism – and the empowering of capital from the 1980s. It created a growing polarization between 'core' and 'peripheral' workers. This has been exacerbated by the impact of the 2008 financial crisis and 'austerity' economic policies. Recently, jobs have been growing fastest at the top (including professionals, technical, managerial) and bottom (unskilled) ends of the labour market and shrinking in the middle (including skilled trades and administrative and secretarial work).

We do, however, need to keep these developments in perspective. Non-standard forms of work have always been a feature of the UK economy, ranging from the casual work of dockers, navvies and other groups, seasonal labour, through part-time homeworking and the 'black economy' and 'cash-in-hand' labour. Moreover, as Edgell has shown, the range of modern-day non-standard work experience was extremely diverse and generalization across the sector is difficult (Edgell, 2006, pp. 126–51). Whilst few commentators dispute that change towards non-standard employment relationships is occurring and has accelerated since the 1980s, nonetheless 'standard' or 'traditional' full-time and formally contracted forms of work with job tenure do still predominate in the early 2010s. It is also the case that not all of the employment rights legislation of the Fordist era has been swept away in the deregulation mania, that Blair's administration made significant changes (such as the minimum wage in 1999) and other sources of support for workers (such as European Union Directives) have emerged to bolster job security, employment rights and manage risk. The 'end of work' theorists point towards an important shifting pattern within UK labour markets, involving a clear erosion of workers' employment rights and more insecurity, but we have to wait to see if irregular and insecure work supplants more traditional forms of labour in the future. What is clear is that work patterns are increasingly becoming polarized and without radical policy changes (for example raising the minimum wage; investing further in vocational and skills training; increasing female employment levels) the gap between higher income, 'work rich' households (frequently with two main earners) and low income, 'work deprived' households looks set to grow even wider in the future.

2

The Meanings of Work

The meaning of work in people's lives has been the subject of considerable debate and discussion. What has been identified as the centrality of work to life – something traditionally associated with the Protestant work ethic – has been perceived to be atrophying by scholars who see in the changing patterns of employment a seismic shift with deskilling and job insecurity loosening people's attachment and commitment to work. This chapter explores these issues.

Meaning in work has been located at a number of levels. Fundamentally, employment is central to people's lives in that it provides for the vast majority the means to their livelihood – the resources to enable individuals and families to be housed, clothed and fed. With the expansion of Britain's welfare state after the Second World War the central role of the wage packet in averting starvation may have been alleviated, nonetheless rising aspirations for higher standards of living continued to be important. Earnings oiled consumption in an increasingly consumer-oriented society. Apart from the basic economic function, employment also had a moral dimension and clearly meant more than just the wage packet for many and perhaps even most workers. A number of studies in the 1950s emphasized the centrality of work in peoples' lives, including Lockwood in a seminal post-war sociological analysis of office work:

> Without doubt in modern industrial society the most important social conditions shaping the psychology of the individual are those arising out of the organisation of production, administration and distribution. In other words, the 'work situation'. (Lockwood, 1958, p. 205)

Studies such as Lockwood's identified that there were *intrinsic* rewards – such as creativity and interest in the work, a sense of purpose, autonomy and independence – as well as the cash and security (*extrinsic* benefits). Around the same time, Galbraith argued that the rewards from labour were unequally distributed:

> The differences in what labour means to different people could not be greater. For some, and probably a majority, it remains a stint to be performed. It may be preferable, especially in the context of social attitudes towards production, to do nothing. Nevertheless it is fatiguing or monotonous or, at a minimum, a source of no particular pleasure. The reward rests not in the task but in the pay. For others, work, as it continues to be called, is an entirely different matter. It is taken for granted that it will be enjoyable. (Galbraith, 1958, cited in Thomas, 1999, p. 168)

Work identity was investigated further by Goldthorpe and others in the *Social Mobility Group* at Nuffield College Oxford in several major studies from the late 1960s. Goldthorpe posited that the work orientation of the elites – in top jobs in social class 1 – was fundamentally different to that of the manual working classes (IV and V). The latter had an 'instrumental' attitude, worked for the money and employment had little meaning for them beyond the economic returns. A crankshaft grinder reflected in 1974: 'My work has been important to me for only one main reason, money – so that my family could live from week to week. My job was and still is a means to an end' (cited in Goldthorpe, p. 1980, 240). In contrast, elites and professionals invariably saw work as their 'central life interest' and sought 'self-fulfilment' through interesting and challenging work. The middle classes (or 'stable, intermediate classes') occupied a point between these extremes, aspiring (though with only limited success) to employment 'in which they could gain some satisfaction of an intrinsic kind' (Goldthorpe, 1980, pp. 237–43).

How then did work forge identities and how, why and to what degree did the meaning of work change from the 1940s to the present? These questions bring us to engage with several specific ideas within the literature, particularly relating to emotion, culture and identity at work. How have the values people attached to work changed over time? Has there been a decline in job satisfaction and in the commitment to work – as some commentators have argued? To what extent were British workers dehumanized, alienated and degraded by their employment – leading to disassociation and deep disaffection? Work was and remains the site of social and cultural power and Marxists (and others – see Donkin, 2001 and Bunting, 2004 for examples) have drawn frequently upon the metaphors of slavery, hell and imprisonment to describe the meaning of work within modern capitalist production. Braverman, for example, in a seminal updating of Marx's deskilling thesis published in 1974, equated the modern workplace to 'dehumanized prisons of labor' (Braverman, 1974). Have there been progressive or retrogressive shifts in the nature, quality and meaning of work in modern society? Have we witnessed deskilling and *deterioration*, or 'upskilling' and *amelioration*? Much of the discussion has pivoted around change in the labour process – the interactions between workers and technology in the production of goods or services (Braverman, 1974; Wood, 1982) – and how such changes have impacted on working-class cultures, shaping collective identities, organization and capacities to resist exploitation in the workplace.

Much recent work focuses on the related but wider issue of *dignity* at work and the extent to which the modern workplace denies this (Hodson, 2001). This discussion hinges upon power and its abuse, upon citizenship in the workplace, upon control, autonomy and agency – or lack of it. Bourdieu has been influential here in arguing a case – based on extensive orally transmitted narratives of French workers – for the widespread existence of 'social suffering' (or 'la petite misère') in everyday life in deregulated, depersonalized and market-driven modern workplaces. Indeed, several prominent commentators have argued for fundamental transformation in the moral dimensions of work – that work has increasingly lost its meaning, that people no longer 'live to work' but have embraced more 'instrumental' and individualized attitudes towards work. This, in turn, has had ramifications for social class awareness, with negative implications for working-class solidarities, occupational communities and collectivism (see Savage, 1999). What is being widely asserted is that the traditional work ethic, or work orientation, has been eroded, 'traditional' working-class communities (such as in mining and shipbuilding) have atrophied and class has lost its meaning. Some go further to argue for 'an end to work', associating the shifts towards service sector, non-standard and less secure work in the modern era with diminished attachment and *commitment* to work, with a shift in focus toward consumption defining the individual in a more affluent age (Beck, 2000; Cassells, 1997). For some this represents a profound loss and a disaster; for others an opportunity to develop a more civilized and enriching work–life balance (see Donkin, 2001).

As an historian, I think a case might be made for these discussions
to be more firmly based in empirical evidence and contextualized in a
more balanced appraisal of the past which implicitly forms the benchmark for such interpretations. Lack of historical context has been the
concern of a number of work sociologists who argue that this blights our
chances of understanding and getting some perspective on continuity
and change and contributes to some of the prevailing myths regarding
work (Bradley et al., 2000, p. 188). With this in mind, the first part of
this chapter explores the meaning of work for the immediate post-war
generation c1945–1970s. This is a period when structural change in the
economy and labour market was relatively modest – the proportion of
the total labour force employed in manufacturing hardly changed for
example (Savage, 1999, p. 26). Any evaluation of the meaning of work
also needs to be grounded in the narratives of workers themselves.
Here we might hope to find discursive shifts across time (intergenerational) and space that elucidate the meanings of work and the debates
on 'the death of work' – as Callum Brown did in a pioneering study
of religiosity in the twentieth century (Brown, 2000). Thus the main
source material analysed here are subjective, qualitative accounts
generated by workers themselves – oral testimonies, autobiographies
and memoirs – as well as a series of 'classic' workplace ethnographies.
The latter were usually the product of sociologists, anthropologists
and journalists living and working within specific occupational communities – such as Huw Beynon, Polly Toynbee and Ruth Cavendish
in assembly-line work. Such personal accounts and ethnographies tell
us much about workers' feelings, providing an insightful barometer of
the complex and ever-evolving world of work – its significance, joys
and frustrations.

The argument advanced here is that work means different things to
different people; there are a plurality of meanings attached to work
which is complex, multi-layered and contingent, influenced by social
class, gender, ethnicity and age. It is further posited here that talk
of a collapse of the work ethic – the moral dimensions of work – is
premature and that most people in Britain continued to have work-
centred lives in the second half of the twentieth century and into the
early twenty-first century and derived much significance from their
work. Long-standing divisions and inequalities have also persisted,
as has the importance of class and gender in identity formation.
The ramifications of the loss of work through unemployment and
redundancy from the Second World War to the present – explored in

Chapter 7 – speaks volumes for the continuing and pivotal importance of work in people's lives in contemporary society.

The 'work ethic' is often spoken about. Before going any further,
however, we should make it clear what is meant by this. Michael Rose
has noted that 'the term *ethic* implies that individuals have a moral
involvement in work' – an 'inner need' – and he highlights several
features of this: firstly, employment commitment: 'duty' to work, as
opposed to dependency; secondly, work centrality and career orientation: work is more important than any other aspect of life – 'the
prime source of meaning and personal identity'; thirdly, deferment
of gratification: work comes first; and fourthly, conscientious effort
('something is not worth doing unless it is going to be done well'),
irrespective of the financial rewards (Rose, 1988, pp. 132–4). In the
UK these ideas go back to the work of Samuel Smiles in the 1850s
and the pioneering research of Max Weber who famously associated
the Victorian period with a strong work ethic linked to Protestantism.
V.S. Pritchett nicely captured the centrality of work to one family in
1945:

> They were all workers in this family. Everything was work to them. Uncle
> Tom was always sawing and hammering. He had made the chests of draw-
> ers and the tables in his house. Aunt Annie scrubbed and cooked. Cousin
> Gladys was always sewing and even when she came in from her factory, she
> had, as they said, 'something in her hands' – a brush, a broom, a cleaning
> cloth or scissors. Jim was a worker too. He worked at the post office in the
> middle of town. (V.S. Pritchett, *The Night Worker*, 1945, cited in Thomas,
> 1999, p. 138)

At mid-twentieth century there may still have been a dominant (or
hegemonic) work ethic connected to the 'breadwinner' ideal or duty,
but the meaning of work varied widely across space, gender, class
and ethnicity with many diverging manifestations and intersecting
identities – or 'intersectionality' (see Strangleman and Warren, 2008,
p. 179; Kirk and Wall, 2010, pp. 226–7).

'I work for the money': work, wages and livelihood

There are many ways in which work gave meaning and shaped lives.
At a very profound level work provided a livelihood and defined the
standard of living, and for a large segment of the labour force this
was the main (but not only) reason for going out to work. Doing work

provided the resources for the family – to maintain a presence above the poverty line – as well as the 'readies' for consumption as expectations for more and better quality leisure time grew in the post-war period of relative full male employment. Work cannot be disconnected from the extrinsic rewards as income meant so much. The sociologist Ferdinand Zweig commented in 1952: 'From what the workers say themselves it might seem that the wage packet is the most important factor in liking or disliking a job' (Zweig, 1952a, p. 102). In 1969 in his introduction to the second volume of his collections of short workers' autobiographies Ronald Fraser made this point forcefully:

> Money is of self-evident importance, a primary concern. It is a lack which even in those cases where 'good money' is earned, as in the trawlerman's case, is filled only at the expense of long hours and of great physical and mental strain. Money, we seem to be hearing is what work is about… Lack of money, where money is the socially validated measure of all human activity and worth, is a derogation of a person's possibilities, a human lack… A man who has less is less of a man. (Fraser, 1969, pp. 8–9)

One of Fraser's subjects (a factory worker, Dennis Johnston) had a dig at those who tried to elevate manual work to some sort of noble activity:

> People who speak grandiosely of the 'meaning of work' should spend a year or two in a factory. The modern worker neither gives anything to work nor expects anything (apart from his wages) from it. Work, at a factory level, has no inherent value. The worker's one interest is his pay packet. (Johnston in Fraser, 1968, p. 12)

A factory metal worker (a crankshaft grinder) reflected in a similar fashion in the early 1970s: 'Success at work from my point of view, and most working class people that I know, is measured by the amount of money that is on your pay-slip at the end of the week' (Case 664–0780; Goldthorpe, 1980, 240–41). A clerical worker spoke in similar tone:

> In common with the other jobs I've had it has no value as work. It is drudgery done in congenial surroundings. You feel dispensible, interim: automation will take over it one day, the sooner the better. You are there for the money, no other reason. You begrudge the time. (Philip Callow, cited in Fraser, 1968, pp. 58–9)

Sillitoe's anti-hero Arthur Seaton in the classic working-class novel *Saturday Night, Sunday Morning* (1958) nicely exemplified such attitudes in his disinterest in the factory job he had and preoccupation with making his 'fourteen quid' a week to fund his binge drinking, womanizing and fashionable clothes:

> 'I like your room,' she said, her eyes on the open curtain of his wardrobe. 'Are all them clo'es yourn?' 'Just a few rags,' he said. She sat up straight hands in her lap. 'They look better than rags to me. They must have cost you a pretty penny.'... 'I get good wages,' he said... and spend 'em on clo'es. It's good to be well dressed.' (Sillitoe, 1958, p. 185)

Thus wages were consistently the single most important issue identified in attitudinal surveys as most important to workers (see Table 2.1 below), and significantly the main cause of industrial disputes and strikes in the post-war decades (see for example the 1953 *Research Services Survey*, cited in Kynaston, 2007, pp. 425–6). Frequently, workers linked earnings to improving family living standards in articulating work orientations (Goldthorpe, 1980, pp. 240–1). And the importance of the wage applied to disabled people as well as non-disabled people (Barnes, 2000, p. 48), to women as well as men.

So a prominent motivation for taking employment in the formal economy was the income – whether this was seen as the main wage, or a supplementary one; working for 'extras'. In an oral interview, Doris Gibbs explained why she worked in the 1960s: 'When the children were very small, we didn't have any money... my mother looked after the baby and it bought us a new carpet and took us on holiday and things (interview by Neil Rafeek, 18 Dec 2002, SOHCA/019).

Table 2.1 Main reasons given for working by gender, 1999 (%)

	Women	Men
Need money for basic essentials	44	67
To earn money to buy extras	15	3
To earn money of my own	10	5
I enjoy working	13	10
Working is the normal thing to do	5	8
To follow my career	7	6
For the company of other people	3	0
For a change from my children or from housework	2	0

Source: Hinds and Jarvis, 2000, p. 105. Copyright © Institute for Social and Economic Research.

One comparative study in the early 1980s has also identified the UK at that point as having a strong 'money motivated' work ethic and a relatively low 'attachment' to work – in that it was not considered central in life in the way that it was in the USA and Japan for example (Yankelovitch et al, 1985, p. 398). These conclusions, however, have been challenged, not least by those who argue that such research was motivated and influenced by the political rhetoric of Thatcherism – which had a vested interest in creating a false image of a decline in the work ethic as an excuse to tighten labour discipline and attack the trade unions. As we will see, the meaning of work and the culture of work in the UK was far more complex. Significantly, as Rose has pointed out, studies have consistently shown that even if they found that they could afford not to work, 60–70% of people usually say they would still *want* to work (Rose, 1988, p. 129).

'La petite misere': marginalization, degradation and alienation at work

In order to earn the means for subsistence and to satiate consumption expectations many workers had to endure brutal working conditions and many petty indignities, assaults on self-respect and injustices at work, even in the period of relatively full male employment post-Second World War. From oral evidence garnered from very different places, Studs Terkel, Pierre Bourdieu and Alessandro Portelli – amongst others – have stressed the ways modern work can be both life-enhancing and deeply alienating, oppressing the spirit in multitudinous ways (Terkel, 1972; Bourdieu, 1999; Portelli, 2011).

The publication in 1974 of Harry Braverman's *Labor and Monopoly Capital* triggered a resurgence of the labour process debate that goes back to Marx's *Capital* and beyond. Marx posited:

> As the division of labour increases, labour is simplified. The special skill of the worker becomes worthless. He becomes transformed into a simple, monotonous productive force that does not have to use intense bodily or intellectual faculties. His labour becomes a labour that anyone can perform. (Cited in Tucker, 1978, p. 214)

Whilst Marx laid emphasis on the impact of mechanization and the nascent factory system in the nineteenth century, Braverman identified a more profound deskilling dynamic within the capitalist workplace associated with Taylorist and Fordist work regimes in the twentieth century. The new, largely North American-inspired 'scientific' mass production systems entailed tighter managerial control and monitoring, close work study and surveillance as well as job fragmentation and more detailed division of labour (see McIvor, 2001, pp. 93–108). This eroded worker discretion and autonomy which sucked the creativity, significance and meaning out of work experience. The new methods were designed to raise productivity, enhance competitiveness and hike up profits. Fundamentally, the combination of conceptualization and execution by workers was attacked, and a concerted attempt to draw knowledge from the craft artisans to management was an integral feature of the new work regimes. Fordist workers were expected not to think, but just to perform, following the instructions of management and the dictates of the production planning department and time and motion analysts. Braverman commented:

> The attempt to conceive of the worker as a general-purpose machine operated by management is one of many paths taken toward the same goal: the displacement of labour as the subjective element of the labour process and its transformation into an object. Here the entire work operation, down to its smallest motion, is conceptualized by the management and engineering staffs, laid out, measured, fitted with training and performance standards – all entirely in advance. (Braverman, 1998, p. 124)

The empirical evidence indicates that an erosion of manual skill was widespread within employment in Britain in the twentieth century. Deskilling, as Paul Thompson commented in *The Nature of Work,* was 'the major tendential presence within the development of the capitalist labour process' (Thompson, 1983, p. 118; and see McIvor, 2001, pp. 52–8). In manual work, flow line processes, automation and prefabrication, combined with work study and 'scientific management', changed the way that work was performed in industries as diverse as shipbuilding, engineering, steel making, food processing (epitomized by McDonalds), printing, wood-working, construction and coal mining. Allan Tyrell started work in 1958 as an apprentice wood machinist and went on to ply his craft at a number of high-end companies, including at the BBC, at Harrods and in piano-making. He recalled: 'The quality and the skill that was needed was out of this world'. His work-life narrative was full of references to the pride and self-esteem he derived from working on complex wood-carving jobs, using 'thousands' of different types of hardwood and a wide variety of tools, machines and processes. He witnessed, however, the transition to mass production in his trade. He recalled in an interview in 2010:

> When I went into the job market [after being made redundant from the BBC job], it wasn't there, the skills were not required, we'd come into an age now, whether it was my fault or not, we'd come into an age where everything was mass-produced, the beautiful carvings and mouldings were not being put into homes. The wonderful staircases and balustrades, and handrails, and all the paraphernalia that goes into nice homes, were simplified, streamlined and mass-produced. And I really struggled. And then, I was struggling for a while, and then I finally got a job – how the mighty fall – I got a job at Maxilla Nursery. Around the corner here, yeah, as a part-time caretaker. (Britain at Work interview by Dave Welsh, 29 June 2010)

Allan later returned briefly to his trade, but as an unskilled band-saw operator doing standardized cutting of plywood boards and flooring sheets in bulk. 'I knew it was a bad firm', Allan commented, and he ended up having a bad accident at work and being sacked whilst off sick.

The post-war growth of the electronics sector created jobs, though these were largely for semi-skilled assembly workers, whilst in printing the work was transformed with the advent of computer technology and desk-top printing. Coal mining changed with the coming of power-loading and automatic shearing, though actual control over the labour process was more difficult for management to enforce in some coalfields because of geological conditions – such as in Scotland. Here, as Perchard's work has shown, the 'politics of speed-up' was influenced more by the constant threat of pit closures from the 1950s (Perchard, 2007a). Steel-making, textile production and car-making were amongst those occupations that became heavily automated, whilst the building of ships and houses was fundamentally changed with the shift to welding and the prefabrication of components and units (for example with oil tankers). An English steel worker interviewed in the mid-1990s spoke evocatively of the impact of technology on creativity in the job of steel-making:

> Being a sample-passer was different from what it had been in my father's day. The skill had gone out of melting. It was skilled work in my father's day, semi-skilled in mine. Computers, clocks and gauges had all come in. It took the art out of steel-making. It became boring. No challenge. Originally it was you against the furnace. The equipment had taken the skill out of it. (Cited in Blackwell and Seabrook, 1996, p. 34)

Chemical manufacture also became heavily automated in petrochemical plants such as ICI Billingham and Wilton and in their polythene manufacturing plants (Walker, 2007, p. 48).

Similar tendencies were evident in offices and in shops. The growth of large retail outlets and supermarkets precipitated wholesale deskilling of shop workers, making the traditional five or six-year grocery apprenticeship obsolete. All-round knowledge and experience was replaced by shelf stackers and till operators. Clerical work also suffered from the same processes, with work deskilled and intensified through technological change (word processors) and organizational innovation (for example call centres; performance-related pay). As Knox and McKinlay have commented: 'The effect has been to narrow both the range and scope of clerical work and, at the same time, enhance the power that the organisation has over the individual' (Knox and McKinlay, 2008, p. 59). In banks and financial services, new technologies such as adding machines, direct debits, telephone and internet banking and automated cash dispensing machines drove along fundamental changes in work methods associated with a shift from a 'service' culture to a 'sales' culture. John Grigg, a London bank clerk (later assistant bank manager) in the 1950s and 1960s, commented that mechanization made the job similar to factory work: 'It was very much like that, working in front of these adding machines, except that you wore a suit instead of overalls'. He noted the working hours were generally longer than factory work: 'It was quite exhausting in many ways' (Britain at Work interview by Roraima Joebear, 28 June 2010). The compensations were cheap mortgages and good pensions for bank employees. The growth of part-time contract staff (replacing the notion of 'a job for life') and performance-related pay added to the pressure. John took early retirement aged just 52 when job cuts were being made in the late 1980s in the banks with the onset of computerization. Ironically perhaps, his manual-working father had encouraged John to go into banking because it was judged at the time (around 1950) to be a much more secure career than factory work and anything that involved 'taking your coat off' to work.

Professionals, then, were also not immune from profoundly deleterious changes in the nature of work. Witness, for example, the attack on the autonomy of teachers from the late 1980s as the state imposed national testing at ages 7, 11 and 14 and the 'national curriculum' was introduced. Teachers complained they were losing their discretion to design courses and were subject to more inspection, monitoring and self-evaluation (Draper, 2008, pp. 527–30). District nursing provides another example. Dougall's work has charted the relentless attack on nurses' autonomy as the job became increasingly specialized, regulated and controlled between the 1940s and the 1980s (Dougall, 2008, pp. 344–6). Whilst some new skills were created in these work reorganizations, they too could be subject to fragmentation as the relentless logic of profit maximization proceeded.

Associated with deskilling and work intensification, *alienation* (which might be defined as an increasing detachment and disassociation from work which had come to lose its intrinsic meaning) was evident across vast swathes of the labour force working in the decades after the Second World War. This was especially notable in unskilled labour and routine, repetitive manual and clerical work. Alienation was exemplified, perhaps, in the car assembly plants and in the modern-day call centres. One visitor to Ford's car plant in Dagenham in 1948 commented: 'masses of men fixed to the assembly-line ... showed the enslavement, the dehumanisation, the degrading and humiliation of man as a whole person ... the horror' (cited in Kynaston, 2007, pp. 408–9; see also Beynon, 1973). The lack of meaning in some work also seeps from the autobiographical narratives of many of the workers collected for a *New Left Review* project in the 1960s. One factory worker recalled:

> Despite the relatively improved conditions, what have we got? We're not 'pushed around'; the time passes. But that's all. We spend a third of our lives in the factory, but there is no overall purpose or meaning to it other than the money. Back from one holiday, we start counting up the weeks to the next; no other dates qualify for significance except the date when we are free. There is no sense of achievement about the work. (Cited in Fraser, 1969, pp. 294–5)

Sillitoe's main character in *Saturday Night Sunday Morning* exemplified this deep disinterest in work, which to him was boring and meaningless. On the first page of the novel the work is referred to by Arthur Seaton as 'monotonous graft in the factory' which the Saturday night boozing was required to have 'swill out of your system' (Sillitoe, 1958, p. 1). There was little sense of attachment to the work here: 'the factory did not matter. The factory could go on working until it blew itself up from too much speed' (Sillitoe, 1958, p. 45). This was dehumanized toil: 'Back to the treadmill. Monday was always the worst; by Wednesday he was broken in, like a greyhound' (Sillitoe, 1958, pp. 24–5). The boredom was happily accepted by Seaton, who relished having what he regarded as an easy job where he could earn 'a cool fourteen nicker' without any thinking and not too much physical effort on his lathe (Sillitoe, 1958, p. 32). The work had little meaning:

> The minute you stepped out of the factory gates you thought no more about your work. But the funniest thing was that neither did you think about work when you were standing at your machine. You began the day by cutting and drilling steel cylinders with care, but gradually your actions became automatic and you forgot all about the machine and the quick working of your arms and hands. (Sillitoe, 1958, p. 38)

This was expressed evocatively later in the novel when Seaton reflected on his 'drugged life at the lathe' (Sillitoe, 1958, p. 170) and how his eight years in the factory felt like a 'life sentence' (Sillitoe, 1958, p. 190). Lack of 'freedom' ('treadmill'), imprisonment ('life sentence') and 'slavery' are frequently recurring metaphors in such accounts used to emphasize and evoke just what work felt like.

The depersonalization of work was another recurring theme in work-life narratives, evident, for example, in the 'number' metaphor. A sheet metal worker reflecting on his working life for the Goldthorpe social mobility studies in the early 1970s noted of his failure to advance: 'the persons in higher authority were not willing to give anyone a chance to better themselves. Whatever I did, I was just a number to most people' (Goldthorpe, 1980, p. 225). And Margaret Gray, a Scottish textile worker, recalled:

> An' ah jist didnae like the changes. They sort o' forced you into doin' things that you wouldnae do normally... It went against the grain... They didnae seem to bother about ye. The atmosphere was different. You wis jist a number in the end, jist a number, and they couldnae hae cared less. (Interviewed by Ian MacDougall, 31 Jan 1997, SWPHT Collection)

This sense of alienation on Margaret's part was sharpened by a feeling that 'outsiders' brought in to run the company did not have *experience* ('hadn't a clue'), and a deep sense that the personal and paternalist touch in management was gone and that the workers were no longer valued:

> Ah mean, they would walk through the shop floor and they would never look right or left or say good morning or anything, which, it doesnae take much to say good morning, ye know... They looked upon you as if ye were dirt at times. As ah say, ye wis jist a number.

This repetition of the 'number' metaphor evoked dehumanization and speaks volumes about the changes in the meaning of work for a significant group of people employed in the declining manufacturing industries in post-war Britain. Duncan Adam, a textile mill manager in the Scottish Borders (Peebles) where Mary worked reflected on his first contact with one of the company owners, Sir Henry Ballantyne: 'He says, "your father was a warper.".... He had known ma father, he wasn't jist a number. He'd known ma father and he was welcoming me into the business. It was quite nice.' In contrast he described the new owners who replaced Ballantyne as 'ruthless' and bemoaned the shift in company ethos:

> Ballantyne had been a family business ... He knew ma father ... You could approach anybody ... After, the whole thing was divorced. They weren't interested in the shop-floor. All they were interested in was money. And anything that was in the way of making money — chop. (Interviewed by Ian MacDougall, 8 Nov 1996, SWPHT Collection)

Reflecting on this passage, one gets a sense of a degree of inevitablility in this kind of critique of change in work in the narratives of individuals reflecting back in older age, and, invariably, after retirement from work. There are several possible ways that this might influence the way work-life narratives are constructed. Firstly, people tend to become more conservative and set in their ways with the passage of time: invariably a 60-year-old will distrust changes in the nature of work that would have been warmly embraced in their youth. Duncan Adam articulated this when asked what he felt about the changes in his working life:

> Sad. Sad. Sad to see the decline and as you get older you resent change. You know, the changes in the mill, rationalization and all that, everything, you know, you saw it as progress and it was a necessity. But there's something inside ye, ye resented it a wee bit.

Recalling work days in an oral interview some time after retirement might also influence the way narratives are constructed. The actual experience of alienation and/or joy through work may have receded somewhat, whilst the events are being recalled through the prism of contemporary experience and the knowledge of what has happened to work conditions in the interim. Experiencing relative isolation and perhaps social exclusion in older age, for example, may lead respondents to emphasize nostalgically the positive socializing and camaraderie aspects of work. Demotion to lesser status and poorer paid work with advancing age and reducing capacity to do heavy manual work could also be embarrassing and alienating (Zweig, 1952a,

p. 23). Overbearing control and tyrannizing over employees, leading to humiliation and a sense of low esteem and loss of worth also degraded the experience of work for many workers, whilst casual employment, with its insecurity (and sometimes corruption), as on the docks, lowered self-esteem (Hill, 1976, p. 34).

Drawing upon such experiences in US and British factories, ethnographers and sociologists produced evocative accounts of the degradation and deskilling of labour within Fordist work environments. The studies by Cavendish, Beynon and Wight are examples. What was being discovered was that work had lost its meaning to many people and, stripped of opportunities to express themselves through employment, they increasingly adopted an instrumental attitude towards their everyday work (Wight, 1993, pp. 235–8). As a cleaner at Ferrantis electrical engineering company in the 1970s commented: 'Ye didnae have to think, ye know, ye just did it' (Margot Russell, cited in MacDougall, 2000, p. 136). Around the same time a warehouseman reflected: 'You're not thinking, you're just doing what they tell you'. He left to take up a more interesting job as a trucker 'where there ain't nobody looking over your shoulder' (cited in Thomas, 1999, p. 155). A female watch assembler at Timex, Dundee, expressed this sense of alienation crisply when she commented in an interview in 1994: 'you were like a battery hen' (cited in Knox and McKinlay, 2008, p. 60). Similarly, the journalist Polly Toynbee reflected thus on a spell working in a cake factory in 1971:

> Anyone who has worked at all in a factory knows how deathly conveyor belt work is. At first it is difficult to keep up, and when you're tired it's quite merciless. After a while, when you have become fairly used to it, the fact that you can't work faster is also infuriating... I often wondered what people thought about, working on assembly lines all day. The answer is nothing... the monotony permeates every corner of the brain. The rhythm deadens every thought. (Toynbee, 1971, pp. 35–6)

She continued later in her study:

> The nobility of work is a bizarre concept. In all the jobs I saw and did, in almost all of the jobs for the working classes, I found little that wasn't stultifying, and degrading to any normal human intelligence. (Toynbee, 1971, p. 138)

Disillusionment, disappointment, a collapse of trust, a deterioration in working relationships are amongst the themes articulated in such 'alienation narratives' by workers and ethnographers alike.

Identification with and commitment to work

The deskilling and degradation of work thesis has been challenged
and there is much empirical evidence to indicate that the processes
could be mediated and resisted, and that change did not just flow in
one direction. Rather, ameliorative mutations and the 'upgrading' of
work coexisted in tandem with the destroying of traditional skills.
'Revisionists' argued that deskilling was not ubiquitous, nor work degradation the inevitable consequence of change in the labour process
over the course of the twentieth century (see McIvor, 2001, pp. 10–12).
As observed already, one argument of the latter is that at a macro
level more creative, autonomous and meaningful jobs – in administration, management and the professions (Reich's (1992) 'symbolic
analysts') – have been growing at a faster rate than the erosion of
skilled manufacturing jobs or creation of new deskilled production
line employment. The deskilling thesis has also been criticized for
having an erroneous benchmark based on craftsmanship which was
not representative of the majority of the labour force. Strong work
groups and trade unions could also resist change – mediating work
degradation, so that managerial changes were delayed or modified.
Thus traditional skills were adapted and persisted, as Penn has shown
for engineering (Penn, 1982; 1985). Workers may well have been more
significant agents in the restructuring of work – especially in the
1950s, 1960s and into the 1970s when the trade unions were at their
most powerful (see Chapter 6).

Work reorganizations and technological change, moreover, might
involve the reconstitution of skill in new expertise sets (and mind
sets). For example, in printing the shift from composing to computerized desk-top publishing was labour-shedding, creating a smaller
workforce, but with a different range of skills and competencies, pivoting around the role of data manager (Watson, 2008). Pringle's 1988
oral interview-based study, *Secretaries Talk*, threw up a similar pattern that did not neatly fit the deskilling thesis. She argued that with
word processing in the 1980s copy writing and shorthand skills were
lost, and more time was spent in routine keying in. This impacted
negatively, with a narrower range of skills in the typing pool, though
secretaries benefited from gaining useful skills and the time saving
capabilities of the new technology. In surveys a majority expressed
enhanced satisfaction with word processing compared to typing, and
overall there was no downward spiral of proletarianization (Pringle,
1988, pp. 189, 193–4): 'Secretaries retain skills and initiatives and, in

some contexts, considerable power' (Pringle, 1988, p. 194). Clearly, change in the nature and organization of work was more uneven and complex than Braverman and other Marxist labour process theorists conceptualized. This, in turn, had implications for work identities and how people extracted meaning from their employment.

Whilst the evidence from workplace studies and workers' own testimonies indicates that many workers experienced and articulated a deep sense of alienation, expressing disassociation, detachment, a blatantly instrumental attitude to work and emphasizing the wage packet as the primary motivation, clearly the meaning of work for many went beyond the extrinsic rewards. This was evident from the range of work-life stories from across the occupational spectrum provided to Goldthorpe and his team of social mobility researchers in the early 1970s (see Goldthorpe, 1980, pp. 217–50). Spending so much time in the workplace inevitably gave this part of a person's life meaning – and this might be largely negative, positive, or, as Zweig argued in 1952, frequently a combination of qualities: 'the ambivalence of love and hate is nowhere more strongly expressed than it is in the attitude to work' (Zweig, 1952a, p. 105). And for many, especially though not exclusively skilled craft workers and professionals, the *intrinsic* rewards of work were evident with work maintaining a central function in providing meaning and purpose to life. The dominantly positive and celebratory representations of work in popular culture during the 1930s, the war and the immediate post-war years – from Orwell's *The Road to Wigan Pier* and Grierson's documentary films (such as *Coal Face*, 1935, and *Night Mail*, 1936) to J. B. Priestley's wartime broadcasts and Brandt and Marzaroli's photographs of noble toilers may have also served to bolster such constructions.

Moreover, even where work was repetitive and boring, the camaraderie and socialization at work could provide compensations whilst high levels of satisfaction and commitment to work could be maintained for a whole host of reasons. Hill's 1976 study of dock work in London provides an example, as does Sykes' 1973 study of Scottish navvies. As one jaded and demoralized unemployed worker in the later 1960s reflecting back on his working life said: 'there isn't a job I've ever done, however tedious, however laborious, but what I have not extracted some small degree of pleasure from, known some sense of pride in' (Fraser, 1968, p. 276). In one survey of building workers in 1946, 70% of labourers indicated 'definite liking' for their work, compared to 82% of skilled craftsmen (cited in Kynaston, 2007, p. 426). Glyn Wright's 1995 poem 'Where the Sexes Meet' evokes something of the hierarchal nature of factory work and the pervasiveness of managerial surveillance, whilst also pointing to the agency of workers expressed through covert socializing:

> The metal shop whiffs of grease, old handrags.
> We arrive here dressed as ourselves and button up
> Uniform blue overalls to hammer, weld, strip down,
> Bash out conveyors that line the factory floor
>
> Foremen are brown coats. Managers swank
> In spotless white, fierce with creases, prowl
> the yards, the cubby holes to catch you out.
> Think they're up to all the dodges
>
> Women are wrapped and knotted in white aprons,
> Packed in rows across the factory floor, seated
> At belts that never stop whilst their overseer
> Scans them from a platform made by us
>
> The air's chocolate over there, butter, jam.
> That's where the sexes meet when machines break down,
> Where you chat to each other between ovens,
> Across conveyors, when backs are turned.

(Cited in Thomas, 1999, p. 139)

And whilst the *British Social Attitudes* surveys indicated *money* as a main reason given for working, they also consistently found the majority of people (68% of men and 70% of women in 1992 for example) indicated that work meant more to them than the earnings alone (Kiernan, 1992, pp. 90–1). The self-employed registered particularly high levels of job satisfaction, with over 70% of them indicating that they 'enjoyed working' in the 1992 survey.

What then do workers' testimonies and workplace surveys and ethnographies tell us about work satisfaction and commitment and how work forged identities in the immediate post-war period? And did this change with the shift from the 1980s from an industrial to a post-industrial economy?

'Work is all important', a painter and decorator reflected in 1974, 'Everything takes second place to it' (cited in Goldthorpe, 1980, p. 240). Similarly a welder at the Swan Hunter shipyard at Wallsend in north-east England commented in an interview in 1992, 'Work governs your existence' (Bradley et al., 2000, p. 180). From road sweepers to lawyers, people defined themselves through their work, priding themselves on their skill, productivity, earning power, craftsmanship, strength, endurance, adaptability, graft, professionalism, service to the family, the community and society. In tandem with the prevailing alienation narrative, this is evident in the majority of the 40 work-life autobiographies published in *New Left Review* from the mid to late 1960s. Work done well provided a source of satisfaction – an emotional hit – as well as commanding respect, whilst being part of an occupational group conferred status amongst peers. Many workers felt a strong sense of ownership of their jobs: that they belonged to them and that they were part of a community. For example, Strangleman has shown how important this was for railwaymen in his seminal study of occupational culture in that sector, emphasizing strong work values, a sense of 'service' and pride in performing 'to the best of their ability' before privatization changed this from the mid-1990s (Strangleman, 2004; Strangleman, 2002, sections 3.2–3.5;). Kirk has also argued that railway workers he interviewed frequently evoked the positive metaphor of 'family' – as for example with a 50–year-old female train manager in North-West England:

> We joined a company, a railway company; British Rail became your family. They were an extension of your family; you hurt one, you hurt them all... it's a community. I joined it. (Kirk, 2008, p. 51)

Martin Eady, a London railway carriage examiner, provided an evocative and solidly positive work narrative in an oral history interview in 2010, remarking on the intrinsic job satisfaction, camaraderie and high level of control and autonomy on the job in the 1970s and 1980s: 'It was fairly heavy work. It was very dirty, obviously because you're spending your entire working shift under a train. But me, I quite enjoyed it. A very good atmosphere in the depot, a good crowd of people' (Britain at Work interview by Dave Welsh and Roraima Joebear, 20 May 2010). Martin went on to recount numerous anecdotes of his working life, referring to the banter, rituals, joking around, the respect for elder craftsmen, the racism in some workplaces, the drink culture, the 'fiddles' and the routine use of bad language: 'It was great fun', he reflected, 'there was a lot of laughs'.

Miners also had a strong, well-defined work identity. The 1956 anthropological study of Yorkshire miners by Dennis, Henriques and Slaughter, *Coal is Our Life*, emphasized the deep emotional attachment to and pride engendered from the work:

> In the pit itself, among his workmates, the miner is proud of doing his job as a good man should, and to a great extent a man becomes identified with his particular job... Pride in work is a very important part of a miners' life. Old men delight in stories of their strength and skill in youth. (Dennis et al., 1956, p. 73)

Tom Ellis, a North Wales miner (who started work underground in 1947 and rose to become a mine manager) commented in his autobiography that miners' work identities were forged in the freedom from authority they held at the point of production:

> That we worked entirely unsupervised was an aspect of our work which made a great impression on me, the discretion given to us no doubt fostering the sense of responsibility within the team and its pride in, so to speak, delivering the goods. I gradually came to realise that the pride in his craft, which was characteristic of the miner, stemmed partly from the considerable personal discretion he exercised in how he went about his work...I was happy in my work and confident that I had made the right choice of career. (Ellis, 2004, pp. 38–9)

Whilst declining in numbers, skilled craftsmen frequently articulated high levels of job satisfaction and joy in work and developed a strong 'sense of occupational community' (Hill, 1976, p. 38). This was connected to a range of things, including the wider variety of work, the level of thinking (conceptualizing) that had to be put in to it and the degree of autonomy exercised at work (especially by the self-employed craftsman). As one glazier confidently asserted in 1946: 'Mine is a job on its own. Not everyone can get an eighth of an inch off 57 feet of glass' (cited in Kynaston, 2007, p. 426). A skilled steelworker described his promotion to the 'suit and tie' role of 'sample-passer' – essentially supervisor of the smelting process – as 'the greatest day of my life' though he hastened to add, 'apart from getting married' (Blackwell and Seabrook, 1996, p. 35). He evoked what the job meant to him:

> Eventually I became a sample-passer in 1966. I was picked out by management. I felt big. I was over the moon. It wasn't the power, it wasn't the money. It was an achievement. That's what I wanted to be, because that is what my father was. (Cited in Blackwell and Seabrook, 1996, p. 34)

Experience, attitudes and feelings about work varied widely. More positive narratives of work emerge from craftsmen, supervisors, managers and professionals, whilst many manual workers derived a deep sense of satisfaction from enduring and resisting tough and demanding work regimes. This is evident in Hill's study of the London dockers in 1971, where he observes:

> Those dissatisfying characteristics of industrial work tasks which are notoriously typical of many factory jobs were markedly absent from the foremen's jobs, while even the manual dock workers perceived their work to be relatively free from most of these sources of deprivation. (Hill, 1976, p. 57)

Dockers regarded themselves as skilled and were somewhat unusual in the degree of control and autonomy they exercised over their labour – factors which clearly contributed to a generally positive work orientation and 'intrinsic work satisfaction' (Hill, 1976, pp. 58–9, 67). For others, exhausting and dangerous work might be stoically tolerated for the sake of the family. John Oswell, a London van and lorry driver from 1962–1997, described the autonomy he enjoyed working alone on the road: 'You're left alone basically. And it's a responsibility I think because what they're saying to you is "there's a job – go and do it and you're doing it on your own"'. He worked most of his life for Esso as a tanker driver: 'It was a wonderful job. I loved it. I loved going to work on a Monday. Other people say "Oh Monday's come around again, I can't stand it". I used to love it! I couldn't wait to get Sunday out of the way and go to work on a Monday' (Britain at Work interview by Dave Welsh, 15 Jan 2011). His work-life testimony is peppered with references to his rate of earnings at different jobs and his search for job security – which came with the Esso job (where he worked for the last 24 years of his working life). A recurring motif was the need to 'earn a living' to support his family. His was a classic male 'breadwinner' narrative. When he took what he described as a 'horrible job' in 1973 that he 'absolutely hated' he rationalized this with the comment: 'The money wasn't very good and the hours were awful and I didn't like the job at all but I had to take a wage home. I had to put money on the table because I had two kids to feed. So I took this job'.

For others, a pivotal element in job satisfaction was the individuals with whom you worked. Work provided a source of social contacts, drinking partners and mates. A London sheet metal worker Frank Cooper (who started work in 1939) responded in an interview in 2010 to being asked 'where were the best places you worked':

> Oh I think they were all good. The enjoyment is the blokes that you work with. I still have some contact with different people that I worked with at different times. I was talking to a fellow who lives at Kingsbury, actually, on the telephone the other day. He said I saw somebody the other day who told me you were still alive, he said! And we had a chat and he's ninety-two. And he was a sheet metal worker I worked with. I think the enjoyment is the people you work with. Yes, when you go to work you do meet up with some miserable bastards, but by and large they're not. You have a laugh and a joke and, y'now. I think that's great. (Britain at Work interview by Peter Atherton, 10 March 2010)

Other work narratives enable further consideration of these ideas about the meanings of work. For example, the Scottish oral historian Ian MacDougall interviewed eleven female textile workers in Peebles. These testimonies are witness to a rich and varied work experience – though the length of interview transcriptions, from less than 3,000 words to almost 30,000 words, signifies much about the differing performances and power of recall of narrators. What is evident is that the type of job being done conferred a certain status and meaning; there was a distinct pecking order of jobs in the female labour market, with professional occupations (e.g. teaching) and clerical and shop jobs at the top, working in textile factories of intermediate status, and domestic service at the bottom. As one Borders textile worker (Wilma French, born 1938) pointed out: 'they used tae say if ye worked in a shop ye were kind o' posh, in these days'. She hastened to add, 'but the wages were nae good' (interviewed by Ian MacDougall, 6 Dec 1996, SWPHT Collection). The Peebles work-life narratives are suffused with a great deal of job satisfaction. Effie Anderson worked in the mills from the early 1940s to around 1980. Her narrative identifies gendered job segregation and subordination in employment (for example, there were no female supervisors), the tendency towards work intensification in the 1960s and 1970s with changing technology and the requirement to work more looms (from one to four), as well as the increasing insecurity of the work as time went on (she was made redundant in her mid-50s). Nonetheless, she indicated in her testimony that she wished for no other work (she had hated domestic service in her early teens) and had found the job financially rewarding and intrinsically satisfying: 'Ah enjoyed ma work. Ah did enjoy ma work' (interviewed by Ian MacDougall, 28 Nov 1996, SWPHT Collection). Similarly Myra Little (born 1936) noted: 'Ah thoroughly enjoyed ma stake warpin'. Tae me that wis an experience, it really wis. But ah like a' these sort o' complicated things that you've tae think on. Somethin' that you're goin' tae achieve somethin' at the end o' it' (interviewed by Ian MacDougall, 18 Dec 1996, SWPHT Collection). These were not narratives of alienation, but rather very positive stories, frequently with detailed descriptions of the labour processes and friendships forged in the factory. In textile communities such as Peebles, Stirling, Dundee and Paisley, women workers were invariably more upbeat in their memories of work and its importance to them. The focus of their work-life narratives was as much work-centred as family-oriented, though clearly work identities were shaped by and refracted through gender (see Chapter 3).

It appears clear, therefore, that work had multiple meanings (often not mutually exclusive), and that for many and perhaps even most people in the later twentieth century work continued to hold significance beyond the wage packet. Writers, academics and creative artists invariably placed work at the centre of their world. Freud, for example, commented: 'I could not contemplate with any sort of comfort a life without work. Creative imagination and work go together with me; I take no delight in anything else' (cited in Thomas, 1999, p. 179). Noel Coward put it more flippantly in 1963: 'Work is much more fun than fun' (cited in Thomas, 1999, p. 140). Moreover, intergenerational change could be in the direction of job enrichment, rather than denigration. There continued to be a moral dimension to work with attitudinal surveys showing that some people felt jobs were becoming more skilled and that they expressed a wide range of reasons for working beyond the financial rewards – such as a sense of achievement, independence and creativity (Gallie, 2000, pp. 289–90). Clearly for many people, and probably proportionately more than before the Second World War, work continued to be *enjoyable* and rewarding and to provide dignity, self-respect, satisfaction and a sense of worth.

Nowhere was this more evident than amongst the burgeoning ranks of professionals whose work narratives often clash sharply with those recalling their working lives of pre-1950, or those of their parents. Given the radically changed job profile of men and (particularly) women in Britain in the second half of the twentieth century this is hardly surprising. For women, personal upward social mobility and intergenerational shifts from domestic service to the factory and shop work, and from there to the office and into the professions, increasingly via higher education, were often (and again not surprisingly) articulated in a positive light. The dehumanization of work thesis might be criticized for being male-centred. Despite persisting inequalities, historically the direction for female labour has undoubtedly been towards more status, power and independence in employment over time as well as towards access to a wider range of jobs and higher status (and paid) positions. As a consequence, paid labour was much more important and meaningful to most women's everyday lives in the 2000s compared to c1950. Access to and working within higher education provides an example. Ann Mair, employed as a programmer in the early years of computerization in the late 1960s at the new University of Strathclyde in Glasgow, represented a female worker benefiting from the creation of new skills with the coming of computers. Reflecting on that period and her work as the first computing officer for the Department of Politics she noted: 'we were the state of the art, we really were' (interviewed by Neil Rafeek 23 Dec 2002, SOHC/019). Similarly, Karen Morrison took advantage of strong demand for labour in the 1960s and 1970s to enhance her career, becoming a university academic department secretary, explaining: 'It just promised probably a better career, a better working environment, *more interesting,* I mean I was bored to tears where I was' (interviewed by Neil Rafeek, 25 Nov 2002, SOHC/019). Morrison's narrative is that of an articulate woman who progressed from routine office work to department secretary and then department administrator: 'I forged the way if you like.' Despite being forced to leave her job temporarily at a university in 1968 when she was pregnant (because there was no provision then for maternity pay), she went on to a fulfilling career. She commented:

> It was just kind of tacit, that a secretary was a secretary and you were, you know, my phrase is 'I'm only paid up to here', under my chin, I'm not paid to think from there to there ... So I increased my involvement and was allowed to do so which has been very rewarding for me and I think, *I think*, I hope to the benefit of the department. I can't say in the sixties that I would have been able to do what I'm doing today, I don't think I would have been given the opportunity. I would think it would have been seen that only an academic could do this.

Pam Osborne had a similar career trajectory in London. Born in 1946, she started work as a typist for an airline (British Eagle) in 1964. After a fragmented early working life in several jobs she left work to bring up two children, returning to the labour market in 1979. Thereafter she progressed to working at Brunel University, where she became research administrator and finally the Pro-Chancellor's PA in 2000. She reflected: 'Oh it's lovely at Brunel. It's lovely'. Along the way she experienced the revolution in office technology which came with computerization and the web. She commented: 'Technology is fantastic. It has its place. But I still think you can't beat the personal touch ... I'm an old-fashioned PA ... Office roles have changed so much now' (Britain at Work interview by Ruth Sheldon, 12 June 2009). The depersonalization of work was the only significant negative reported in her generally positive and very detailed work life narrative which oozed with pride and self-esteem.

The growth of the service sector and professional jobs, as well as the significant expansion of public sector employment, also altered perceptions and experiences of work. The resulting workplace environment was much safer and less health-eroding than much manual work (see Chapter 5), and for many the work involved the application of complex skills and long training after several years in further and higher education. The son of a joiner, Willie Dewar trained as a draughtsman, undertaking his apprenticeship during the Second World War. In his narrative he articulated a close attachment to the work and to the product. He also may have over-emphasized the danger because he felt a need to defend his masculinity and show a parallel with the risks that wartime combatants faced:

> Some people said they would have quite willingly worked for nothing in the locomotive industry because it was an interesting, interesting trade to be in. And the loco, I always say a locomotive is a living thing. You know it spits back at you, it throws oil at you ... it burns you and it will also kill you. (Interviewed by Arthur McIvor, 9 December 2008, SOHC/032)

Moreover, widening higher education admission and upward mobility provided access – eventually – to creative, people-centred and enriching careers for a larger segment of the offspring of the working classes. Alan White, born in 1938 and raised in Edinburgh, was the first of his family to enter librarianship from a manual working background. He reflected in 1996:

> I liked working with the public ... I reckoned in my modest way I was quite good at it, I got a lot of fun out of it, I enjoyed myself, I enjoyed the variety that working with a wide cross-section of the public can bring. And to the day that I retired, I retained that liking. I was very, very lucky. I mean, I landed in doing something that I enjoyed doing and I enjoyed doing it with a wide cross-section of people. And I've never regretted my decision whatsoever. (Interviewed by Ian MacDougall, 22 August 1996, SWPHT Collection)

His narrative emphasized his pride in doing the job well and being recognized by his peers (he became President of the Scottish and UK Library Associations). Similarly, Ron Thompson's work-life narrative stressed his love of journalism, the 'buzz' and romance of getting the 'scoop' or 'exclusive' and his enjoyment of the range and variety of the work and, in later years, his independence and autonomy as he moved into television journalism with Grampian TV (interviewed by Ian MacDougall, 7 July 1999, SWPHT Collection).

For some professionals, such as lecturers and librarians, there were increasing frustrations linked to work intensification, rising stress levels and the increasing bureaucratization of the job. One Scottish male librarian (Andrew Fraser) reflected critically on committees and administrators more interested in resources than providing a service (for example when the mobile libraries were scrapped). Nonetheless, his generally positive work narrative stressed the pleasure he derived from over 45 years working in the public library service in the Lothians (interviewed by Ian MacDougall, 23 May 1997, SWPHT Collection).

For some of these workers, employment was injected with meaning and significance by a sense that they were providing a service to the public and to society as teachers, social workers, nurses, doctors and civil servants. Respect was earned as valued members of the community. Witness, for example, the excitement embedded within this reflection by an economist Roger Sandilands on Glasgow as an environment in which to work:

> I felt for someone who's interested in doing Economics it [the city] seemed a living laboratory of economics in action in terms at least of the kinds of *real problems* that economists should be interested in; unemployment, inequality, poverty, poor housing, social problems in general...I loved it, it was what I wanted to do and I just blossomed. (Interviewed by Neil Rafeek, 1 November 2002, SOHC/019)

'Death of work'? The meaning of work since 1980

How have work identities changed in the modern era since the 1970s? Has association, attachment and meaning deepened as labour markets mutated from industrial to post-industrial jobs, with the surge in the numbers of professional, creative and managerial posts? Or has computerization, scientific management, flexible work systems and the proliferation of deskilled, routinized and more insecure 'McJobs' drained intrinsic value from work? Partly as a reaction to the neglect of identity and agency in structuralist accounts of work such as Braverman (1974), and prompted by wider changes in the economy and the emergence of more non-standard forms of work with deindustrialization and deregulation, research has increasingly focused on attitudes and emotions at work. A dominant interpretation has been that with the expansion of temporary, part-time, insecure and non-standard 'modern' employment, as well as growing unemployment, work no longer functions as a primary means of identity – especially as far as men are concerned. Traditional work cultures and workplace solidarities have evaporated in a context of global free market capitalism where workers are more isolated and individualized. To Sennett,

Casey, Beck, Gorz, Bauman and others the work ethic has atrophied, with traditionally strong work identities being 'degraded' and work no longer occupying a pivotal position in people's lives. Increasingly in this new world people look toward the family, leisure and to consumption for meaning in their lives, in place of their work (see Strangleman, 2007 and Strangleman and Warren, 2008, pp. 292–4).

Evidence of this *diminishing* orientation towards work is present in personal and oral accounts. Indeed, these discourses act as a kind of barometer of mutating work identities over time. This was expressed, for example, in unfavourable comparisons between attitudes to work of the older and younger generations. An English steel worker interviewed in the mid-1990s commented: 'We worked as a team. Got on well together. Today it's not the same ... Young people take no interest in work now' (Blackwell and Seabrook, 1996, pp. 32, 35). Nan Stevenson, an office cleaner, interviewed in 2002 eighteen months before her retirement, articulated a similar sharp sense of changing work culture and in her occupation a *diminution* in younger workers' attachment to and pride in the work:

> They've not got the same interest in their job now that they did. You kept working and kept an interest in your job ... You come in here, you take a pride in how you scrubbed that room 'Oh that looks nice'. They don't do that now. (Interviewed by Neil Rafeek, 28 Nov 2002, SOHC/019)

To this respondent the meaning of work had altered from her generation to the next – the moral dimension had eroded. She recognized the improvements in wages and productivity that came with mechanization of the cleaning job, but still looked back to the more interesting, sociable days at work in the 1960s when the work was simpler and less stressful: 'Everybody kind of all worked together ... They were happy days then, they were happy days then. You looked forward to coming to your work in those days, so you did.' Similarly, a female train cleaning manager recalled days when a train would be sent out – 'it sparkled' and was 'pristine':

> From the top to the bottom everyone cared ... Now they get on, do a quick sweep, a bit of a wipe of the windows, stick it through the mechanical wash. That's clean? (Cited in Kirk, 2008, p. 51)

There is an element of wistful, nostalgic yearning for a kind of 'golden age' of a more meaningful past work life here. Strangleman has referred to this in his studies of railwaymen where he detected in his oral interviews a 'nostalgia for a lost workplace', though he also

warned against scholars drifting in to 'an unreflective nostalgia our-
selves' (Strangleman, 2002, sections 2.33, 3.1; Strangleman, 2004).
Daniel Wight also found that such nostalgia for a lost era of committed hard graft pervaded the Central Scotland coal mining village
he studied as an anthropologist in the 1980s. He found really significant differences in orientation to work between the older and younger
generations in the community. This identification of different levels
of emotional attachment to work between the older 'veterans' and
younger, new generation workers was a recurring motif in work-life
interviews – indicated, for example, in Bourdieu's *The Weight of the
World* (1999). This slippage in work commitment might be expected,
given the growing lack of reciprocity with erosion of job security,
short-term contracts and the growth of out-sourcing in the modern
market-driven economy. Strangleman commented that the situation
in the railways was complex: 'a dynamic, heterogeneous working-
class culture which changed subtly over time – and across generations'
(2002, section 3.2).

In the early years of the twentieth-first century it was perhaps the
call centre that epitomized the almost apocalyptic vision of meaningless, degraded, monotonous and dehumanized work. Fernie and
Metcalf argued in an empirical study of several call centres in the late
1990s that they exemplified the close control and surveillance that
Foucault theorized (adapting Bentham's idea of the panopticon) was
characteristic of the modern workplace. To Fernie and Metcalf, these
were the new 'sweatshops':

> The possibilities for monitoring behaviour and measuring output are
> amazing to behold – the 'tyranny of the assembly line' is but a Sunday
> school picnic compared with the control that management can exercise
> in computer telephony. Indeed, the advertising brochure for a popular
> call centre software package is boldly titled TOTAL CONTROL MADE
> EASY. (Fernie and Metcalf, 1998, p. 2)

Call centre workers' oral testimonies frequently incorporated this
alienated, disconnected, work-as-drudgery narrative (see Taylor
et al., 2002; 2003). As one Scottish call centre worker commented:
'I think I'll probably be stuck in jobs that I don't want for the rest of
my life, that's the way I see it... working is important but my job isn't
important. I work to live, not live to work... My job isn't important.
Keeping it is, but it's not a factor in my life' (interview E-I-14; ESDS
Online Archive, Project SN4815). Another reflected that home life
and going out were 'more important', with work designated as 'not

very important' (interview E-I-13; ESDS Online Archive, Project SN4815). A particularly scathing and emotional indictment of such work came from a former building society call centre manager in Glasgow, Catherine McBean, who recalled of the late 1990s:

> In the call centre, people were monitored every second of the day. And they were rated on their call rate and the duration of the calls, you had to make the calls as short as you could; how many calls they had answered, and that was all monitored, in computerized monitoring of the calls and the terminals – they all sat in front of a terminal on the phone. And (pause), I remember one day being in my office and watching this girl. She had her headphones on and she was tethered, with the headphone wire to the phone and she got up off her chair and started pacing up and down the floor. I thought to myself that's like a dog in a yard, in a kennel pacing up and down there. And I thought, this is not right. People can't go to the toilet, they don't feel they can go to the toilet without having an impact negatively on their performance levels. And, the pressure of the situation. I thought we shouldn't be treating human beings like this. I really, really didn't like it. And I began to have problems dealing, living with that. So, there came an opportunity for me to take voluntary redundancy. I didn't have to. And I'm not blowing my own trumpet when I say I was quite a star in the place. I could have gone on, but I said (pause), 'I don't want to be a part of this'. And I took the voluntary redundancy and left [in 1998]. (Interviewed by David Walker, 21 February 2011, SOHC/042)

This narrative strongly evokes the panopticon nature of this employment, with the high level of performance monitoring and self-exploitation evident, as well as the assault on personal dignity, expressed powerfully through the deployment of the 'dog and kennel' metaphor.

With such changes in the economy, in work organization and the fundamental shift towards more non-permanent work contracts and job insecurity, there were signs that expectations about work and the meaning of work were mutating, together with the identities that were forged in the workplace. The qualitative *British Social Attitudes* surveys which mushroomed from the mid-1980s picked up on these changes in work orientation and commitment. In Russell's comparative study of Britain, Germany, Sweden and Italy at the end of the 1990s, for example, it was found that the UK recorded the lowest levels of commitment to work by a substantial margin and that over time (1989–1997) work commitment in Britain eroded more sharply than elsewhere (Russell, 1998, pp. 85–9, 94). This was associated strongly with the growth of job insecurity, deregulation and the removal of legal 'protections' in the labour market (and *not* with levels of unemployment – see Chapter 6), with Russell arguing that what employers gained in flexibility they paid for in terms of lower productivity and a diminished work ethic and eroded attachment to the company (Russell, 1998, p. 93). Concurrent with these experiences, however, were countervailing tendencies – with higher educated, creative and professional employees increasingly demanding more intrinsic rewards from their work and some embracing 'downsizing' and a more sustainable work–life balance (Russell, 1998, p. 90). This represented a shift towards 'post-materialist' values. Such evidence may well lend support to the polarization thesis – the idea that work deprivation has grown at one end of the labour market and work enrichment at the other end.

What is clear is that the 'degradation' and 'end of work' theses are far from proven, as the empirical work of a number of contemporary sociologists demonstrates (see Strangleman and Warren, 2008; Kirk and Wall, 2010). A flaw in such hypotheses is a tendency to romanticize and over-simplify the past – assuming a fixed and stable work identity 'benchmark' (sometimes implicitly associated with skilled craft production) characterized by a firm attachment to work. Work cultures and identities historically were always more fluid, contingent and heterogeneous. Relatively few workers before the Second World War experienced the work satisfaction, creativity and control of the professions and skilled craftsmen (who constituted perhaps 15–20% of the total labour force in the 1930s). Moreover, there is plenty of evidence to suggest that work continued (and continues) to provide meaning for a significant segment of the labour force. It is important not to over-extrapolate from the experience of call centres and the like. Hodson has shown how the struggle over 'dignity at work' remains a contested terrain, with workers (and their trade unions) operating as active agents in maintaining self-respect and self-worth in the face of technological change and managerial assaults designed to deepen their control and increase the profit margin (Hodson, 2001).

This chimes with some of the *Social Attitudes* survey work – such as Russell, who argued in 1998 that whilst work commitment in the UK was diminishing over time, this applied particularly to 'extrinsic characteristics of work', such as earnings, whilst 'the emphasis placed on intrinsic rewards remains stable and high' (Russell, 1998, p. 94). Whilst their reliability is somewhat questionable, *Social Attitudes* surveys on levels of job satisfaction (as in Table 2.2) – whilst indicating

Table 2.2 Job satisfaction by gender, 1989 and 1998 (%)

	1989	1998
Very satisfied		
Women	37	35
Men	38	29
Fairly satisfied		
Women	47	45
Men	42	49
Not very / not at all satisfied		
Women	13	19
Men	17	22

Source: Hinds and Jarvis, 2000, p. 106. Copyright © Institute for Social and Economic Research.

a marked diminution in male job satisfaction in the 1990s – do not support the concept of a deeply alienated workforce.

Kirk and Wall's recent book, *Work and Identity* (2010), based on extensive oral interviewing across three very different groups of workers (110 interviews of teachers, bank workers and railway employees), provides a riposte to the 'end of work' theory (Kirk and Wall, 2010; see also Kirk, 2008; Wight, 1993). They argue that despite neo-liberalism and the post-1980 reforms bringing the market into education and challenging the autonomy and professional identities of teachers, nonetheless traditional workplace values were resilient to change and teachers continued to find meaning in 'public service' (Kirk and Wall, 2010, pp. 122–3). The case appears less convincing for bank workers where the nature of work has changed fundamentally with the transition from banking to selling (or 'from tellers to sellers') and the growth of financial sector call centres (as with the building society call centre example above). Nonetheless, the narratives of many bank workers continued to indicate that 'work remains a major source of meaning and belonging' (Kirk and Wall, 2010, p. 148). Even in the railways, despite growing estrangement and disassociation from the work under privatization, there remained a strong 'residual' meaning, associated with notions of 'duty' and 'public service', camaraderie (significantly the 'like a family' metaphor recurred across several of the cited testimonies) and pride in the job (Kirk and Wall, 2010, pp. 156–61, 174–5). Whilst there were pressures exerted upon traditional and dominant work cultures from the 1980s, 'work',

Kirk and Wall argue, 'remains central to identity formation' (Kirk and Wall, 2010, p. 98). They conclude that orally transmitted work histories indicate that prophesies of the 'end of work' are premature and that work experience 'still figures in fundamental ways as a site of identification in the lives of most of the men and women with whom we spoke' (Kirk and Wall, 2010, pp. 226–7).

Conclusion

What appears evident is the persistence into the twenty-first century of a multi-tiered labour market in which the experience of the fortunate and privileged contrasted with the poor and deprived, with age, social class, ethnicity and gender continuing to influence and limit employment opportunities. In turn, this shaped workers' attitudes, and the ways in which they constructed their employment stories and narrated their working lives as participants, drawing out different messages, discourses and signifiers from their labour. Work meant different things to different people and this could change over a life course as the job evolved and as new techniques, forms of work organization and technologies were introduced. For many, there were negative connotations with work devoid of inner meaning, where workers lacked control, autonomy or space to express their capacities, knowledge, discretion and skills. Such 'alienation narratives' abound – and not just within the mass assembly line occupations (where research has perhaps been most extensive). The empirical evidence also supports the view that deskilling and work degradation was a prevailing experience for many workers and that this impacted on their attachment and orientation to their work.

At the other extreme a wide swathe of workers (and not just the skilled craftsmen) found purpose, joy and meaning in their work, which gave structure to the day, forged identities, gave a sense of belonging and was a source of much pride and self-esteem. This was perhaps most evidently the case for the growing number of professional and creative workers in the economy. To some degree at least, these differences in emotional attachment to and the intrinsic meaning of work reflected class and status differences within society. As Hill has observed:

> The lower down the occupational hierarchy a group is placed, the more likely its members are to experience work as something that is meaningless and lacks the capacity to provide positive satisfaction of their needs and desires, as something that is truly 'alienating'. It can be argued that

this is one of the most fundamental aspects of the social inequality of modern society. Conversely, the higher the occupational and class position of
the group, the more work is likely to be found to be meaningful, stimulating and satisfying. (Hill, 1976, p. 57)

Whether negative or positive, or the many hues of grey between, what
is evident is that work was a deeply *emotional* experience. Whilst
many experienced degeneration in their working lives, the evidence
does not support the view that there was *universal* degradation of
work in Britain or wholesale 'abandonment' of traditional work values. Up-skilling and deskilling happened concurrently with new technologies and economic change (Strangleman, 2004, pp. 74–6). Work
continued to be a site of real meaning and significance and, perhaps
for most workers, of pivotal importance in their identities.

That said, clearly there were widespread assaults upon respect and
dignity at work through mismanagement, evasive monitoring and
other forms of abuse and misuse of authority (see Bourdieu, 1999;
Hodson, 2001). There was clear and evident erosion of the 'service'
ethic in privatized sectors such as the railways (Strangleman, 2004)
and much evidence of alienation in the most routinized of occupations – such as assembly-line work and 'post-industrial' call centre
jobs. And there was real tangible loss in what Blackwell and Seabrook
termed the 'dematerialisation of work' as the traditional manufacturing industries collapsed and new computerized technologies spread
(Blackwell and Seabrook, 1996, p. 194). A struggle for security, dignity and respect at work characterizes the contemporary workplace
and in many respects this situation has worsened with neo-liberalism
and the turn to deregulation of labour markets and as the free market prevails, globalization continues and the disempowering effects
of persistently high levels of unemployment bite deeper. Violence of
sorts continues to be inflicted upon workers in the modern workplace
though this is now more connected to the pace, intensity and mean-
inglessness of the work – more of an assault upon mental energy than
physical capacity. And the meanings that are derived from work are
affected accordingly. Whether all this amounts, as some theorists have
argued, to the 'end of work' as job insecurity intensifies and attachment to work atrophies in the modern, globalized labour market,
remains to be seen. What is undeniable is that social inequalities in
earnings and wealth have widened sharply since the 1980s and there
has been an increasing polarization of the labour market, reflected
in a widening divergence between those fortunate enough to enjoy

their work and those alienated by it. Such lived experience continues to shape work identities and the meanings people derive from their employment. Increased security and citizenship in the workplace, the reduction of over-work, narrowing the wage gap, the elimination of work deprivation and a better work–life balance remain important aspirations and objectives in the early twenty-first century.

3

A Man's World?

In the immediate post-war period and despite the influx of women into war-related work, employment remained dominated by men. In the 1950s and 1960s, women were widely perceived to be participating in employment in a temporary and subordinate capacity before getting down to their life's role of bearing and nurturing children. This chapter investigates the gendered nature of work and gender identities at work.

The first section focuses on male identity and the expression of masculinity in employment. How did the kinds of jobs undertaken by men incubate and forge masculine values? How did male peer pressure on the job work? Was there a spectrum of masculinities in the post-war workplace with a dominant, or 'hegemonic' mode of masculinity – as Connell and Messerschmidt (2005) have argued in a seminal contribution to this field? And how, why and to what extent did male dominance in the workplace decline? Heavy industry communities such as Merseyside, Tyneside and Clydeside developed a reputation for a particularly masculinized, aggressive, 'hard man' culture, reflected in, amongst other things, hard drinking and gang warfare (see Johnston and McIvor, 2004; Young, 2007; Bartie, 2010). Work experience and the wider cultural environment provided important sites for the incubation, reinforcement and reproduction of *macho* values and attitudes – especially those encapsulated in the 'hard' working man of this era. However, there was a range of experience and what is argued here is that it is more useful to talk about masculinities rather than masculinity.

The second section explores the relationship between femininity and work, women's changing relationship with the labour market and the struggle for gender equality in employment and the workplace in the period 1945–1970s. The final section investigates mutating gender relationships and gender identities at work and examines the extent to which work identities have converged over the past thirty years or so. Oral evidence and other personal narratives provide important insights into gender identities at work – and some of the pioneering investigations have been based on oral interviews, such as Elizabeth Roberts. Hence, amongst a range of sources, this chapter draws upon personal testimony and oral histories (including some my own field-work with Ronnie Johnston) and upon discourses in fiction, workers' memoirs and autobiographies.

Masculinities at work

In the early twentieth century male identities were wrapped up in the notion of the man as the breadwinner. To be a man was to fulfil this role of providing for the family and the culturally created way of doing this was through a lifetime of hard graft in employment (an ethos reinforced regularly by the church, school, and state). The value of male and female labour indicated the relative worth placed on each within what was an intensely patriarchal society. Before the Second World War men in full-time employment typically earned double on average what women in full-time employment earned. The prevailing cultural norm was for women and men to occupy 'separate spheres' – for an adult woman's place to be in the home with primary responsibility for the family and the man to dominate the public sphere of paid employment, trade unions and politics (for an overview see McIvor, 2001, pp. 174–99).

The unusual labour market circumstances of wartime constituted a challenge to these entrenched notions of masculinity because women were replacing men in the labour force and subverting traditional gender roles. Summerfield's (1998) study of women workers in the Second World War and Summerfield and Peniston-Bird's (2007) nuanced account of the Home Guard demonstrate this clearly. Whilst men who joined up and became uniformed combatants were exalted as 'real men', others who were conscientious objectors, unfit or forced to stay in their wartime jobs as 'Reserved Occupations' could have their masculinity undermined by accusations of malingering, coward-ice, 'taking the easy option' and by women's more evident presence on the shop floor and the rising status of women generally in wartime (see Rose, 2004). However, there were limits to the extent to which the traditional gender order was challenged during the wartime emergency (Johnston and McIvor, 2005). Twice as many men served in the Reserved Occupations as combatants and new research suggests that despite the challenge from women and the elevated masculinity of the uniformed combatant, masculinity was sustained – at least within working-class communities – and indeed may well have been bolstered in the home front workplace (see Chand, forthcoming, 2013; Robb, forthcoming, 2013). Significantly, men continued throughout wartime to dominate the toughest, heaviest, most dangerous jobs and a clear sexual division of labour persisted – with female workers only penetrating to a limited extent the all-male bastions of the dangerous heavy industries. Full employment and high earnings in wartime, moreover, rolled back the emasculating experience of the 1930s, years of high unemployment and insecurity which had seriously challenged the role of many men to 'perform' as breadwinners. And men in wartime had their masculine credentials bolstered by the pervasive propaganda that their skills and experience was vital for the war effort – that they were doing their bit in vitally important Reserved Occupations. There was certainly little sense of emasculation amongst a cohort of Scottish wartime reserved workers interviewed in the late 2000s. One commented: 'You look on it as pride that we did something to stop the Germans' (interview, Wendy Ugolini with George Cross, 7 Nov 2008, SOHC/032). A Glasgow locomotive factory worker reflected:

> You just felt you did your job and that was the job you would do. If you were called up you would just have another job. There was no feeling that I should have been in the Army or I should have done this. You had a job to do, you did it and everybody was quite happy... You could have volunteered, you might not have got away but the fact was you were doing a job to help the war effort and you were quite happy to do that. (Interview, Arthur McIvor with Willie Dewar, 9 December 2008, SOHC/032. See also Chand, forthcoming, 2013)

Moreover, the immediate post-war years saw a concerted effort to roll back the challenge to masculinity that the wartime penetration of women into the male-dominated workplace ostensibly represented. There was the disappointment of the failed Equal Pay Inquiry (in 1946) and the resurrection of segregated gender roles in the idea that the proper place of women was in the home. The notion of 'separate spheres' revived to again dominate the cultural landscape of the 1950s. Hostility to female employment on the part of men was widespread in the decade after the Second World War as men struggled to reassert and bolster their dominance in the workplace (Segal, 1997, pp. 299–300). Memories of mass unemployment in the 1930s may have influenced such attitudes. Whilst the gendered 'separate spheres' idea did not go unchallenged (as we have seen there was a growing influx of married women into the paid, formal economy, especially in part-time employment), and was slowly eroding (Brooke, 2001), a distinct sexual division of labour continued to exist, with men being centred in the world of paid work and production in the 'public sphere' and women predominantly in the private domain of home, family and reproduction. Women were the 'house wives' whilst men were still invariably the sole or primary breadwinners. Moreover, the workplace was an important site for the incubation and forging of male identities. In her seminal study of masculinities, Segal has made the point that work 'is one of the main anchorages of male identity' and that 'men's engagement in paid work, in "skilled" work, is central to the social construction of masculinity, or, as the contrasts in men's working lives would suggest, of masculinities' (Segal, 1997, p. 297).

Since the mid-1970s, important historical research has been undertaken which examines gender relations and the concept of femininity throughout history. Within this strand of work – much of it undertaken by feminist historians – women are examined as gendered subjects across a wide range of spheres, such as at the workplace, within the political arena, as members of the family, and more broadly within the culture of Victorian respectability. However, despite this stream of research, both mainstream historians and those specifically interested in the issue of gender, have tended, at least until relatively recently, to shy away from putting *masculinity* directly under the spotlight. Studies such as those of Willis, Cockburn, Michael Roper and Connell have shown how employment was clearly central in forging masculinities – in making men. Masculinity at work has recently been brought further under the spotlight in a series of studies, including oral-history projects that have focused specifically upon male-dominated industries, including engineering, dockwork, railways, shipbuilding and coal mining (Ayers, 2004; McKinlay, 1991; Strangleman, 2004; Johnston and McIvor, 2000a; McIvor and Johnston, 2007). This work has extended our understanding of male identities in the workplace considerably, though much more work needs to be done.

Masculinity at its core involves an assumption of power or superiority by men over women. Historically, the 'essence' of masculinity has been variously located with reference to notions of the man as *provider* (probably the most enduring representation); to physical prowess; toughness; homophobia; risk-taking; aggression and violent behaviour (including violence against women); a competitive spirit; a lack of emotional display; dispassionate instrumentalism and only limited involvement in fathering. Whilst the home and consumption were designated feminine domains, production was widely regarded historically as a highly masculinized sphere. Closer analysis, however, reveals a more complex and fluid picture. Theorists tend now to perceive a range of masculinities that can be prevalent at any given moment, and see such masculinities as being socially constructed and subject to significant change over time. There is also disagreement over a precise definition of what masculinity entails, recognition that few men actually 'fit' the norms and that some of the stereotypical 'core' attributes are not necessarily exclusive to men (see, for example, Watson, 2000). As Segal has persuasively argued, masculinities are unstable and changing:

> Masculinity is not some kind of single essence, innate or acquired. As it is represented in our culture, 'masculinity' is a quality of being which is always incomplete ... It exists in the various forms of power men ideally possess: the power to assert control over women, over other men, over their own bodies, over machines and technology. (Segal, 1997, p. 123)

Segal goes on to make the important point that 'masculine identity is never fixed. And some men never did acquire the appropriate gestures and display in the first place' (Segal, 1997, p. 133). This chimes well with Eileen Yeo's nuanced definition:

> Masculinity might be defined as the models and practices of manliness that prevail in a social group at a particular historical moment ... There is no solid masculinity (or femininity for that matter) but rather multiple masculinities which also exist in relation to each other, in historical situations of unequal power. Masculinity is fractured by class, race and ethnicity in settings where some versions of manhood are privileged and others subordinated. (Yeo, 2004, p. 129)

Part of the price men paid for assertion of their masculinity within patriarchal capitalism was their colonization of the most hazardous and health-eroding jobs, including the armed forces and underground work in mining. Protection of what was widely assumed to be the 'weaker sex' was frequently enshrined in law, through, for example the Factory Acts, Mines Acts and Special Regulations in 'dangerous trades', such as working with lead. Men, by contrast, were considered to be able to look after themselves. Women's lives after marriage were invariably dominated by debilitating and repetitive unpaid labour within the home – which could have its own negative effects upon physical and mental well-being. Women's health was also adversely affected by repeated childbirths, obstetric disasters and the unequal distribution of income and resources within the family. However, the domination of heavy industry jobs by men meant that it was male workers who were *disproportionately* exposed to the toxins and life-threatening hazards of paid employment for much longer periods. Ironically, perhaps, whilst relatively well paid work in the dangerous heavy industries empowered male workers as 'providers' who made 'sacrifices', male workers' health could be undermined as part of this process too. This will be explored in more depth in Chapter 5 when we turn our attention to the impact work had upon the body.

Manly work: traditional industrial masculinities and the hegemonic 'hard man'

Working-class masculinities were nurtured in the tough street culture of the neighbourhood and the recurrent brutality of school life. Many boys' games centred around the acting out of heroic roles – emulating the glamourized danger faced by cinema and comic book heroes, including Tarzan and John Wayne. Actual bodily harm was risked for the sake of peer group status. Competitive, adolescent bravado was also evident in the male-dominated environment of the manual workplace. 'Manual labour', Willis commented in 1977, 'is suffused with masculine qualities' (Willis, 1977, p. 159). The socialist labour activist Jimmy Reid famously noted during the 1971 Upper Clyde Shipbuilders' work-in: 'we didn't only build ships on the Clyde, we built men' (cited in Bellamy, 2001, p. 199). A cult of toughness characterized the heavy industries and young male workers adapted to this and absorbed it through peer pressure. Campbell has noted how Scottish mining communities were saturated 'with a discourse of manliness', with male youths encouraged by older miners to avoid displaying emotion (such as crying) and to play fighting games because, as one said, this was 'the training you got to be hard men' (Campbell, 2000, p. 238). On the docks, young workers learnt from experience, as one London docker recalled:

> I started out as a youngster working in my uncle's gang – all me mates did the same, cos' that way you'd pick up stevedoring from the old hands. It was like an apprenticeship really – you kept on getting clouted until you

could hold your own and the gang didn't have to carry you any more. You should have seen those old timers work – it was beautiful – they could shift 400 tons of cement from craft without sweating enough to take off their 'chokers', while we young 'uns were stripped. But that was how you learned the trade. (Hill, 1976, p. 29)

Jim Phillips has commented on how the status of dockers was enhanced within the community by acceptance of risks in what was a highly dangerous occupation, citing the example of the London docker Jack Dash who worked naked from the waist up (nicknamed 'nature boy') and who made light of a death-defying fall 50 feet into a ship's hold (Phillips, 2005, pp. 62–3). Similarly, Ayers has explored the incubation of manly identities amongst Liverpool dockers in the post-Second World War period (Ayers, 2004, pp. 153–68).

The transition from dependent to wage-earner marked the coming of manhood and conferred a privileged position within the home. John Oswell took up a printing apprenticeship in London after leaving school aged 15 in 1962. He passed over 'more than half' his pay packet to his mother, reflecting later: 'But it didn't worry me – I was just...you know...I was at work and I was one of the men wasn't I' (Britain at Work interview, by Dave Welsh, 19 Jan 2011). Tommy Coulter, a Scottish miner, commented:

> Once you were a producer, ah think it's maybe like something similar tae the animal kingdom, now the lion has tae get the grub first. Ah think once yi' wir a producer and handing in, contributing more tae the household you got maybe a wee bit better treated than a younger brother or whatever you know or a sister. (Interview by Neil Rafeek and Hilary Young, SOHC 017/C21)

Dangerous, dirty, dusty and physically exhausting work, with the constant stream of injuries and deaths in the pits, metal works and the shipyards hardened boys up, de-sensitizing them to danger and socializing them into a competitive, macho environment. Miners were not immune to fear, but daily exposure to risk toughened them up. Any sign of weakness, emotion and vulnerability could lead to being pilloried: the butt of jokes, scathing banter, vicious nicknames and sometimes very public humiliation – such as chalking the ship's hull. One such comment on a ship's hull on Clydeside referred to 'Big Dave: Big Girls Blouse' (Bellamy, 2001, p. 139). The Liverpool Labour politician Derek Hatton reflected on how his early years in the all-male world of the fire service (following his father's occupation) honed his macho attitudes. He recalled falling asleep on the shoulder of one of his workmates, commenting: 'they didn't stop ribbing me about it for weeks and neither did Dad' (cited in Segal, 1997, pp. 125–6).

For other lads, apprenticeship constituted the transition to adulthood. Here was where the young worker learnt the trade and all the informal, unspoken workplace culture that went with it. Being an apprentice represented a stage between childhood and full manhood. Convention had it that apprentices should not get married or be allowed to become a full member of a trade union until they had served their time. This transitional status was evident in the home too, where earning a wage elevated the 'manly' status and privileges of young workers. Thus the entry of a son into work became the point at which maternal influence waned and the gendered norms of a *machismo* workplace were transmitted down through the generations. Richard Hoggart reflected on this in 1957 commenting that on leaving school and going to work a son 'is, probably for the first time, close to his father and finds his father ready to be close to him: they now share the real world of work and men's pleasures' (Hoggart, 1957, p. 50). Ken Hancock, a miner who started work in 1968, recalled in an interview in the 1990s: 'The first day at work, you feel you've become a man. You grow three inches, all the way around' (cited in Blackwell and Seabrook, 1996, p. 146).

These transitions were captured in some of the social realist fiction, as well as in oral testimonies and workers' memoirs. In his autobiography *Growing Up in the Gorbals*, Ralph Glasser recalled listening to the men at Dixon's Blazes (a large iron and steelworks in Glasgow) relating: 'Grim anecdotes of terrible things – of men crippled for life, or killed outright. The concluding words of one of these tales gave me nightmares for a long time: "there was nothing left of the poor bugger but his feet"' (Glasser, 1987, p. 5). This was a brutal world in many respects, though one mediated by the black humour, swearing and 'patter' characteristic of these work communities as well as the street. The edge was taken off the danger and the degradation of employment by this repartee, epitomized, perhaps in the comedy of the ex-Clydeside shipyard worker Billy Connolly. There was much macho tale-telling of great feats, of accidents narrowly missed or of gruesome deaths and mutilations. Injured men would earn cryptic nicknames – such as 'bracket-head' for the shipyard worker who was injured by a falling object from above (interview by Ronnie Johnston, 22 December 1998, SOHC/016/A6). Asbestos workers joked that they could never be cremated as they would not burn; others that they rushed to eat an injured man's sandwiches after he was taken off to the Infirmary. Story-telling of 'great feats of strength' also abounded, including the one about the riveter who over-hit a rivet, sending it clean through a 12 inch hull, shooting across the river Clyde, killing two sheep on the other side. Competitiveness was a deeply-rooted feature of the male workplace and a way of affirming masculinity. Competitions punctuated the agricultural calendar; Bill Brack proudly recalled his physical prowess in his record-breaking tree planting in the Ae forest in the Scottish Highlands, reaching 2,400 in one day (MacDougall, 2000, pp. 239, 236). A London dock crane driver recalled:

> Now the essence of uh efficiency in the dock, we were all piece work. Now you could have uh a lovely team of good labourers, workmen, underneath you but if you hadn't got a good crane driver then everybody suffered. So you had to be [...] extreme[ly] capable to get jobs in the better gangs. I was the first crane driver ever to land over eighteen hundred [tons] of butter in one day from one gang. I also landed five hundred tons of flour in one day, with the gang. Now these were extreme quantities, [...] but I must be fair and say that when it come to the butter job that record of mine was broken twice in the same week, because the other crane drivers all decided to have a go and they beat it by a hundred or two here and there you know. Now that's what happens. It's a great competitive world you know, but it was crane driving at its best, there's no doubt about it. (Toby Butler, *Dockers* Memoryscape, Lovell's Wharf, London excerpt: A.S. Ellis http://www.memoryscape.org.uk/Dockers%20transcript.htm)

Working in manual labour was widely regarded within such communities as the pinnacle of masculine endeavour. As Strangleman has noted, there existed a tension between 'productive' and 'non-productive' workers (Strangleman, 2004, p. 73) and manual workers looked down with disdain upon effeminate clerical workers and those who did not work with the tools. Roper's study (1994) of post-war management in the manufacturing industry in the UK indicates a strong association between manual labour, getting your hands dirty and manliness. As one manager noted: 'If you weren't running around hitting bits of iron with hammers and wielding a spanner you weren't a man' (Roper, 1994, p. 117). In the mines some managers were accepted by the men whilst others were reviled. One of Perchard's interviewees, Bill Marshall, recalled how a fellow under-manager at Seafield Colliery was treated with disdain, including having his office door urinated on (Perchard, 2007a, p. 371). Meldrum, a shipyard rigger character in H. Munro's 1961 novel *The Clydesiders* expressed his dislike for the 'pen-pushers' forcefully:

> 'The bastards', he whispered. Inside him distrust of sedentary men smouldered to madness. His fists bunched...The rigger found himself gazing vacantly at the crowns of two clerks perched on high stools...He felt no kinship. To him they were two sheltered specimens of a *soft* breed whose activities could hardly be classed as *real* work and whose semi-indolent existence was supported entirely by the sweat of hard-grafting chaps like himself...Arrogant behind his own dirty face he saw their clean ones as an affront. And automatically hated them. (Cited in Bellamy, 2001, pp. 174–6)

A generation earlier, Walter Greenwood's hero in the novel *Love on the Dole* (1933), recalled his transition from the 'cissy' world of office work to an engineering factory, where there were 'great muscular men dwarfed to insignificance by the vastness of everything...Phew! But they were men' (Greenwood, 1933, p. 48).

In the post-war years men placed much esteem on hard graft and the ability to survive tough work conditions. Reflecting on the work environment in the *Daily Mirror* print room in the 1970s David Dyett said: 'The regulars would watch you to see if you looked as if you were going to work or not. If you weren't going to work they wouldn't help you' (Britain at Work interview, by Tom Vague, 28 May 2009). In a seminal piece of social anthropology Alan Sykes described the highly individualist, anti-trade union, macho world of the navvies working on a hydro-electric site in Scotland in 1953: 'To be known as a hard worker was something to be proud of...Men who worked hard were praised, while poor workers were regarded with contempt' (Sykes, 1973, p. 212). Like dockers, the navvies closely guarded their independence and autonomy and almost strutted their masculinity, honed through hard, unrelenting physical graft. Sykes observed:

> There was little pride in skill, but considerable pride in being able to work long and hard in bad conditions. The navvies boasted amongst themselves of the feats of hard work they had achieved or seen others achieve. The younger ones frequently tried to show off by emulating such feats and by competing against each other at work. For example, one young navvy after much boasting worked three successive twelve hour shifts – a straight thirty-six hours without a break. Financially he gained nothing as he spent the next two days in bed, but the feat aroused much interest in the

camp and added greatly to his reputation as a worker... Such feats were performed for fame. (Sykes, 1973, pp. 212–3)

Being a man also involved standing up for your rights against authoritarian management and the bosses – whether individually (as with the navvies) or collectively, through the union. The synergies between class and masculine values could be dynamic. Women participated in protest, resistance and industrial action too, but the labour movement was heavily dominated by men up to the 1970s and male activists invariably assumed leadership and superiority (see Chapter 6). Moreover, a fiercely independent work culture characterized metal working and mining – exhibited in high strike proneness and things like taking illicit tea breaks and 'idle days'. Activists such as Jimmy Reid exploited masculine solidarities in the shipyards as well as class consciousness. Part of the appeal was for workers to act 'as men' in the protection of their right to work and bring home a decent wage to support the family. Banners during a 1956 strike against redundancies at the British Motor Corporation read 'BMC: Be a man and come out on strike'. Reid's famous speech at the mass meeting of UCS workers at Clydebank in 1971 included the comment: 'We build men. They have taken on the wrong people and we will fight' (cited in Bellamy, 2001, p. 199). In the charged *machismo* atmosphere of the yard mass meeting this fighting talk struck a chord and there were no dissenters when the call for hands to be raised was made. The oft-seen photograph of eight male leaders of the UCS campaign, linking arms together with Tony Benn during the demonstration at Glasgow Green in 1971, provides an enduring image of such class-conscious male solidarity. Ranks were closed where management or external forces were threatening the very basis of men's role as providers (wages), their prerogative to work and their control and independence at the point of production. Whilst more work requires to be done to disentangle the dynamics of these processes, it is apparent that such class-based camaraderie coexisted in the traditional heavy industries within a workplace environment characterized by *machismo* attitudes, sectionalism and competitive trials of strength and skill.

Oral and autobiographical evidence thus provides us with useful insights into the way that work was *perceived* by men and what it signified to them. The heavily industrialized and proletarianized urban conurbation of Clydeside constitutes a revealing example. Here male workers' personal accounts were frequently tinted with pride in the labour process and the hardships that were endured in the workplace.

There is a recurrent 'heroic' discourse here. In his memoirs, the 'Red Clydesider' David Kirkwood noted of shipbuilding workers:

> These men – the finest, the most expert craftsmen in the world – had lived their lives in their work. Their joy as well as their livelihood lay in converting the vast masses of Nature's gifts into works of art, accurate to a two-thousandth part of an inch. (Kirkwood, 1935, p. 251)

Whilst such accounts of skilled workers extolled the masculine attributes of creative craftsmanship, others glorified muscle, strength and physical endurance. In an interview a former steelworker recalled the rough and violent environment of the Hallside Steelworks on Clydeside where he worked in the 1960s:

> It was a very macho culture ... It could also be quite violent too. But it was, you would say, very much an old-fashioned west of Scotland man's world, definitely ... When the work was there, there was such a demand for men that they would take in anyone. So guys quite often recently released from prison, and they included the occasional psychopath, literally, would wind up working beside you ... You had to be able to look after yourself ... had to be prepared to stand up and say you were prepared to fight. A couple of times I was in fights and I didn't choose them but if you backed down, that would be it. Everyone, everyone would stamp on you from then on, so you had to do that. But once you'd done that, that was OK. (Interview by Neil Rafeek, with Stewart McIntosh, SOHC/019)

In another example of workplace violence between men, James Boyle, an apprentice in a large iron works in Glasgow (Dixon's Blazes), recalled an incident at work when he was about 15, around 1955:

> My tradesman and a rigger were having a heated argument and I unfortunately interrupted them to my regret. The rigger unceremoniously gave me a good punch on the jaw that sent me tumbling down a flight of steel stairs and told me to shut my mouth until I was asked to open it. (Interview by David Walker, 10 January 2009, SOHC/023/01)

Whilst oral testimonies reflected the existence of a wide range of managerial styles, from exploitative to consensual, workers could reach composure in accounts stressing stoic struggle against profit-maximizing managers, employers and foremen and the toleration of tough, dirty, hazardous and dusty work environments. Tom Ellis, a North Wales miner, recalled of the immediate post-war years:

> It was a time when there was a national shortage of fuel and miners were being urged to work ever harder, each pit boasting its own 'Stakhanovite'

who filled an incredible tonnage and who was rumoured to earn an equally incredible wage, as well as making a paragraph in the local paper. Colliery management basked in the reflected glory from the muscular exploits of their best men. (Ellis, 2004, p. 51)

An Ayrshire miner Alec Mills (born 1933) commented: 'You found out that men and management in general were always at loggerheads in the coal mining industry...If you were a *weak* man you would have did what the boss said' (interview by Arthur McIvor and Ronnie Johnston, 19 June 2000, SOHC/017/C1). Miners undertook what was amongst the most dangerous of all jobs (see Chapter 5) and their work fostered machismo attitudes. 'Yes we were a bit macho', a Scottish miner Tommy Coulter recalled in an interview in 2004, continuing, 'we thought we were the greatest and we knew that was the case...' (interview by Neil Rafeek and Hilary Young, 12 January 2005, SOHC/017/C21). Another Ayrshire miner said:

> That's what you done till aince you got a place eh on the run, ken among the men, ken...I was drawing when I was 18 year old...I was drawing 100 hutches a day. No kidding you, I was like steel. I was a hard man then... Oh we were down there first go in the morning and last away, ken. Aye we made good money then, ken. (Thomas McMurdo, interview by Ronnie Johnston, 11 July 2000, SOHC/017/C20)

Another important aspect of masculinity was the camaraderie of the workplace. Textile mills and other female-dominated workplaces offered similar opportunities for socializing, but the male bonding aspect was frequently consolidated by contact with workmates out of work hours in the street and in the pub. As Mullen has noted, hard drinking and heavy smoking have for a long time been 'strong symbols of male virility and *machismo* in traditional working class culture' (Mullen, 1993, p. 177). The distribution of wages also sometimes took place in the pub. In such circumstances, it was very difficult not to conform. As shipyard worker Joe Curran commented in 1964: 'Even the man that didn't want a drink was more or less forced to have one' (cited in Bellamy, 2001, p. 106). Moreover, within this culture, being able to tolerate the toughest work conditions, take the greatest risks and hold one's alcohol were celebrated as praiseworthy male attributes. Robert Gladden, a Middlesbrough steel worker from 1942 to 1989, reflected on the drink culture in his workplace:

> You learnt to drink there. Eventually you would sup about fourteen pints a day – eight in the afternoon, six at night. You soon sweated it out again.

> They'd go in to a pub at two o'clock after a shift and order four pints at a time. The first two they'd drink straight down. (Cited in Blackwell and Seabrook, 1996, p. 32)

And the pubs were where working-class men spent much of their leisure time, as Wight noted: 'the pubs were at the centre of the men's domain, in contrast to the home which was the women's sphere' (Wight, 1993, pp. 155–6). Drinking also reflected a man's earning capacity, with 'big drinkers' equated with hard workers. One of the last miners in a pit village in central Scotland proudly told a researcher in the early 1980s: 'I'm the top machine worker in Scotland, put that on your form...aye...you know...status'. He went on to comment on how he welcomed the reverence, 'you know, when you stand at the bar and say 'I'll buy you's a round' (Wight, 1993, p. 163).

Whilst a range of masculinities coexisted, this type of *hegemonic* masculinity undoubtedly characterized most heavy-industry communities up to the middle of the twentieth century, and perhaps for some time beyond, as the social anthropology of Daniel Wight suggests and the 2000 movie *Billy Elliott* nicely caricatures. Wight has shown how miners in central Scotland were expected to be 'strong' and 'tough', both physically and emotionally – expressions of which were protecting female relatives and never crying (Wight, 1993, pp. 42–3). Other attributes which enhanced masculinity in the mining village where Wight lived from 1982–4 were ownership of cars and large dogs (especially Alsatians and pit bull terriers) and meat-eating (particularly steaks and hot curries).

The pay packet was the symbol of power, holding the potential of diversionary recreation and, for married men, mandatory sex. As Walter Greenwood's fictional hero Harry Hardcastle put it in *Love on the Dole*: 'There'd be a flutter on the two-thirty; football match this afternoon, the public house tonight and a long morning tomorrow with the missus' (Greenwood, 1933, p. 49). Moreover, bringing home a wage invariably meant for the young male worker a quite different treatment in the home: more respect and preferential treatment as befitted the transition from dependent to proto-breadwinner. It was a matter of pride for new young male workers to be 'put on their own can', meaning that they were now responsible for buying their clothes out of what was left of their wage after their mothers had taken their housekeeping money. Richard Fitzpatrick, a chemical process worker, referred to this in an interview:

> It wis a job and it was money and as I said I didnae smoke and I didnae drink. Ma father gave ma mother thirty bob, I gave her thirty bob and I

went ma own can at eight and eight pence and I bought all my own clothes and everything, went aboot like a millionaire a few times. (Interview by David Walker, 13 August 2004, SOHC/022)

Furthermore, assuming full breadwinner status, with a dependent wife, sharpened men's sense of entitlement and power within the home and the marital relationship. Gaitens portrayed this evocatively through one of his fictional characters in *Dance of the Apprentices*:

Mr Macdonnel, looking marvellously fit and untired after a long, hard day's shovelling on the concrete-board of a big navvying job, greeted neither his wife nor boy... Mr Macdonnel strode with unnecessary, frenzied haste into the lobby, divested himself of cap, jacket and waistcoat, and dashed back towards the jawbox, rolling up his shirt-sleeves, baring his breast, his hob-nailed boots, streaked with clay, whitish with concrete, thudding violently the floor. His every motion bragged that he was the breadwinner; his hefty gestures, as he soaped and splashed at the tap, were like shouts of 'I'm heid o' the hoose! I'm boss here!' His tough, middle-sized physique hummed with self-esteem which egregiously pervaded the little kitchen. (Gaitens, 1948, p. 9)

This vivid literary representation was undoubtedly something of an exaggeration of reality: a stereotypical caricature that hid a wide range of masculine identities within working-class communities. The same might be said about the writing of Sillitoe, exemplified, perhaps in the misogynist 'angry man' character Arthur Seaton in *Saturday Night and Sunday Morning*, an influential, widely read novel (1958) and subsequent film (starring Albert Finney in 1960) with which many young working-class men identified (Segal, 1997, p. 13).

Connell in *The Men and the Boys* (2000) reminds us that working-class culture is full of *Stakhanovite* examples of working men pitting themselves against the accepted effort limits of wage labour – such as the miner who loaded 'sixteen tons of number nine coal', or another worker's fatal attempt to compete with a steam hammer (Connell, 2000, p. 188). A competitive spirit was part-and-parcel of machismo work culture, as was a high tolerance of danger and a propensity to take risks in manual employment in mid-twentieth century Britain. This was justified to some extent with the argument that sacrifices were made for the sake of the family. Hence this was part of fulfilling the breadwinner ideal. Moreover, protecting oneself could be construed as a sign of weakness and an affront to masculinity. Hence the early reluctance to wear safety helmets, goggles and respirators. In effect, generations of working-class men whose lives were ordered by productionist values in the traditional heavy industries were also a party to the erosion of their own resources of health (see Chapter 5). What is hard to understand is the extent to which workers were reluctantly taking risks because of peer pressure, trying to impress their fellow workers with their manliness, to maximize earnings in a volatile and uncertain market environment, or because they felt pressure from supervisors and managers keen to impress their bosses and squeeze out profits. Not complaining and taking risks singled the worker out to foremen and managers who had a say in any future promotion opportunities. Not grumbling about poor working conditions also meant workers did not cost the firm money to make machines safe (guards), for the supply of barrier creams, safety equipment and for absence from work. In industries characterized by cyclical unemployment – such as shipbuilding and construction – a reputation as a 'good worker' could be crucial when lay-offs came round. Masculinity in the post-war workplace has to be understood, therefore, within a wider context of unequal power relations and the exploitative actions of employers and managers – themselves frequently acculturated to a machismo work culture through their own upbringing (see Roper, 1994).

Femininity, the household and work, 1945–80

If a dominant discourse of masculinity associated with the breadwinner ideal prevailed in working-class communities in the immediate post-war period, then the corollary of this was a dominant mode of femininity – a set of ideas and practices that infused and structured women's working lives. Traditional discourses of femininity associated the core role of women with the 'duties' of the family and the unpaid work of the household. The widely accepted view was that paid employment should cease for women on marriage and the birth of children at which point a woman should become a full-time housewife and devote her life to the family and motherhood. Other behaviour was not deemed 'respectable'. At the extreme, this was believed to fit with the natural, biological attributes of women as nurturers and carers. Femininity was associated with the binary opposite characteristics of manliness – emotional display and irrationality, softness, weakness, inferiority, dependency. Ailsa Brockie, a trainee nurse in Glasgow in the mid-1950s recalled:

> Once you got married you weren't really, you were unclean almost. I
> think you would maybe get a job in out-patients but you were not really

considered totally one of the staff anymore...if you got married you left and that was that. (Ailsa Brockie, born 1936, Glasgow 2000 Lives Archive, Glasgow Museums)

In the 1940s and 1950s such sex-typed roles and prevailing assumptions about women's central responsibilities as mothers were still widely accepted, despite the transgressions that had occurred in wartime (Bruley, 1999, pp. 121–2). The Second World War marked key changes for women, though the extent to which wartime constituted a discontinuity in working lives has been the subject of much debate. A key research question has been whether wartime experience replicated patterns of class and gender subordination at work, or marked a liberating episode, altering fundamentally the meaning of work in women's lives. In a seminal monograph Summerfield has argued that the Second World War was a cathartic experience for many women, though experiences varied across a spectrum from 'stoic' to 'heroic' women and wartime changes in the division of labour were not, in the main, sustained thereafter (Summerfield, 1998). A similar argument has recently been developed for Ireland (Muldowney, 2007). Clearly many women welcomed the opportunities war brought to do a wider range of work, replace men and participate in the wartime economy. Many experienced a strong attachment to the job and commitment to more challenging and fulfilling work whereas to others, it was a case of having to put up with it, looking forward to the opportunity to return to the home and family duties. Nancy Williamson, one of the few female journalists in post-war Scotland summed up the contradictory impact of wartime experience neatly:

> I know a lot of people hated it, loathed every moment... But I can't say I did. I made a lot of good friends, I had some very interesting experiences, and as I say, I gained a lot of self confidence... And I think if it hadn't been for that, I wouldn't have been able to do the job of a journalist. I'd have been far too shy. (Interviewed by Ian MacDougall, 28 Oct 1996, SWPHT Collection)

This is a more modernist narrative, transgressing traditional ideas of gender normative behaviour.

Zweig's 1952 study of women in Britain, *Women's Life and Labour* – albeit somewhat impressionistic, judgemental and condescending (women he claimed 'loved repetitive jobs') – provided a snapshop of mid-twentieth century attitudes towards female domesticity and paid employment. He was struck by 'the sense of inferiority which many, if not most, women have. They accept man's superiority as a matter of fact' (Zweig, 1952b, p. 156). Zweig recognized the monotony of unpaid domestic labour, commenting on 'the drudgery of the work at home ... often in her home her spirit is crushed and her self-confidence broken'. He continued:

> A woman regards herself primarily as a helpmate to man, but that concep-
> tion may in practice be taken too far and her status of a helpmate deterio-
> rates to that of a servant or a little slave. And how many examples have I
> seen of that? Having the worst jobs in industry, a woman has also the worst
> jobs at home, the job of fighting constantly with dirt, filth and dust, the job
> of carrying excessive loads in her shopping, of pinching and scraping. The
> most menial jobs are again allotted to her. (Zweig, 1952b, pp. 154–5)

Middle-class households perhaps subscribed strongest to the ideal, with the sole male breadwinner and female full-time housewife the norm at mid-twentieth century. Working-class families, however, as Glucksmann (2006) has shown in her development of the concept of 'total social organization of labour' (TSOL) were increasingly adapt-ing expectations to allow for the earning of a 'supplementary' or 'com-ponent' wage, primarily through part-time employment and a return to work after children reached a certain age – the so-called bi-modal pattern of employment. What is evident, though, is that it was widely expected that a woman's life on adulthood would be dominated by unpaid domestic labour. 'Here I am', a married woman of 41 with four children told Zweig in 1952, 'working for them all day and they think I am just their slave' (Zweig, 1952b, p. 26). As Galbraith put it in 1979: 'the servant-wife is available, democratically, to almost the entire present male population' (cited in Edgell, p. 154). And mar-ried women remained responsible for almost all household domestic work as well as any paid employment they undertook. In part, this 'double burden' was facilitated after the Second World War by reduc-ing family size, domestic labour-saving technology and the increasing purchase of some goods and services outside the home (Crompton, 1997, pp. 128–9). Crucially, this pattern was compatible with and did not challenge male roles as the primary breadwinner.

Zweig was amongst those who argued that in the post-war years paid work was not a primary source of identity for women, rather home and family remained most important (Zweig, 1952b). Family appears to have continued to be the main focus and aspiration for many young women, who expected to only be working for a short period before marriage and children – unless absolutely necessary financially. Segal has made the point that 'women...may also *experience* their jobs differently from men – at least young women in factory jobs who are oriented primarily to future prospects of marriage' (Segal's emphasis; 1997, p. 299). Roberts' (1995) and Bruley's (1999) oral history based research also confirmed this picture of a return to and the persistence of traditional gendered attitudes and an acceptance of customary segregation and the sexual division of labour (Bruley, 1999; Roberts, 1995, pp. 124–40; see also Kynaston, 2007, pp. 416–23).

To Roberts, work meant different things to women than men in the post-war period up to around 1970: 'married women did not view work in the same way as men did' (Roberts, 1995, p. 131). Whilst the idea was growing that married women had a right to paid work, nonetheless in Roberts' view essentially women developed very different connections with and attachments to paid employment than men, because women, 'with few exceptions...were mothers first and workers second' (Roberts, 1995, p. 139). Hence, she posits, 'married women preferred part-time work, given their preoccupation with the well-being of their children' (Roberts, 1995, p. 122). Roberts explains the marked expansion of married women's employment post-1945 as a result of 'mixed motives': financial necessity for some; women's belief that it was 'their duty to do so' given the labour shortages; changing societal attitudes and the removal of stigma; a desire to socialize ; 'greater aspirations' – linked to consumerism: domestic appliances, cars, clothes; family holidays (Roberts, 1995, pp. 124–9). One Lancashire woman reflected: 'I went out partly for my sake. I was just vegetating at home and I felt I needed an interest again, and we needed the money' (Roberts, 1995, p. 127). Married women themselves in their oral testimonies frequently validated their employment by reference to how their wage enabled the purchase of 'extras'. In another Lancashire woman's case it was simply to afford a nice 'continental pushchair' for the baby – though instead of the six weeks she intended, she ended up working for nine years (Roberts, 1995, pp. 128–9).

Male attitudes towards wives working also ranged widely, from the traditional to the more progressive, though there appears to be a growing acceptance of wives' employment, especially where this could be rationalized on well-being, social or economic grounds in ways that maintained men's sense of still being the *primary* breadwinner (Roberts, 1995, pp. 129–31). As one married Lancashire man commented: 'I modified my views in the 1960s. I accepted the fact that she [his wife] needed some other interest outside the home. She used to get depressed at home on her own' (Roberts, 1995, p. 130). Economic and social reasons were frequently entwined in women's own personal accounts and whilst older women tended to be more traditional in their outlook, with home-centred lives, younger women were more adventurous, ambitious and transgressive of entrenched gender norms.

So in the immediate post-war period the historical sexual division of labour reasserted itself. Indeed, this was legitimated in the welfare reforms which *assumed* the role of men as the providers and women as unpaid domestic housewives: 'During marriage', the 1942 *Beveridge Report* noted, 'most women will not be gainfully employed' (cited in Hinds and Jarvis, 2000, p. 101). Within two years of the end of the war two million women had left their wartime jobs. The closure of wartime nurseries and crèches accelerated this, as did the high cost of childcare (Bruley, 1999, pp. 120–1) and the attitudes of men. Having a non-working wife was a sign of respectability and status, whereas the opposite could challenge a core part of masculine identity – the capability to provide for the family. One woman recalled in an interview in the mid-1990s how she finished work in 1946 on the birth of her daughter: 'I wanted to go back to work, but my husband wouldn't hear of it' (cited in Bruley, 1999, p. 120). She returned to part-time paid work ten years later. Mary Williams' experience was similar. She recalled in an oral interview in 2010 how she worked as a young woman in the 1950s as a bus conductor for London Transport and that a key motivation was to save for a deposit on a small house. She stopped to have children, supplementing the family income thereafter by taking in lodgers, ironing shirts for a local laundry and selling Avon cosmetics. This was frustrating, as Mary recounted: 'As soon as the kids had got up just the littlest bit, I wanted to get work away from the house. I wanted out. I wanted gone from it. As soon as I could, I got a job in the schools and the school meal service' (Britain at Work interview by Kathleen McIlvenna, 5 Sept 2010).

Myrdal and Klein's 1956 study, *Women's Two Roles*, captured these trends. They noted a tension in the 1950s between gender roles and a tendency for women to play the game to preserve masculine sensibilities:

> The pattern of male superiority is still so strong that the pretence, at least, of feminine weakness and intellectual inferiority has to be kept up ... It is not a genuine belief in the superiority of men but a convention that masculine illusions in that respect must not be disturbed. (Myrdal and Klein, 1956, p. 139)

In her study of women tobacco manufacturing workers – based on oral interviews in 1980 – Anna Pollert reflected that her subjects 'still considered themselves as dependent on a man, and their pay as marginal to a man's' (Pollert, 1981, p. 84). One of the respondents reflecting on the equal pay issue commented: 'But men will feel downgraded. I expect to be supported by my husband if I'm married, but if I was earning as much as him – he wouldn't feel he was supporting me – he'd be downgraded' (Pollert, 1981, p. 85). As far as the men in the factory were concerned Pollert found 'the crux of their attitude was that the woman's place was in the home, or in a "feminine" job such as nursing' (Pollert, 1981, p. 79). Pam Osborne, a Londoner born in 1946, left her employment as a typist in 1970 for nine years when she became pregnant. She recalled: 'You were expected to give up work and look after the children. There just wasn't any maternity leave. And so that was what was expected and you did it'. She added that there were few other possibilities for child care 'because you were expected to look after your own children', adding, 'I thoroughly enjoyed doing my own childcare'. She recalled how in the 1960s when she started work women had few employment rights and it was difficult to be independent:

> They had to be backed by a man. They couldn't get finance on their own or anything like that. They had to have a male guarantor. And I guess it was a case of we sort of knew our place. That sounds terribly old-fashioned ... The women that were career women were often looked upon as being very hard and not really very nice. Very pushy. But I think it was because they had to be. There weren't that many career women. It was generally accepted that women got married, had babies, didn't work. And most women did the office work. You didn't really get anybody that was in managerial that was female. Very few. (Britain at Work interview by Ruth Sheldon, 12 June 2009)

Catherine McBean became a manager in a building society in Glasgow in the late 1980s and earned more than her husband, something he didn't like at all:

> My husband was an engineer, service engineer, and at that particular point in time he really didn't want me ... he didn't like it because I was earning more than him, he really didn't like it and we had a few rocky times then but we managed to sort it out ... he had a problem with the fact that I was earning more than him. (Interview by David Walker, 21 February 2011, Glasgow Working Lives, Glasgow Museums / SOHC/042/21)

In an important article in 1991, Hakim also argued that the work orientations of women differed from men; that they continued to exhibit a conscious choice and preference for a 'homemaker career' and that they showed a great deal of satisfaction with their participation in the formal economy, despite low status and low wages (Hakim, 1991). To Hakim, women had markedly lower expectations of and commitment to work than men and this facilitated higher levels of satisfaction with the jobs they ended up in – for example with homeworking for money, widely considered to be flexible enough to fit around child care and other domestic 'duties'. Women were thus making rational choices to work part-time and combine home-making, rather than taking on full-time employment.

This interpretation has not gone unchallenged, however. Differences were less evident, if at all, with the younger generation of women from the 1980s and where women were better qualified and doing the same or similar work as men (Phizacklea and Wolkowitz, 1995, pp. 11–12). In their case study of homeworking in the 1980s and 1990s – dominated by black and ethnic minority women working full-time – Phizacklea and Wolkowitz take issue with Hakim's view, arguing persuasively for 'a complex interaction between structure and agency', positing:

> The vast majority of these ethnic minority women have not 'chosen' to pursue a career over the homemaker role; they work full-time through financial necessity, a necessity which is linked to higher rates of black male unemployment, larger family size, lower household incomes and the necessity of working longer hours to bring home something approximating a living wage. (Phizacklea and Wolkowitz, 1995, pp. 12–13)

For these women workers, the meaning of work was similar to that of mothers who worked in the 1930s because of the low wages and labour market insecurity of their unskilled husbands. Material circumstances and structures of power continued to constrain choice and agency, whilst the situation was changing over time.

Post-war married women's working lives were invariably dominated by housework and family even where they combined such with some part-time paid work. Ann Oakley's seminal work, *Housewife* (1974) was the first in the UK to explore domestic work like any other labour process. It was based on interviews with 40 London women. The investigation found that whilst some aspects of the job (such as child care and cooking) could be rewarding and there was some control and autonomy exercised in the pace and timing of tasks, still in the main this was repetitive, monotonous, unskilled work. Amongst the most despised aspects were the endless rounds of washing up, ironing and cleaning. Such routine housework Oakley equated to factory assembly-line work (see also Cowan, 1989, p. 7). The job encapsulated many of the attributes of alienated labour – meaningless, low status, long working hours (Oakley found an average of 77 hours worked in her sample of young married mothers), fatiguing, boring, socially isolated. 'Loneliness', Oakley noted, 'is an occupational hazard for the modern housewife' (Oakley, 1974, p. 88). Little respite was achieved, moreover, from labour-saving household technologies, or from more input into unpaid housework from husbands – at least up until the 1980s (Edgell, pp. 159–60). Apart from some very specialized tasks – such as household repairs – the evidence indicates that a strict gender demarcation prevailed in most households. Studies such as Young and Willmott's (1973) which suggested the emergence of a more symmetrical family in the early 1970s was not supported by strong empirical evidence, nor by subsequent research. Ken Hancock (a National Union of Mineworkers branch delegate) commented in an interview in the mid-1990s: 'It's a man's world. There's no use trying to get around it. It's a bloody macho, sexist world'. (cited in Blackwell and Seabrook, 1996, p. 148)

The growth of part-time employment opportunities (usually defined as employment for 30 hours a week or less) after 1945 for women was one factor which drew more women into the formal, paid economy. Perhaps commitment to such work was liable to be diluted, compared to full-time permanent career workers. However, whilst they may have lacked employment rights in such subordinate part-time positions, for some this represented liberation of sorts. This was expressed by Margaret Crawford (born 1936) who took a part-time job as a local librarian, initially working 18 hours a week because this fitted with her family responsibilities (she was married with two children). She was an untrained library assistant who worked alone running the local library at Hurlford, Ayrshire, and described her work in very positive tones, using phrases like 'rewarding' and 'satisfying'. Positive elements for her were the contact with the public and especially with school children, the joy she got from encouraging reading, the 'service' to the community and the control she exercised over her own work environment:

> I found, well, you can have the place the way you liked it. I mean, especially the first few years really, there was nobody pressurising in any way, nobody standing over you... As long as things were going ok you were left just to run it the way you did. (Interviewed by Ian MacDougall, 3 March 2002, SWPHT Collection)

The development of the post-war library service provided a field where middle-class women found some employment security and decent promotion prospects. Dorothy Milne recalled a number of deputy and chief librarians who were women in the 1940s and 1950s and she herself rose from assistant librarian in Aberdeenshire to chief librarian in West Lothian in 1941 (interviewed by Ian MacDougall, 10 May 1999, SWPHT Collection).

Other oral testimonies elaborated on women's entry into the male-only domains of a pretty rigidly segregated workplace in mid-twentieth century, and not just in the heavy industries. One example would be journalism which was a very macho world of hard drinking and heavy smoking reporters and editors, operating in a stressful environment to tight deadlines. On the *Edinburgh Evening News,* as a journalist Bill Rae recalled, the only women involved in the fifties were a couple that worked specifically as features writers on the women's page, called 'Eve's Circle' (interviewed by Ian MacDougall, 3 Sept 1996, SWPHT Collection). One of the jobs such female journalists were given were the 'church notes', a practice that reflected the gendering of religious belief. Exceptions might be rationalized as being masculinized, as Bill Rae noted: 'Any women reporters that I ever did come across on jobs, they always seemed kind of hard to me. [laughs]... They had the sort of hard crust....' One of these 'transgressors' was Nancy Williamson who was a journalist for 15 years from 1947. Whilst she noted the clear division of labour (female reporters did not do Saturday sport or the court reporting in the 50s and early 60s), she did not express resentment towards this and went on to deny any overt discrimination (interviewed by Ian MacDougall, 28 Oct 1996, SWPHT Collection). Again, there is a contradiction here between the evident structural subordination of women and lack of opportunities (compared to men) in the labour market and the more positive recollections of those narrating their experiences of employment. Her narrative was one that expressed a strong identification with her work and much joy and satisfaction derived from the labour process.

Were women any less attached to paid work than men in the 1950s and 1960s? Did they identify differently with employment as a consequence of socialization into feminine roles and their lived experience? The Stirling Women's Oral History Project undertaken in the mid-1980s provides some pointers on this. The 80 Stirling life history testimonies illuminate the frustrations linked with discrimination against women in the workplace, the internalization of separate gendered roles, the prevalence of the marriage bar, unequal pay and subordination. However, as Stephenson and Brown have argued, these narratives also demonstrate that the work ethic of women was more similar to men than had been previously thought, contrary to the interpretations of other scholars, such as Roberts (Stephenson and Brown, 1990). The lengthy nature of their work memories in these interviews suggests strong identification with their paid employment. Women gleaned much satisfaction and joy out of their paid employment, and much pride and self-esteem in the use of their skills. Key issues that emerged from the oral testimonies of Stirling women were the camaraderie and sociability aspects of work. This was a site for socializing, song and gossip, of friendships and contact which was much missed in later life, and recalled wistfully (perhaps somewhat nostalgically) and positively in oral interviews. When asked how she felt about her work one Stirling department store worker (a clerk and cashier) said: 'I liked it very much. I must admit I thoroughly enjoyed all my years....' (Stirling WOHP, Transcript X2). Evidently, there was a conflict between the material reality of structural and deep-rooted subordination of women at work within an intensely patriarchal capitalist economy and society, and the ways that women actually perceived and narrated their work experience.

Some oral testimonies of women workers in London generally support these assertions. Marie Henderson worked from 1948 to 1993 and reflected in an interview in 2007 how she had enjoyed her employment and how central to her life it was. Revealingly she referred to the guilt that many women of her generation felt about paid employment, repeatedly noting 'I don't regret it'. She started as a textile machinist in a factory in the East End of London:

> I became a sample machinist, because your work would be good to present to others, you know... I don't regret working as a machinist, because we did have some fantastic times, you know. You, it wasn't like this today, 'I'm bored', you know. We had to go to work to earn our money, and if we didn't go, we didn't get paid. (Britain at Work interview by Lucy Kerr, 3 May 2007)

Pam Osborne (cited earlier) worked for a while in a large office typing pool in a company called Minimax. She recalled:

> ...Generally very happy. It was very happy working there. Like all places, you get the odd miserable person, but generally I was very happy working at Minimax. And they did look after us. (Britain at Work interview by Ruth Sheldon, 12 June 2009)

She reflected: 'I became technological. I sort of grew with it. Which was really good'. Her testimony is interspersed with positive work identifiers: the work was 'fun', 'fantastic'; 'the people there were very, very nice'; 'I loved working there'. Mary Williams migrated from her home town Derry to work as a bus conductor in London Transport in the 1950s. She commented:

> They had a fantastic atmosphere in the garage. You felt comfortable in it ... there was a feeling of camaraderie. It was both between the driver and the conductors and between the people who were catching the bus. There was a fantastic feeling of being at home, being right in the middle of where you wanna be ... What I loved about the job, really, was the shift work. You'd never see the same people and very regularly they'd change the route so that you'd have to learn another route. If you liked variety, we had it. (Britain at Work interview by Kathleen McIlvenna, 5 September 2010)

Mary's work-life history has an almost epic quality and it is impossible to do it justice here. She had children, but her narrative is definitely a work-centred, rather than family-centred one, despite her career being broken with numerous jobs. From the buses, she moved to school meals, then to offices, ending up employed for nearly twenty years in the civil service working for the Metropolitan Police as a typist and receptionist until retiring in 1994. She then devoted her time to volunteer work with disabled and refugee children. There is a clear sense of ownership and belonging associated with the way women such as Mary narrated their working lives.

As employees, then, women shared many of the joys and frustrations of work with men and clearly, like men, there were a range of diverging identities and orientations to work coexisting at any one time. Roberts' view may be now seen as somewhat uni-dimensional and requires some refinement. But there remains much power in her argument – based on one of the most extensive oral history projects ever undertaken – that whilst the period 1940–1970 was a 'transitional' one, traditional notions of femininity prevailed in working-class communities. Regarding married women in employment, Roberts has asserted: 'with few exceptions, they were mothers first and workers second' (Roberts, 1995, p. 139). This was despite a societal shift in the direction of recognizing that women not only had a right to employment, but also 'a duty to do so'. Whilst identities were changing and a range of femininities were evident in this period of flux, still continuities should not be lost sight of. Traditional notions of male and female roles, of the masculine and the feminine, proved remarkably persistent and difficult to break down.

Changing gender identities

Neither masculinity nor femininity were fixed constructs at any point in time, rather a range of gender identities (masculinities and femininities) coexisted across a spectrum and mutated as time passed. Not all men bought into the 'hegemonic masculinity' of the manual working classes – what Pahl has termed 'emotionally controlled, power-seeking providers' (Pahl, 1995, p. 190) – even at mid-twentieth century. And many women transgressed gender normative behaviour. Segal has commented that different individuals exhibited a range from extreme masculinity, shading through androgynous to more feminine traits (Segal, 1997, pp. 66–7). In a recent analysis Brooke has argued that gender identities were more fluid in the 1950s, with women increasingly identifying with paid employment and traditional modes of masculinity eroding (Brooke, 2001 see also Abrams, 1999). To Brooke, the 1950s 'destabilized established understandings of working-class masculinity and femininity'. One contemporary survey that points in this direction is that of Ferdynand Zweig, who commented in 1961:

> Somehow related to this is the process of softening in the worker, I would venture to call it his feminization. The worker's world was formerly known for its masculinity – now he has mellowed considerably. The women around him imbue him with feminine values. He accepts his wife as his companion on more or less equal terms, especially when she goes out to work and earns her own living. All this means that the worker is moving away from his mates. (Zweig, 1961, p. 208)

In the Scottish context, Abrams has challenged the stereotype of the uncaring and detached father, arguing using oral evidence that there was markedly more active participation in family life amongst the post-war generation (Abrams, 1999). Clearly a wide range of identities and relationships existed; other masculinities and femininities were on display and attitudes changed over time.

Certainly the notion of the 'passive' female worker was more myth than reality. Working-class women had a long tradition of resisting managerial exploitation, initiating strikes and participating in strikes, for example in textile manufacturing, where women were particularly well organized. The equal pay strike of female upholstery stitchers at

Ford's Dagenham plant in 1968 (recently made into a movie, *Made in Dagenham*), which led directly to the equal pay legislation in the UK in the early 1970s, was preceded and followed by many less well publicized confrontations with management on equality issues, such as the abolition of the marriage bar, wage parity and other rights for female workers. For example, a female clerk in local government in Barrow Town Hall recalled the struggle in the 1950s in her workplace:

> We were going to have equal pay because a lad came in at the same time as you, same age, same job and he would get so much extra a week. We fought like mad, in fact the man that came around the office for the union dues used to dread coming, we wouldn't let him out! So they got equal pay, and that was our first victory and I do reckon that it was our little clique that really ground them down. And we fought like mad for married women to be kept on and six months later I got married [in 1958] it came in that they would take married women on. (Cited in Roberts, 1995, p. 132)

In an interesting article engaging with Portelli's pioneering ideas about memory, Liz Leicester has recently explored the little known Leeds clothing workers' strike in 1970. This dispute involved women downing tools for equal pay in the face of their male-dominated trade union, the National Union of Tailors and Garment Workers (NUTGW), who refused to make the strike official. One female shop steward commented:

> I sometimes think there isn't a lot of sympathy with women workers, you know, it's more or less a man's union. You see we've only one lady on the branch committee ... All the others are men ... They in their hearts, really think a woman's place is in the home. (Cited in Leicester, 2009, p. 48)

Whilst lack of support from the NUTGW hindered the strikers, there was a clear sense that it was the employers who were culpable for the historic undervaluation of female labour. Traditional notions of femininity were being challenged here. One of the female leaders, Gertie Roche, commented:

> At every meeting it has been obvious that the women are intensely involved, unleashing years of resentment. Do the employers realize that at last we are moving into the twentieth century? Almost every day reference is made to equal rights for women. Do they think this has no effect on the women who form 78% of the industry's labour force? Many have families to feed and homes to tend. Think of the organization and determined effort necessary to keep this up year after year. The revolt is due, not to a

handful of left-wingers but to something far deeper – 20 years of neglect by the employers. (Cited in Leicester, 2009, p. 49)

An important feature of the Leeds strike in 1970 was the organization of 'flying pickets' by the women, years before the miners used such tactics to such devastating effect from the mid-1970s to the mid-1980s.

Notions of masculinity, always fluid and contingent, were also changing over time. Brooke has made the point that 'softer' modes of masculinity were most prevalent in the newer 'sunrise' industries and on the new suburban housing estates (Brooke, 2001). Clearly the reality was more complex than the dominant *machismo* discourse implies. The 'hard man' culture may well reflect the prevailing experience in some traditional working-class communities (such as on Clydeside and Tyneside), but this is hardly representative of the UK as a whole in the post-war period. Something of a divide existed between what might be termed 'rough' and 'respectable' masculinity in the workplace. Some craftsmen prided themselves on never breaking a wage packet, and passed their earnings on intact to their wives. More typical, though, was taking 'pocket money' for drink, cigarettes and a bet, and passing the remaining 'housekeeping' money over, hence never admitting the full content of the wage packet. This unequal distribution of resources in the home represented an important aspect of masculine power. In an oral interview a carpenter revealed a glimpse of both a dominant and an alternative, less masculinized work culture in the Clydeside joinery trade in the 1960s:

> The unions were quite agreeable then to bonus work, which meant that everybody was hammering away as fast as they could at floors, ceilings... Being the finer type, and not being exposed to high pressure work like that, I was allowed to work in a workshop and make up the likes of doorframes and window frames. (Interview by Ronnie Johnston, 19 January 1999, SOHC/016/A8)

This was the kind of worker who distanced himself from the rougher kind of working-class culture. His social life revolved around Burns nights, Masonic Lodge meetings, golf, and amateur dramatics. Interestingly, though, this particular respondent was also a top class amateur wrestler. Indicative of the coexistence of rough and softer masculinities and the fluid boundaries between acceptable and unacceptable behaviour is Jimmy Reid's plea for responsible behaviour during the 1971 Upper Clyde Shipbuilders work-in when he demanded 'there will be no bevvying' (drinking). For some, as they got older, the bravado of working without protection in hazardous work environments in search of higher wage packets gave way to a determination to protect themselves from insidious and longer-term bodily damage. The miners who tried to shield their lungs by using nylon stockings and brassieres over their mouths as dust masks clearly weren't that bothered about preserving their masculine image (Archie McLaren, interview by Ronnie Johnston, 29 June 2000, SOHC/017/C5). Moreover, as previously noted, fictional representations may well have exaggerated the prevalence of 'hard man' or 'aggressive' masculinity. This case has certainly been made in reference to the classic Clydeside 'hard man' novel, *No Mean City* and to Sillitoe's work. Daniels and Rycroft have made the point that in *Saturday Night, Sunday Morning*: 'The factory floor, and work generally, is represented almost entirely as a male preserve' when most manufacturing in Nottingham (where the novel is based) was actually dominated by women in the 1950s (Daniels and Rycroft, 1993, p. 468).

If a range of masculinities and femininities coexisted around the 'traditional' breadwinner/housewife paradigm, then there was also significant change in attitudes over time. The shift was towards more liberal and egalitarian attitudes towards gender roles. There were discernible differences between generations, with a larger proportion of younger workers rejecting the 'old ways' and embracing sexual equality. In part, this may have been connected to the increasing tendency in a period of full employment and economic restructuring for sons not to follow into their fathers' occupations. The broad shift was from manual to 'pen-pushing' non-manual labour. Improving housing standards and smaller families also helped prompt a reorientation of recreation for men from pub to home, hence neutering one of the principal sites of male bonding. Over time, deindustrialization and the growth of the service sector also reduced the numbers employed in the heavy industries, whilst economic insecurity dragged earnings in these occupations downwards, making it less tenable to equate manual work with masculinity. With work restructuring in manufacturing, some of the most fundamental roots of masculine power and identity (based on skilled craft work) could be challenged and eroded. Pahl has argued this led to the 'deposing' of men from their central role in employment (Pahl, 1995, p. 191). Cockburn (1983) has examined this process for printing. Another example would be carpet manufacture, where Sayce, Ackers and Greene have shown a gender 'identity crisis' ensued when work reorganization and deskilling in the 1990s undermined the craft masculinity of the weavers. In this case, however, the process was contested and mediated, with male domination of the work surviving, albeit with some marked erosion in status and self-esteem (Sayce et al., 2007).

How were male identities expressed in non-manual workplaces? Was there a heavily gendered work culture in the growing non-manual jobs in offices, banks, the health and education sectors? How did men adapt to working in what were regarded as more 'feminized' work environments – such as the office? Clearly manliness was not just associated with manual labour: Different masculinities emerged in other non-manual and managerial occupations. Collinson and Hearn have developed the idea of 'multiple masculinities/multiple workplaces' to conceptualize 'the diversity of men's workplace power, status and domination' (Collinson and Hearn, 1996a, p. 73). They make the point that there is relatively little research on manliness in non-manual workplaces compared to manual labour. However, they perceive certain contexts as capable of incubating and honing masculinities, such as the aggressive sales and entrepreneurial cultures of insurance and financial consultants (Collinson and Hearn, 1996a, pp. 69–70). Other male-dominated professional occupations – such as doctors and lawyers – are suffused with macho beliefs, fuelled by high earnings and a high pressure work environment. Such middle-class masculinities were incubated in competitiveness, ambitiousness, technical expertise and exercising authority (Segal, 1997, p. 94). For Segal: 'the bureaucratic masculinity linked to a middle-class work culture, on the other hand, emphasizes duty and self-discipline' (Segal, 1997, p. 95). And Connell makes the point that masculinities are just as capable of being incubated in the middle-class workplace as the working-class one – though the patterns are somewhat different. In extreme cases, one manifestation of this was sexual harassment in the office.

Management (heavily populated by men), Collinson and Hearn argue, 'reflects specific masculinities' which might be equated to 'a form (or forms) of hegemonic masculinity' (Collinson and Hearn, 1996a, p. 71). Here dominant men exercise power over other male workers and over women. An example might be the blatantly 'macho' culture of American managers in the North Sea oil and gas industry (see Beck et al., 1996). One of the most comprehensive studies has been Roper's 1989 analysis of masculinity within the generation of post-Second World War managers in manufacturing – the 'organisation men'. Roper shows post-1945 corporate culture to be very 'macho' and these men to have a well-defined sense of themselves as male bread-winners, believing in a well-defined sexual division of labour, with wives in a 'servicing' domestic role. These men defined their manliness through tough decision making and wielding of authority and control in their spheres of work (Roper, 1994, p. 220). And somewhat like manual workers they defined themselves by reference to other sectors considered less manly – such as the financial services sector – 'effete city gentlemen' (Roper, 1994, p. 215). However, in their orally transmitted narratives Roper detected much bravado and tough talk but an underlying fragility or vulnerability: 'organisation men rarely felt equal to the cult of toughness they so ardently promoted'. Their identities were undermined by economic and technological change too: 'the post-war generation presented an image of hard masculinity based on its practical expertise in mechanical engineering, but microchip technologies threatened to render this kind of skill obsolete' (Roper, 1994, p. 216). This led to insecurities and ambivalences – a kind of fractured and shifting masculinity: 'they felt less manly than "self made" entrepreneurs, paternalistic inheritors and (as one man expressed it) the "horny-handed sons of toil" whom they managed' (Roper, 1994, p. 223). Perchard (2007a) has made the important point, however, that managers were a wide and varied group, so it is difficult to talk of characteristics of managers *en masse*. There were underlying class tensions, for example, between production managers, largely drawn from the shop floor and working-class backgrounds (and invariably with a defined masculine culture), and more administrative managers, predominantly from middle-class backgrounds (Perchard 2007a; Tiratsoo, 1999). These divisions were also evident during the 1984–5 miners' strike in the clashes between some colliery managers who sided with the NUM against Sir Ian MacGregor and his acolytes (Perchard and Phillips, 2011).

What is clear is that 'gendered power regimes' and a range of dominant masculinities existed across both manual and non-manual workplaces (Collinson and Hearn, 1996a, p. 73). Nonetheless, male identities were fluid and there remain issues with generalizing about male behaviour. Collinson and Hearn argue:

> Masculinities in contemporary workplaces are characterized by contradictory tensions. On the one hand, men often seem to collaborate, cooperate and identify with one another in ways that reinforce a shared unity between them; but on the other hand, these same masculinities can also be characterized simultaneously by conflict, competition and self-differentiation

in ways that highlight and intensify the differences and divisions between men. Given these deep-seated tensions, ambiguities and contradictions, the unities that exist between men should not be overstated. They are often more precarious, shifting and highly instrumental than first appearances suggest. (Collinson and Hearn, 1996a, p. 72)

With economic restructuring and the diminution of dangerous manual labour, as well as the end of military service, it has perhaps become more difficult for men to find the opportunity to express or display their masculinity – at least physically. For some, this has to be found in sport or maintaining fitness regimes outside of the workplace; for others in continuing to assert their domination in the home. Others have shifted from traditional masculine attitudes to embrace more progressive views – accepting the right of women to paid employment and a career beyond home and family, whilst becoming more emotionally involved in the family and embracing a different work–family balance themselves. Zweig noted the germination of this shift in his 1961 study of family life and work, though he commented that it was occurring more rapidly in newer industrial communities than the older, traditional working-class areas based on the 'heavy' industries (Zweig, 1961, p. 205). Labour market trends – the decline in male economic participation rates and growing job insecurity – have undoubtedly contributed something to this erosion of male identification with paid employment, whilst the opposite process has been occurring for women. Gendered identities have concurrently witnessed blurring and something of a convergence. Legislation on equal pay, opportunity and sex discrimination at work in the 1970s helped to change attitudes. In 1984, *Social Attitudes* surveys in Britain were still showing large minorities (45% of men and 41% of women) supporting the idea that a woman's place was in the home whilst men's place was in paid employment. By the end of the century *Social Attitudes* surveys showed that such beliefs had changed, leading Hinds and Jarvis to comment: 'the traditional notion of women as housewives seems to be all but extinct' (Hinds and Jarvis, 2000, p. 103). Goodwin has made the important point, however, that 'men's attitudes also vary between groups of men and as such they cannot be treated as a homogeneous group' (Goodwin, 1999, p. 133). The same could be said for women. Race, class, education and age were all significant variables affecting attitudes.

Goodwin's detailed quantitative analysis of a cohort of 33-year-old males in 1991 shows the extent of shift in men's attitudes away from traditional masculine views of gender roles, towards gender egalitarianism. 85% of men in the sample agreed 'men and women should all have the chance to do the same kind of work', whilst around 96% believed 'women should have the same chances as men to get some training or have a career' (Goodwin, 1999, p. 122). The group most likely to retain strong traditional masculine views were the manual working class – the least educated, most likely to be members of a trade union and usually in full-time employment and with a strong work ethic. Those with the most liberal views regarding gender roles were in higher occupational status jobs, better educated and most likely to hold non-standard jobs – including contract, self-employment and part-time work (Goodwin, 1999, pp. 118–22, 197).

Moreover, the tenacity of established notions of masculinity was reflected in the slow pace at which men responded to the rising economic participation of women by contributing more of their time and labour to unpaid domestic work. Studies did show a tendency towards Young and Willmott's (1973) 'symmetrical family', especially amongst the younger generation and the middle classes (Crompton, 1997, pp. 86–8). But change was at almost a glacial pace until very late in the twentieth century. Young and Willmott calculated in 1973 that men spent almost 10 hours in domestic work, but women employed full-time spent 23 hours (Edgell, p. 165). Studies thereafter indicated slow change in the direction of gender equality (Hochschild, 1990; Gershuny, 2000). Rising unemployment in the 1980s, however, did not automatically coincide with a significant increase in male unpaid domestic work because of the persisting sense that such activity was emasculating (see Chapter 7).

Questions about the contemporary significance of masculinity and the role of work in forging or undermining masculine values today are really beyond the scope of this book. Attitudinal surveys appear to indicate that the younger generation (under 30) almost completely subscribes to the idea of sexual equality in the workplace. Some recent work has also shown that the transition towards more non-standard forms of work (such as home-based contract work with irregular hours) is facilitating shifts in the sexual division of labour within the family, thus challenging traditional notions of masculine roles (Osnowitz, 2005). Other studies, however, indicate significant vestiges of gender inequality persisting – for example showing that 'performance standards are stricter' for women employees than men (Gorman and Kmec, 2007) and indicating differences in sleep deprivation in dual income households with babies (Maume et al., 2010). Whilst change has been marked, nonetheless, in an employment context where still almost twice as many men as women are working full-time there remains a strong association between men and paid work in the early twenty-first century and between men and the notion of being a breadwinner, with all the connotations of power and privilege which that entails within the home and family.

There also remains significant segregation based on gender within the labour market, with men continuing to dominate the top positions in the economy, though this has narrowed markedly over time (Hakim, 1998; see Chapter 1, Table 1.5). Simpson's recent work indicates that where men have entered fields of work dominated by women (such as nursing, primary school teaching, cabin crew and libraries) 'they adopt a variety of strategies to re-establish a masculinity that has been undermined by the "feminine" nature of their work' (Simpson, 2004, p. 349). McDowell's study of 'white working class youths' also suggests masculine identities were adapted and survived employment change from manual to more insecure and non-standard service sector work – with her subjects showing a strong attachment to the breadwinner ideal – and indeed to the traditional work ethic (McDowell, 2003).

In *Social Attitudes* surveys women and men continued to show divergences in their reasons for working and in their work orientations. Women emphasized 'financial freedom', rather than 'financial necessity'. In 1999, 67% of men said their main reason for working was 'need for money for basic essentials such as food, rent or mortgage', against 44% of women, whilst substantially more women (15%) than men (3%) said their main reason was 'to earn money to buy extras' (Hinds and Jarvis, 2000, p. 105). Where there was a clear *similarity* in attitudes between men and women in *Social Attitudes* surveys in the 1980s and 1990s was in relation to job satisfaction – perhaps a somewhat surprising finding given structural subordination of women in the labour market and lower levels of pay (Hinds and Jarvis, 2000, p. 106).

As far as men were concerned, the household also continued to command secondary importance to paid work – though significant differences existed between the younger and the older generations. In 1998, whilst around 80% of those aged 18–24 disagreed with the statement 'a man's job is to earn money and a woman's job is to look after the home', only around 45% of those over 50 disagreed with this statement (Scott et al., 1998, pp. 30, 31, 35):

> The British public are among the most liberal in their views on gender roles, but they can hardly be said to have abandoned traditional views.

Moreover, although the trend is clearly one of increasing support for less traditional roles over time, attitudinal change is really quite slow ... In practice, gender roles seem remarkably resilient. (Scott et al., 1998, p. 35)

A considerable gap certainly still existed at the turn of the century in gender roles and in attitudes. Time budget surveys demonstrated an increasing tendency for men to devote more time to childcare and household duties – though the gap remained significant even where both partners were in employment (Gershuny, 2000). In the 1992 *British Social Attitudes* survey it was found that in households where both the man and the woman worked full time, it was mainly women responsible for 'general domestic duties' in 67% of the cases and in only 24% were such duties shared equally (Kiernan, 1992, p. 101). The gender division was still particularly marked when it came to the 'core' routine tasks of shopping, cooking, cleaning, washing, ironing and childcare (women's roles), whilst men dominated the doing of household repairs and, somewhat idiosyncratically, dishwashing after the main evening meal (Airey, 1984, p. 133; Kiernan, 1992, p. 102). Crompton concluded her survey of the domestic household division of labour in 1997:

Changes in the gender division of market work, that is, women's entry into paid employment, have been achieved much more rapidly than changes in the gender division of non-market work (domestic labour). The most recent work suggests that a slow process of adaptation is under way, although it is likely that some gender stereotyping of household tasks will persist, as will the greater identification of women with the home in general. (Crompton, 1997, pp. 90–1)

Table 3.1 Earnings by gender, UK, 2011

Gross weekly pay	
men	£538.5
women	£445.1
Hourly pay	
men	£13.23
women	£11.92

Source: Adapted from data from the Office for National Statistics, *Labour Force Survey*. Licensed under the Open Government Licence v.1.0.

'Meaningful symmetry in the sense of gender equality in paid and unpaid work', Stephen Edgell commented in 2006, 'is a long way off' (Edgell, 2006, p. 167). The fact that women have been losing their jobs faster than men in the economic recession since 2008 only serves to emphasize this point. The gender gap in hourly pay and earnings (see Table 3.1) also remained stubbornly persistent into the 2010s.

Conclusion

The British workplace was dominated by men in the immediate post-Second World War period and to all intents and purposes this was a 'man's world'. Working lives were gendered – patterned by prevailing traditional cultures of masculinity and femininity, which saw men's role as the breadwinner, with lives centred on paid employment, and women's role as the home maker, with lives dominated by unpaid work pivoting around the family. Women's employment was largely segregated and undervalued, with women still earning in the 1950s little over half that of men on average – and this did not change until well into the 1970s.

In an economy still dominated by manual labour, the inherent dangers, physicality and harsh, brutal realities of the workplace acted to incubate a dominant mode of masculinity in working-class communities. This was especially marked in the so-called 'heavy industries', including coal mining, shipbuilding, iron and steel, transport, construction and sections of engineering. Here we see *machismo* attitudes forged in an almost exclusively male, tough and physically demanding work culture, created and reproduced in a not dissimilar way to how military service incubated masculine identities. In the manual work environment, masculinity was cemented in enduring filth, brutality and risk-taking at work, and those who deviated and objected were pilloried and outcast as 'soft', effeminate and sometimes castigated as endangering the team (or compromising the capacity to maximize piecework earnings) through their unwillingness to risk their own safety. At its extreme, masculine identities at work endangered lives, sapped energy and undermined health, just as other expressions of virility and *machismo* did, notably heavy drinking and smoking (Mullen, 1993, pp. 176–7). This represented a *sacrifice* of sorts by such working men and provided another important justification for male power and male dominance within the home and family. This behaviour could be rationalized, moreover, by comments that men were working for the family, or to give the kids 'a better chance'. Trade unions were amongst the conservative institutions that failed to aggressively attack masculinity in the workplace and resisted gender equality in employment in the immediate post-war decades – a process that Sylvia Walby associated with a strategy of 'patriarchal closure'. The unions will be explored further in Chapter 6.

Non-manual service sector workplaces in the immediate post-war period were also invariably dominated by men as were positions of power, status and authority in the workplace, including management and the higher professions. We know less about how such work incubated masculinities and how male identities were sustained in these different 'pen-pushing' work contexts. However, the work of Goodwin, Roper and Collinson and Hearn, amongst others, have elucidated how masculinities were reproduced in middle-class occupations, how some men subordinated both other men as well as female labour, and how 'gendered power regimes' operated and were sustained in offices and other white-collar occupations. There were different patterns here, but still a culture of male power, competitiveness and superiority over women.

There were signs of change and evidence of a wide variation in attitudes and experience, even as early as the 1950s (Brooke, 2001). In reality, a range of masculinities and femininities coexisted within a diverse and sometimes contradictory and complex workplace culture, where relationships, identities, attitudes and behaviour varied widely. Attitudes towards sexual equality in the labour market also clearly became more progressive over time, influenced by the feminist movement and by progressive equal opportunities legislation from the 1970s. Belatedly, the trade union movement embraced change and shifted to a more pro-active policy on gender equality in the workplace from the 1970s (see Chapter 6). The 'hard man' mode of masculinity atrophied and gave way to 'softer' styles of masculine behaviour in the workplace and a growing acceptance of gender egalitarianism. Traditional notions of the feminine role also morphed dramatically as women's relationship with the labour market changed. These transformations were especially evident amongst the younger generation. By the 2000s, Britain was amongst the most liberal of countries in terms of gender equality in the workplace, though clearly vestiges of sexism and misogynist attitudes persisted and inequalities – for example in access to top jobs and in wages – doggedly continued.

Masculinities and femininities clearly continue to be diverse and fluid, whilst the gendered nature of employment and unpaid household tasks has definitely been breaking down – and continues to do so into the twenty-first century. However, the empirical evidence suggests there remains some way to go before the last vestiges of traditional attitudes towards gender segregated roles are completely shaken off and the gender neutral labour market and household is established, with equal opportunities, earnings and choices for both women and men.

4

The Colour Bar

I am confronted by the colour bar every day. Some jobs are given to coloured people but there is no prospects of promotion. When I look around the city of London I do not find educated coloured men working in banks, as bus inspectors, as policemen. (Asian worker)

It's true to say we are not only fighting discrimination on the part of management but we have also to educate some of our own members too. (Trade union official)

At the beginning the unions tried hard to block them, to stop them coming in but that seems to have stopped. However, the shop stewards would certainly not agree to immigrant apprenticeships – I mean for Pakistanis. (Personnel manager)

The above are all extracts from interviews undertaken in 1966 and 1967 for the Daniel Inquiry on *Racial Discrimination in England* (1968). Race and ethnicity divided workers and patterned people's experience of work in post-Second World War Britain, constituting the basis for subordination and for privilege. This chapter explores the experience of work through the lens of race and ethnicity, examining work cultures and identities and the nature of discrimination and prejudice in the post-war workplace. It focuses upon the personal and emotional experience of black and minority ethnic groups and migrants, and the responses of the 'host' nation, including employers and majority white workers and their collective organizations. The subaltern structural position of such marginalized workers in British labour markets is relatively well known (see Chapter 1). The aim here is to explore discourse and experience – to unpick prevailing attitudes and investigate what it was like for immigrant labour in Britain after the Second World War. This discussion is located within a literature that is dominated by the idea of segmented labour markets and which emphasizes the host nation's jingoistic hostility towards and discrimination practised against migrant labour. Ken Lunn's seminal work, however, has challenged this stereotypical 'negative' view, indicating the existence of a range of opinions towards black and minority ethnic (BME) workers, of much toleration and cross-race solidarity, significant differences within local labour markets, and the need to contextualize what he terms 'complex encounters' (Lunn, 1985; 1999).

Generally speaking, there has been a division within the literature between more traditional 'modernist' theoretical perspectives and more recent 'post-modernist' approaches (Mason, 2000, p. 112). Richard Hyman provides a classic structuralist interpretation:

> Racism creates divisions within the working class which can be viewed as conducive to the stability of capitalism in that concerted working class action is inhibited. Some writers would argue that both racism and sexism are at times cultivated for this very reason. (Hyman, 1989, pp. 34–5)

Other studies have emphasized the range of experience within the diverse migrant and BME community in the UK, the agency of BME workers and pointed to marked changes in attitudes and experience over time. The notion of 'intersectionality' is important here as race, gender and class combined to produce multiple disadvantages in the labour market. An increasing body of research on experience in particular local labour markets in the post-war period is refining and developing our understanding – and more such work is clearly needed at the local and community level (see, for example, Phillips et al., 2007).

White migrants

In the immediate post-war period there were very few people of a non-white ethnic background living and working in the UK – perhaps in the region of 100,000–200,000 in the mid–late 1940s (Daniel, 1968 p. 9). However, Britain did have a number of settled white immigrant communities, with the Irish, Jews, Italians, East Europeans and others well embedded in the labour market. Irish migration to the UK reached massive proportions in the 1950s with one estimate suggesting net migration to the UK of 16% of the Irish population (Baines, 2007, p. 336). Assimilation of the Irish was facilitated by equality of educational opportunity after the Education Act of 1918, though there continued to be significant differences (albeit narrowing over time) between the experiences of 'settled' second and third generation Irish migrants, Protestant Irish immigrants and Catholics, and new arrivals after the Second World War.

Discrimination against Catholics and an 'ethnic hierarchy' in employment had its roots in the labour market in Northern Ireland. Here historically Protestants had monopolized government positions and top private sector jobs, occupying a privileged position within the labour market. Restrictions on Catholic employment were widespread. Mary Williams got typing and shorthand certificates from her school in Derry in the early 1950s but recalled:

> No jobs were available for Catholics and that's what I was. You would go in to ask them or get in and be interviewed and the interview would finish up with 'and what religious denomination are you?'. And you'd answer them and then they'd say, 'we'll let you know'. You never could get a job. (Britain at Work interview by Kathleen McIlvenna, 5 September 2010)

As a consequence Mary migrated to find work; firstly to New York, then to London to work as a bus conductor for London Transport. In large private companies in the North of Ireland, such as Harland & Wolff, Short Brothers, Mackies and Sirocco Engineering, only between 1% and 6% of total employees were Catholic as late as the 1970s (Darby, 1987, pp. 54, 68–9). Less than 15% of top civil service posts in Northern Ireland were held by Catholics and a 1971 survey of the Belfast Corporation Electricity Department found 61 Catholics in a total labour force of 1,346. Even in counties such as Fermanagh with a majority of Catholic residents, only 32 Catholics had jobs with the county council out of a total of 370 employees (Darby, 1987, pp. 54–5). Attempts at reform, such as the creation of the Fair Employment Agency (FEA) in 1976, may have been symbolically important, but were pretty ineffective in changing things, as Darby has shown (Darby, 1987. pp. 57–67). There were few complaints and only 18 positive cases of discrimination proven by the FEA in its first 7 years (1976–83). Catholics continued to be ghettoized in more vulnerable, poorly paid and insecure jobs and suffered disproportionately from unemployment in Northern Ireland in the 1980s recession. Unemployment rates rose to around 10% for Protestants and 25% for Catholics – who also experienced markedly more long-term unemployment (Jenkins, 1988, pp. 316–9).

Catholic disadvantage in the labour market in Northern Ireland may not have been totally attributed to discrimination, as a number of 'revisionist' scholars argue (Darby, 1987, pp. 55–6). Demographic factors may have played a part – there were fewer job opportunities in the more Catholic dominated west of the country. However, the weight of evidence suggests that sectarian ethnic discrimination was the primary factor creating wide differences in experience in the labour market in post-war Northern Ireland, and the evidence for this in the towns and cities – including Belfast – is irrefutable (Jenkins, 1988, p. 319; Darby, 1987).

'Sectarian ethnicity' transferred with migration from Ireland to the UK mainland and resulted in markedly fewer Catholics in managerial and professional occupations and proportionately more in the bottom end of the employment spectrum in lesser skilled manual jobs. This followed a long-standing historical pattern. The Irish navvy squads who worked on the Scottish Highland Hydro Electric Schemes as tunnellers (the 'tunnel tigers') in the 1940s and 1950s were a case in point (see Sykes, 1973; also Cowley, 2001). Certainly the practice of some companies of not employing Catholics continued long after the Second World War, with school attended used as a recruitment filter to determine religious affiliation. This was evident, for example, on Clydeside in companies such as Harland & Wolff and Weirs. Robert Gear – an engineer (born 1943) – referred to this in an interview:

Q. Were there any questions about what school you'd been to?
In Weirs? (laughs) oh aye, oh aye, there absolutely was. They always asked you that and if you said Holyrood [a Catholic Secondary School in Glasgow] they just threw your [application] paper away. Weirs was terrible. Then they got token Catholics coming in, but it's fine now though. (Interviewed by David Walker, 23 March 2011, Glasgow Working Lives, Glasgow Museums/SOHC/042)

Protestant Irish migrants to the UK mainland, by contrast, tended to fill the better paid, more secure skilled and supervisory positions. An asbestos insulation lagger, Hugh Cairney, recalled how jobs in the shipyard communities on Clydeside prior to the 1950s were clearly demarcated by religion:

When my father was a young boy, sixteen and that looking for work, if you were a Catholic in the shipyards you didnae get employed. You got

employed as a labourer or something like that but you didnae get employed
to learn a *trade*, and the only thing at that time going was the insulation,
you can go to that – we werenae a trade, *we're still no' a trade*. (Interviewed
by Neil Rafeek, 26 March 2005, SOHC/016)

Not only did this mean a clustering of Catholics in lesser skilled,
poorer status jobs, but also the more life-threatening ones, both in
terms of injury risk and chronic occupational disease (see Chapter
5). In Scotland, Tom Devine has recently asserted that such economic disadvantage in the labour market for Catholics had disappeared by the end of the twentieth century, when it can be said there
was a level playing field in terms of employment opportunity and
job status (Devine, 2000). However, recent work has challenged this
argument. Whilst overt discrimination was much less in evidence
on the mainland by the 1950s and continued to decline, it had left
a legacy, as Boyle has shown in an important recent book, based on
new oral interviews (Boyle, 2011). For example, older age groups
of Irish Catholic migrants in West Scotland continued to experience disadvantage in the 2000s, with a markedly higher proportion
in lower status manual occupations (Abbotts et al., 2004; and see
Boyle, 2011).

There were, however, some Catholic-dominated employment enclaves
where favouritism and discrimination operated in the opposite way.
Dockwork was one example. A London docker recalled in the 1970s:

> Take the Big Boot gang – got all the cream on those ferry boats at 34 shed,
> but you had to be a green scarf (Catholic) to get in there. Any time Father
> X [the local priest] found someone in trouble – you know, the kiddies with-
> out clothes or the wife sick – he told the shipworker and that man got a
> couple of days with the gang. (Hill, 1976, p. 19)

Around the same time a Clydeside shipyard rivet heater (Michael
Denny) used his Catholic connections to move to a better job. He
recalled:

> The manager in the shop was a guy called Gordon Woods and I knew he
> was a very staunch Catholic and he'd seen me in the chapel as an altar boy
> and, this is true, I went tae him and I said 'Mr Woods, you don't know me
> but I've been stuck on this rivet heating and I would dearly love a shot at
> the welding'. [Mr Woods] 'Jist bring your gear through'. I used him. I think
> this goes on a lot. You know folk say ye've got tae have a funny handshake
> [Orange Lodge / Masons] but it works both ways and it worked for me

that way. (Glasgow Museums, Glasgow 2000 Lives interview with Michael Denny)

In 'Monklandsgate' in 1993–4 it was alleged that a Labour control-led council in Lanarkshire (Monkland East, which was dominated by Catholic councillors) divided resources unequally favouring Catholic dominated Coatbridge and not Protestant dominated Airdrie (even allegedly handing out job applications to favoured candidates on green tinted paper instead of white).

Immediately after the Second World War, significant numbers of the Polish armed forces (that had been based in the UK) settled in the country (around 160,000) and over 100,000 'European Voluntary Workers' (EVW) – mostly East Europeans – were recruited to UK jobs (in agriculture, mining, construction, textiles, clothing and brick-making for example) from displaced person camps (Baines, 2007, pp. 339–40; Patterson, 1963, pp. 62–3). Most were men, but over 20,000 were female workers, mostly drawn in to textile production in Northern England (Webster, 2000, p. 258). This was part of a post-war government recruitment drive to address acute labour shortages and reconstruct the economy. Many of the EVWs were treated par-ticularly badly, being demoted from their former professions to low paid, unskilled and low status labouring or routine clerical jobs. They were on temporary contracts, subject to repatriation if their work was no longer needed. As Webster noted, the conditions of their entry into the labour market: 'subordinated them to dominant white eth-nicities in Britain' (Webster, 2000, p. 260) – though she also notes an important distinction between them and black migrants in that whites were not seen as a threat to racial purity (Webster, 2000, pp. 262–3). Polish immigrants and EVWs clustered in what Patterson described as jobs characterized by their 'intrinsic unpleasantness, or because of low pay, long hours or seasonal fluctuations... low status or insecurity' (Webster, 2000, p. 63). This was a pattern with immigrant labour. One example was the brick-making trade in Bedford and Peterborough, the subject of a later study of EVWs in the 1970s by Blackburn and Mann, 1981, pp. 138–49).

EVWs were met with a great deal of hostility and resentment, and were ghettoized into jobs that were below their capabilities and expe-rience. One noted: 'English people didn't like us so much' (Webster, 2000, p. 267). Another reflected: 'From beginning they treat us not really good. They treat us like a second-class citizen. Sometimes they ask us why we not back to Poland' (Webster, 2000, p. 267). One daughter of a Latvian surgeon recruited to a textile mill articulated the culture shock of her new factory employment:

> I couldn't even imagine you know what a mill looked like really, and as soon as I walked in – you know all your eyelids were full of cotton and it was terrible dust and noise. And I thought – my God!... I was ready to go back. But then I thought, well, I decided for myself to come over here, and if other people can do this job, definitely I can do it. So I make my mind up that I was determined to do the job, which I did. (Cited in Webster, 2000, p. 271)

The labour market insecurity of EVWs was worsened in some cases by trade unions imposing rules to restrict promotion and 'redundancy priority clauses' to ensure migrant workers were the first to be laid off (Patterson, 1963, p. 62; Phillips et al., 2007, pp. 143–7). The receptivity of the labour movement to such migrant workers has been a much debated issue. The dominant interpretation emphasizes the negative and hostile reactions of the UK trade union movement towards this post-war wave of white migrants (Kay and Miles, 1992). Ken Lunn has challenged this view, arguing that it is based largely on institutional and policy sources, and that at a local and workplace level assimilation was much less problematic and there was much camaraderie and support and little evidence of overtly racialized reactions. He provides examples of this within the Scottish coalfields regarding Polish labour. 'The strength of the local labour movement', Lunn argues, 'helped facilitate the relatively harmonious settlement of those Europeans who agreed to accept and abide by the terms of that culture' (Lunn, 1999, pp. 74–5) In contrast, Phillips, Hallett and Abendstern's recent study of the experience of EVWs in the post-war Lancashire cotton industry in 1946–1951 indicated a range of responses, though enough underlying prejudice, discrimination and 'trade union jingoism' to challenge Lunn's interpretation of smoother and more cooperative relations between the dominant endogenous white workers and incoming migrants at the local level. They argue for a more nuanced picture in evaluating responses to migrant workers, located within the context of the memory of job insecurity in the 1930s Depression and the local economic environment (Phillips et al., 2007, p. 150). Hyman has also made the pertinent point that controlling entry to occupations and excluding or restricting 'outsiders' (on ethnicity or gender) was an understandable reaction by host nation workers and their trade unions given the insecurity of the labour market (Hyman, 1989, p. 250).

Black minority ethnic migrants

Before the Second World War, there was a black population of perhaps 10,000 – 20,000 in Britain, mostly living in port cities where black seamen had passed through and settled (Wright, 1968, p. 40; Sherwood, 1985, p. 116). Liverpool was one such place. Here the 'settled' port community was bolstered by West Indian volunteer workers brought in during wartime, thus increasing the black population of the city from around 500 in 1939 to some 3,500 by 1945. This was part of a process whereby black migrant workers were attracted from the colonies to work in the wartime economy, as well as being recruited to the armed forces (notably the Air Force where 5–6,000 worked as ground and air crew by the end of the war), where the colour bar was officially lifted several weeks after the outbreak of war. We still know little about the experience of such workers. However, detailed study of two groups – a Honduran contingent of lumbermen brought in to work for the Forestry Commission in Scotland and the experience of Indian lascars in the merchant marine – has highlighted the embedded institutional racism of wartime Britain (Sherwood, 1985; Sherwood, 2003). Gross mistreatment (including pitifully low wages, no leave and inadequate accommodation in isolated camps) eventually led to the Honduran migrants striking for better conditions and being forcibly repatriated in August 1943. The Indian lascars were more enduring, with around 50,000 serving in the Merchant Navy during wartime. Their experience was also characterized by systemic underpayment of black workers in contrast to whites, condoned by the jingoistic and notoriously racist National Union of Seamen. Lascars' wages in the British merchant navy during the war were between three and four times lower than white seamen's wages (Sherwood, 2003, p. 46). Around 6,600 Indian lascars lost their lives working in the British merchant navy during the Second World War. The concept of wartime equality of sacrifice had little resonance here.

One of the first extensive post-war studies – Richmond's *Colour Prejudice in Britain* (1954) – examined the experience of black immigrants in Liverpool. Whilst welcomed in wartime, tensions grew in the immediate post-war years as servicemen returned to their jobs and the economy faltered in 1947. Black immigrants were sacked and turned down for employment elsewhere on Merseyside as racism revived and what one 1946 report called 'discriminatory treatment by employers against coloured colonial subjects' spread (Richmond, 1954, p. 43). Indeed, the Richmond study found evidence of widespread and systemic racial prejudice and discrimination (Richmond, 1954, pp. 47–90, 158). One Jamaican volunteer worker recalled his experience towards the end of the war:

> Instead of being given a square deal we are treated as of no account. After two and a half years we are given the worst kind of jobs. I have spoken to the foreman about same and he says we cannot be trusted with any other kind of work... The reason for all this is there is hardly any work for the men employed...When a job do come in the white men are given the cream... the management seem to have forgotten when they depend on us... I did not come here to be messed around but to put my shoulder to the wheel and get everything over as early as possible that we can all get back to a normal life. Unless we all fight shoulder to shoulder regardless of colour and creed that will never happen. (Cited in Richmond, 1954, p. 56)

The situation was worsened by the particularly poor employment prospects on Merseyside in the immediate aftermath of the war – which led to the region being officially designated as a 'Development Area' due to the high levels of unemployment. The tensions culminated in the race disturbances in Liverpool in 1948, which included physical violence against blacks (Richmond, 1954, p. 152), predating the better known Notting Hill riots by a decade. In part, at least, this reflected white workers sense of labour market insecurity, influenced in turn by memories of the mass unemployment of the 1930s. 'Fear that such a situation will be repeated still exists', Richmond noted in his study, and 'it is this fear which, more than anything else, leads white workers to resent the negro' (Richmond, 1954, p. 147).

Following the British Nationality Act 1948 (which confirmed British citizenship for those born in the Commonwealth countries) large-scale migration from the British colonies and Commonwealth began, with a steady flow from the arrival of the *SS Empire Windrush* in 1948 until the early 1960s. By 1969 the black population of Britain was estimated at 1 million and by 1985, 2.4 million, with the majority groups being Afro-Caribbean and Asian. The flow was restricted somewhat with tighter immigration controls from the passage of the Commonwealth Immigrants Act (1962), but the upward trend in net migration resumed from the early 1980s, with net immigration peaking at 171,000 in 2001 (though the majority now came as 'dependants' rather than primarily as 'workers'). The last quarter of the twentieth century and the early twenty-first century also saw larger numbers of white immigrants from European Union (EU) countries (Britain became a member of the later European Economic Community (later the EU) in 1973).

Immigrants were attracted by better job opportunities and earnings in the UK and came to fill labour shortages, predominantly being slotted into unskilled jobs in manufacturing, public transport and the NHS created by technological change and those jobs deemed too dirty or unsociable or poorly paid to recruit local labour (Braham et al., 1981, p. 91; Mason, 2000, p. 95). As one manufacturing company manager (who first recruited black workers in 1956) put it: 'You can't get white people to do the menial tasks that have to be done in any foundry, not even the floating workers like the Irish' (cited in Wright, 1968, p. 43). Another manager commented: 'It wasn't easy to obtain unskilled labour. Non-coloured labour won't have it. It's hard work under rather bad conditions' (cited in Wright, 1968, p. 43). BME workers also occupied some of the most dangerous and life-threatening jobs, as Lee and Wrench have shown (1980, pp. 551–66). This was highlighted in 2004 with the drowning of 23 illegal Chinese immigrants who were cockle picking in Morecambe Bay.

London was the most important labour market in the UK for immigrants. In 1991, 45% of all Britain's BME population were in Greater London, where they represented 20% of the total population (Mason, 2000, p. 99), with other significant concentrations of BME workers in the West Midlands, Greater Manchester and the Yorkshire textile towns (such as Bradford) where employers sought to increase their competitiveness with cheaper labour. By the 2000s there was roughly the same number and proportion of black ethnic minority immigrants (4.6% of the labour force) as white ethnic minority immigrants (4.7% of the labour force) living and working in the UK. However, white immigrants fared considerably better than black ethnic minority immigrants in terms of the quality of jobs, extent of unemployment and wage levels (Baines, 2007, pp. 343–6). Amongst the lowest earners in the worst jobs were Pakistani and Bangladeshi immigrants.

Many of the first wave of black migrants found they could not use their skills and qualifications and were forced to downgrade expectations. John Grigg worked in the banking sector in London and he noted how in the 1950s bank managers 'were not very happy at all to have Asians or black people working for them'. He recalled how when he was acting branch manager he was phoned by the Regional Office to ask for permission to send 'a light skinned Asian' to fill a branch vacancy (Britain at Work interview by Roraima Joebear, 28 June 2010). Prejudice on the basis of skin colour made it difficult for BME migrants to get work, or at least work that matched their skills, experience and qualifications. Lily Crawford migrated from Jamaica to London in 1951 hoping to find work as a trained beautician. 'Nowhere would have me', Lily recalled, 'because they weren't accustomed to black people'. At one place a potential employer felt obliged to ask the rest of the white staff if they would work with a black woman. Lily eventually found employment at Morris' beauty parlour run by a Jewish migrant owner who empathized with her difficulties (Britain at Work interview by Dave Welsh, 18 March 2008). Door-to-door selling (or 'peddling') was a common first occupation for many male Asian migrants, sometimes in conjunction with a more regular full-time job – as with Ujager Singh, an Indian migrant to Coventry in 1937 (Virdee, 40). This could be demeaning work. Kabul Singh Heer, another Punjabi migrant to Coventry who arrived in 1938 reflected: 'I really felt ashamed going door to door – I felt like a beggar' (Virdee, 2006, p. 41). Bashir Maan, a Pakistani immigrant to Glasgow in the early 1950s recalled:

> I started peddling too with them, because there was no other way, no other job available … most of them were in peddling in the fifties, but in the late fifties what happened was that the country was going through a very prosperous spell, this country, and people here, the indigenous population was moving on to better jobs, jobs with social hours and better pay. They were leaving the jobs with less pay and unsociable hours, so there was a vacuum there, so the employers needed labour and they couldn't get their own labour, so they were forced to recruit immigrants. (Interview by Neil Rafeek, 9 May 2003, SOHCA 019)

Similarly Akbar Kahn, a Pakistani migrant to Coventry who arrived in 1954, reflected: 'The English did not work in the factories and foundries … It was our men who worked there, they did not survive – some died inside. They were making cast iron. The English did not work there' (Virdee, 2006, p. 43). (Actually *some* did, but it is the perception that they did not that is significant here.)

Maan commented on how south Asians moved into work in chemical factories and the buses because of the unpopularity of these jobs and, later, moved into local retail despite initial prejudice:

> Now the trouble they found was that no customers would come in during the day, so they had to keep their shops open till late at night to make a

living. During the day if a person saw, at that particular time, a black face behind the counter, they would walk out. (Interview by Neil Rafeek, 9 May 2003, SOHCA 019)

Maan's testimony is representative of a strong 'self-help' narrative that can be detected in many black migrants' personal accounts where the emphasis is on personal struggle to overcome an alien and inhospitable culture and to succeed in the face of intense discrimination. Ujager Singh reflected: 'When you have your own business you can make more money than if you work for someone else' (Virdee, 2006, p. 40). Another Indian migrant to Coventry (Kewal Singh, who arrived in 1958) reflected: 'We Indians kept on working no matter how hard the work was' (Virdee, 2006, p. 47). For many migrants the pressure to work long hours and to conform to management pressure was influenced by the need to support families back home. Such narratives contrast sharply with the focus in endogenous white 'activist' work-life accounts, where the binary opposites of management as villains and workers and their unions as the heroes frequently features (see McIvor, 2010, pp. 109–11).

Different immigrant groups gravitated to particular industries, often with a snowball effect through 'chain migration' over time. Kevin Searle's recent study based on extensive oral interviewing of the Yemeni immigrants who worked in the Sheffield steel industry is a good example (Searle, 2010). Before the Second World War Yemenis were the largest Muslim immigrant group in the UK, mostly working as seamen, with important clusters in Cardiff, Liverpool and other sea ports. After the war Yemenis swelled the unskilled workforce in the metal working industries of Sheffield, Birmingham and Manchester. Language was a significant obstacle and they experienced much racism and discrimination, which Searle's respondents evocatively recall. One outcome was a marked failure to attain promotion or any significant upward mobility during their working lives (Searle, 2010, pp. 73–113). 'They keep us bottom ladder' was how one Yemeni worker in Sheffield put it (Searle, 2010, p. 73). As Searle points out there was a marked 'racial division of labour on the shop floor':

> The restrictions on Yemeni promotion and the relative mobility of the white workforce meant that racial disparities soon emerged between a permanent Yemeni lower class and a transitional, white mobile class, with opportunities to flee the least desirable jobs. (Searle, 2010, p. 108)

Not that this was just accepted. Searle shows how Yemeni individuals and the community organized to resist racism (this was the subject

of a BBC documentary (http://www.bbc.co.uk/nationonfilm/topics/
family-and-community/south-shields-yemeni-riots.shtml) – albeit
with little evident success. For some, this involved defending themselves with knives in workplace confrontations. Another got his own
back another way, recalling:

> I worked on a 12 hour shift from six o clock in the morning to six o clock
> in the evening, and I had to take a pot up in the crane to piss into. I used
> to throw the piss out of the crane cab over the workers who didn't like us
> Arabs. (Searle, 2010, p. 86)

At mid-twentieth century a colour bar existed within segments of
the British economy, with widespread and deep-rooted discrimination operating against black minorities. Some employers indicated
to Employment Exchanges in the 1950s a 'no coloureds' or 'NBI'
(no blacks or Irish) policy (Ohri and Faruqi, 1988, pp. 61–2). A West
Indian painter and decorator who came to the UK in 1950 was told by
a foreman: 'Sorry but this shop is closed to you blokes', whilst a West
Indian motor mechanic who applied to work in a garage recalled: 'I
was told straight off that no coloured were wanted' (Daniel, 1968, pp.
71–2). Another was told by a manager: 'the men in this shop do not
work with coloured' and was shown the door (Daniel, 1968, pp. 72).
Bhajan Singh Atta (an Indian migrant to Coventry in 1955) recalled:
'We were thought of as second class people ... they all used to look at
us with contempt ... There used to be a board in front of the factory
stating no vacancy for the black man ...' (Virdee, 2006, p. 51). Others
were told there were no vacancies whilst at the same time taking on
white workers or continuing to advertise the same post (Daniel, 1968,
p. 73). Doug May, a white worker, recalled such discrimination against
a black friend in the early 1960s in Bristol:

> We walked around the streets of Bristol in actual fact we went to all differ-
> ent factories to try and get a job and ... we tried a number of places one day
> and eh, my friend Barry he said 'Well, go on in on your own.' I said: 'What
> for?' and he said: 'Just go in on your own'. And it was Bulldog Linings
> which was a company out at Brislington and I went in and I said 'are there
> any vacancies for trade union ... eh ... for fitters?' and yeah, I was given a job.
> Barry went in quarter of an hour after I went in and he was told 'no vacan-
> cies'. I didn't take the job subsequently because I didn't like what they'd
> done for a start and I mean he was a good mate of mine for six months
> and they'd turned him down basically on colour, there was no other rea-
> son to turn him down. I mean, if anything, he was probably better on the

tools than me ... but em ... shouldn't say that should I (laughs). (Interview by David Walker, 6 September 2005, SOHCA/022)

Discrimination based on skin colour was rife. Peter Wright's study in 1961–4 for the Institute for Race Relations (IRR) indicated this clearly, as did the Political and Economic Planning (PEP) Racial Discrimination Inquiry in 1967 which found over half of all West Indian immigrants and over a third of all Indian and Pakistani immigrants surveyed reported personal experience of discrimination against them in the labour market. Patterson's study of Brixton in the period 1955–61 found a wide range of attitudes amongst managers and within the local community, including extreme racism. An example of the latter was one building contractor's agent (ex-NCO in the colonies) on a large site employing some 2000 men:

> I've had 300 blacks through my hands in the last two years. As workers I find them slow, lazy and aggressive... Occasionally they're violent... I am sorry for them, but they are not up to the work here. They are only a generation away from the jungle, trying to be Western and failing. They're cunning and have an inborn animal instinct... They make money by graft, letting rooms and living off women, and the smart ones take jobs as a cover. (Patterson, 1963, p. 118)

One outcome was that black ethnic minority immigrants were frequently 'downgraded' in terms of job status, invariably forced to work in the lowest paid, unskilled jobs. This was the case, for example, in the West Midlands foundries in the 1950s, as Duffield has shown (Duffield, 1985). Reid's study of 735 black immigrant workers in Manchester in the mid-1950s found only 1% in skilled jobs, 44% in semi-skilled and 55% in unskilled jobs (Patterson, 1963, p. 70). Patterson, however, claimed: 'I myself found no great evidence of genuine downgrading'(Patterson, 1963, p. 71). Cecilia Wade, a Caribbean migrant to London in 1956, recalled her experience of the labour exchange:

> I took my references from home saying I was a teacher. This woman at the counter said, 'Oh you were a teacher back home were you? Well you won't get teaching here!'. I said, 'Well what have you got to offer?'. 'Nothing at the moment. Come back next week.' The following Monday I went and she looked me up and down and said, 'All I have to offer you is Lyon's Tea Shops or there is a job going at a hospital in Clapton. Which would you prefer?'. I said, 'I don't know much about Lyon's Tea Shop because, as I said, I was a teacher and I'm looking for clerical work.' 'Oh! You won't get clerical work here.' She was positive. (Cited in Bruley, 1999, p. 125)

One inquiry in the late 1960s found only 7% of formerly non-manual immigrants in non-manual jobs in the UK (with 51% taking unskilled manual jobs; Daniel, 1968, p. 62). The same survey found that about a third of skilled manual immigrants also found themselves having to demote to unskilled work. Brooks' study of London Transport in 1975 found that experience varied, but much downgrading was evident, including those 'who were previously in non-manual, supervisory or teaching employment' (Brooks, 1975, pp. 40–1). Many BME women found themselves clustered in the particularly insecure, low paid and marginalized homeworking sector where they were disproportionately represented compared to white women.

Employers and white workers widely believed that black workers did not have the capacity for positions of authority and were averse to the idea of black workers as foremen and supervisors. Many were unwilling to accept BME workers as equals (Deakin, 1969, pp. 220–1). This was the product of a widespread belief in subordinate capacities linked to colonialism, not dissimilar to attitudes held by men towards female workers in textile factories a generation earlier. 'Bars on the promotion of coloured labour to supervisory positions', Deakin noted 'became fairly general throughout industry' (Deakin, 1969, p. 197). Harold Stevens, a West Indian from Barbados, was the first black worker on his shift at ICI in the 1960s. He recalled how he faced racist jokes and white workers 'picking fights'. He said, 'it was rough for about the first two years'. He was also passed over for promotion in ICI despite having worked longer than others promoted to coordinator or foreman. He reflected, stoically: 'That's the way it goes. If the foreman don't think I'm good enough then that's up to him' (Nichols and Beynon, 1977, pp. 86–7).

A Jamaican immigrant Wallace Collins (who worked in London for eight years from 1954–62) recalled a similar experience in his autobiography published in 1965. A skilled cabinet maker, he faced prejudice and disbelief about his abilities which grew to open hostility and jealousy towards his craftsmanship and supervision of four other black workers. He was sacked after refusing to back down and defending himself when threatened by a white co-worker. He commented: 'I felt used and discarded, as I lugged my tool box out the shop that Friday evening, and in fact was oozing with bitterness'. He recalled one of his fellow workers saying: 'Wallace, if you were white you would be foreman in this shop'. He reflected ruefully: 'The lessons I learnt in that job were, it doesn't pay to be too interested in the white man's work, lest you be accused of being geared to do him out of his job; and it is wise to make yourself as inconspicuous as possible' (Collins, 1965, p. 75). He drifted through a series of jobs and became thoroughly alienated by the whole experience, thinking of little but the wage packet at the end of the week (Collins, 1965, pp. 94–5). Later, after a spell of unemployment for over a year he recalled an incident which influenced him to leave what he termed 'antique Britain' (Collins, 1965, p. 76) after eight years and move again, this time to Canada (in 1962). He was sent by the Employment Exchange to report to a building site foreman:

> I showed him my job card, which stated clearly that I was a carpenter. He looked at the card in my hand, then at me and pointed down in the hole. 'I want someone to finish off this hole, can you handle a pick and shovel?' I said no, to which he replied, 'sorry mate'... The ordinary man in the street was bellowing against the migrant like cantankerous fishwives... In my various jobs I noticed how bold employers became in their prejudices against the migrant. (Collins, 1965, pp. 120–1)

In some cases white workers objected to the employment of blacks and other ethnic minorities – as in nursing in the mid-1950s (Lunn, 1999, p. 77) – and threatened to strike if black workers were taken on – as at Central Buses in London in 1954 (Brooks, 1981, pp. 126, 128; Patterson, 1963, pp. 145–7). In February 1959, 680 workers at Sterling Metal Works foundry at Nuneaton near Coventry downed tools in protest against the employment of Indian workers on particular jobs (Virdee, 2006, p. 50). The local newspaper referred to them as the 'colour bar strikers' (*Coventry Evening Telegraph*, 11 February 1959). In another Coventry workplace the opposition of white workers led to exclusion from the better paid jobs, as Sohan Singh Cheema (an Indian migrant who arrived in 1954) recalled:

> When we were employed by management, people objected and asked why coloured people had been employed. These people threatened to strike. Therefore the management said that we could work as cleaners instead of in the foundry. We always used to get unskilled work. (Virdee, 2006, p. 51)

Some bus companies operated a blanket colour bar employment policy (Nichols and Beynon, 1977, p. 85). This was reported to be worse in the West Midlands – where there were a series of strikes on immigrant employment – and other provincial towns in the 1950s and early 1960s than in London (Patterson, 1963, p. 146; Lunn, 1999, p. 78). In 1955, two Transport and General Workers' Union branches at Bristol bus depots had voted against black drivers and the bus company management continued to maintain a 'whites only' policy. The Traffic Manager commented:

> We shall go on engaging white labour before coloured labour. This is the policy of the management of the company in the light of the experience in other cities and towns where they have engaged coloured labour and their labour situation has deteriorated because it is then no longer regarded as a white man's job and the white people start leaving and they find themselves more short of labour than they were before. (Cited at Dresser: http://www.bbc.co.uk/legacies/work/england/bristol/article_2.shtml)

This was challenged several years later in Bristol in 1963. The resulting bus boycott led to the first black drivers and conductors being appointed (Dresser, 1986), and, by 1968, the first black bus inspector (Deakin, 1969, p. 202).

Some rail companies had similar racist attitudes and refused to employ black station guards (for example at Paddington and Euston Stations), whilst two of the biggest railway goods depots still operated a colour bar in 1961 (Patterson, 1963, p. 90). One British Rail spokesperson said:

> There is no doubt that passengers prefer having European guards and ticket collectors. It is the same throughout industry. White men are preferred to coloured men for reasons of intelligence and education. (Dresser: http://www.bbc.co.uk/legacies/work/england/bristol/article_2. shtml)

The first black station guard to be appointed at Euston happened in 1966 (Deakin, 1969, p. 203). A London Transport worker (Martin Eady) recalled how when he started in the early 1970s there were established communities of Jamaican and Barbadian railway workers: 'They worked permanent days and they did some of the heavier maintenance, and in those days they were completely separate from us'. Martin found it odd, given the left-wing political background of many of these migrant workers from the West Indies, that they were not more active:

> I said: 'why don't you get involved in the union?' And of course, racism was the short answer. They hadn't been welcomed. They'd been recruited into the union, so the union were quite happy to take their money, but in the main they had been badly treated, although the union always denied that. (Britain at Work interview by David Welsh and Roraima Joebear, 20 May 2010)

Bill Siepmann, a London Transport railway guard employed from 1978, recalled black colleagues reminiscing:

> Those I was friendly with, sometimes they'd tell you stories about the old days and it must have been really, really hard and just absolute non-stop racist abuse, basically. But as usual, there were covert forms of retaliation. Pissing in the station foreman's teapot was one I remember. (Britain at Work interview by David Welsh, 2 July 2010)

In 1976–7, a National Front cell existed at Upminster railway depot in London and the *NF News* was sold on the news stand there.

The prevailing discrimination extended in many workplaces to forcing a 'whites first' policy, with black workers prioritized for sacking and redundancy in times of economic downturn (breaching the usual 'last in, first out' principle), sometimes with the approval of the trade unions (Patterson, 1963, pp. 62, 109, 147; Duffield, 1985, pp. 159–66). Employers and managers frequently took the line of least resistance – exploiting the 'reserve army' of cheap immigrant labour where they could, and tolerating white workers and trade union polices to restrict entry to maintain harmonious industrial relations. The employers' movement either ignored the issue entirely, or campaigned to minimize government intervention in their 'managerial prerogative'. The Director of the powerful Engineering Employers' Federation commented in 1967: 'we have in our industry to our knowledge little evidence of a serious state of discrimination' (Deakin, 1969, p. 210). The Confederation of British Industries (CBI) only made its first statement on racial equality in 1967 and went on to oppose the extension of the Race Relations Act to cover employment (as did the TUC) a year later (Deakin, 1969, pp. 196, 210). The government also virtually ignored race as an industrial relations issue – evident, for example in the silence on this matter in the wide-ranging Royal Commission on Trade Unions and Employers' Associations (Donovan Commission, 1965–8).

For their part, the trade unions played a pivotal role in the shaping of workplace discrimination and race segregation in the post-Second World War period, though their responses and policies ranged widely. Duffield has noted how black migrants tended to flow into areas where the trade unions had no presence or were weak (as in London and the West Midlands), whilst where the trade unions were strong they could limit such 'dilution' of labour:

> Where trade unions were well organized in private industry they were usually successful in controlling the entry of black workers, restricting them

to labouring or other menial jobs and confining their employment to time of labour demand ... the typical response of employers to union pressure of this nature was one of acquiescence. (Duffield, 1985, p. 160)

The Massey Ferguson tractor plant in Coventry is a case in point. In an area of high black immigration, there were only 10 black employees out of a total workforce of 6,800 in the mid-1970s (Wrench, 1987, p. 170). In the West Midlands foundry industry BME workers were segregated in the low paid, insecure and unskilled jobs created by the expansion of mechanization to the foundries after the war. Discrimination also operated covertly because of the widely prevailing practice of recruitment through 'word of mouth' favouring the relatives and friends of the majority white workforce. Corruption and bribery were also rife through a system of BME worker recruitment in many plants dominated by management-controlled black intermediaries (the 'go-betweens', 'straw bosses' and 'uncles') to whom fees would have to be paid to get work (see Duffield, 1985).

Wrench has also argued that the trade unions contributed to racial disadvantage through both proactive policies and through inaction, notably with the TUC's *laissez-faire* policy of refusing to develop any specific policies to address the issues of its black membership in the 1950s and 1960s (Wrench, 1987, pp. 160–86). As Vic Feather (General Secretary of the TUC) noted in 1970: 'The trade union movement is concerned with a man or woman as a worker. The colour of a man's skin has no relevance whatever to his work' (cited in Wrench, 1987, p. 165). Empty resolutions passed by the TUC from 1955 onwards outlawing racial prejudice and discrimination were meaningless when they were not backed up with any positive action. The TUC also remained committed to immigration controls and opposed to the passage of Race Relations legislation up to the 1970s. Some individual unions, branches and officials – for example in the West Midlands – worked to support strikes against the employment of black labour and to restrict entry through the 'quota' system. Examples included the National Union of Seamen, the Confederation of Health Service Employees and the TGWU.

On their part, many BME workers expressed their frustration through collective organization and strike action. In 1965, for example, 500 Indian TGWU members went on strike for a fortnight to get a sacked shop steward reinstated (Duffield, 1985, p. 167). In one case in 1967–8 in a foundry in the West Midlands 21 Indian TGWU members threatened with redundancy went on strike in protest, but to no avail (Ohri and Faruqi, 1988, pp. 80–1). Sarwan Singh Gill recalled how black workers were paid a lower rate in the 1950s at Dunlop in Coventry until: 'Later on when more [Asian] labour came we formed a union – then we were given the equal pay' (Virdee, 2006, p. 51). In some cases, as Fryer has noted, strikes were in the face of trade union hostility to BME workers (Fryer, 1984, p. 385). There were also a series of strikes by black workers in the 1960s and early 1970s in response to trade union collusion in racist practices (e.g. at Courtaulds Mill and Mansfield Hosiery, Preston in 1972) or against discrimination which did not get official trade union support (as at Woolf Rubber Company and the Coneygre Foundry, Tipton, 1967–8). In the latter strike, members of the Amalgamated Union of Foundry Workers crossed the picket line (Wrench, 1987, p. 166). Manual craft and general unions were amongst the most racist in this period. Examples of trade union failure to support black union members in disputes continued well into the 1970s, most famously, perhaps, at Imperial Typewriters, Leicester, in 1974 where around 400 Asian workers came out on strike over the company cheating on its bonus payment system. The TGWU in this case refused any support, leaving the black strikers to struggle on for three months. And racist attitudes continued to surface amongst trade union shop stewards and officials. In 1978 an official of the National Society of Metal Mechanics commented:

> Don't get me wrong, I'm not racist but I think everyone who enters this country should be given a test to make sure they can read and write properly. I don't blame employers being selective about whom they employ. (Cited in Wrench, 1987, p. 171)

In his assessment of trade unions and racism (published in 1987) Wrench concluded: 'black workers in this country have served the unions far better than the unions have served black workers' (Wrench, 1987, p. 162).

The labour relations conflicts noted above were indicative of a growing propensity of BME workers to resist exploitation and fight for equal opportunities and improved work conditions in the 1960s and 1970s. At this point BME workers were proportionately just as likely as white workers to be members of trade unions (Wrench, 1987, pp. 161–2), though Indian and Pakistani workers were less well organized and few BME workers were office-holders within the unions (Deakin, 1969, p. 206). By the 1980s union membership density for BME workers was significantly higher than white workers. Partly in response to the racist attitudes of some trade unions, BME workers also developed their own organizations and – like the coal miners – could usually rely on very high levels of community support in their struggles with employers. Amongst the most prominent were the Black Trade Unionists' Solidarity Movement and the Indian Workers' Association.

The evident failures of the labour movement on racial disadvantage were counterbalanced to some extent by extensive evidence of solidarity and support for racial equality across many workplaces and workers' organizations. Lunn has made the point that the record of the trade unions on race was mixed, ambiguous and complex over 1945–79. He argues for a more balanced perspective: 'challenges to populist racism could be reinforced by trade union positions and declarations but also undermined by the individual and group actions of trade union members' (Lunn, 1999, p. 76). For example, in response to the racism within the bus depots in the mid-1950s the TGWU passed a formal resolution in opposition to 'any form of colour bar', though it remained committed to immigration control (Lunn, 1999, pp. 78–9). Whilst the TUC and the main manual workers' unions supported immigration controls and failed to develop proactive anti-racist policies and attack discrimination directly in the 1950s and 1960s, the record of the white collar unions was much better, whilst locally union branches were capable of actively pursuing a race equality agenda – as in London Transport from the early 1960s (Lunn, 1999, pp. 79–82). Deakin's authoritative study in 1969 argued that the trade union movement: 'displays a vast diversity of behavior', though he concluded, 'but in practice they have often alienated the coloured worker' (Deakin, 1969, pp. 208–9). In part, this reflected the wide range of views amongst majority white members, whose attitudes need to be understood within the context of their own exploitation and precarious, insecure position within a capitalist production system based on profit maximization. This particularly applies to manufacturing communities facing deindustrialization, restructuring and large-scale redundancies – as Phillips and colleagues have argued for the cotton towns of North-West England:

> Antagonism towards BME workers in the Northern textile districts, for example, was as much rooted in the powerlessness of native labour over the economic system and the 'crisis of cotton culture' as in racial prejudice. (Phillips et al., 2007, p. 150)

Whilst racism was deeply entrenched within both the workplace and the trade union movement, it was challenged and was increasingly resisted in the 1960s and 1970s when the policy crumbled in the face of growing radicalism, civil rights movements and the cultural revolution. The unions became more supportive and an increasing number of BME migrants joined the unions. More trade unions became solidly anti-racist, subscribing to the universal 'brotherhood of workers' idea and in reality a wide range of views and policy coexisted. One trade union branch secretary described by Patterson as 'the most liberal' she interviewed commented:

> We won't tolerate colour bar or discrimination among our members. But the West Indians can't expect feather-bedding just because of their colour. They'll have to learn to mix in and adapt themselves to our ways if they're to be accepted. They must lose their chip-on-the-shoulder attitude and realize that if someone calls them 'Sambo' or 'Blackie' he doesn't usually mean to be offensive. They should answer them back in the same spirit as 'Ginger' or 'Shortie'. A factory isn't a school for young ladies and nicknames are usually personal. (Patterson, 1963, p. 141)

According to a survey in 1966, 22 trade unions had some negative rules or agreements relating to 'coloured', 'immigrant' or 'foreign' labour (Ohri and Faruqi, 1988, p. 88). Others, however, were much more progressive, with the National Association of Local Government Officers (NALGO) standing out in the earlier period (Ohri and Faruqi, 1988, pp. 90–1; Wrench, 1987, p. 178).

What is evident is that racial prejudice remained deeply embedded within sections of the white British workforce in the immediate post-war decades. Despite being a shop steward at British Leyland (car manufacturers) in Coventry, my father's racism (perhaps incubated in his youth on Merseyside in the 1940s?) provoked memorable disagreements between us in the family home in the mid–late 1970s. A northern textile mill worker commented thus about West Indians to the ethnographer Dennis Marsden in the mid-1960s when asked 'what do you think about the colour bar then?'

> I think they should put 'em in quarantine for six months when they first come here. They're not civilized some of 'em. I know some's all right, but they come here and they've got all sorts of uncivilized habits, living together in one house. And when you talk to 'em they are just like animals. All they can think of is sex'. (Cited in Jackson, 1968, p. 90)

The Political and Economic Planning (PEP) researchers in the 1960s went on to prove systemic discrimination by 'testing' employment practices using 'dummy' English, Hungarian and black immigrant applicants (Daniel, 1968, pp. 77–8). These findings were confirmed by the next PEP Report by Smith in 1976 (Smith, 1981, pp. 177–80), which found that around 30% of 'posing' black immigrants failed to get a job interview as a consequence of discrimination (with the white Italian 'control' group suffering from around 10% discrimination). Smith also showed a higher likelihood of ethnic minority immigrants to be employed on unpopular shift-working, especially the night-shift. Other researchers found discrimination extended to second generation ethnic minorities – including black graduates in the early–mid 1970s. In one study, 68% of direct job applications by black graduates were rejected against 18% of white graduates; whilst of 'milk round' applications, 81% of black graduate applicants were rejected after the first round, as against 36% of white graduate applications (Ballard and Holden, 1981, pp. 163–76). The 1967 PEP Report noted: 'Difficulties with regard to employment, often directly linked to discrimination or prejudice, are the most widespread single source of disappointment with life in Britain for coloured immigrants' (Daniel, 1968, p. 57).

Another survey was commissioned by the Institute of Race Relations in 1963. It focused on two of the areas of greatest BME concentration: Greater London and the West Midlands. It too found immigrant workers disproportionately clustered in the lower end of the occupational hierarchy. In the West Midlands, for example, only 2% of West Indian immigrants were professionals, managers, supervisors or self-employed (the labour force average was around 20%; Deakin, 1969, p. 73). Whilst there was more diversity in employment in London, still there was a marked over-representation of immigrant labour in unskilled labouring jobs (Deakin, 1969, pp. 74–8). Over half of all restaurant and cafe workers in London in the 1970s were immigrants (Braham et al., 1981, p. 103). Everywhere, it was rare for a black worker to be in any position of authority over white workers and chances of promotion were extremely limited (Deakin, 1969, p. 197; Wright, 1968, p. 21). Patterson's detailed study of Brixton in South London (based on around 400 interviews in the community between 1956 and 1959) showed this hostility towards black immigrants being promoted to positions of authority over white men in the workplace to be one of the most persistent of discriminatory practices (Patterson, 1963, p. 149).

All this was linked to widespread prejudice – for example in refusing to believe black immigrants could be skilled – and fear of wage undercutting, taking jobs and strike-breaking by workers and disrupting industrial relations by the bosses. White workers raised irrational fears of diseases being spread by what they regarded as black workers' poor hygiene and personal habits (Wright, 1968, p. 71). One of the racist slurs in the Huddersfield textile mill Marsden investigated in the late 1960s was that blacks were more likely to have venereal disease linked to their voracious sexual appetites (see also Segal, 1997, pp. 168–204 on fear of the 'unclean' and phallus envy). One West Indian mill worker commented sarcastically to a white worker who offered him a sweet: 'You never take fuck all I offer you. *Your* hands clean?' (Jackson, 1968, p. 91). Some workplaces which did recruit ethnic minorities laid down 'quotas' to appease worried white workers. Patterson found a 10% quota was common in South London in the early 1960s (Patterson, 1963, p. 129). 'Throughout the field of employment', the Institute of Race Relations Report in 1969 concluded, 'discrimination is widespread and pervasive' (Deakin, 1969, p. 221). Not surprisingly average wages levels lagged behind the white majority. Surveys suggest BME group men earned around 15–20% less on average than the white majority right up to the 1980s (Blakemore and Drake, 1996, p. 132).

Things were beginning to change, albeit slowly. The public sector, where discrimination had been markedly less blatant than in the private sector, led the way. The civil service had been a heavy recruiter of BME labour in the 1950s and 1960s and of almost 18,000 BME civil servants in 1969, 850 were in professional and executive grades (Deakin, 1969, p. 201). As Deakin noted: 'public accountability is not of such a searching quality as to eradicate discrimination, but it does limit its scope and inhibits to a degree those who would practice a policy of discrimination' (Deakin, 1969, p. 204). In the face of a massive labour shortage in the post-war years the NHS recruited large numbers of BME workers, including as GPs and nurses. Immigrants constituted one in six GPs in the 1970s (Braham et al., 1981, p. 103), occupying a professional status that was unusual within the racially segmented British labour market. Still, within the medical profession vertical and horizontal segregation was evident, with clear underrepresentation in top medical jobs (with relatively few immigrants making it to consultant status) and over-representation in least popular fields, such as geriatrics (Braham et al., 1981, p. 93). Jones and Snow's recent oral history based study of BME immigrant clinicians in Manchester since 1948 provides much evidence of the influence of race in the patterning of job opportunities and promotion prospects in the NHS (Jones and Snow, 2010). This study found that immigrants were employed to do the most menial, lowest paid and low status jobs in the NHS – such as the cleaning, whilst BME nurses found themselves disproportionately engaged in the least popular low status specialisms, such as mental health, midwifery and geriatrics (Jones and Snow, 2010, pp. 55–8). White nurses went into surgical wards or obstetrics and had more favourable shift patterns, for example being employed on fewer night shifts than BME workers.

Access to the labour market was clearly patterned by race and ethnicity, both in terms of the availability and the status of jobs. Phizacklea's work has shown how BME women had markedly worse jobs that white women – though the gap was not as wide as that between white and black men (Phizacklea, 1988, p. 46). One area where Asian women were clustered was in the 'sweatshop' conditions of the clothing industry in inner cities like Birmingham, often working illegally in grim conditions with no unionization. 'They are under constant pressure', Raghib Ahsan from the Midlands Low Pay Unit noted in 1984: 'It is hard to believe that we are living in the 1980s. Industrial conditions are more like the 1880s' (cited in Wrench, 1987, p. 179). Black workers were also more vulnerable in the labour market – unemployment rates amongst blacks quadrupled in the 1970s, whilst rates doubled for whites (Braham et al., 1981, p. 104; see Chapter 6). The clustering of immigrants into the lower echelons of the labour market can be predominantly explained by racial prejudice and discrimination (though other factors had some impact, such as language and age). And prejudice and discrimination was systemic amongst employers, managers, foremen and white workers and their trade unions in the 1950s and 1960s. This was most prevalent before, but certainly continued long after, the outlawing of such discrimination in the first Race Relations Acts (1965; 1968). It was easier to exploit people when they had lower expectations, were less well organized than endogenous workers, had lesser employment rights and may well have had a more instrumental view of work – for example as a means to send money home (Grint, 1991, p. 242).

Experience, however, varied widely. For example, Indian migrants gained access to somewhat higher level jobs and experienced lower levels of unemployment in the 1980s recession than most other BME groups. Unemployment figures indicate that access to the labour market was particularly difficult and precarious for West Indians and Pakistani/Bangladeshi men, whilst Indian men fared notably better (with unemployment rates in the mid-1980s at 15% compared to the average for white ethnic male workers at 11%). The latter was at least partly the product of different work cultures and levels of qualifications across ethnic minorities, with Indian men notably better qualified (Grint, 1991 pp. 237–8). The Ugandan Indian migrants who came in 1972–3 were particularly well qualified and quickly established themselves as part of the urban elite. As a Sikh woman, Disha Parkash, observed:

> A lot of academics came from Uganda in to Glasgow at that time, at that point a lot of doctors you know…medical doctors with their families…People were very kind of rural and 'villagey' until the Ugandan Asians came and that kind of changed everything. The whole aspect of life changed in our community, in the Sikh community. They were very, very, modern Sikhs you know so they kind of changed the outlook for everybody. (Interview by David Walker, 20 June 2008, Glasgow M74 Project, SOHC 023/15)

Nonetheless, prejudice and discrimination based on skin colour was common. Jamal Hasan was a community and youth worker in the East End of London in the 1970s and early 1980s. He recalled:

> When I came to this country in 1972 I realized that Asians, black people and anybody who came from a colonial background were still perceived as subservient to the whites. It seemed to be generally thought that white people were superior and we were inferior…Not only was racism very apparent, but institutional racism was very deep rooted. (Britain at Work interview, 7 April 2006, anonymous interviewer)

Challenging racial discrimination in employment

How far has racial and ethnic discrimination in the labour market eroded since the 1950s and 1960s? Undoubtedly the civil rights legislation of the 1960s and 1970s (Race Relations Acts of 1965, 1968, 1976) combined with broader social and cultural changes and direct action from within BME communities and the growing anti-racist movement have had a positive impact in reducing prejudice and disadvantage. BME workers were not simply the passive victims of abuse, prejudice and discrimination. There was a long history of resistance, challenge and transgression, individually and collectively through community and workplace groups, as well as through protest, campaigning and political mobilization (Mason, 2000, p. 110). The first Race Relations Act (RRA) of 1965 was based on US civil rights legislation and made discrimination and segregation in public places illegal (Blakemore and Drake, 1996, pp. 13, 119). The amended RRA of 1968 incorporated discrimination in employment and housing. Discrimination was not, however, made a criminal offence but rather cases were taken through a conciliation procedure in the newly established Race Relations Board. Hence, the system was not punitive, lacked the powers of its US equivalent and handled few cases in its early years – just 150 or so per annum in the early 1970s when reported instances of racial discrimination in employment recruitment alone numbered in the thousands (Blakemore and Drake, 1996, pp. 119–20). Nonetheless, the 1960s RRAs were symbolically important in laying down a marker and shifting public discourses on the acceptability of race inequality. Procedures were tightened somewhat with the RRA 1976, which created the Commission for Racial Equality (CRE), recognized 'indirect' discrimination, passed the employment discrimination cases to industrial tribunals to arbitrate and introduced criminal liability for race discrimination. By the early 1990s the number of race discrimination cases being heard by the industrial tribunals had increased almost tenfold compared to the early 1970s (Blakemore and Drake, 1996, pp. 121–5). Still, however, the CRE lacked the punitive sanctions to force better practice upon the more recalcitrant employers and uncertainty over its role limited its impact.

Some studies of more settled immigrant groups were reporting that the initial hostility and opposition of host communities was evaporating as early as the 1960s – such as Patterson's 1963 Brixton study which indicated that social acceptance and assimilation was beginning in the workplace, though still rare within the wider community (Patterson, 1963, pp. 152–3). Patterson identified generally positive trade union attitudes by the early 1960s as pivotal in this process and asserted that 'a minority of exceptional individual migrants have begun to move up from the bottom of the industrial ladder and to undermine the British workers' notion of coloured workers as "Lascars, coolies and cane-cutters in far-away lands"' (Patterson, 1963, p. 153). Brooks' study in 1975 also noted that over time, initial hostility to the employment of blacks in London Transport dissipated, though this was 'grudging' and a long, slow process (Brooks, 1975, pp. 130–2). Sheila Emmanuel migrated from Dominica to join her husband in London in 1967. She worked in catering in London Transport for a few years then became a bus conductor. Whilst her work narrative in an interview in 2011 was generally positive, Sheila recalled two specific incidents of racist abuse from passengers and one physical assault which left her with a minor injury after she was dragged off the bus into the road (Britain at Work interview by Myrna Shoa, 14 Jan 2011). She reflected of her thirteen years working on the buses: 'I enjoyed my job on the bus apart from when you find some people are aggressive'. Martin Eady started working for London Transport in February 1973 and commented on changing attitudes and more intolerance towards racism amongst his generation of fellow workers. Nonetheless he recalled a discussion with a trade union 'chairman' after a branch meeting who offered to arrange a transfer from Ealing Common depot because, as he put it, 'Oh that place is full of fucking coloureds'. Martin continued: 'Not all the people in the union were racist by any manner or means at all, there were good anti-racist people in there at that time, but there was a prevailing view particularly amongst the older generation' (Britain at Work interview by Dave Welsh, 20 May 2010).

The labour movement belatedly played a part in this process towards racial equality and elimination of discrimination in the workplace. Indicative of change was the reversal of the TUC's traditional pro-immigration control stance in 1973. Lunn has charted this shifting terrain as the TUC moved towards a much more aggressively pro-equal opportunities, anti-racist policy (Lunn, 1999, pp. 82–6). In part, this was in response to the rise of the British National Party (BNP) and race relations tensions within society more broadly. Martin Eady was instrumental as an NUR union representative in rooting out the BNP from the Upminster train depot in the late 1970s and was active in the Rail Against the Nazis movement – a splinter from the highly effective Anti-Nazi League formed in 1976. Whilst there continued to be plenty of evidence of residual racism within the trade union movement – for example in poor representation of BME workers in trade union hierarchies – attitudes and policies were changing, indicated, for example, in widespread support across the labour movement for the Asian Grunwick strikers in 1976 (see Chapter 6). As Lunn has argued in a balanced appraisal of the evidence up to the late 1970s: 'In some senses the labour movement led by example in challenging the politics of racism; in others, it continued to replicate the institutional racism which had been constructed over some hundred years' (Lunn, 1999, pp. 86–87). Wrench found in the mid-1980s that the prevailing situation was 'mixed', with 'both positive and negative aspects':

> The trade union leadership has made progressive shifts from an archaic position; progressive activists have made their voice heard; some unions have devoted some resources to equal opportunities and anti-racism. On the other hand, it is clear that a real barrier to future progress is still the ignorance, the defensiveness, the misguided colour blindness and indefensible racism of some men and women in positions of power and influence in the trade union hierarchy, as well as within the rank and file. (Wrench, 1987, p. 185)

As far as lived experience of the workplace went, the picture also remained uneven into the 1980s and beyond. The recurrent Policy Studies Institute national surveys of ethnic minorities elaborated on differences in experience within the diverse ethnic minority population and reported some upward mobility (for example through self-employment) whilst continuing to stress endemic and persistent discrimination and chronic prejudice based on skin colour (Modood et al., 1997, pp. 1–2, 83). My work colleague David Walker began employment in London Transport's Chiswick Works in 1979 and he recalled being introduced to a young British Afro-Caribbean fellow worker:

> He offered me his hand and said 'people call me Sooty.' Taken aback I said 'what's your real name?' He said 'Geoff' I said 'OK, I'll call you Geoff.' Always stayed with me that – terrible. People actually called him Sooty! I always made a point of calling him Geoff and asking others 'have you seen Geoff?' or 'did you hear what Geoff did'.

Racism revived and deepened in periods of economic recession. This was a pattern since the economic crisis of 1947–8 which sparked the first significant post-war racial conflict in Merseyside (Patterson, 1963, pp. 44–5). Racism surged again in the 1980s economic downturn (Jenkins, 1988, p. 333). Ohri and Faruqi's study in 1988 found 'systematic, rather than incidental, discrimination' taking place, and concluded: 'structured racism operating in the organisation of the economy continues to have a deliberate and powerful impact on the lives of black people' (Ohri and Faruqi, 1988, p. 62). For example, skilled craft apprenticeships in the early 1980s went to white applicants at more than three times the rate when compared to similarly qualified black applicants (Ohri and Faruqi, 1988, p. 72). Some groups fared better than others. West Indians, Pakistanis and Bangladeshis continued to be seriously disadvantaged in the labour market, whilst other groups, including Chinese, Indians and African Asians had employment profiles and earnings not dissimilar to the white majority (Modood, 1997, pp. 2, 84; Mason, 2000, p. 102). Whilst 30% of the white male labour force were professionals, employers or managers, only 19% of Pakistanis and 14% of Caribbeans were (Modood, 1997, p. 100). Burton has also shown significant differences existed in occupational welfare provision – with only 21% of male Pakistanis and Bangladeshis in occupational pension schemes in the early 1990s, compared to 43% of male white, Indian and black workers (Burton, 1997). The wage gap between white workers and BME workers also remained significant – particularly for women. One estimate in the mid-1990s indicated that BME women workers earned on average 23% less than white women (Sly, 1994). The lower status of Pakistani and Bangladeshi workers was also reflected in particularly wide differentials in earnings (Modood, 1997, pp. 113–4). At the same time, significant upward mobility was evident in almost all ethnic minority groups (with the possible exception of the Bangladeshis), mirroring the general shift in the labour market . Modood sums this process up as a 'lessening of disadvantage', though by no means it's disappearance (Modood, 1997, pp. 139, 142).

The Commission for Racial Equality was similarly cautious about the extent of change, arguing that there remained a significant gap in the mid-1990s between companies having policies against racial discrimination on their books and actually implementing them (Burton, 1997, p. 506). There appears to have been considerably slower progress on eradicating racial discrimination than gender discrimination up to the 1990s, whilst BME female workers were amongst the most disadvantaged. Other studies have shown a marked narrowing in labour market disadvantage for black and minority ethnic male workers, but little change for BME female workers (Ignaski and Payne, 1996). One area of marked change – which owed something to the Race Relations legislation – was growing penetration of the non-manual sector, where a similar proportion of total employed BME and white workers was achieved by the early 1990s (Blakemore and Drake, 1996, p. 132).

What is also evident, however, is significant change and diversity *within* particular groups – making generalization difficult. Age was an important variable, for example, with significant differences in orientations to work and experience between the older and younger generations. Dale, Fieldhouse, Shaheen and Kalra's 2002 study of Pakistani and Bangladeshi women, based on oral interviews with 41 women in Oldham, showed that the meaning of work was very different to younger women born and educated in the UK, who were much more involved in paid employment than their mothers, who generally led very traditional family-centred lives. The ability of the latter to engage in market activity was constrained by lack of educational qualifications, language and heavy family responsibilities. Young Pakistani and Bangladeshi women, on the other hand, generally did not see their work careers as conflicting with their religion or with their domestic role, but 'as a means to independence and self-esteem' (Dale et al., 2002, p. 22). When the interviewer asked a 21-year-old

Bangladeshi woman (in full-time employment) what work meant to her she replied:

> Freedom and being a person, an individual. When you are in work you are seen as a different person than at home. At home you have to listen to others and you are like a child obeying orders, at work you can be professional and mature... work means socializing and making new friends... it's good when we have meals and go out and have a good gossip. (Dale et al., 2002, p. 14)

Another 27-year-old, married Pakistani woman indicated that paid work meant empowerment within the home, commenting: 'Equality in a relationship. I don't think it comes naturally just because you are working. It just puts you in a better bargaining position' (Dale et al., 2002, p. 16).

In the 1990s and 2000s research focused much more on delineating and explaining the plurality of experience within the ethnic minority community and the complexities of the 'ethnic penalty' in contemporary society. Racism, however, though clearly less extreme than it was in the 1950s and 1960s, remained doggedly persistent. The *British Social Attitudes* surveys consistently posed a question about the degree to which BME workers 'are not given jobs these days because of their race'. The results in the surveys of 1983, 1987 and 1991 indicated that between 60% and 69% of those surveyed perceived such discrimination existed (Airey, 1984, p. 128; Young, 1992, p. 181). One EU survey in 1997 found that around one-third of the UK population admitted to being racist (Grint, 2000, p. 228). Attitudes were becoming more progressive, but deeply engrained racist beliefs proved difficult to change.

Conclusion

A colour bar and ethnic hierarchy existed in Britain in the two decades following the Second World War, reflected in the exclusion of BME workers from many workplaces and their integration on markedly disadvantageous terms into generally low paid, low status jobs. In the 1950s and 1960s there existed a deeply segmented labour market based on race and saturated with prejudice and discrimination against migrant 'others'. This built on an established pattern of ethnic prejudice and discrimination, evident in the treatment of the Catholic Irish and the first post-war wave of white migrants, in schemes such as the European Volunteer Workers.

Recent scholarship, however, suggests that we need to guard against vague categorizing, overgeneralizations and stereotyping. There has been a growing recognition of the range of attitudes, views and policies of the 'host' population towards migrants in what Lunn has described as 'complex encounters'. There is also a sense that prejudice and discrimination needs to be contextualized and understood within prevailing power relations in capitalist production and the dynamics of local labour markets. In this reinterpretation and critique of crude structuralist and modernist explanatory frameworks, the BME community emerge as divided, diverse, fluid and as active agents exercising choices bounded by constraints. Our understanding of economic disadvantage has also been sharpened by a sense of intersectionality – the interplay of class, race and gender. In the process, the appraisal of the roles of key institutions in labour markets – such as the trade unions – have been subject to revision. The labour movement was not homogenous and represented a wide spectrum of attitudes and opinions. Whilst there was much evidence of racism in the early period up to the 1970s in many workplaces and many trade unions, these were also the organizations that were capable of exposing unfair and discriminatory practices of managers and employers keen to exploit vulnerable labour. From the 1970s on, the labour movement shifted to become a key element of the progressive coalition of pressure groups and social movements fighting against racism in employment and in society.

Grint concluded his balanced evaluation of racism and ethnicity in labour markets in the 1990s thus:

> And while racism remains a critical problem for society it is the case that patterns of inequality are changing in response to increased human capital by minorities (specifically educational qualifications) and to labour market restructuring (specifically the decline in unskilled jobs). The consequences of this are beneficial for some groups – Afro-Caribbeans, Indians and Chinese but not for Pakistanis or Bangladeshis for whom the future remains bleak. (Grint, 2000, p. 265)

Change over time has been uneven. Some ethnic minority groups have benefited more (such as Jews and Indians) from the structural shifts in the economy from manufacturing to service jobs than others, whilst analysis of labour markets suggests the persistence of some kind of 'ethnic penalty' or 'racial disadvantage'. London, for example, has developed a distinct racial division of labour in cleaning, hotels, retail, catering and food processing where workers are recruited to low paid and insecure jobs because of their ethnicity, not their skills (Holgate, 2005, p. 464). Certainly wide differences in labour market experience by ethnicity and race continues to stain the present-day UK labour market, though the pattern is more complex and multi-layered than a simple white/black divide (see Table 1.6).

5

Bodies

They only wanted healthy and strong people in the factory. If somebody was slim or had been working in an office then it was difficult for him to get a job in the factory. They used to feel the muscles of the worker before the job was offered. It was like when a butcher in India checks the goat before buying it, to see how much muscle that animal has on it. (Darshan Singh Briya, cited in Virdee, 2006, p. 45)

Being a man with no education – the only thing you had was the muscle in your arm and what experience you got with metal, and a very willingness to work. I would go in and say to people 'Yes I'll do that in that time.' And whatever it took to do that I would do it. Silly now, looking back through the years, you know. (Interview by Ronnie Johnston, 1 February 1999, SOHC/016/A9)

This was how an Indian migrant to Coventry (he came over in 1956) and a Clydeside sheet metal worker expressed aspects of the embodiment and physicality of their employment and the nature of work regimes that impacted upon their bodies. There is a recognition of the central importance of the body, a sense of dehumanization and evident regret vented here (and in other such personal testimonies) that the prevailing productionist ethos had caused damage. Bodies bore the brunt of competitive pressures at work: of trauma, chronic disease, fatigue and stress. The body and emotion are largely absent from most scholarship on the history of work, though recently attention has been growing (see, for example, Wolkowitz, 2006) and there has been an important strand of research upon occupational health and safety for some time. This chapter engages with this historiography, exploring embodiment in the workplace, work-health cultures

149

and the changing ways that work interacted with the body, both positive and negative, in Britain since the Second World War. It draws upon considerable fieldwork, including oral interviews conducted by Ronald Johnston, myself and others (Neil Rafeek; David Walker; Andrew Perchard; Angela Bartie; Susan Morrison; Hilary Young) on occupational health in the post-Second World War period.

Employment and the body

Undeniably, work was and continues to be good for the body. At a very fundamental level, work is a cornerstone of good health, fitness and well-being, for a number of reasons. Employment provided the resources which determined standards of living and gave purpose and structure to lives, things that were essential for mental health. Undertaking work can be life-enhancing, contributing to a real sense of purpose and fulfilment, undoubtedly improving self-esteem, physical and mental health, as the studies of the deleterious effects of losing work clearly indicate (see Chapter 7). Work is now recognized as pivotal to happiness in indices of well-being touted as alternative (and more appropriate) measures of a society's 'wealth' to Gross Domestic Product (GDP). The therapeutic and healing value of work has long been accepted, for example in the treatment of those with learning difficulties and other mental health disabilities and illness, including depression (see Long, 2006; Turner, 2010). Workers felt valued and significant as a consequence of their employment; of being associated with productive lives and of actively contributing to society. Moreover thinking jobs could sharpen the intellect, whilst manual jobs could hone a muscular and fit body – as Orwell famously observed of the Wigan miners in the mid-1930s. A Barnsley miner, Joe Kenyon, recalled in his autobiography:

> Our pits used muscle and blood. Our blood. A trammer had to be fit, broad backed and short ... strong in muscle and bone and a bit weak in the head. At the age of fifteen I joined a Health and Strength Club ... That way I developed a strong back and strong muscles in my arms and legs. For me, being only five feet four, tramming was a doddle. (Kenyon, 2003, p. 80)

Robert Gladden, a Middlesbrough steel worker from 1942 to 1989 observed: 'You felt very fit after a shift. It was hard, enjoyable work. It was like body-building, shovelling for eight hours a day. You didn't feel tired; you stayed nice and slim' (in Blackwell and Seabrook, 1996, p. 32). Similarly a Harlan County (USA) coal miner reflected in an interview with Alessandro Portelli on the older generation working in the pre-mechanized pits:

> In those old pick and shovel days, they were pretty tough men. I mean, the men's lifestyle, the way of working, the arms, the hands, the muscles, the big shoulders. Now what we would consider very hard work, those men could do with ease, because the kind of work they did at the mine, really developed, developed them. My father weighed two hundred pounds and he was five feet eight, and he could bounce a refrigerator on his back. (Portelli, 2011, p. 139)

Skilled craft workers might enjoy being absorbed in the conceptualization and execution of a complex labour process and revel in the relative autonomy they exercised over the pace and rhythm of work, with evident positive consequences for their mental health. The socialist author, Robert Tressell (Noonan) evoked this nicely through his main character Owen when he was planning and decorating a 'drawing room' in the famous novel *Ragged Trousered Philanthropists*. Many professional, academic and creative non-manual workers similarly enjoyed the health-enhancing qualities of work undertaken with much independence, under little direct supervision and overt pressure. Employment, moreover, brought an income which directly impacted upon ability to pay for health insurance, medical treatment and the resources (such as food and housing) which were basic to the maintenance of health and well-being, as well as bringing other non-wage benefits (for example holidays and a pension) and opportunities for socialization. Exit from work through retirement, redundancy and long-term unemployment remains an important cause of social exclusion, isolation and poverty, and has been associated with ill-health and premature mortality (see Chapter 7). In almost all its forms, work could *potentially* be good for the body (and loss of work detrimental) – and sometimes we have perhaps been guilty of forgetting this in our haste to brand the capitalist workplace as generically and *intrinsically* unhealthy and dehumanizing.

That said, it is also true – and the evidence is irrefutable – that Fordist production regimes invariably involve an extension of control over and monitoring of the body and, in many types of manual work, high levels of risk, injury, and exposure to chronic occupation-related diseases, with subsequent risk of disability. In the modern non-manual workplace the pressure and intensity of work, as well as its inherent instability, could also impact adversely on health – hence the contemporary stress at work epidemic. Moreover, *relatively* healthy and safe workplaces in the UK in the early twenty-first century have had to be fought for and were (and remain) subject to contestation and a power struggle, as wages and work time have been (and continue to be). In the second half of the twentieth century there remained many hazardous and health-threatening occupations, labour processes and work environments coexisting with a fundamental neglect by employers of the potential of the workplace as a site of good health practice (on the latter, see Long, 2011). Occupational ill-health, injury and disease could be the product of many factors. The extent of medical knowledge prevailing, the efficacy of the monitoring and regulatory framework and prevailing attitudes and identities come to play here. At the core of this issue, however, lies an unequal power relationship in which the competitive market system encourages those with power to exploit those with little power, putting profit before health. Managerial pressure *and* the prevailing work culture could also incubate self-exploitation, with a high risk-taking ethos prevalent within manual labouring jobs at mid-twentieth century (especially those that were front-loaded with bonus systems and where workers, once injured or killed, could be easily replaced).

Undeniably work could and did impact adversely upon the body, not least where the profit motive or productionist culture induced managerial abuse, bullying, harassment and work intensification which made it difficult to sustain a healthy work–life balance and the dignity of labour. As two medical researchers reflecting upon the causes of coronary heart disease noted in 1949: 'existing conditions of work impose strains which, when endured too long, are beyond physiological tolerance' (J.A. Ryle and W.T. Russell cited in Bartley, 1985, p. 137). Bodies could be prematurely exhausted. Jim Ward, a builder who worked on the construction of the Sizewell A nuclear reactor in East Anglia in the 1960s (completed 1966), reflected on the work of the boilermakers on the site:

> They worked hard, and it was a rough job they were doing...dangerous, and of course, another short working life. I think, after about sort of...40 or so, round about that age, it was noticeable, at that age, that you'd get a little bit of a shake on...which you don't realize in normal work... so, it was a short working life for most. (http://www.buildingworkersstories. com/project-4/)

Overwork could lead to physical and emotional fatigue, stress, exhaustion and, in extreme cases, to breakdown and depression. And the latter may well have been compounded in the recent past as the long-term historical trend in the UK of reducing working hours has been reversed for significant groups of workers (see Bunting, 2004; Donkin, 2001). Whilst working hours fell after the Second World War, the data suggests little change in work hours in the UK from the 1970s to the late 1990s, when male workers in the UK worked more hours than any others in Europe (Gallie, 2000, p. 308). A long working hours culture re-emerged in the 1990s and 2000s, not least amongst professionals where new communications and IT technologies (such as the mobile phone, the laptop and easy internet access) blurred the boundaries between work and home, to the detriment of family life and health (see Bunting, 2004). Given these technologies, control and regulation of working time becomes virtually impossible. One outcome of longer hours and work intensification in the modern deregulated economy has been rising levels of work-related stress – which will be examined in the final section of this chapter.

Interpretations of the impact of work on the body have ranged widely. At one extreme is the traditional view that science and technological change inevitably bring progress, and with state regulation controlling the worst excesses of competitive capitalism modern work regimes have progressively improved – for example in removing much of the dangerous physical toil and some of the drudgery from heavy manual and repetitive tasks with mechanization and automation. Coal mining might be a case in point. Factories have also become intensively regulated, machinery guarded and risk assessments for health and safety impacts are now commonplace. Against this view, modernists, many influenced by Marx, argue that within a capitalist framework where power is exercised unequally workers' bodies have been exploited to accumulate profit. In this interpretation, corporate capitalism, grasping petty entrepreneurs and a colluding state have been largely responsible for the carnage of industrial 'accidents', chronic disease, stressed out and broken bodies.

More recently, the post-modernist turn has seen a refocusing on discourse and a fundamental rejection of such meta-narratives on the grounds that they fail to take into account the agency of actors and the range and diversity of attitudes, culture and policies – in this case of employers, managers, workers, their organizations and the regulators. The debate over asbestos provides an example of the range of views (Tweedale, 2000; Bartrip, 2001; Bartrip, 2005; Johnston and McIvor, 2000a; McCulloch and Tweedale, 2008). Foucault has been influential in positing the notion of the controlled and docile body (utilizing the Benthamite concept of the 'panopticon'), subject to the overt and covert surveillance of management (in the penal system) and this has been applied to the modern workplace by labour sociologists and others. Bourdieu similarly places the body at centre stage in work relations, though he gives more credence than Foucault (for example in his deployment of the notion of 'habitus') to agency and resistance. To Bourdieu bodies were both subjects and agents; bodies could be passive, but they also could be reactive, dissenting, transgressing and resistant (Wolkowitz, 2006, p. 16). In reality, power relations in the modern capitalist controlled enterprise subject to the vagaries of the market undoubtedly narrowed the range of choice and patterned people's lived experiences. However, there was a *dynamic* relationship here and this could embrace contradictory changes over time. Bodies and minds could be sustained, honed and improved by work (and hence empowered by it) as well as compromised, damaged, burnt out and destroyed by it. The Japanese have a term for death through overwork: *karoshi*, the absence of which in Western vocabulary is indicative, perhaps, that we don't like to recognize the more brutal impacts of work on the body.

The body in the mid-twentieth century workplace, 1945–70

As in other aspects of employment, the Second World War and its immediate aftermath brought significant improvements in standards of health and safety in the workplace. The growth of trade union membership (see Chapter 6) extended protection over workers at the point of production, whilst the post-war Labour government and tight labour markets with virtually full male employment provided a conducive environment to curtail the worst excesses of managerial abuse and exploitation. The National Insurance (Industrial Injuries) Act 1946 extended the Welfare State in the workplace, with streamlined processes and improved benefits compared to the old Workmen's Compensation Act (Bartrip, 1987). Nationalization brought renewed efforts to provide decent medical coverage in the workplace – such as the 'flagship' Mines Medical Service – an innovator, amongst other things, of preventative x-rays for workers to monitor exposure to and damage from dust inhalation. The social medicine movement attracted a cadre of highly motivated doctors and other medical professionals into the field, determined to extend research and medical knowledge to occupational health. Archie Cochrane, who headed the government's Pneumoconiosis Research Unit and pioneered the mass epidemiological studies of pneumoconiosis and tuberculosis in the early 1950s in the Rhondda Valley in South Wales using the newest x-ray techniques, would be a good example. And the international community had some impact – not least the growing work of the International Labour Organization (ILO) in information gathering, publicizing work-health hazards and passing basic safety conventions through which it aimed to standardize practice globally. Whilst the latter had a limited and uneven impact on countries keen to protect national sovereignty (and competitiveness), the UK was one of the leading countries in the world by 1950 – ranked third (after Bulgaria and France) in terms of the numbers of ILO health and safety conventions it had ratified (41 out of 90, compared, for example, to the USA which had only ratified 6; Williams, 1960, pp. 383–4). This all appears to have had a positive impact. In the UK the rate of fatal workplace injuries – inflated during the wartime emergency – fell by a half from the wartime peak in 1941 to 1950 and the non-fatal injury rate by some 40% (Annual Factory Inspectors Report for 1950, pp. 40–1).

Nonetheless, despite a focus in the 1940s on the 'healthy factory' (Long, 2011), which built on more than a century of world-leading work hazard regulation and control by the state, still manual workers in the UK in the immediate post-Second World War period were subject to a wide array of pressures and assaults upon their bodies and minds – both traumatic and chronic. In the period 1945–49 almost 2,000 workers were killed in Britain each year on average as a result of work-related accidents and many more seriously injured, mutilated and rendered disabled (McIvor, 2001, p. 132; we have no reliable figures for non-fatal injuries because of serious under-reporting). In the 1950s, deaths ran at an average of 1,564 per annum and by the 1970s the death toll remained an average of 758 per annum (Gallie, 2000, pp. 302–3). The 'traditional' heavy industries saw the greatest carnage, with the highest death and mutilation rates amongst coal miners, seamen and fishermen, iron and steel workers, shipbuilders, construction workers, and agricultural and forestry workers. Figures provided in the *Registrar General's Decennial Supplement on Occupational Mortality* for 1951 for accidental deaths (excluding deaths in the home and motor vehicle accidents) provide a rough guide to incidence. Amongst those occupations with more than three times the average standardized mortality rate (SMR) for accidental deaths were slaters and tilers, various categories of underground mine workers and quarrymen, seamen, railway shunters, pointsmen and level crossing men, platelayers, construction workers, well and mine sinkers and tunnel miners. Topping the list, however, were members of the armed forces, an occupational group with obvious risks that tends to get neglected in the literature on occupational health and safety (see Reilly, 2010). Not surprisingly, occupational mortality from injury was extremely low amongst non-manual occupational groups. This was another significant – and somewhat neglected – area of class inequalities in health. Clerks and typists, for example, recorded a workplace occupational mortality rate of less than a third of the average SMR, registering something like 25 times less risk than coal face workers of accidental death (*Registrar General's Decennial Supplement on Occupational Mortality*, England and Wales, 1951, Pt 2, Vol 1, HMSO, 1958, 145–9).

Oral testimony and personal reminiscence is particularly illumi-nating in reconstructing occupational health cultures – including the attitudes and perceptions of workers in dangerous occupations like the heavy industries. See, for example, Alessandro Portelli's richly evocative recent oral history of the mining communities in Harlan County, Kentucky, where death, injury, disease and bodily damage were common recurring themes in the narratives of his 150 interview-ees (Portelli, 2011). Similar evidence for the UK evokes the grim post-war working conditions in mining, iron works and shipyards, as well as the heavy toll such work exacted upon the body and the *limited* influence *in practice* that the state had in the workplace. Oral histo-ries challenge the idea that technology was universally positive in its impact and that statutory controls were everywhere effective. What emerges is evidence that the law was frequently flouted as employers and managers put profit and production before workers' health and well-being. However, this was a complex process, with structure and agency intertwined within unequal power relations. On occasions, managers flouted market logic to protect workers' health and well-being – and sometimes lost their jobs as a consequence (as Perchard, 2007a, has shown for nationalized coal mining). Workers themselves could also collude in this process, for a variety of reasons, including job security. Sometimes such 'self-exploitation' was a product of a system which rewarded extra productivity with wage incentives and bonuses; sometimes it was through fear of losing their jobs or jeopardizing promotion prospects; sometimes it was for personal gain; sometimes because workers were not told or made aware of the dangers to their health or the *degree* of risk; and sometimes because of entrenched custom and practice and the belief that the risk seemed acceptable and the outcomes (particularly regarding the risk of disease rather than injury) too far ahead in the future to worry about. Bodies were vulnerable in all sorts of ways and for many who had lived through the 1930s and the war occupational health and safety was just not a priority in the daily struggle to make ends meet. In the older, 'traditional' heavy industries, company closures and redundancies undoubtedly added to the pressures upon workers not to complain on health and safety issues – to conform and to keep quiet.

Inhaling death: asbestos and coal

The use and abuse of asbestos provides a pertinent and chilling example. The risk to health of inhaling asbestos fibres was first officially recognized in the UK by a female Factory Inspector, Lucy Deane, in a report published in the *Annual Factory Inspectors' Report* for 1899. The first statutory regulations aimed at controlling exposure came in 1931, though working with asbestos was not finally banned in the UK until 1999. Work-life histories illuminate the complex interplay of managerial pressure, corporate greed, regulatory failures and prevailing work and health cultures that coalesced to germinate the asbestos tragedy (see Johnston and McIvor, 2000a). Joiners in construction and insulation engineers (known as laggers) in the shipyards recalled working amongst a fog of asbestos fibres in the 1950s and 1960s and the blatant flouting of safety precautions by both management and men. They were most closely involved with asbestos use and amongst the first to recognize its dangers to health. Jimmy Burns worked as a thermal insulation engineer in Southend from 1948. He recalled:

> I remember spraying blue asbestos on potato barns for a crisps company in 1960 with all these little kids just standing around watching ... Since the building boom after the war the stuff was put up everywhere ... We're paying for the post-war building boom now. (Cited in Chappell, 1983, p. 472)

Jimmy was sacked several times for trying to enforce the 1931 Asbestos Regulations and improve health and safety conditions in the places he worked.

The nature of their work, though, normally required that laggers worked alongside other trades people. For example one lagger remembered how the nature of the work put other tradesmen in danger:

> We used tae insulate the boilers actually on the boat, and the place was covered in asbestos when we were dain that ... the dust just a' floated. It floated round and everybody got their share. (Interview by Ronnie Johnston, 15 March 1999, SOHC/016/A13)

A retired ships' plumber, who is now suffering from asbestos-induced pleural thickening, recalled how he had got his daily exposure to asbestos: 'I was working in amongst it. Engine rooms, boiler rooms... it used to come down like snow' (interview by Ronnie Johnston, 22 December 1998, SOHC/016/A2). There was a widespread lack of understanding amongst the workforce regarding the extreme health risks inherent in asbestos from the 1930s through to the 1970s. It was a common sight in the shipyards to see young workers playing with asbestos cuttings, and an ex-shipyard labourer recalled how in the 1960s:

> They were throwing this 'monkey dung' (asbestos cement paste) about and that, and hitting folk in the passing just for a game you know. Nobody knew how dangerous it was. These blokes were laggered in it head-tae-foot. (Interview by Ronnie Johnston, 2 February 1999, SOHC/016/A18)

James McGrath, a Glasgow docker (born 1926), now also with pleural thickening, recalled of the late 1970s:

> Some of the jobs were terrible but they lasted a week. You wouldnae have went in tae it in a million years cause... blue asbestos and white asbestos in hessian bags... you know... but you didn't know and nobody told you. There was one guy frae down there, a guy called Todd, he was a pipe coverer... and he took this asbestosis and he told everybody and he wanted tae come in and talk tae the dockers but the foremen wouldn't let him come in just tae tell us about the stuff, [foremen said] 'Naw, naw, communist,' you know, things like that... daft. (James McGrath, interviewed by David Walker, 12 August 2009; Glasgow Dock Workers Project, Glasgow Museums)

The wearing of masks was eventually made compulsory when asbestos was present. However, many employers continued to issue their workers with unsuitable or ineffective masks (such as the paper 'Martindale' masks), many of which were uncomfortable to wear for any length of time – usually because the straps cut into the back of the worker's head or they restricted breathing excessively. A heating engineer recalled that masks were often not available on site: 'If you waited for the mask coming you would never get done... But eh, we accepted it.... It was a general trend in the building trade that you just carried on with the job, you know' (interview by Ronnie Johnston, 9 January 1999, SOHC/016/A5). Uncontrolled use of asbestos – long after the risks were known – left a grim legacy of rising respiratory disease and lung cancer rates, with mesothelioma the main killer (see Tweedale, 2000; Johnston and McIvor, 2000a). According to the Health and Safety Executive, deaths from mesothelioma rose from 153 in 1968 to 2,321 in 2009. Currently, building construction workers are amongst those most at risk because of their widespread exposure to working with the mineral in the 1950s, 1960s and into the 1970s.

Underground mining remained one of the most risky places to work in post-Second World War Britain. Whilst the problem of mine explosions had declined considerably, in underground mining workers continued to face substantial dangers, not least from rock falls and accidents associated with the moving machinery as the job became increasingly mechanized with the transition from pick and shovel to automatic shearing and power loading. Seven major disasters occurred in the six years post-nationalization (1947–52), including the explosion at William Pit in Whitehaven in 1947 where 104 men died (Ashworth, 1986, pp. 555–6). In the immediate post-war years deaths in the industry regularly topped 400 per annum, with much higher disabling injury rates. Miners continued to register particularly high standardized mortality rates from accidents and respiratory disease. The toll on the body in the mines varied enormously, however, across the different coalfields, collieries and the workforce (Ashworth, 1986, pp. 557–8; McIvor and Johnston, 2007, pp. 38–60).

Zweig's 1948 study of British miners, *Men in the Pits*, evokes the impact work had upon the body. He commented on how a miner could lose an average of four or five pounds in weight per shift from energy use and sweat loss and observed the prevalence of blue scars ('spider's webs') from work injuries and coal dust impregnation all over older miners' bodies (something that Orwell had noted earlier in Wigan, talking of marbled skin like 'Roquefort cheese'). 'Nowhere else', Zweig observed, 'can you see the same relative numbers of disabled men as in a colliery village' (Zweig, 1948, p. 6). Visual impairment (nystagmus) was widespread amongst the older men in the pit villages in the mid-twentieth century. The spine and back were other vulnerable areas, as one Lanarkshire miner, reflecting on his transfer to a Fife pit with high coal seams in the early 1970s recalled:

> We went up to Fife. Fucking eight feet high man! You thought, 'what the fucking hell... we wore knee pads; they [the Fife miners] didnae. They stood and fucking shovelled, man, because it was that high, y'know. But we, we couldnae shovel standing up because the old back was knackered, y'know. (Interview by Ronnie Johnston with John McKean, SOHC/017/C10)

The damage the job wrought upon the body was seared into miners' consciousness and emerged in personal accounts and interviews where injury, death, illness and disability were frequently recurring themes. Alan Napier, a Durham miner, recalled lost comrades much like a wartime combatant:

> The lads on the 'C' drift where I was in there – there's only one left alive. All of them died *young*. Hank and all of them. Hank collapsed and died. Wally Purvis, Clemensey, all *big hitters*. All gone. Them's the empty chair in the club. And they all worked in the same flat. (Interview by Neil Rafeek with Alan Napier, 31 March 2004, SOHC/017/C43. 'Flat' is a term for an area of the pit underground)

In autobiographies and oral testimonies, coal miners recalled a postwar work regime within the newly nationalized mining industry where – despite the rhetoric of a health and safety-conscious NCB – production was routinely prioritized over health and safety (see McIvor and Johnston, 2007). New power cutting and loading technology alleviated some problems but caused others, whilst statutory safety provisions were widely ignored or subverted at the coal face. Witness, for example, Bob Smith's sensitive evaluation in his autobiography of the mixed benefits of mechanization in the pits:

> It seemed that all improvements in coal getting brought new problems. The new machines which cut and automatically loaded coal in a continuous cycle were extremely noisy and produced masses of dust. Ventilation was never good, and the air always hot and humid. In those conditions men sweated heavily, and the dust settled on them thick and black. Only their eyes and teeth stayed white. The air bags which were supposed to control the ventilation and bring fresh air in to us were often torn by debris or falling coal, and did not really do their job well. We were supplied with masks but at first they were crude and inefficient. Later models were better, but without doubt they did hinder a man's breathing, and a lot of men found they could not wear the masks when doing heavy work. And in spite of all the mechanisation it was still, as always, very heavy work. (Smith, 1991, pp. 87–8)

There were, however, competing discourses relating to the impact of work upon the body. Employers and the state frequently denied responsibility, deflected blame and minimized risk. For example, the Mines Inspectorate for the Scottish Division claimed in 1953 that of all pit accidents for that year, 'nearly half of the accidents were avoidable by ordinary caution which suggests that workmen were often ready to take a chance' (*Report of HM Inspector of Mines, Scottish Division,* for 1953, p. 5). Similarly, the Mines Inspectors Reports detailed many instances of miners being killed through undercutting seams too deep or failing to support their working area adequately (*Report of HM Inspector of Mines, Scottish Division*, for 1949, p. 36; 1952, p. 5). In response, the union leader Abe Moffat castigated the Mines Inspectors for blaming the victims, arguing that the technological solutions to the dust problem underground (including water sprays on the drilling and cutting machines) were not being implemented by the NCB because of the cost (Moffat, 1965, p. 239). Workers' choices were constrained by having to work within a framework dictated by management in relation to investment (or non-investment) in technology and the payments by results wage payment systems which incentivized maximizing production at the expense of health. Understandably, given the context, workers cut corners and took risks. Another miner (John McKean) recalled that management turned a blind eye to the practice of not putting in the stipulated number of timber roof supports – except when the Mines Inspector called: 'See the next day they'd let you go into the same fucking place with no doubties [supports] as long as that fucking coal was coming out, you know what I mean?' (interview by Ronnie Johnston, 29 June 2000, SOHC/017/ C10).

Masculinity and risk-taking at work

What is difficult to disentangle is the extent to which workers were reluctantly taking risks in their work because of peer pressure, trying to impress their fellow workers with their manliness, to maximize their income in an unstable market environment, or, because they felt directly or indirectly pressurized by management, or because they had become inured to danger. Entrenched work habits were difficult to erode. When machine guards, ear defenders, safety helmets and protective goggles were first introduced in construction, shipyards, wood yards, steel works and mines many workmen initially resisted wearing them. Allan Tyrell (a London wood machinist) noted of his work in the late 1950s and into the 1960s how 'although Harrods were very good, again they didn't supply things like ear defenders, the guards were there, but no-one ever used them' (Britain at Work interview, by Dave Welsh, 29 June 2010). Wood machinists were renowned for losing fingers or parts of fingers on the job and Allan's credentials as a qualified wood machinist were once challenged by a prospective employer who doubted his experience because he still had all his digits intact. In part this attitude towards protective gear was because early versions of protective clothing and machine guarding were either uncomfortable and/or could interfere with productivity and hence earnings. However, wearing masks, helmets and goggles was also seen by many workers as a sign of personal weakness and an affront to manliness (see Chapter 3). Workers were also agents in this and were capable of taking decisions that undermined their own health and safety, especially if procedures affected earnings. An ex-miner reflected in the 1990s: 'The safety rules were broken by the men themselves, because they wanted the money' (cited in Blackwell and Seabrook, 1996, p. 145). Workmates and supervisors might question a worker's masculinity if they failed to take risks and 'conform' to accepted practices. Joe Kenyon worked in Barnsley coal mines from 1929 to 1960 eventually becoming a workmen's (safety) inspector after nationalization, responsible for inspecting the site of accidents. He recalled being accused of requiring 'iron jelloids' from a supervisor (overman) because he complained that part of the seam was unsafe. Shortly after the roof collapsed, vindicating Kenyon's caution (Kenyon, 2003, pp. 100–1). The wood machinist cited above (Allan Tyrell) recalled:

> It might sound petty, when I was at Samuel Putneys [early 1960s] I wanted ear defenders. I didn't know what a safety guard was because … well, no one knew what a safety guard was 'cos none of the old boys … 'safety guard? I've never heard of a safety guard. Didn't do me any harm!'… And when I wanted ear defenders, because the noise was so loud it was, the decibel reading was like a jet engine, and I was treated like a pariah. I was laughed at, I was stupid and that. Never got them. The only time the safety guards come out … when we had word that this time next week at four o'clock, after he's been down the pub, this factory inspector would come round to look at the safety guards, so we'd get them out, and have to rub them down with wire wool, grease them up and try and get them into position … And he'd walk around; well he'd stagger around with the boss, and after about ten minutes he'd be gone. Take them off 'cos it hindered the workers, and it was back to square one. (Britain at Work interview, by Dave Welsh, 29 June 2010)

Whilst critical of management negligence and 'greed for production' Kenyon commented on workers' 'own disregard for safe working habits'. He recalled in his autobiography the tragedy of two mining shaftsmen: 'Jack and Sam, being so familiar with the job, became contemptuous about wearing their safety belts'. Jack slipped, grabbed

Sam to try to save himself and both of them together with a trainee plunged down the shaft. The trainee was saved by his safety harness whilst the two older and experienced men fell to their deaths (Kenyon, 2003, pp. 117–8, 158–9).

What is apparent is the coexistence of two important degenerative pressures upon health and the workers' bodies with the intertwining of capitalist exploitation and masculine values. This could produce somewhat surprising outcomes. For example, at the Red Road high rise flats building contract in north Glasgow in the mid-1960s, trade union officials had great difficulty getting the joiners cutting asbestos boards to wear protective masks. One shop steward recalled being told to 'get to fuck' when he tried to warn the joiners that the asbestos dust they were producing from sawing the boards was putting themselves and other workers in danger. Good money was being made on the job and the employers (in this case Glasgow Corporation Housing Department) were condoning unsafe working practices in order to get the flats built quickly. The incident led to some improvements, but work was not stopped on the site, nor was an alternative form of insulation used. Tragically, decades later a large number of these so-called 'white mice' were diagnosed with fatal asbestos-induced cancers (Johnston and McIvor, 2000a, pp. 99–104).

An important issue here though was that the use of a mask or respirators made it more difficult to breathe and hence to work effectively and thus to maximize earnings on piecework. For most workers in the 1950s and 1960s, when the choice came between using a respirator which restrained productivity and doing without, but getting higher wages, the latter course was taken. This was compounded by the fact that the risks of dust disease also seemed distant – a long-term possibility, as one miner noted about masks:

> We did'nae wear them. You did'nae think of the future, we just thought from day to day, well, you did'nae think you were going to get ... silicosis or nothing like that. (Interview by Ronnie Johnston with Bert Smith, 5 July 2000, SOHC/017/C14)

Doing dangerous work was to a large extent taken for granted in many working-class communities after the war – when sons frequently followed fathers in coal mining, iron and steel and shipbuilding communities. Bill Sirs commented on working in a steel rolling mill that: 'I quickly became accustomed to the routine and the danger' (Sirs, 1985, p. 48). He worked in the industry from 1937 until

1963, becoming a crane driver and a trade union leader. He recalled this anecdote:

> I faced some dangerous situations. Always being an athletic type, I rarely used to climb up the stairs to my crane; instead I had a rope which I shinned up and down like a monkey (something which I would not recommend anyone else to do). On one occasion the fuses in the cab arced; there was a tremendous, blinding flash behind me and in seconds the whole cab was on fire ... The cab was a death trap, so I threw out the rope and escaped in the only way possible. I was very lucky on that occasion. (Sirs, 1985, p. 50)

Taking risks and earning big money were exalted masculine values. An example would be the much lauded 'big hewers' – the 'champion' highest producers and earners – who seemed to exist in all British mining communities. Exposing the body to risks could be justified on the grounds that this was a worthwhile sacrifice for the sake of the family (Johnston and McIvor, 2000a, p. 77). The wife of a machine operator who worked in the Turner's Asbestos Cement plant in Clydebank for around eight years up to the mid-1960s commented: 'He was frightened to walk out of the job because he was married with a family' (interview by Ronnie Johnston, 22 March 1999, SOHC/016/A26). Her husband was well aware that he was risking his health: 'I knew it was dangerous before I went in there 'cause there was people complaining but when you have two of a family to bring up it was better than walking the streets. I never was idle in my life' (interview by Ronnie Johnston, 22 March 1999, SOHC/016/A26). Similarly, some miners would try to hide their encroaching breathlessness and where they failed to attain financial compensation or benefits might return to work underground knowing full well that this would worsen their respiratory problem. To such men fulfilling the breadwinner role dominated their thinking, surpassing any concerns they might harbour over the long-term damage that might accrue to their bodies. Some workers (as in the extract at the beginning of the chapter) recognized this in later life. This points to both a deeply ingrained work ethic amongst such male manual workers and a fiercely competitive workplace environment where risk-taking was commonplace and helped to sustain and bolster working-class masculinity (see Chapter 3). This was so elsewhere too, as Connell has noted of Australian miners and Portelli of the Harlan County miners in Kentucky, USA:

> Pressure from the company hierarchy would meet a cultural disposition amongst the workers. One union worker recalled: 'I would always think to myself, "let's try to beat that other shift. If they loaded 400 tons, let's get 450"'. (Portelli, 2011, p. 143)

Trade unions and the body

By the middle of the twentieth century trade unionism was well entrenched in the British workplace and the movement provided pivotal protection for workers' bodies at the point of production. A critical interpretation of union policies on health has pointed to a tendency to neglect the body in an economistic prioritization of the wage, job security and financial *compensation* policies, rather than *preventative* strategies (Beaumont, 1983, p. 42). *Mass Observation* noted in 1942: 'In view of its evident importance to production, the extent to which industries and unions concern themselves with the health of their workers is noticeably slight' (*Mass Observation*, 1942, p. 203). In the wartime crisis, when risks were reconfigured, this might be understandable, but criticisms of trade union ambivalence on occupational health issues persisted thereafter. A radical Scottish occupational hygienist, Robin Howie, commented in an interview in 2001: 'In my own experience trade unions have not been as concerned with things like health and safety as they are about the fact that the job is still there and what the wage rates are' (interview by Neil Rafeek, 20 Sept 2001, SOHC 017/C45). One suggestion is that the unions absorbed and reflected the 'macho' attitudes of their dominant male workforce, rather than vigorously challenging this high-risk workplace health culture – and there may be some support for this thesis in relation to the asbestos issue, where the response of the unions was initially ambivalent (see Johnston and McIvor, 2000a, pp. 165–72). Even as late as the 1980s the trade unions were divided on the issue (Chappell, 1983, pp. 471–2). A strong pro-asbestos group persisted, notably within the ranks of the TGWU, whereas other unions, notably the GMB and UCATT supported a total ban. Understandably, perhaps, given the insecurity of the 1980s economic recession and advancing deindustrialization, many workers thought jobs more important than their health.

However, recent research has persuasively reasserted just how proactive and aggressive the trade unions were in occupational health and safety. Melling (2003) and Long (2011) have demonstrated how compensation was entwined with prevention and health education. In an important study of the health policy of the Trades Union Congress 1914–60, Long has argued:

> A more fruitful way to assess trade union responses is to see the pursuit of compensation and the pursuit of health as complimentary, not competing. It is not the case that the TUC prioritised compensation payments over the pursuit of health. (Long, 2011, p. 212)

Recent case studies of occupational health in the UK chemicals sector by Walker (2007), in relation to the respiratory disease byssinosis in cotton textiles by Bowden and Tweedale (2003) and on coal workers' respiratory illness (pneumoconiosis, bronchitis and emphysema) by McIvor and Johnston (2007) all demonstrate the pivotal role played by the trade unions in twentieth century occupational health campaigns. Whilst there were tensions between branches, local and sectional interests – including fears that regulation might precipitate job losses in 'declining' heavy industries and a constraining pressure from a high-risk masculine culture in the workplace – the union movement, nonetheless, clearly and unequivocally worked to protect members. Their activities even extended into campaigning on public health issues, such as the scourge of tuberculosis. An editorial in 1957 in the journal *Occupational Medicine* exhorted, 'trade unionists nowadays are extremely health-conscious' (*Occupational Medicine*, July 1957, no. 7, p. 65). The view of one trade union representative in 1955 that the Trades Union Congress was 'the custodian of the health and welfare of the working class' was more than just empty rhetoric (TUC *Annual Report*, 1955, p. 377). This was supported by at least one former company manager:

> ...particularly from 1945 onwards, if an operative found himself exposed to something that he considered dangerous he would take it up with his union shop steward who would then take it up with the management who had to have a proper look at it. I think the unions were very active and effective in promoting health and safety. (Interview by David Walker with Brian Watson, 8 October 2005, SOHC/022)

Walker has made the point that:

> To criticise the trade unions for not doing enough or of prioritising wages over health is to perpetuate the false premise that an equality of power existed between the trade unions, the state, and the employers. (Walker, 2007, p. 269)

Moreover, many risks were not fully understood by workers and trade union members. Where the risk to health had been immediate and obvious, such as in the many areas of the chemical industry, the workers did not refuse to wear protective clothing and masks (Walker, 2007). Early versions of anti-dust masks were also often hopelessly inefficient. Attitudes were changing and the TUC and some trade union branches were increasingly becoming more active from the mid-1970s in campaigns to re-educate their members to tolerate a lower risk threshold and abandon time-honoured *machismo* work practices, such as not wearing helmets and not using masks or respirators.

Dangerous trades

Other manual occupations were characterized by high levels of risk to life and limb. Like mining, working at sea was another extremely hazardous job at mid-twentieth century, with a particularly high work-related death rate – indeed in fishing in the 1950s and 1960s the death rate was almost double that of coal mining. Peter Martin – a cook on trawlers out of Grimsby after the Second World War – recalled: 'Fishermen are tough – they've got to be, otherwise they wouldn't be able to carry on and work the way that they do' (Martin, cited in Fraser, 1969, p. 82). On board the men would work up to 18-hour days, sometimes for several weeks on end, exposed to the elements and vulnerable to injuries as a consequence of outdated and dangerous equipment (such as exposed winches) and low railings. Fatigue was endemic and injuries to the hands commonplace. 'When I look back on more than twenty years on trawlers', Martin commented, 'I can't help being angered that, for the benefit of the country, men are allowed to go to sea to be injured and killed without any thought being given to their welfare' (Martin, cited in Fraser, 1969, p. 86). Working in the North Sea oil and gas industry was also fraught with dangers – and the site of the world's worst oil industry disaster when 167 workers lost their lives on the Piper Alpha platform in 1988. A survivor, Kevin Topham, recalled:

> There were some in the lower accommodation cabins. They were trapped in. They never did get out. They were just drowned in there because the doors, the doorframes, were all metal, and these evidently twisted... and consequently one couldn't open the door. One crew member, friend of mine, Ivan Mitchell, he's still got scars on his hand where he fought to get out through his cabin door which was twisted, and he did manage it through superhuman effort in the end. (Interview by Hugo Manson, 18 October 2000; Lives in the Oil Industry, Archive ref. F10593/A)

Iron and steel works were also notoriously dangerous, though the injury risk differed markedly across the metal-working community (Bradley, 2011). Hot splashes and the inhalation of silica dust were amongst the hazards identified in Patrick McGeown's evocative autobiography, *Heat the Furnace Seven Times Over* (1965). An ex-steel worker from the west of Scotland noted that few could tolerate the work at the furnaces: 'About one steel worker in ten could stand up to them successfully' (cited in Fraser, 1969, pp. 56–7). Dorothy Radwanski, one of very few occupational nurses in industry in the 1960s, described conditions in the foundry at the North British Locomotive Works in Glasgow thus: 'the air was very black; the men were absolutely black. I was absolutely shocked and I said to somebody "it's like *Dante's Inferno*"' (interview by Neil Rafeek, 22 October 2001, SOHC/018/ B6). As late as the mid-1970s, a Scottish occupational hygienist Ian Kellie commented that conditions in the Scottish steel industry were 'appalling' and that he was 'astonished' at the high incidence of silicosis (interview by Neil Rafeek, 5 December 2001, SOHC 018/B1; on silicosis see also Morrison, 2010). The problems could be heightened in remote areas far from the public gaze. Perchard's work on the aluminium industry in the Scottish Highlands has shown how bodies were damaged by the furnaces emitting toxic fumes and carcinogens, causing occupational asthma, emphysema and chronic pulmonary congestion (Perchard, 2011, pp. 191–244).

The possibility of serious injury at work was widespread: As Sandy Doig, (Factories Medical Inspector in Scotland, 1943–70) put it in the late 1960s: 'It is pretty safe to say that there are very few factories without some risk to health' (*Glasgow Herald*, 31 Jan 1968). 'We were selling our health', one textile factory worker commented in 1969, recalling an accident he had where the machine had to be dismantled to retrieve his trapped and mangled foot (cited in Fraser, 1969, p. 95). Risks varied significantly, however, across manufacturing (see Table 5.1) as the Factory Inspectorate observed.

Nor were the big employers necessarily the worst offenders. One quite comprehensive local authority survey of occupational health and safety across more than 10,000 workers in an industrial region of Glasgow in 1953 found the worst standards and highest injury and disease incidence amongst the smallest companies (Johnston and McIvor, 2000a, p. 58). Nichols found the same results in his analysis of workplace injuries in the later twentieth century as did Robinson and Smallman (Nichols, 1999, pp. 97–100; Robinson and Smallman, 2006). Trauma to the eyes was particularly prevalent in manufacturing. The Factory Inspectorate estimated in 1950 about 200,000 eye injuries sustained in factories each year (Annual Report of the Factory Inspectorate, 1950, p. 59). In one engineering firm in Govan, Glasgow, there were more than 300 referrals a year to the Glasgow Eye Infirmary in the early 1950s – an excellent example of the NHS having to patch up the work-wounded (*Glasgow Herald*, 14 Jan 1954,

Table 5.1: Accident frequency rates in manufacturing, 1950

Tinplate manufacture	6.47
Iron and steel founding	3.95
Shipbuilding and repairing	3.32
Iron and steel extraction	3.28
Non-ferrous metal extraction	3.09
Construction	2.64
Electricity generation	2.57
Oil refining	2.53
Chemicals	2.30
Cotton	1.54
Aircraft	1.00
Tobacco and cigarettes	0.82
Light & electrical engineering	0.80
Printing	0.74

Source: *Annual Report of the Factory Inspectorate*, 1950, p. 37.

p. 6). Whilst there continue to be significant gaps in our understand-ing, several important studies in recent years have elucidated our knowledge of the work–health interaction in these notoriously danger-ous occupations. There remain, however, serious gaps in the literature and a really urgent need to focus study on trauma in the workplace and how workers responded to and navigated the injury/mortality risk in the post-war workplace.

Together with the high levels of death and disability through injury in the workplace, workers' bodies were also damaged by a cluster of chronic occupation-related diseases. Endemic health problems associ-ated with work had been identified by medical professionals and in lay epidemiology for centuries and the most blatant diseases and toxins had been recognized by the UK government for compensation pur-poses, starting with a modest list of six occupational diseases in 1906 'prescribed' under the amended Workmen's Compensation Act. By the 1950s, the official prescribed list of occupational diseases drawn up by the state for compensation purposes included a wide range of toxins, gases, chemicals, muscular disorders and respiratory ailments. The latter were probably the most significant; indeed coughing was ubiquitous within working-class communities where the inhalation of noxious, toxic and irritating dusts, fumes and chemicals was common-place. The pneumoconioses – such as silicosis, asbestosis, byssinosis and coal workers' pneumoconiosis – were amongst the most wide-spread and amongst the most dreaded of work-related ailments. One medical professional estimated in 1958 that over two million British workers were disabled to some degree by respiratory illness caused by what they inhaled in their workplaces (Dr Barnett Stross, Labour MP and radiologist; *Hansard*, 30 July 1958, pp. 1,540–1). Miners, again, suffered disproportionately. Within the coalfield communities pneumoconiosis caused by the inhalation of coal and rock dust reached record levels post-Second World War, with death rates peaking in the 1945–55 period, and newly diagnosed cases around 1960. The recurrent introduction of new chemicals and compounds also posed unknown health risks, as David Walker has shown, leading to outbreaks of dermatitis, tissue and bone damage and new occupational cancers – such as bladder cancer (Walker, 2007).

One problem was that general practitioners were not in a good position to diagnose employment-related diseases such as these because of the neglect of occupational health in their training. The situation was worsened by the compartmentalizing of occupational and public health – the former administered post-war through the Ministry of Labour and the latter the Ministry of Health. Despite wide support from the trade unions and the British Medical Association, the Dale Committee (1951) enquiry determined that the time was not right for an integrated National Health Service and Occupational Health Service (largely on cost grounds). In the wake of Dale, several industrial health surveys were initiated (to expand empirical research findings) in the 1950s, including the Govan, Glasgow enquiry in 1953, Halifax in 1957–8 and the Potteries in 1959 (Williams, 1960, pp. 401–6). They uncovered high levels of ill-health, occupational disease and desperately poor standards of cleanliness and hygiene, and health-sapping work environments made worse by poor ventilation and inadequate dust control. Work conditions were deemed particularly conducive to respiratory damage, eye injuries, repetitive strain injury and dermatitis. In Halifax, the Industrial Health Advisory Committee enquiry was particularly critical of the lack of preventative action to minimize risks and share medical knowledge. It found there were no full-time factory medical officers employed in the city's industries, and only four part-timers and 23 factory nurses – mostly in the largest factories. One commentary on the Halifax survey noted:

> The NHS provides for the medical care of all those that fall ill, but much less is done to try to keep people well in the workplaces where they spend much of their lives... It is both more profitable and more sensible to spend

money on keeping people well than to grant sick leave. (*Manchester Guardian* editorial, 26 March 1958, cited in Williams, 1960, p. 402)

All the 1950s occupational health enquiries found a range of experience, with the worst conditions in the smallest workplaces (where trade unions were weakest). Few of the latter had anything but rudimentary occupational medicine services. The occupational health expert Donald Hunter estimated in 1959 that only 4% of factories employing less than 100 workers had the services of a doctor on site, whereas about half of the largest factories employed company doctors (Hunter, 1959, p. 20). What was also evident was a gulf between the relatively unhealthy and unsafe workplaces of the traditional heavy industries, primarily located in the north of England, in Wales and in Scotland, and the better environmental conditions in the newer 'sunrise' industries in London, the South East and the Midlands. Hammond's study using Factory Inspectorate data showed, for example, a fatal death rate from industrial accidents per 1,000 workers in the mid-1960s at almost 25% higher for Scotland, Wales and Northern England compared to London and the South East of England. Standardized mortality rates from mesothelioma (the main asbestos-related disease) in Scotland in the 1980s were running at 31 per cent above the UK average (with Clydeside almost double the UK average). Statutory injury benefits were three times higher in Scotland, Wales and Northern England than London and the South East and, linked to this carnage, there was a significantly higher proportion of the disabled in the traditional industrial heartlands of South Wales, Clydeside and Tyneside (Hammond, 1968, Tables 5.2.3–5). In part these discrepancies in experience reflected economic structure (a larger proportion of the working population employed in the most dangerous 'heavy' industries), but prevailing health cultures were also important.

In Scotland, the particularly bad occupational health and safety record led to a long preoccupation with what became known as the 'Scottish anomaly' by the Health and Safety Executive. One HSE study in 2006 found Scotland's fatal injury rate in workplace accidents was almost 50% higher than England (HSE, British Partnership in Health and Safety, 2006). Workplace sickness rates were also higher in Scotland (*The Herald*, 23 September 2012, p. 12). Deeply entrenched attitudes proved hard to erode, as one Clyde shipbuilding safety officer commented in 1977: 'Safety is always uphill work in a traditional industry like shipbuilding where men are set in their ways...It takes time' (cited in Bellamy, 2001, p. 74). Important here though was that workers were hardly encouraged to act differently. There was a lack of knowledge of dangers, lack of support for learning, lack of emphasis on the use of safety equipment and an overall lack of company investment in health and safety training. Safety officers were far from being empowered by their employer to get the workers to change.

Occupational ill-health and injury was thus an important source of health inequality in the post-Second World War period, affecting the working class much worse than the middle and upper classes, with male manual workers affected disproportionately, compared to non-manual workers. Unskilled male manual workers in the hazardous heavy industries faced the highest risks, with ethnic minorities also disproportionately exposed to unhealthy work, given the discrimination they faced in the labour market in the post-war decades (Phizacklea and Wolkowitz, 1995 and see previous chapter). As one Indian migrant to Coventry, Chuhar Singh Jandu recalled:

> The general working conditions were very bad – there was not much point complaining about health and safety. We were just happy to be here. Generally in the foundries and other engineering factories around Coventry the working conditions were atrocious. The wages were low, long hours and dirty working conditions. Most people wanted to make a good living and the only way they could do that was by working long hours. (Virdee, 2006, p. 48)

Significantly, long before mesothelioma was officially recognized as a prescribed occupational disease, the Registrar General's data on occupational mortality in 1951 defined labourers and unskilled workers making asbestos goods as having by far the highest standardized mortality rate (SMR) for cancer of the lung (at 85% greater than the average SMR from lung cancer; *Registrar General's Report*, 1951, p. 144). There was also a marked gender imbalance, a reflection of segregated labour markets for women and men and related patriarchal attitudes which saw men dominate the more dangerous trades. Official figures suggest 80–90 per cent of all serious work-related disabilities and disease at mid-twentieth century afflicted male workers (*Annual Report of the Factory Inspectorate*, for 1950, pp. 47–50, 63). However, this ratio changed as the traditional heavy industries declined and may well have been an underestimation, as chronic work-related disease could remain undetected in women until long after they had left employment on marriage or childbirth.

The UK's state-prescribed occupational diseases list also included tuberculosis – long regarded as the classic disease associated with poverty and overcrowded slums. TB was scheduled under the National Insurance (Industrial Injuries) Act in 1951 for certain specific health workers, including nurses, TB sanatoria workers, social workers and asylum officers. This created a significant precedent in the UK because no other disease prevalent in the general population had ever been defined officially as an occupational disease – and hence subject to compensation under the Industrial Injuries Act. It marked the culmination of a long campaign going back at least to the 1920s on the part of the TUC and several constituent trade unions to shift medical and popular understanding of the aetiology of TB to recognize that overcrowded workplaces and contact contagion in the course of employment were important causal agents (see McIvor, 2012). This campaign utilized growing medical knowledge, including epidemiological studies of nurses, which demonstrated to the satisfaction of the statutory body (the Industrial Diseases Advisory Committee) the markedly higher rate of TB incidence amongst specific occupational groups. This built upon an earlier recognition – going back to the 1920s – that there was a synergistic relationship between forms of pneumoconiosis (notably silicosis caused by dust inhalation at work) and TB. What happened in industries like slate quarrying, stone masonry, metal mining and cutlery grinding was that weakened lungs with tissue damage caused by dust inhalation at work lowered resistance to the TB bacillus.

The scheduling of TB as an occupational disease in 1951 was somewhat unusual – a divergence from an otherwise markedly conservative policy of statutory regulation and monitoring of chronic work-related disease and a tough (that is on the workers) regime of medical surveillance over the damaged body in industry. Tweedale and Hansen (1998) have shown how conservative the Pneumoconiosis Medical Panels were in diagnosing asbestosis from the 1930s to the 1960s. These Panels comprised of physicians who made an assessment of causation and the degree of respiratory impairment – by the percentage they judged individuals respiratory capacity was diminished. McIvor and Johnston (2007) have shown a similar cautious pattern in relation to the long campaign – from the 1950s to the 1990s – to get bronchitis and emphysema scheduled as occupational diseases (and hence subject to compensation). Insurance companies were embedded in all this and not averse in the 1950s and 1960s to using callous delaying tactics in the knowledge that liability to compensation pay-outs were much reduced if the victim died (as in the infamous case of Charlie Coyle in 1955–6; see Johnston and McIvor, 2000a, pp. 7–8). What the TB scheduling of 1951 demonstrates is something of the porous nature of occupational health and the difficulty of disentangling causation when bodies drift across different spaces so that diseases could have their origins in employment, or in the home, the family, in personal habits and lifestyle, or the wider environment, or exacerbated by poverty and deprivation (see McIvor, 2012). Multiple causation was recognized later in the case of bronchitis/emphysema and smoking (and enshrined in the compensation 'model' for miners, with differential payments depending upon smoking history and a series of other variables), as well as with stress. Thus the boundaries become blurred. Sexually transmitted diseases (STDs), including AIDS, for example, are clearly spread widely within the community through lifestyle choices, though just as clearly these are unequivocally occupational diseases associated with sex industry workers (Scambler and Scambler, 1999; Wilton, 1999). They have not been and are unlikely in the foreseeable future to be officially recognized as such and scheduled for compensation purposes. This demonstrates the socially constructed nature of occupational disease (Dembe, 1996).

Responsibility and blame

So why were work-related diseases, injuries and death rates so prevalent in the British workplace at mid-twentieth century? Interpretations range across a wide spectrum, in part reflecting wide divergences in contemporary views and a range of discourses in the literature from the medical, state, employers' and workers' perspectives. At one extreme are those that argue the inevitability of 'accidents' or high levels of disease given the lack of medical knowledge at the time and berate scholars who fall into the trap of hindsight (Bartrip, 2001). Others have continued a long tradition of 'blaming the victim', drawing upon the ideas of some psychologists about 'accident proneness' or 'careless' workers (see for example The British Safety Council, *Common Causes of Factory Accidents*, c1970) or, as in the case of the Robens Report into workplace safety in 1972, finding workers culpable through their own 'apathy' and indifference (Nichols, 1999, pp. 86–90).

Other contemporary accounts, such as the National Institute of Industrial Psychology's (NIIP) survey of 2,000 accidents in the late

1960s, placed responsibility squarely upon employers and management-designed work systems, including payments by results wage systems that placed an incentive on overwork (NIIP, 1971). Some work sociologists – particularly, though not exclusively, those writing in the Marxist tradition – have argued that understanding occupational injury and ill-health is dependent upon locating this 'within the social relations of production' (Nichols, 1999, p. 90) and that capitalist modes of production are intrinsically corrosive of health because of the dominance of the profit motive (Navarro and Berman, 1983; Kinnersley, 1973). Others, interpreting this as excessively deterministic, have argued for a more complex and contingent blending of structural factors with a degree of workers' agency (for example in the ways workers express their masculinity in the workplace – see Chapter 3) and identify a wide range of employer and managerial strategies on health and safety (see, for example, Melling, 2003). The latter ranged from the socially responsible 'welfarist' acutely tuned to the health and welfare of their employees, to the grossly negligent, authoritarian profit-maximizers who treated employees as little more than commodities. There were also significant differences emerging in the 1950s and 1960s between the extensive occupational medicine services in the workplace in the public sector, compared to the private sector (Johnston and McIvor, 2008). Medical provision in the privately owned shipyards, for example, atrophied sharply after the Second World War.

What is critically important is the degree to which workers' choices – however significant – were constrained and shaped within a competitive market and an unequal power relationship at the point of production in a context where workers were invariably undervalued and exploited. Experience differed widely, but this should not distract us from the underlying tendency within competitive, free-market capitalism to put shareholders and the profit margin before people's health and well-being. Nichols' work has perhaps been particularly influential here in emphasizing the 'social determinants' of injuries sustained at work – the influence of the business cycle, labour markets, work intensification and the profit motive (Nichols, 1997). Corporate irresponsibility was widespread, from the boardroom denials of the asbestos multinational Turner and Newall to the condoning of 'macho' management in the North Sea oil industry (Tweedale, 2000; Beck et al., 1996; Brotherstone and Manson, 2011; McCulloch and Tweedale, 2008).

One other factor was of major importance in explaining the persistence of high casualty and disease rates in the post-war British workplace: the structural flaws in statutory provision and the regulatory framework. Only about half of all the UK's workplaces were covered by the health and safety legislation in the immediate post-Second World War years – agriculture, for example, was not regulated until the Agriculture (Safety, Health and Welfare Provision) Act 1956, despite the sector having injury incidence levels way in excess of manufacturing and second only to shipping and mines. In part, this reflected the historic pattern of government only responding to pressure from public opinion – for example after major mining pit disasters – and from the labour movement. It was no coincidence that the sector with the strongest and deepest tradition of collective organization and strike activity – mining – was also amongst the most systematically regulated in terms of health and safety. Uniquely across UK industry at mid-twentieth century, coal mining included the statutory appointment of workmen's safety inspectors (from 1911). Across manufacturing, voluntary workers' safety committees were thin on the ground in the 1950s, despite being recommended by the ILO and supported by the trade unions. Only about 4,000 such committees existed across Britain's 230,000 factories in 1960, representing less than 2% of the total (Williams, 1960, pp. 440–1).

A number of studies pointed to the way corporate crime was widely accepted and condoned, with low penalties (derisory fines) for breaches of Factory law which consequently failed to act as a deterrent (Williams, 1960, p. 5; Jones, 1985). State policy for its workplace inspectorate emphasized persuasion and education of recalcitrant employers, rather than punitive punishment. In part, as Williams argued in his seminal 1960 study *Accidents and Ill-Health at Work*, this reflected a wide public disinterest in occupational health (Williams, 1960, p. 5). In a monograph Long has carefully reconstructed the long campaign, spearheaded by a number of voluntary agencies, to establish a national Occupational Health Service integrated into the NHS (Long, 2011). As Long has shown, the Trades Union Congress played a pivotal role in the movement to create the 'healthy factory' and by the 1940s was lobbying for the merging of occupational health with public health in a combined 'service' which would include a full preventative programme within the workplace (Long, 2011; see also Johnston and McIvor, 2000b). However, this idea failed to gain sufficient political support and was never implemented. If successful, it might have done much more to erode the high-risk workplace health cultures that pervaded the heavy industry workplace, to have systematically introduced effective preventative public health measures through the work-place (such as x-rays and inoculation) and to have focused research efforts more widely on the work–health interaction, rather than the prevailing narrow focus on specific occupational diseases, like pneumoconiosis. Despite wide support – and precedents in other places such as Scandinavia – the NHS and occupational health remained largely separate. One consequence was the continuing marginalization of occupational health – indicated, for example, in the big discrepancy in the numbers of civil servants employed as factory inspectors (largely focusing on safety rather than health) compared to medical inspectors (a ratio of more than 10 to 1 in the 1950s; Williams, 1960, p. 413).

Moreover, an overreliance by the state upon 'scientific discourse', or professionally-generated medical knowledge, constrained effective regulation. There was a deep-rooted and long-standing belief in the idea that hazards could be regulated and controlled, evident, for example, in the tendency to lay down 'threshold limits' of exposure (measured by particles per cubic inch in the air captured by filters in 'dust counting' machines) – as with silica, vinyl chloride, coal and asbestos dusts. These were later found to be inadequate and of limited effectiveness and revised to be more stringent (see, for example, Walker, 2007, p. 141). In the meantime this provided workers with a false sense that they were being protected and were secure and not exposed to risk.

The very process of getting an occupational disease officially scheduled (and hence subject to compensation) was incredibly restrictive, relying upon positive proof of linkage (and convincing a panel of medical experts: the Industrial Injury Advisory Committee), rather than erring on the side of caution and the concept of *reasonable probability* (which the TUC campaigned for). In this context, medical knowledge was socially constructed and, it has been posited, tended to reflect powerful industrial and corporate interests – as in the case of the Asbestosis Research Council (Tweedale, 2000). Daykin and Doyal have argued:

> Occupational health research and practice have indeed frequently served the interests of employers at the expense of workers: by minimising the scale of work-related illness; limiting compensation costs; prioritising the maintenance of production over the protection of health; ignoring and devaluing workers' experience of occupational ill-health and focusing on individual behaviour in explaining work-related illness. (Daykin and Doyal, 1999, p. 7)

Significant change was not to come until the 1974 Health and Safety at Work Act and that fell far short of what radical reformers pushing for an integrated public health and occupational health service wanted.

Trends in occupational health and safety, 1950–2010

How then did the nature of workplace risk in the UK in relation to injuries and ill-health change over the second half of the twentieth century? This is not easy to measure accurately. As Gallie (2000) has pointed out, we have consistent reported data for work-related injury fatalities but the reporting of non-fatal injuries has changed significantly since the Second World War, making the construction of long-term time series difficult. There is marked under-recording in the injury statistics, as not all 'accidents' were reported. The official data also seriously under-record fatalities from occupational diseases, where there can be a very long time lag between exposure and death. Undoubtedly the figures, which derive from the Health and Safety Executive and its predecessor agencies, also under-recorded prevalence amongst the most vulnerable, casualized, least secure, poorest paid workers in small companies or working with subcontractors (Wolkowitz, 2006, pp. 102–3). The mortality data for trauma (though not chronic disease) is more reliable. In the early 1950s there were around 2,000 recorded work-related trauma fatalities a year, giving a fatal injury rate per 100,000 workers of 10.5. Thereafter fatalities fell steadily. By the 2000s, workers were more than ten times less likely to be killed at work from an 'accident' than in the 1950s (see Table 5.2 below). The trend is broadly confirmed with the less reliable figures for reported non-fatal work injuries, which according to the HSE fell fourfold from 336,701 in 1974 to 85,110 in 2009/10 (http://www.hse. gov.uk/statistics/history/fatal.htm).

This pattern of declining mortality and improving occupational safety was the product of several factors. Clearly of key importance were the structural shifts in the labour force – the sharp decline of employment in the most dangerous manual trades such as mining, agriculture, shipping, fishing and heavy manufacturing and rise of the more benign (at least in terms of physical hazards) office and professional non-manual jobs. However, the HSE only attributes about 35–50% of the improvement to structural change in jobs. Whilst they fail to specify who or what were the other ameliorative forces, clearly, contrasting the 1950s with the 2000s we might posit that improved

Table 5.2 Fatal injuries to workers 1974–2010

Year	Fatalities	Fatality rate (per 100,000 workers)
1974	651	2.9
1981	495	2.1
1986–7	407	1.7
1996–7	287	1.1
2000–1	292	1.0
2009–10	152	0.5

Source: Contains public sector information published by the Health and Safety Executive and licensed under the Open Government Licence v1.0. Accessed at http://www.hse.gov.uk/statistics/history/fatal.htm.

vigilance on the part of the trade unions, better health education and awareness, a more critical investigative media, a changed health culture in the workplace and improved policing and regulation (following the Health and Safety at Work Act 1974 and subsequent European Union Directives) all had an impact. What is also important in explaining occupational health and safety trends in the UK is that risk was increasingly exported to less developed countries where labour was cheaper and regulatory regimes weak or non-existent (see, for example, McCulloch and Tweedale, 2008). Decommissioned ships full of asbestos insulation, for example, were sold to India for scrap. To what degree employers and management attitudes and policies changed in the UK is also less clearly evident (and more research is definitely needed here). One post-Second World War colliery manager, Tom Ellis, commented ruefully on a significant gulf between the attitudes of enlightened colliery managers such as himself – who believed in 'a symbiotic relationship working for good between workman and manager' and what he termed 'the reactionary attitude of the industry's management per se' – including the National Coal Board whose main preoccupation was production (Ellis, 2004, pp. 122–3; and see Perchard, 2007a; McIvor and Johnston, 2007). Trade union pressure, workplace campaigning and the need to maintain good public relations undoubtedly had some impact in facilitating change. As one ex-ICI plant manager commented:

There was the social conscience of the companies concerned and ICI being a big company wanted to have a good image as a good employer so there was various pressures to improve health and safety. I know my own health and safety, I mean as a plant manager, obviously you wandered around the plant and you tended to be around when things went wrong. So again, whereas at the beginning I hadn't thought much about it, by the 1970s everybody's safety consciousness and health consciousness increased, it was a natural process. (Brian Watson, interviewed by David Walker, 8 October 2005, SOHC/022)

The Health and Safety at Work Act, 1974

The most important change since the Second World War in the regulation and control of workplace dangers took place in 1974 with the passage of the Health and Safety at Work Act (HSWA). What impact did this have? Prior to the HSWA there were a series of laws which regulated minimum standards of health and safety in specific workplaces such as the Factory Acts (updated in 1961), the Mines and Quarries Acts (updated in 1954) and the Nuclear Installations Act (1965). The law covered such things as temperature, ventilation, lighting, fumes, dust, first aid, washing and toilet facilities, workplace cleanliness and the guarding of hazardous machinery. Some limited regulation had also been introduced for office workers in 1963 after a long trade union campaign. Standing alongside these laws were more specific legal regulations on particular hazards, such as the Construction Regulations (1966) and the Asbestos Regulations (1969). The operation and limitations of this complex and fragmented body of health and safety legislation is beyond the scope of this chapter. However, amongst the weaknesses of the pre-1974 regulatory system were its uneven coverage (with some 8 million workers not covered by any regulation in 1970) and the way specific regulations could be superseded quickly by technological change, such as mine shearing technologies or asbestos spraying, and new products, as in the chemicals sector. There were also issues about the inadequate resourcing of the inspectorates designated with the duty of enforcing the law, the ineffectiveness of policing by inspectorates and criticism of their tactics of prioritizing persuasion and education rather than punitive measures. In part this was a reaction to the law courts who proved reluctant to impose heavy fines, and thus a financial deterrent, upon corporate criminals who breached the law.

The HSWA 1974 rationalized this system by replacing the individual statutes with one that comprehensively covered all employees, designed to encompass all problems of safety, welfare and health at work. It introduced the main institutions currently responsible for

British health and safety at work: the Health and Safety Commission and the Health and Safety Executive. Crucially, the HSWA introduced a new principle of 'shared responsibility' for workplace health and safety between employers and employees. It was the statutory duty of employers to: 'ensure, so far as is reasonably practicable, the health, safety and welfare at work of all his employees', whilst workers had the 'duty' to adhere to the health and safety regulations, work together with the employer, not mistreat anything and 'take reasonable care of your own health and safety and that of your workmates' (Eva and Oswald, 1981, pp. 43–4). The law was enforced by a cadre of HSE inspectors with powers to enter any workplace and issue Prohibition and Improvement Notices stopping a specific job, or section or complete workplace. Those breaking the law (employers, workers and manufacturers) could be taken to court by the HSE and fined, or have a custodial sentence of up to two years imposed.

The new system was an improvement, but had several flaws. It allowed alternative arrangements to be made in some special cases – including, significantly, the North Sea oil industry. As Beck, Foster and Woolfson have shown in their research, what made this extractive industry unique was the fact that the North Sea oil production regime was transplanted almost intact from the USA. This included most of the technology, many of the management structures, and, crucially, a dominant 'gung ho' attitude towards health and safety in many of the platforms (Beck et al., 1996, pp. 56–63). It was also the case that it was the Department of Energy, and not the Health and Safety Executive, which was responsible for safety on most of the oil platforms from 1974. These factors, it has been argued, combined with the emphasis placed on extracting the oil as *quickly* as possible, led to a neglect of health and safety offshore in many installations, culminating in the Piper Alpha disaster in 1988, where 167 workers died. Tragically, it took this disaster to transform the health and safety culture in the offshore oil industry and to radically change the extent and nature of the offshore regulatory system.

Sprinkled throughout the HSWA section on employers' responsibilities is the phrase 'so far as is reasonably practicable'. Essentially this involved a risk against sacrifice calculation and as Eva and Oswald have argued the law courts continued to interpret this in the employers' favour. The courts threw cases out, or imposed small fines which hardly acted as a deterrent (Dalton, 1998, pp. 56–8). The average fine for health and safety crime was just £99 in 1977–8 (Eva and Oswald, 1981, p. 56) and no employers were jailed under the HSWA before the mid-1990s (Dalton, 1998, pp. 35–6). Moreover, employers generally insured themselves against this risk. Weak enforcement also continued to be an issue. The Inspectorate was spread thinly, with less than 500 field inspectors in 1980, meaning each covered some 1,000 workplaces, making routine preventative visits to every workplace on average only every four years (unless specifically called in). The economic recession from the late 1970s and government public spending cuts in the 1980s only made matters worse. A wide gulf continued between the statutory regulations on paper and actual practice far away from the regulators' gaze at the point of production. For example, a heating engineer could remember slip-shod procedures in his firm well into the late 1980s:

> If we went down tae strip a boiler we just took it [the asbestos] off with a hammer and chisel, you know. There was nae masks or anything at that time, you know. If you came out for a breather they were asking you what you were dain sitting outside, you know. You were spitting up black for maybe a week, you know, when you came out. (Interview by Ronnie Johnston, 22 December 1999, SOHC 016/A6)

Three years after the passage of the HSWA the system was supplemented with regulations that permitted unionized workers to set up safety committees with their employers. This had long been an aspiration of the trade union movement and was achieved, partly as a quid pro quo for union support for incomes policies, as part of the Labour government's Social Contract. However, the sharp decline in trade union membership in the 1980s restricted the impact of this enabling legislation. In 1986, the Reporting of Injuries, Diseases and Dangerous Occurrences Regulations (RIDDOR) came into operation, compelling employers to report any injuries resulting in absences from work of more than three days. However, the statistics subsequently collected under RIDDOR suggest the continuation of substantial under-reporting of non-fatal injuries. Moreover, the stipulation that employers should investigate reported accidents when company safety representatives made such a request was also undermined by the erosion in trade union membership.

European Union Directives improved matters somewhat. In response to growing European pressure the Management of Health and Safety Regulations 1992 were passed with the aim of addressing some of the shortcomings of the 'shared responsibility' principle. This compelled employers and self-employed to carry out 'risk assessments' of potential workplace hazards and to determine what

Table 5.3 Fatal accidents at work in Europe by member state, 2007

	Fatalities	Standardized mortality rate
Austria	117	3.8
Belgium	47	2.5
Denmark	41	2.0
Finland	21	1.3
France	435	2.2
Germany	387	1.8
Great Britain	183	1.3
Ireland	29	1.7
Italy	404	2.5
Netherlands	61	1.8
Portugal	226	6.3
Spain	332	2.3
Sweden	34	1.4
EU 15	2322	2.1

Source: Contains public sector information published by the Health and Safety Executive and licensed under the Open Government Licence v1.0. Accessed at http://www.hse.gov.uk/statistics/european/fatal.htm.

measures should be taken to comply with the employer's or self-employed person's duties under the 1974 HSWA. Criticisms continued, nonetheless, of the shortcomings of the regulatory framework, leading, for example, by the late 1990s in some quarters to a campaign to introduce a new crime of 'corporate killing' to penalize employers more directly and hence provide a more effective deterrent (Dalton, 1998, pp. 35–6; Woolfson and Beck, 2005; see the Corporate Crime & Governance website: http://www.gla.ac.uk/faculties/socialsciences/corpcrime/links.htm). This new offence would mean there would be no need to locate and charge the 'controlling mind' of a company, but that the company itself would be held responsible, with the possibility of its directors being sent to prison.

Whilst serious shortcomings in regulation persisted and economic pressures continued to make workers vulnerable, nonetheless workplace injury mortality rates fell steadily after 1974 (see Table 5.2). Comparative statistical data (see Table 5.3) – whilst subject to some issues relating to inconsistency in data collection across different countries – certainly suggests that Britain's workplace safety record contrasted favourably with other European countries by the 2000s.

Occupational disease 'epidemics'

The situation in relation to long-term trends in occupational health (as opposed to safety) is less clear cut. As Snashall has shown, a cluster of occupational diseases were declining in incidence and virulence from the 1970s – such as pneumoconiosis, dermatitis, tenosynovitis and the beat conditions, TB and leptospirosis – whilst others were increasing, including mesothelioma, asthma, vibration white finger and stress (Snashall, 1999, p. 3). The picture is an uneven one. The HSE admitted itself in the late 1990s that it had prioritized safety issues and not paid enough attention to chronic ill-health and disease caused by work (HSE Consultation Document, 1998, p. 4). To some extent new hazards, toxins and diseases – such as those associated with chemicals (like vinyl chloride monomer, benzene and chromates), musculoskeletal disorders, repetitive strain injuries (associated for example with computer use), and stress – have replaced old ones. Dembe (1996) has argued that definitions of occupational disease are socially constructed with recognition of a condition as an occupational disease dependent upon a range of social, economic, technological and political factors. Hence TB was only 'recognized' belatedly as an occupational disease in 1951 and bronchitis in 1993. Watterson has identified how 'old, new and silent epidemics' of occupational diseases have coexisted and persisted, arguing that the neglect of workers' bodies has been the product of 'the relative invisibility of occupational health epidemics and the low priority afforded to them' (Watterson, 1999, p. 107). He asserted:

> There are also epidemics that are recognised but are viewed by workers as part of the job, such as back pain for nurses and building workers, damaged knee joints for carpet layers and miners as well as colds and flu for teachers. In times of insecure or poor employment conditions these are likely to remain unchallenged. (Watterson, 1999, p. 110)

Moreover, given the long incubation period for many classic occupational diseases – including occupational cancers – the peak of disability and death rates could occur some considerable time after the initial contact and exposure to toxins and carcinogens. This was the case, for example, with asbestos-related diseases, whose symptoms could emerge 30, 40 or more years after initial contact. Hence, death rates from mesothelioma started to accelerate from the 1970s, peaking in the 2010s as a result of high exposure rates in the 1950s and 1960s before a new phase of regulation kicked in from the 1969 Asbestos Regulations and subsequent controls over the importation of and working with the mineral (though white asbestos – widely considered to be less carcinogenic than other forms – was not finally banned until 1999). As already noted, scholars differ widely in their interpretation of the asbestos tragedy. The evidence strongly indicates, however, that this is a classic example of vested interests in the form of powerful multinational corporations conspiring to put profit before workers' health, aided by the effective collusion of the state. Whilst the worst unhealthy working practices have become controlled in the UK (and other well-regulated economies, such as the USA), in practice the problem has been increasingly transferred to other poorer countries where multinational companies could benefit from weaker regulatory regimes, little trade union interference and cheaper labour costs. This happened worldwide with asbestos, as McCulloch and Tweedale have shown in their important study, *Defending the Indefensible* (2008). Chemical manufacture provides another deeply tragic example – with the US multinational Union Carbide responsible for one of the worst occupational and environmental health disasters in history with the lethal gas leakage from its plant in Bhopal in 1984, responsible for at least 3,787 deaths (with some estimates as high as 11,000) and almost 4,000 severe and permanently disabling injuries. The scale of the disaster was exacerbated by failures of both local and national government in India – the latter putting attracting investment and jobs before adequate regulations and safeguards. Mukherjee's recent oral history of the disaster gets behind these mortality statistics to explore the human story of what was one of the world's worst occupational and environmental health disasters (Mukherjee, 2010; see also Shrivastava, 1992).

The recession of the 1980s and Thatcherite policies of deregulation combined with the empowerment of capital and neutering of the trade unions also had degenerative impacts upon occupational health and safety – at the very least slowing down the pace of progress and at worst contributing to overwork and workplace ill-health – as in the North Sea oil and gas sector. More intensive Japanese production methods transplanted to the UK, for example, resulted in higher levels of stress, exhaustion and a rash of new repetitive strain injuries (Hodson, 2001, p. 117). The disciplining effect of mass unemployment facilitated work intensification, insecurity and stress. For example, the cost-cutting switch to one-person operation with the loss of thousands of guards' jobs on the London Transport trains in the 1980s led directly to more accident deaths. Bill Siepmann recalled the empowerment of management which came at this time and which could compromise health and safety. As a new Health and Safety representative he came across a 'dodgy train' – one of the older 1938 stock: 'I told the driver to refuse to take the train out. Which he did. And management came down on me like a ton of bricks' (Britain at Work interview by David Welsh, 2 July 2010). Bill feared getting sacked, but his judgement was vindicated when within three weeks the train crashed, smashing into the roof of a tunnel.

Electronics, another rapidly growing sector from the 1960s, threw up significant health hazards, including exposure to toxic chemicals. In a way similar to some asbestos-related diseases, the health effects of exposure to such chemicals could take a long time to show up. In addition, many of the chemicals used in some of the processes were carcinogenic. Amongst these were chromic acid, trichloroethylene, carbon tetrachloride, and other chemicals which directly affected the main organs, such as arsenic and zinc oxide. On top of this were new risks from exposure to gases and vapours, and the even more threatening danger of exposure to ionizing radiation. Fears over the impact of chemical inhalation (ethylene-glycol ethers) in the making of silicon chips in IBM led to a media exposure which forced the HSE into an inquiry in 2001. The results were inconclusive. In addition, performing detailed repetitive work in electronics under strict time pressure resulted in a high incidence of stress-related complaints (Geiser, 1986, pp. 38–49) – something which is discussed in greater detail in the final section of this chapter.

Standards of occupational health and safety were clearly subject to the vagaries of the market and the wider political and regulatory environment. Whilst the data indicates a clear and unequivocal improvement since 1950, the current economic recession and cut-backs in the HSE's budget and staffing have reversed this trend. A recent report by O'Neill and Watterson at the Occupational and Environmental Health Research Group at Stirling University has shown that fatal and major workplace injuries rose in the UK by around 8% between 2006 and 2011 (despite reduced economic activity), whilst the number investigated and prosecuted by the HSE fell sharply (*The Herald*, 23 September 2012, p. 12). It is not only workers' pockets that are bearing the brunt of the current economic recession, but workers' bodies too.

Disabled bodies and shattered lives

Ill-health and injury associated with the workplace resulted in high levels of suffering and hardship, much of it preventable. Williams noted that even the more generous benefits of the National Insurance (Industrial Injuries) Act 1946 only amounted to roughly half the fully incapacitated workers' previous salary (Williams, 1960, p. 33). As the pressure group Clydeside Action on Asbestos argued, this made those affected 'victims twice over' – once as a result of the actual physical harm and secondly as a victim of an unfair system of financial compensation. Toxins, carcinogens and injuries sustained at work could have devastating impacts upon workers' bodies, with deep ramifications for individuals, families and communities. There were markedly differing levels of impairment, however, and a wide range of experience, with effects and coping strategies varying significantly across a wide spectrum of personal tragedies. Difficulties could be exacerbated, moreover, because rehabilitation services were also very limited in the 1950s and 1960s. At worst, the outcomes could involve quite fundamental *mutations* in lifestyles, behaviour and identities. Impacts included erosion of physical and mental capacity, loss or change of employment, declining income and standards of living, a collapse of status and self-esteem, a drift towards social exclusion and towards dependency and marginalization as citizens. These transitions were more sudden and traumatic in some cases than others, depending on the nature and pathology of the disease(s) and injuries and the individuals concerned (Johnston and McIvor, 2000a, pp. 177–208; McIvor and Johnston, 2007, pp. 273–308).

Recently, disability studies have done much to establish that those with impairments in our society are *socially* oppressed, excluded, marginalized and lacking citizenship. This scholarship has developed strong critiques of the state, medical profession and lay policies towards the disabled community in Britain in the nineteenth and twentieth centuries (e.g. Blaxter, 1976; Oliver, 1990; Hughes, 2002. See Chapter 1). However, much of this analysis of the disabled has been constructed from studies of the congenitally impaired, such as those with mental illnesses, those with learning difficulties, and those with loss of faculties such as sight, hearing and speech. Occupational injury and disease hardly features in the literature. And it is hard to convey the physical and psychological pain, emotional trauma and suffering that went along with the damage caused by unhealthy and unsafe workplaces (see McKessock, 1995).

Respiratory disease provides a pertinent example. As we've seen, breathing impairment was widespread across the coalfields and in other heavy industry communities (such as quarrying and iron and steel) in the immediate post-war years. But what did this mean to those who were affected and their families? The most chronic and disabling form of pneumoconiosis, Progressive Massive Fibrosis (PMF), was associated with severe breathlessness, chest pain, wheezing and coughing, which worsened as the disease progressed. One South Wales doctor described the disease in 1961 as 'concrete in the lung' causing progressive loss of respiratory function which was severely disabling and could be fatal:

> The air spaces are slowly strangled and eventually if enough are strangled then the man himself is strangled and loses his power to expand his chest and he drops from say a 2 half inch expansion down three quarters of an inch...and that is the overt sign that you have of this process. (Interview with Dr Thomas, Audio/374; South Wales Coal Collection, University of Swansea)

Multiple respiratory and other work-related disabilities were common in the coalfields. Joe Kenyon noted of Barnsley pit communities in the 1950s: 'Very few families were not touched by death or serious accident at some time or other. Every village had its quota of men and young lads with broken backs, a leg or an arm missing, hands crushed and useless' (Kenyon, 2003, p. 89). A South Wales miner, Mostyn Moses, suffering from a combination of pneumoconiosis, bronchitis and emphysema commented: 'I have been spitting up dust like black lead from my lungs, like black slurry. Then I started seeing blood and now they tell me I've got tuberculosis as well' (cited in *Saga Magazine*, March 1998, at www.deadline.demon.co.uk/archive/saga/980301.htm). Death could ultimately accrue through respiratory failure and/or cardiac failure. There was and remains no cure for pneumoconiosis.

Because of the sharp loss of earnings, some workers opted to hide the extent of their disability and continue to work, risking further damage. One doctor described re-employment efforts in lighter, more suitable jobs for disabled miners as 'unsuccessful' and commented in the early 1950s: 'They are compelled by economic pressure to carry on with their job' (McCallum, 1953–4, p. 105). A South Wales miner (whose father had died of pneumoconiosis in 1969) continued to work for nine years after being diagnosed with pneumoconiosis in 1971 and being advised by his GP to leave the coal face:

> Q. So when you were told in 1971 that you had pneumoconiosis why did you not want to leave the face then?
>
> A. [Long pause]. Young family. Money. Not greedy but just y'know. No money. It was a big drop in the wages see. Yeh. A minimum wage compared to a coal face worker or a hard heading man. A hell of a big difference. (Interview by Susan Morrison with John Jones, 15 September 2002, SOHC 017/C27)

In some workplaces the mutual support system saw younger and fitter fellow workers carrying the older and disabled. As one Scottish miner noted: 'You carried lesser men, gie them a hand, wee dig out and that, but you couldn't cover them all but by and large did a good job covering the weaker elements in society in them days' (interview by Neil Rafeek and Hilary Young with George Bolton, 12 January 2005, SOHC 017/C23). The common experience, however, was a slide into relative poverty and degrees of social exclusion – increasingly those affected were house-bound, isolated and unable to operate as independent citizens.

A Durham mining union official, David Guy, reflected on the restricted opportunities that faced those with lung impairment as the pits closed:

> As long as they were able to work, or get to work in some shape or form, the management were pretty sympathetic to people in poor health, especially if it was caused by the work at the pit and there was a tendency for the union and the management to work together to try and fix them up in jobs which they could cope with. Once the pit closed that type of sympathetic approach wasn't there any longer by employers outside the industry – I mean the first thing they make you do when you apply for a job is to get you medically examined and in the vast majority of cases people were told: 'You're not fit enough to work for us, how the hell did you manage at the pit?'. So that's resulted in a high percentage of people in the mining communities relying upon sickness benefits, industrial injuries benefits. So I think we've been able to monitor that much better than what we would have done had the pits still been operating. I think the pits *masked* a lot of that, whereas now they're out there now, the reality is there isn't any sympathy for you if you've got a form of disablement. Employers want to take on people who they are going to be able to exploit to the maximum, so they don't want anyone who's got a bad chest or who have spinal injuries or neck injuries or arthritis, there is a reluctance of employers to employ people in

that category. (Interview by Neil Rafeek with David Guy, 8 March 2004, SOHC 017/C44)

To some extent the social exclusionary impacts of disability were mediated by the highly supportive, tight-knit coal mining communities, where miners and their families could also draw upon the support of their trade union and the pioneering welfare work of the Coal Industry Social Welfare Organization. Other workers were not so fortunate and found that work-related disabilities plunged them into a vicious downward spiral of economic and social deprivation, mental ill-health and mutation in identities that fundamentally affected their lifestyle. Victims, dependants and their families had to deal with the trauma of diagnosis, curtailment and loss of employment, physical deterioration and, invariably, the deeper psychological implications of dependency and loss of self-esteem. Mildred Blaxter described this in her pioneering mid-1970s study of disability as a process of 're-evaluating identity', which could be either a sudden discontinuity or a longer-term process of 'drift' (Blaxter, 1976; Barnes and Mercer, 2003, p. 63). Personal accounts and oral testimonies suggest that the essence of manhood could be deeply shaken by occupational disability and subsequent loss of work, and the drift into varying levels of dependency (e.g. McIvor and Johnston, 2007, pp. 297–303).

Management policies and workplace culture within patriarchal capitalism clearly did damage workers' bodies and undermine health and well-being in many ways. In his autobiography Abe Moffat talked of his younger brother incapacitated with pneumoconiosis and emphysema: 'a physical wreck before he reached the age of fifty' (Moffat, 1965, p. 232). Some noted the impact of occupation-related disability on their sex life. A 65-year-old miner admitted bluntly that his lung condition meant he was 'too fucked to have sex' (interview by Ronnie Johnston, 29 June 2000, 017/C10). A retired insulation lagger commented that he was impotent as a result of his asbestos-related disease (interview by Ronnie Johnston, 26 January 2000, SOHC 016/A14). The diminution of libido is a documented consequence of loss of employment for some male workers, recognized as early as the 1930s (Bourke, 1983, pp. 132–3). However, coupled with this is a loss of pride brought about by not being able to perform as a man in other senses associated with loss of independence and the 'provider' role. Billy Affleck, a 50-year-old Ayrshire miner, made this clear:

It was a big blow to me to be told that I'd never work again. Eh, your pride's dented, ken. I mean when your out and your wife's to come out and say to you 'Come on I'll get that...' Wee jobs outside eh, that you're no fit to do, and your son or whatever eh will say to you 'Right come on...' It definitely hurts your pride. (Interview by Arthur McIvor and Ronnie Johnston, 19 June 2000, SOHC 017/C2)

Another asbestos worker reflected on how difficult it was adapting to the speed dictated by his lung condition, and of the reversal of bread-winner roles:

> My wife's got a wee part-time job three mornings a week. And I've seen her going out about half past twelve and I've just finished the last bit of my washing, just ready to put my clothes on. (Interview by Ronnie Johnston, 18 March 1999, SOHC/016/A7)

A 60-year-old railway track worker disabled by a work injury which left him blind in one eye commented on being taken off his job as a track supervisor: 'They've changed the rules now; they've took all that off me. What it is, because they've more or less made me impotent in the gang, do you know what I mean'. Significant in this narrative, as Kirk (the interviewer) noted, was the deployment of pronouns – 'them and us' and use of the 'impotence' metaphor, suggesting something of a cri-sis of masculinity (Kirk, 2008, pp. 49, 51). And the widow of a quantity surveyor who had died of mesothelioma commented on how almost to the last her husband had tried to play out his masculine role:

> He really didn't drive very much by himself at this stage. Men are funny things. We would get in the car together here and we would drive out the gates, and then we would pull in and stop and I would take over. Men eh, don't like to give in. (Interview by Ronnie Johnston, 22 March 1999, SOHC 016/A21)

In extreme cases, masculine frustration boiled over into rage and violence, as was the case with this ex-lagger with an asbestos-related disease:

> I get what would you say, flash backs. And then I rare up. Frustration. You want to take it out on somebody so it's your wife. So she phones the police and you've got all that squabble. (Interview by Ronnie Johnson, SOHC 016/A16)

Clearly, within such a work-dominated *machismo* culture in the manual industries, encroaching disability, old-age and/or the removal of employment could have deep social, physical and psychological effects. This might be summed up as social exclusion and emascula-tion. It appears that the impact upon the male psyche could be even more damaging where loss of the provider role was combined with physical deterioration in health as a consequence of industrial injury, disability or disease. Massive adjustments had to be negotiated in this forced transition from independent provider in a male-dominated work environment, to socially excluded dependant, often confined within what was still perceived by members of this generation as the woman's domain in the home.

Rita Moses, the wife of a South Wales miner suffering from multiple respiratory diseases noted: 'There's no quality of life for him. He loved his garden and to go for a walk and a drink. Now he can hardly do anything... We've got three sons and two daughters. My Mostyn was a fit and healthy man then' (cited in *Saga Magazine*, March 1998, at www.deadline.demon.co.uk/archive/saga/980301.htm). A 58-year-old disabled miner from Ayrshire remarked: 'I swam a lot. I played golf. I wasnae a bad golfer...And eh, you cannae do them things now. You cannae compete in these things anymore'. Others lamented being unable to dance, or walk up to the pub, or do household chores. 'We used to love going to the dancing. Now if a dae one turn around the hall I'm buggered' commented one ex-shipyard plumber with an asbestos-related disease (interview by Ronnie Johnston, 22 December 1998, SOHC 016/A2). An occupational asthma sufferer interviewed in 1998 reflected on the impact his disability had: 'I've had no social life since about 1980. Eh, people unfortunately don't want to know you when you're, you're ill like, y'know. People stopped coming. I was very disappointed' (interview by Ronnie Johnston, 1 February 1999, SOHC 016/A9). An ex-marine engineer with an asbestos-related disease reflected: 'I led a very full social life...I no longer do that. I have shut myself off from life completely' (interview by Ronnie Johnston, 9 May 1999, SOHC 016/A12).

Clearly occupational disability impacted upon pride, identity and self-esteem, so the effects upon mental health could be as devastating – sometimes more so – than the physical impairment. George Burns, a Durham ex-miner with chronic bronchitis reflected: 'I shouldn't feel like that but that's my nature and I take it badly because I could do it and when suddenly you can't. I think 'well, I'm a bloody right off here, waste of time really... 'it's hard to accept, *it's so hard*' (interview by Neil Rafeek, 28 April 2004, SOHC 017/C40; narrators emphasis). A lorry driver with an asbestos-related disease testified:

> The depressions's bad...You just want to greet your eyes out and everything, y'know. Then you sort of reminisce, all your past life. Y'know,

as if you're going to die, y'know. And you remember all the good times. And you just think... You can get a violent one. You just flash up stuff. (Interview by Ronnie Johnston, 23 March 1999, SOHC 016/A4)

'All my thoughts are negative', the wife of a 64-year-old electrician with mesothelioma stated: 'I cannae see a future' (interview by Ronnie Johnston, 15 March 1999, SOHC 016/A13).

The oral testimonies of such disabled workers thus help us to understand how work could impact upon the body and upon identities, and how individuals and families navigated the *transition* from fit, independent and capable worker, able and willing to carry their own weight, to a slower unfit worker, increasingly dependent upon others. Partners and wives – most frequently women – might have to adjust to becoming full-time carers, with limited state support and much anxiety and stress on top of the financial hardships. This *emotional history* has hardly been explored, clearly merits more attention and is likely to become an important research focus in the future. Bitterness, frustration, embarrassment, anger and violence as well as stoic and even heroic toleration and resignation to one's fate are likely to feature significantly in this, with a range of emotions evident from the oral testimonies and other narratives of disabled workers reviewed briefly here.

There is also, however, a further and very different identifiable impact of such experience. For some workers, chronic illness or injury was radicalizing, enervating and politicizing. Alan Napier, a mining union official and Labour councillor in Durham, commented:

You can see the ones who were lucky to be alive mind, but they can't get the words out, they can't breathe properly. And in the main, the ones who are in their eighties are bent at right angles... So you can see the legacy, you can see the legacy of the pit. So you can understand the anger we've got. (Interview by Neil Rafeek, 31 March 2004, SOHC 017/C43)

Knowledge of bodily damage, pain and premature death, and perceptions of injustice and exploitation, drew some into political activism – to campaign to punish those responsible, to prevent the same thing happening to others and to get decent levels of compensation. This was evident with rank and file trade union activists – such as John Todd and Alan Dalton in the Transport and General Workers' Union – in growing 'official' trade union activism on health and safety (which accelerated from the 1970s) and in the emergence of important new voluntary agencies, such as the Society for the Prevention of

Asbestos and Industrial Diseases (SPAID; formed by Nancy Tait in 1979; see McDougall, 2013) and local groups like Clydeside Action on Asbestos (founded in 1986).

Occupational health in the post-Fordist workplace: the new epidemic of workplace stress

With changes in the economy and in technology with the growth of the service industries in the second half of the twentieth century, the emphasis in occupational health shifted from physiological impacts to psychological ones; from the body to the mind. The use of the body at work has fundamentally changed, as Wolkowitz has shown, from making goods to 'interpersonal interactions', with a heavy emphasis across a number of employment sectors in 'emotional labour' (employment that requires interaction with people and the expression or suppression of emotions; Wolkowitz, 2006, pp. 1–2). Concomitant with Britain's changing industrial and occupational landscape, old illnesses were gradually being replaced by 'new' illnesses, such as repetitive strain injury (RSI), Sick Building Syndrome and the inchoate complaint of stress (see Taylor et al, 2002; Taylor et al, 2003; Murphy, 2006; Wainwright and Calnan, 2002). There has also been a growing recognition that traditional studies of work and health interactions have frequently been rather narrowly conceived, neglecting 'the current epidemic in stress, overwork and depression' (Wolkowitz, 2006, p. 2) and the experience of marginalized groups, for example the health experience of female workers and of unpaid work such as domestic household labour and caring (Daykin and Doyal, 1999, pp. 1–2). Isolation has emerged as one of the deleterious mental health impacts of a range of work situations, including homeworking (increasingly being populated by Asian women) and domestic labour – something which Oakley identified as associated with the work of the 'housewife' in her seminal study in 1974, together with monotony and lack of intrinsic interest. More recently, isolation is an issue for the growing cadre of self-employed workers exploiting the opportunities provided by computer and internet technologies to work from home (see Doyal, 1999).

Several processes are at work here. For one thing, the increasing preponderance of white-collar-related occupational diseases reflects the country's changing occupational and industrial structure. On the other hand, the slow recognition of new industrial diseases demonstrates the historical reluctance of corporate capitalism and successive governments to acknowledge that certain ailments were work-related and therefore potentially liable for compensation. This has been the pattern with, for example, lead poisoning, asbestos-related diseases, coal workers' pneumoconiosis, and with emphysema/ bronchitis caused through working in mines (the latter not legally recognized as a prescribed occupational disease until 1993). The case of repetitive strain injury (RSI) suffered by many typists and keyboard operators and linked to the diffusion of word-processing in the 1980s, illustrates the contested nature of such work-related disorders. Throughout the nineteenth and much of the twentieth century most medics favoured a psychological rather than physiological explanation for RSI, categorizing it as 'occupational neurosis' and even 'mass hysteria' (Pringle, 1988, pp. 189–92). Workers claiming RSIs were widely considered to be malingering; that the illness was imaginary, rather than real. It was not until the 1990s that RSIs (now classified commonly as musculoskeletal disorders – MSDs) were finally accepted as occupational in origin.

It is clear that new industries brought with them unforeseen hazards, and the impact upon health of the high stress, high labour turnover call centres which became quickly established throughout the UK in the 1990s and 2000s is now becoming evident (see Taylor et al., 2002). After musculoskeletal disorders, stress-related complaints formed the second most commonly reported group of work-related ill-health conditions in the UK at the end of the twentieth century, with the rate of reported stress at work doubling between 1990 and 1999 (HSE, 2001, p. 130). Workers in the NHS were reported to be amongst those particularly prone to work-related stress (Wolkowitz, 2006, p. 115). And stress had a range of psychological and physical symptoms, being associated, for example, with depression, anxiety attacks and other forms of mental illness, as well as heightened risk of coronary heart disease, stomach ulcers and some cancers, as well as a contributory factor in unhealthy behaviour such as cigarette, alcohol and substance abuse (Dalton, 1998, pp. 136–7; Wainwright and Calnan, 2002, pp. 3–4). In 1998 a major study by the HSE in the UK called *The Stress and Health at Work Study* (SHAW) found that 1 in 5 of the UK working population believed their jobs were extremely or very stressful, such that this level of stress was making them ill (HSE, 1998). This marked a major departure for the HSE from a previously sceptical and equivocal position regarding work stress (Dalton, 1998, p. 144).

However, as with many other occupational health epidemics, work-related stress was and remains a contested concept. There is a persuasive popular discourse, backed up by many empirical studies, that levels of work stress have been rising since the 1980s. Alan Dalton provides an example of this position, arguing in his 1998 study that 'stress is bad and getting worse', for both workers and managers (Dalton, 1998, p. 135). One TUC study in 1996 (of 7,000 safety representatives) identified stress as widespread and the main occupational hazard for their members (Dalton, 1998, p. 135). It led to a rash of trade union 'work stress' audits to raise awareness and a call for more effective prevention and tighter regulation. Compensation cases were also increasing, supported by trade unions such as UNISON (public sector workers), establishing the principle that employers were responsible for psychological ill-health caused by their work practices (Wainwright and Calnan, 2002, pp. 1–2). Noon and Blyton have argued that work stress is particularly associated with the growth of 'emotion work' and point to a series of studies that mostly support this view (Noon and Blyton, 2002, pp. 194–5; see, for example, Bolton and Boyd, 2003, on airline cabin crew). Studies of call centre workers (such as Taylor et al., 2002; 2003) found work-related stress to be endemic and posited three interconnected factors influencing health and well-being in work: 1. 'proximate' (the labour process and work station); 2. 'ambient' (including lighting and temperature); and 3. 'social' (including employers and supervisors' behaviour and the management of labour, such as deadlines and work quotas). Stress affected both female and male call centre employees and Wolkowitz has called for more attention to be focused on the gendering of workplace stress, as unlike most previous occupational epidemics, this was as prevalent amongst women workers, for example as care workers and in the NHS – where self-reported stress levels reached their highest levels (Wolkowitz, 2006, pp. 105–6). Stress levels were also greater amongst more insecure immigrant workers and non-standard contract workers than 'core' permanently employed staff – though the latter were certainly not immune. Managers, however, were also particularly at risk (Dalton, 1998, p. 135), as were professionals, such as teachers and lecturers, subject to ever-increasing levels of paperwork, monitoring and 'accountability' performance reviews, as well as more short-term and insecure contracts (Wainwright and Calnan, 2002, pp. 12–13). Stress at work has also been associated with contributing generally to higher mortality rates. The new epidemic of workplace stress appears to be breaking new ground in being less tied to social class and to gender than 'classic' industrial disease epidemics have been in the past.

The forces identified with the rise in work-related stress have been diverse. One theory is that this is connected with the fundamental shifts in workplace power from the 1980s and the increase in personal workloads that resulted. Increased pressures were being felt in the UK workplace from globalization, rising unemployment, greater job insecurity, more non-standard work contracts and tighter managerial control and a revival of 'coercive' discipline (the prerogative to manage) with privatization, cost-cutting, downsizing, contracting out and new human resource management systems (focusing on individual responsibility for workloads and greater surveillance). Wolmar, for example, has shown how pressure and speed-up associated with the privatization of British Rail from the mid-1990s led directly to poorer standards of maintenance and a rash of accidents (Wolmar, 2001; see also Strangleman, 2002, sections 2.24–32). The loss of an experienced cadre of older railway workers and the deskilling of railway labour further contributed to this additional risk (Strangleman, 2002, section 2.30). Reorganization or 'rationalization' of work was often cited in workers' self-reporting as significant in causing workplace stress.

On the other hand, many employers and managers continued to be dismissive, challenging trade union claims about the extent of the work stress epidemic and, importantly, contesting culpability, claiming stress to be linked to individual susceptibilities and to pressures outwith the workplace (such as home, family life and relationship breakdowns; Wainwright and Calnan, 2002, p. 6). Responsibility was thus deflected from issues associated with workloads, work intensification, wage incentives, job design, increased monitoring and surveillance and rising job insecurity – causal factors that figured prominently in trade union campaigns and the popular discourse. In a 'revisionist' account of the work stress epidemic Wainwright and Calnan have posited that this 'problem' needs to be kept in perspective and that the reality has been misrepresented and sensationalized because levels of stress may well have been more significant historically, but under-reported before the 1990s. Whilst incidence was never systematically quantified, stress 'neuroses' were a recurring theme in the annual Factory Inspectors' Reports at least from the growth of mass production from the 1920s, and recognized as widely prevalent by some occupational health experts – such as Donald Hunter in 1959, (Hunter, 1959, pp. 60–61). Popular perception – evident in work stress 'victims" personal oral testimonies for example – of a 'golden age' of stress-free work before the 1980s may well be exaggerated.

Wainwright and Calnan argue that the rising self-reporting of stress has coincided with the marked reduction in trade union and labour power since the 1980s and in part represents an individualized alternative to the neutered collective tactics of strikes and industrial action to tackle workplace grievances. This is part of a growing 'culture of victimhood and the therapeutic state' where workers translate worsening work conditions into 'emotional distress' (Wainwright and Calnan, 2002, pp. 28, 32), with reporting swelled by the possibilities of compensation. Changing gender identities might be blended into this mix. It may well have become more acceptable by the 1990s and 2000s for men to express such feelings and self-report stress, whereas previously this would have been considered an affront to their masculinity, policed by peer pressure. One of the difficulties, therefore, is that whilst most physical injury, toxins or carcinogens had clear and unequivocal health impacts, stress is mediated much more by subjectivity and consciousness – with different responses, capacities and variable resilience: 'one person's stressor may be another person's challenge' (Wainwright and Calnan, 2002, p. 29). Wainwright and Calnan's study does help to question widely held assumptions and provides an antidote to uncritical accounts that implicate modern work systems wholesale as inimical to health – just as previous accounts based on wholesale deskilling or 'dehumanization' within Fordist work regimes have done (for example, Braverman, 1974). They conclude: 'It [work] may not be the pathogenic destroyer of health and well-being portrayed in the work-stress discourse'. They continue, however, to insist: 'but for many people the experience of paid employment is one of boredom, unfulfilled potential, frustration, uncertainty, dissatisfaction or alienation' (Wainwright and Calnan, 2002, p. 196).

Whilst Wainwright and Calnan provide a useful counterpoise to exaggerated claims about work stress and contextualize the epidemic, they do, nonetheless, rather tend to lose sight of the material impacts of work upon the body and mind in their preoccupation with discourses. There is, as Wolkowitz, has argued, an 'organic as well as the symbolic level of work experience' and 'each of us has only one body and it feels the pinch' (Wolkowitz, 2006, p. 117). Taylor et al.'s recent investigation of stress in call centres, studies such as Bolton and Boyd's of 'emotional labour' in airline flight attendants' work, evidence of growing levels of violence at work (for example in buses and taxis), ill-health associated with night work and studies of stress levels in the NHS all convincingly point to an exacerbation of work stress levels since the 1980s (Boyd, 2002; Bolton and Boyd, 2003). The evidence associates this with an all-pervasive *intensification* of work in response to market pressures brought on by recession, neo-liberal deregulation, globalization and resulting rising levels of unemployment, underemployment and labour market insecurity. To some commentators, workers have increasingly become 'willing slaves' in an 'overwork' culture that is damaging to health and well-being (Bunting, 2004; Donkin, 2001). Whilst this interpretation may well underplay the extent to which workers are capable of resisting and mitigating the imposition of stressful work regimes, certainly the evidence suggests that whilst old workplace hazards and diseases have declined, new ones have emerged and that work stress is now the most significant of these (see Robinson and Smallman, 2006).

Conclusion

The body was (and remains) positioned at the ecological core of the workplace and was (and continues to be) intimately affected in myriad ways – by the labour process, the wider employment environment and the management regime, and social relations in the workplace. Employment could be benign, could be health-enhancing and could be the harbinger of injury, disease and physical and mental breakdown. Clearly, at mid-twentieth century when the economy remained dominated by manual labour and the traditional 'heavy' industries remained significant, the workplace could be energy-sapping, dangerous and capable of incubating a range of chronic occupational diseases. Perhaps those sectors associated with inhaling toxic dust, chemicals and carcinogens were the most insidious. To a degree, workers' bodies were sacrificed at the temple of Fordism. The legacy was blighted communities of disabled workers, and of untold and unimaginable pain and suffering as individuals and families coped as best they could with fatalities and injured and diseased bodies, together with the identity transformations that could entail.

As the economy morphed, so too did the pattern of employment-related injury and disease. Mortality and injury rates dropped sharply as the UK shifted in the second half of the twentieth century to a service sector, knowledge based economy where non-manual labour predominated in an increasingly deregulated and 'open' market. As an additional 'bonus', the environmental pollution associated with a carbon-based Fordist economy also dissipated. Nonetheless, new threats to the body emerged in this changed employment context, with the discovery of new carcinogens in chemical manufacture, the growth of RSIs, MSDs and workplace stress. The modern-day stress epidemic in the workplace is just one manifestation of a recurring cycle whereby employment has proven capable of both enhancing health and well-being, whilst also simultaneously making workers ill, disabling and destroying minds and bodies. A recent study has shown how developments in more insecure and non-standard work since the 1980s have exacerbated occupational ill-health, including stress, and how this remains a major challenge to occupational health and safety regulators in the UK (Robinson and Smallman, 2006).

In trying to understand and make sense of this, interpretations range widely within the scholarship on occupational health in what is a hotly contested intellectual landscape. Debates have pivoted around the culpability of corporate capitalism, the extent to which state regulation achieved its objectives, the role of medicine and medical research, whether the trade unions were pro-active enough on health and the extent to which workers' cultures and attitudes influenced risky and health-threatening behaviour at the point of production. An embodied history of work needs to take account of how workers are positioned within intersecting exploitative systems of capitalism and patriarchy which constitute threats to their health and well-being. To understand this we need to explore *both* the mechanisms of capitalist exploitation and managerial pressure within the parameters of a competitive market economy and the prevailing, fluid and mutating work cultures and identities, including how gender, race, ethnicity and age intersect to encourage a toleration of overwork and risky behaviour which damages bodies. This is where personal testimony is so valuable. Work-life narratives – including oral testimonies and autobiographies – provide a barometer, laying bare mutating identities and revealing work and health cultures that ultimately impinged upon the body. Wolkowitz's seminal recent study (2006) is an indication that attention is being increasingly devoted to embodiment in the workplace. We require more such work to elucidate our understanding of the complex interactions between work, the body, health and emotions in employment, both past and present.

6

Representation and Resistance

> This branch done a lot. We happened to belong to a trade union. We fought... I mean we walked the streets for 26 weeks to get conditions. We were the ones that forced them to give us tables and chairs to sit down to have a meal with, made them give us a changing room to hang our clothes up. (Hugh Cairney, Glasgow shipyard worker, interviewed by Neil Rafeek, 16 March 2005 SOHC 016/A30)

This is how a retired asbestos insulation lagger who worked in the Clydeside shipyards from 1947 to the 1980s articulated his identification with a trade union. Unions were the main voluntary organizations representing workers and a key agency in the power struggle in the post-war workplace. In a similar vein a West Indian factory worker in London reflected in an interview in 1980:

> I like to be in one [a trade union] because they will help you with the management. You may be working somewhere and the management victimises you and you then have the unions to fight for you, or you might have an accident and the unions will be behind you – things like that. (Cited in Phizacklea and Miles, 1980, p. 121)

These fragments of testimony emphasize the protective function of collective organization, the role of individual agency, the empowerment which solidarity provided, the importance of the local, branch 'rank and file' level and counterpoise 'them' and 'us' – the villains and the heroes in workplace struggles. They nicely frame the main aims of modern trade unionism in capitalist societies: to defend and advance workers' interests. The extracts put primacy on the requirement to resist and 'fight' for workers' rights in a conflictual relationship. Other personal testimonies suggest industrial relations were more consensual, whilst some were more critical and negative towards the unions, regarding them as overly powerful, with much resentment expressed towards being forced to join where 'closed shops' existed. Some personal accounts focused on trade union racism or misogynist neglect of women workers, the distancing of the leaders from their constituency, and what were regarded as their narrow, economistic aims (see, for example, Phizachlea and Miles, 1980, pp. 90–126). Unions are thus popularly perceived across a wide spectrum from villains to saviours, with many hues of grey in between. Individual workers could hold widely differing and sometimes contradictory perceptions of the place of trade unions within society.

In the Second World War and the post-war period trade unions became an established feature of the industrial relations landscape in Britain, assuming an unprecedented level of importance in regulating the workplace and influencing workers' lives. Before the Second World War their existence was still relatively fragile and their coverage and influence (politically and in the workplace) uneven. Unions became firmly embedded in the workplace from the 1940s and were widely accepted as part of the very fabric of British society and politics. This chapter examines industrial relations in the post-war period, explores what trade unionism meant to workers and how it impacted on working lives, locating this within the changing nature of post-war capitalism, employers' strategies and management regimes. How did workers and their trade unions respond to and resist managerial exploitation and protect and advance the interests of their members? Structural inequality may well define the capitalist workplace in the UK, but workers were agents in this too, with different capacities and capabilities to organize and mediate employers' attempts to control and subordinate them.

How these changes have been interpreted and understood vary significantly. For some, post-war capitalism became more humanized and benign, with employers accepting 'social responsibility' and becoming willing to accept the devolution of aspects of work control and take more cognizance of the 'human factor' in employment. To others, capitalism remained at core exploitative and any reforms were 'tactical', designed to ensure the survival and hegemony of private enterprise in a period when nationalization was popular and trade unions more powerful – at least up to the 1980s. The unions themselves were viewed at the time and judged subsequently in varied ways: at one extreme as overly powerful and irresponsibly militant – and blamed for undermining the competitiveness of the British economy and causing its decline;

at the other as critically important agencies in protecting workers' rights and dignity at work, neutralizing the most exploitative aspects of competitive free-market capitalism. What is evident is the diversity of experience within a heterogeneous movement and the divisions within the working classes which fed through into policies which undermined the capacities of trade unions to protect workers.

Trade unions were absolutely pivotal in providing a protective matrix, maintaining and extending dignity and respect at work for vulnerable workers in a harsh and brutal competitive free-enterprise economy. Within the post-war workplace the unions represented the interests of workers in an unequal relationship with employers and managers. This was so because power and decision-making resided at the top and the notion that those who provided the capital had the prerogative to manage as they thought fit was a long-standing and sacrosanct one in Britain. That said, in practice how power was exercised within the UK's market economy ranged widely as British capitalism was no monolithic entity but rather a myriad of competing units operating in diverse, complex and changing markets. Employer and managerial strategies diverged across a spectrum from coercive and unilateral control (where trade unions were not tolerated) through benevolent paternalism to cooperative and consensual joint regulation of the workplace, where trade union closed shops (the compulsory enforcement of full trade union membership in a workplace) were accepted and sometimes welcomed by the bosses. Workplace power was also affected by the broader economic, social, cultural and political environment. In practice, statutory limits had been established to prevent the worst excesses of competitive free-market capitalism – so employers' behaviour was tempered by legislation (for example outlawing child labour and regulating maximum working hours) and government monitoring (as in factory and mines safety inspections). In 1920, Carter Goodrich developed the idea of a power struggle across a shifting 'frontier of control' to define relations between capital and labour and his conceptualization of power and authority ebbing and flowing is a useful one that will be deployed here in our reflections on industrial relations, trade unions and the British workplace after 1945.

Industrial relations, workplace power and the trade unions, 1945–79

The environment in which workers toiled and trade unions operated in the immediate post-war period was a challenging one. The economy was undermined by the costs of war and production capacity had been severely affected by wartime bombing. Managerial incompetence, complacency and nepotism was omnipresent across large segments of the economy and the city, with outmoded attitudes prevalent in many (though by no means all) sections of industry from Boards of Directors through to middle management (Kynaston, 2007, p. 446; see also Tiratsoo, 1999; Perchard, 2007a). At the same time, the production imperatives of wartime had stimulated an expansion of Taylorist and Fordist mass production methods which threatened long-cherished skills and customary work practices. The productivity drive of the immediate post-war years consolidated and extended these developments, with widespread interest in and enthusiasm for American management methods, time and motion study, the Bedaux 'scientific' management system and an attack on 'restrictive practices'. The latter was supported by some trade union leaders. The 1950s and 1960s were to be the heyday of Fordist 'flow' production methods. Concurrently, the economy was restructuring with the shifting of capital from the older, traditional heavy industries to lighter engineering and consumer goods and to the financial and services sector. There was an evident tension between a modernizing economic sector and an obsolete and archaic one. This was further complicated by the expansion of the public sector in the post-war nationalization of swathes of industry, including coal mining in 1947. Whilst private enterprise continued to dominate in this mixed economy, by the 1950s around a fifth of the nation's GDP was generated by the public sector.

The trade unions played a key role in the industrial relations system that developed in Britain in the first half of the twentieth century. After a period of decline and contraction during the interwar period of mass unemployment, the Second World War witnessed a significant surge in workers' power and representation on the shop floor and a marked growth in trade union membership. The unions' wartime role brought them enhanced status and the leadership more respect. Full employment, the extension of public ownership and a more favourable socio-political context facilitated this, including the broadly supportive position of the post-war Attlee-led Labour government. The National Coal Board, for example, was one of the largest industrial concerns in the world, with an output in the 1950s almost matching that of the entire European Coal and Steel Community. The nationalized industries and public sector played a key role in promoting white-collar and managerial unionization too, generally supporting the closed shop and giving all trade unions a voice in formal bargaining structures (for example, see Strangleman, 2004, on British Rail; Perchard, 2007a, on the NCB).

In this new 'social order' workers flooded into the trade unions in the 1940s and membership was up by around 50% between 1939 and 1950 (rising from 6.3 to 9.3 million). This resulted in a sharp shift in the balance of power to the advantage of labour, especially when compared to the 1930s Depression. This was facilitated by state policy, both in wartime and by the post-war Labour governments. For example, as wartime Minister of Labour, Bevin had improved the wages of the low paid, extended trade union recognition and massively increased the scope of collective bargaining, not least through the creation of new Joint Industrial Councils and Wages Boards which provided minimum wages and collective bargaining rights for the lowest paid and poorly organized sectors of the labour force. *Mass Observation* were amongst those who registered the changing balance of power in the workplace and the revival of the shop stewards' movement in wartime (Mass Observation, 1942; see McIvor, 2001, pp. 226–9).

Wages and conditions of work for similar types of labour were becoming more standardized throughout the economy as a consequence of this surge in trade union membership and state intervention in employment, combined with a move to national collective bargaining and reduction in local bargaining. More liberal employment and welfare legislation underpinned these developments, including the symbolic repeal in 1946 of the much resented Trade Disputes and Trade Union Act (1927) which had been passed in the aftermath of labour's defeat in the General Strike two decades earlier. The National Insurance (Industrial Injuries) Act (1946) was also indicative of a changed climate, providing much improved benefits to workers and their families adversely affected by occupation-related accidents and chronic disease. The latter was part and parcel of the post-war Welfare State which directly impacted on working lives, not least in that it placed a floor under wages, extending significantly the 'social' wage. The statutory raising of the school leaving age to 15 in 1947 and to 16 in 1972 also played a part in labour market regulation and the maintenance of full employment. In campaigning and negotiating on these and other issues, the trade unions found themselves drawn into decision-making in a tripartite system of industrial relations (albeit one that allowed trade unions to comment and negotiate only on a limited set of issues) with strong representation at the top level in the corridors of political power for the Trades Union Congress. As Richard Price noted:

> If the underlying structures of social relations remained undisturbed, the actual balance of power at the workplace tended to shift in labour's favour and was protected from counterattack by the political circumstances of the time. The Welfare State and the commitment to full employment in Britain entrenched the power of labour in society. (Price, 1986, p. 215)

All this restrained managerial rights and prerogatives. As Findlay and McKinlay noted: 'Managerial prerogative was the employers' right to hire labour, allocate work, and exercise discipline of the shop floor' (Findlay and McKinlay, 2004, p. 61). Protecting the latter was the primary function of the employers' movement and was enshrined in collective agreements, such as the 'Terms of Settlement' in the engineering sector agreed in 1897–8. At least formally in engineering the unions were powerless to initiate any action until the official disputes procedure had been exhausted. In practice, however, unofficial 'wildcat' strikes occurred which ignored the established collective bargaining and disputes procedures.

The key challenge came on the shop floor where manufacturing industry witnessed a sharp increase in activity amongst shop stewards in the post-war years. Increasingly, as Zweig noted in 1951, employers and managers were forced to acquiesce to shop steward and trade union negotiated agreements on a range of issues previously considered to be the terrain of unilateral management decision-making, including productivity issues, overtime, piecework, bonus payment and seniority promotion arrangements (Zweig, 1951, pp. 15–18; see also Coates, 1982, p. 162). This picked up on and extended the encroachments into managerial terrain that marked the wartime Joint Production Committees (Hinton, 1994). Workers' control and work regulation extended in tandem at both the workplace and the national level with the further extension of collective bargaining agreements on a wide range of work-related matters. As Zweig commented in 1951: 'every single industry works now under a comprehensive code of rules, controls and regulations... freedom of enterprise has gone not only through state interference, but even more so through collective agreements' (Zweig, p. 24). And Arthur Deakin, the general secretary of one of the largest unions at this time (Transport and General Workers' Union) suggested that the trade unions were now able 'to take care of the workers' – unlike in the 1930s when they were relatively powerless (cited in Whiteside, 1996, p. 109). The early post-war gains were also achieved with relatively low levels of strike activity prior to the first significant post-war strike wave of 1957–62. Cronin argues that this period of relative quiescence in industrial relations was the product of broad satisfaction with post-war full employment, little price inflation and steady if modest real wage rises (Cronin, 1979, pp. 139–40). An interwar Depression mentality was evident everywhere, influencing 'the moderate and security-oriented expectations of workers' (Cronin, 1979, p. 139). Cronin continued: 'the aims and expectations of working people were stable and restrained at least into the early 1960s' (Cronin, 1979, p. 141). Gains for workers across the 'frontier of control' were clearly made in the 1940s and 1950s, however, sustained by an expanding labour movement (see Table 6.1 below) shored up by full employment, the legitimization of its power by employment legislation and a post-war consensus in its favour.

Whilst the 1950s represented a period of stability rather than growth in trade union membership (with little change over 1948–65 and a slight fall in trade union density), the influence of the unions at both the national and the workplace level was broadly maintained and even extended. The Conservative administrations of 1951 to 1964 continued to work with the unions in a period of broad political consensus and this facilitated the embedding of union power in this period (Hamish Fraser, 1999, pp. 198–204). Attempts by management to tighten labour discipline could be strenuously opposed, as in the car industry at Ford's Briggs Motors plant in 1955 when the sacking of a convenor led to an all-out strike and at Standard (car manufacturers) where managerial aggression (on so-called 'restrictive practices') and redundancies threatened industrial relations in 1956–7 (Price,

Table 6.1 Trade union membership 1945–1974 (in millions and % of potential members)

	Male		Female		Total	
1945	6.1	45.1%	1.6	24.8%	7.7	38.6%
1950	7.4	54.0%	1.6	23.7%	9.0	43.8%
1955	7.7	55.0%	1.8	24.2%	9.5	44.2%
1960	7.6	53.1%	1.9	25.1%	9.5	43.5%
1965	7.6	51.5%	2.1	26.3%	9.7	42.6%
1970	8.0	56.4%	2.6	31.5%	10.6	47.2%
1974	8.2	59.1%	3.1	34.0%	11.2	49.2%

Source: Bain and Price, 1980, p. 40.

1986, pp. 217–8; Cronin, 1979, p. 140). And employers' hands could be weakened, as in the engineering and shipbuilding dispute in 1957 when the government refused to back up the more hawkish stance by the Engineering Employers' Federation and some of its own Cabinet ministers and contributed to the breaking of its own incomes restraint policy. This was when Frank Cousins, the left-wing leader of the largest union in the UK, the TGWU (Transport and General Workers' Union), had faced down the Tory government declaring: 'Whilst prices rise wages must rise with them' (Kynaston, 2009, p. 649). In the aftermath, Macmillan confirmed his commitment to full employment and industrial peace.

Price has characterized government policy in industrial relations in this period as 'crisis avoidance' (Price, 1986, p. 220) and trade union power was also bolstered by strong public support. In a Gallup poll in 1955 only 18% said they thought unions were a 'bad thing' whereas 67% thought them a 'good thing' (Kynaston, 2009, p. 486). Strike activity was rising from the mid-1950s and the activities of a more assertive 'down tools' labour movement was satirized in the 1959 movie, *I'm All Right Jack*, starring Peter Sellers. The film's scathing ridiculing of the unions and portrayal of them as overly powerful was a message that was much resented by active trade unionists (and one that was to revive strongly in the 1980s). The reality was that Britain was not particularly strike-prone in the 1950s and 1960s, positioned about mid-way in the 'league table' of strike activity in the developed capitalist countries (Wrigley, 2007, p. 219). Moreover (and significantly), far more working days were lost through sickness and occupational injuries than strike activity in this period up to the 1970s.

It is important to place the gains made by the workers and their trade unions in the immediate post-war decades in perspective. Trade union membership remained uneven across the economy – as Table 6.2 indicates – and, crucially, the labour movement remained in many respects a very conservative one, disproportionately representing the interests of the dominant majority male white membership. The movement officially condemned (but in reality condoned and to a degree legitimized) sexism and racism at this time (as we observed in Chapters 3 and 4). This has to be understood, however, in the context of workers' insecurities linked to memories of the 1930s Depression, growing immigration, concerns over loss of orders (and hence threats to jobs) as the Empire disintegrated – all of which required time to digest, understand and accept. In her survey of working-class cultures up to 1960, Joanna Bourke has made the point that: 'Although the

Table 6.2 Trade union density (% of potential membership) by sector/industry, 1965

Agriculture	24.4
Fishing	47.2
Coal mining	92.8
Other mining & quarrying	44.5
Food and drink	31.4
Chemicals	36.1
Metals & engineering	54.2
Cotton, flax & man-made fibres	81.3
Other textiles	32.3
Clothing	32.8
Footwear	72.5
Pottery	62.7
Timber & furniture	36.6
Printing	84.6
Construction	35.7
Gas	69.1
Electricity	71.6
Water	54.0
Railways	83.9
Road transport	86.9
Sea transport	83.7
Port & inland transport	79.7
Distribution	11.5
Insurance, banking & finance	30.3
Health services	33.8
Local government & education	65.7
National government	79.0

Source: Bain and Price, 1980, pp. 43–78.

threat of unemployment as it was experienced between the wars was removed, it never lost its power to compel workers to adopt defensive economic and political strategies' (Bourke, 1994, p. 109). The working classes as a whole were also weakened by internal divisions and the failure of the trade union movement to transcend these and proactively campaign on equal rights and opportunities before the 1970s (Phizacklea and Miles, 1980, pp. 96–8). The number of strikes on such issues by women and BME workers in the 1950s, 1960s and into the 1970s which trade unions failed to make official and provide their support for is testament to this narrow-minded and short-sighted sectarianism. Moreover, the coverage of the unions remained uneven and patchy across the economy. In their study of one particularly militant region, for example, Findlay and McKinlay found that whilst the shop stewards' movement grew on Clydeside it remained 'extremely fragile' up to the 1960s, 'an uneven, partial and hesitant process' and argued for a revision of the popular conception of the post-war era as a 'golden age' for organized labour (Findlay and McKinlay, 2004, p. 65). Whilst some Clydeside workplaces were very well organized – such as Rolls-Royce – such 'strongholds' were not the norm, coverage was patchy and could be 'precarious' (Findlay and McKinlay, 2004, pp. 56–7).

Whilst the principle of managerial authority remained largely intact (indicated in the limited enthusiasm for real workers' control), and bosses retained the authority to *initiate* change in many areas (crucially in labour processes, work organization and technological change), the informal system of industrial relations which extended inexorably in the 1940s, 1950s and 1960s led to a marked expansion of workers' power and participation in decision-making across work-related issues in industry. This was something recognized by the Royal Commission on Trade Unions and Industrial Relations (commonly called the Donovan Report) in the later 1960s. It noted the extent of influence of the unions on the shop floor, the spread of 'protective' (or 'restrictive') practices enshrined in custom and practice and the existence of two connected but separate industrial relations systems at the national and workplace levels. The latter 'informal system' was becoming increasingly significant in the regulation of earnings, creating an issue with upward 'wage drift' from nationally agreed rates. At this point there were around 175,000 shop stewards in British workplaces, and around 3,000 full-time trade union officials (RC on Trade Unions and Industrial Relations, Report, pp. 25–6).

Much depended on whether and to what extent individual bosses and companies were willing to recognize and work with trade unions. Employers were influenced by the structures and environment in which they operated, though they were also capable, as Zeitlin has argued for engineering, of taking 'strategic choices' (Zeitlin, 2004, pp. 123–52). There coexisted a considerable range of different styles of management, industrial relations and work regimes, from the old-style autocratic boss, through liberal welfarist and paternalist employers, to more progressive, bureaucratized and modern managerial systems (see Melling and Booth, 2008). The nationalized industries were examples of the latter, and a real divergence was beginning to emerge between the public and the private sector. As Perchard's work on the nationalized coal industry in the 1950s and 1960s has shown, managerial styles and methods also ranged widely and company managers could be independent social actors and not necessarily the conduits through which the policies of employers or the managing board were transmitted wholesale to the labour force (Perchard, 2007a). In the private sector, company mergers and takeovers frequently provided the opportunity for corporate capital to initiate reorganization, new investment and 'rationalization' – a process identified by one trade union convenor in engineering as forming 'the core of our struggle' (cited in Fraser, 1999, p. 109). Such restructuring represented a constant threat to established work practices and to livelihoods, with the threat of redundancies and work intensification. Changing market circumstances also provided the opportunity for localized and industry-wide employer counter-attacks to contain and roll back the tide of trade union encroachments into managerial decision-making (for example with the privatization of utilities (gas, electricity, telecommunications) and deregulation of public transport).

In relatively remote locations, paternalist company cultures could also continue to exert control over labour. An example would be British Aluminium in the Scottish Highlands. Perchard highlights how 'the company achieved hegemony in their panopticons of Kinlochleven and Inverlochy that has been as culturally enduring as it was, at the time, socially effective' (Perchard, 2007b, p. 65; see also Perchard, 2012). This forged attachment to the firm and an enduring loyalty amongst the workers. One British Aluminium employee, Alexander Walker, reflected in an interview:

> I was a very strong union man... We had disputes with management eh and we always resolved them, because there was never any danger of us going... too far, which I don't think management at the time appreciated, because it wasn't a job, it was a community... although we were really in dispute with the management, we could go and we could sit down with them afterwards and have a drink. (Cited in Perchard, 2007b, p. 64)

Perchard's recent work on the aluminium industry demonstrates in a really nuanced and reflective way how social relations in these communities unfolded within unequal power relations, and where outcomes represented a negotiated settlement, with trade unions and communities mediating the hegemony of the corporation (see Perchard, 2012).

Whilst work regimes varied widely, so too did the penetration of trade unionism and the capacity of workers to challenge, resist and mediate exploitation at work. The power of the trade unions in their heyday has been much hyped and considerably exaggerated. The popular, stereotypical view of union omnipotence in the post-war years needs serious qualification. Union membership was patchy and uneven in the 1950s and 1960s (see Table 6.2 above), with markedly lower levels of organization amongst particular industries/sectors (clerical; retail and distribution; agricultural workers) and amongst female workers and private sector white-collar workers. John Grigg, a London bank clerk, recalled being the only member of the Banking Insurance and Finance Union in the branch he worked at in the 1950s: 'that was frowned upon by other members of staff... Some people thought it was absolutely disgraceful! They absolutely hated trade unions' (Britain at Work interview, by Roraima Joebear, 28 June 2010). A Scottish librarian (Alan White, born 1938) never joined a trade union and his work-life testimony is almost the antithesis of the 'activist' or 'alienated' narrative (interviewed by Ian MacDougall, 22 August 1996, SWPHT Collection). For librarians, this breached entrenched notions of respectability linked to their work ethic. A local librarian in Ayrshire (Margaret Crawford) noted:

> I wasn't a union member... And I'm saying, 'I can't go on strike. Imagine my Brownies passing the library and the library's closed because Mrs Crawford's on strike.' [Laughs] So I didn't go on strike. (Interviewed by Ian MacDougall, 3 March 2002, SWPHT Collection)

In his early days as a journalist Ron Thompson signed the non-union pledge at D.C. Thomson in Dundee with no hesitation as he explained he had no union tradition in his family (his father came from an army background) and was brought up in a non-political, non-religious household. Trade unionism – such a key motif in 'activist' memories and narratives – had no meaning to him in this period of his working life (Ron Thompson, interviewed by Ian MacDougall, 7 July 1999, SWPHT Collection). Even when trade union membership peaked in the mid-late 1970s over 40% of all British employees were not trade union members.

In workplaces where the trade unions did have a strong presence, the narratives of post-war workers provided testimony to workers' ability to challenge, resist and mediate managerial exploitation, and the pivotal protective role the union fulfilled. Tight labour markets helped to shift the balance of power in the workplace. Sillitoe had his working-class factory worker character Arthur Seaton express something of this in the 1958 novel *Saturday Night Sunday Morning*:

> The thousands that worked there took home good wages. No more short-time like before the war, or getting the sack if you stood ten minutes in the lavatory reading your *Football Post* – if the gaffer got on to you now you

could always tell him where to put the job and go somewhere else. (Sillitoe, 1958, p. 27)

Edward Sutcliffe, a northern (Burnley) factory worker recalled in the late 1960s:

> There is much less tension between management and men now; the feel-
> ing of exploitation isn't so evident... The threat of the sack is not so potent
> now; bad-timekeeping is condoned to a surprising extent... and the old
> type of foreman or manager who prowled around looking for idlers is no
> longer present... the iron hand of authority is less in evidence. (Sutcliffe, in
> Fraser, 1969, p. 293)

Robert Doyle, a union official in the warehouse of the print conglom-
erate IPC, described how the strong trade union presence there con-
tained managerial power, notably their aspirations to bring in new
technology to displace labour: 'the printworkers have been highly
successful through their trade union strength in holding on to their
jobs' (Doyle in Fraser, 1968, p. 25). Despite his admission that the
work was 'over-staffed' he negotiated full union consultation on any
redundancies:

> They know, of course, that if they arbitrarily attempted to dismiss our
> members, they would be threatened with a close down of the *Mirror*, *Sun*
> and other sections of the IPC. While we remain strong they have to negoti-
> ate. (Doyle in Fraser, 1968, p. 24)

Another union official (Phillip Higgs) noted in the late 1960s how
the struggle for control over piecework wage payments radicalized
workers: 'The continual battle over rates makes the workers very
militant, for when the rate-fixer comes out to argue with you, you're
immediately faced with the basic element of the class struggle:
exploitation, potential or actual' (Higgs in Fraser, 1969, pp. 112–3).
Price has made the point that by the late 1960s the unions were win-
ning this particular battle: 'The scientific determination of rates had
been subordinated to the manipulation of rates to secure a decent
wage' (Price, 1986, p. 224). But the work of the unions invariably
extended beyond negotiating members' wage rates. At the heart of
the role of the union was resistance to managerial exploitation and
protection and extension of workers' fundamental right to respect
and dignity at work. A toolmaker Jack Pomlet put this very well in
the late 1960s:

> Certainly the union was the organization which we looked to in the strug-
> gle to increase wages, but it was by no means its only function, and perhaps

not even its prime function. For me the union was 'us' and 'ours'. It stood between us and the power of the foremen and under-managers to direct us at will. It was the collective instrument by which we asserted our right partly to control our daily destiny. The union stood between us and that concept of slavery and degradation called 'managerial prerogative'... At the bottom of the instinct for trade unionism lies the instinct of the worker to be a fully integrated creative being, finding his salvation through work. (Pomlet in Fraser, 1969, p. 31)

Sheet metal working was a well-organized sector post-Second World War and one London sheet metal worker, Frank Cooper, commented on how the National Union of Sheet Metal Workers controlled entry to the job: 'If a man came there for a job, the first person he was sent to see was the shop steward. If the shop steward was satisfied that his union ticket was in order, he'd go and talk it over with the foreman and get a start' (Britain at Work interview, by Peter Atherton, 10 March 2010). Strikes to raise wages and protect workers' rights were common in the trade in the post-war years. In one case Frank recalled an unusual strike to get a sacked foreman reinstated:

But no, he was a good bloke and something went on in the factory and they decided to give him his dismissal ... We didn't know why ... When we asked to see the management they said it doesn't affect you sheet metal workers on the floor, get on with your job. We have the right to manage our factory in the way that we think. And we just went out and said unless they told us the reasons why the foreman was sacked we wouldn't return to work.

This dispute laid bare the struggle for control that characterized manufacturing industry in the post-war years, and in this case the power of a strong workplace trade union. The unofficial strike led directly to the reinstatement of the sacked foreman.

Collective organization was capable of providing a meaningful protective matrix. This was demonstrated, for example, in the 1950s and 1960s in construction in Stevenage. In 1951 the unfair sacking of an Irish building labourer (Kevin Murphy) galvanized fellow workers to a 100% strike threat which resulted in his reinstatement. Thereafter, the site became a closed shop with the unions struggling to improve pay, working conditions and health and safety, including successfully opposing the 'lump' system in the town (non-union labour-only subcontracting, with payment by lump sums). Unusually for the building industry, the Stevenage area was characterized by strong trade unionism led by a cadre of experienced and committed activists. As one Stevenage building worker recalled:

> I'm proud to say that I think Stevenage new town was built by 90% trade union labour, and very successfully as well. I'm not talking about getting away with anything at all. I'm talking about working conditions and good relationships with employers. (Ted Oswick; cited at www.buildingworkersstories.com)

Another reflected: 'You couldn't get on without a union card. There was no such thing as the lump or anything like that. They wouldn't allow the lump in here then' (Luke Donovan). And Arthur Utting claimed: 'Stevenage was known as the hotbed right through the unions, one of the best organised areas in the country really' (cited at www.buildingworkersstories.com).

And resistance assumed many forms. There was the all-out strike which increased in incidence from the late 1960s. Hyman's insightful study of strikes in 1972 argued that a key aim of the strike was that 'workers can impose limits to management's control over them' and that was why management regarded strikes as a problem, more so than the actual lost production and profit (Hyman, 1972, p. 160). The six-week 1972 national building strike, for example, won significant improvements in the basic wage (25–30%). Many trade unions used the sectional or rolling strike to spread gains throughout the industry with the minimum of pain to their members (Fraser, 1999, pp. 113–4). Elsewhere individuals or work groups sabotaged management-imposed wage payment systems by going slow or 'working to rule' (Fraser, 1999, p. 133; see also Price, 1986, p. 227). Creating teams or gangs was another tactic that helped to strengthen workers in their struggles with employers – described by one union convenor as 'a powerful weapon in the struggle for control, because the employer can no longer pick on the individual worker' (Fraser, 1999, pp. 116–17). This tactic was exploited very effectively, for example, on the docks (RC on Trade Unions and Industrial Relations, Report, p. 27). The use of the 'closed shop' accelerated sharply (and to a surprising extent with managerial support; see Price, 1986), and this significantly strengthened the unions' capacity to extent their control into managerial terrain. Wrigley has estimated that in the late 1970s some 27% of trade unionists were in closed shops, which were widespread in coal mining, metal working, printing and shipbuilding (Wrigley, 2007, p. 209). Where the unions were strongest they acted as a labour exchange,

controlling entry, and exerted influence over promotion and the allo-
cation of work – on London Transport, for example, through the 'seniority' system (based on date on entering railway employment) and in
printing through the unions issuing 'green cards' to members enabling
them to seek work elsewhere.

Fundamental to the trade unions' role was representation. In the
workplace, shop stewards and convenors supported individual workers in wage, disciplinary and other disputes with management. Martin
Eady, who joined London Transport in 1973, became a shop steward
in the National Union of Railwaymen at a time when they had 100%
membership and management were forced to consult on virtually everything. He recalled representing members in numerous disciplinary
cases and saving jobs where previously they would have been summar-
ily sacked. 'You're a bit like a lawyer in a court', Martin commented,
'They don't have to be innocent. You give them the best chance, as
the defence lawyer for them'. In one case, for example, a member who
came to work 'roaring drunk' and hit a foreman was got off with a
one-day suspension. The offender went on to settle down and eventually worked his way up and became a manager. Martin made the point
that:

> But he could so easily have been bounced out, if he hadn't had the union
> there to represent him. Because it's not ... how good you are in front of the
> management as a union rep. does help, but what's behind you is all the rest
> of the people on the shop floor. (Britain at Work interview by Dave Welsh
> and Roraima Joebear, 20 May 2010)

One shipyard shop steward in the 1960s, Matt McGinn, penned a
poem 'Can O' Tea' to express the solidarity of the community when
one union activist was sacked:

> But the men said I'd been victimised
> For the Union I had organised
> So when I laid down my can o' tea
> A thousand men marched out with me

> (Cited in Bellamy, 2001, p. 164)

Still, the capacity of workers and their unions to regulate work, resist
exploitation and maintain dignity in their employment varied considerably across the economy. Whilst workers' rights were improving
and union power extending, nonetheless there remained a large non-
unionized sector where employment conditions remained poor. We
know far less about industrial relations in the jumble of small firms

and sectors on the periphery of the economy, whilst our vision has tended to be distorted by the big industrial relations confrontations in mining, transport, the docks and manufacturing. In many UK workplaces employers were staunchly anti-union and did not tolerate any interference in their unilateral authority to manage their labour as they thought fit. These were what one worker called 'bloody-minded company managements' (cited in Fraser, 1969, p. 119). One example was the textile company in Brighton that Mike Taylor worked briefly for in 1966–7. Taylor recalled how 40 or so largely immigrant workers put in a 72-hour week of six 12-hour shifts operating the fast-moving machinery in a really stressful atmosphere. There was a high labour turnover and frequent sackings. A national union agreement covered the type of work being done, but this non-union company paid only half the union-agreed wage rate. The work regime was gruelling and demoralizing, leading to what Taylor described as 'psychological degeneration' with workers expressing 'resentment at being treated like dirt, expendable, brought in as objects and pushed out again when we had ceased to serve' (Taylor in Fraser, 1969, pp. 95–6). In response, Taylor organized a branch of the National Union of Hosiery and Knitwear Workers and began recruiting his fellow workers. The company responded in true Victorian fashion by sacking all those who joined the union, reiterating its open shop stance and initiating a lock-out declaring: 'this is a small family firm and a trade union has no place or position in it' (Taylor in Fraser, 1969, p. 98). The workers picketed the factory for eight months, fighting for what Taylor called 'the dignity of labour', before accepting defeat (Taylor in Fraser, 1969, p. 102).

The Fidelity Radio factory in North Kensington became something of a cause celebre in the 1970s. It employed around 450 mainly Asian and Caribbean workers, roughly 50:50 men and women. There was no union and work conditions were appalling. A key issue was the very low basic wage, which was supplemented with a complicated and arbitrary bonus system (which represented around half of total earnings) which was utilized by management to discipline the workforce. So overtime was systemic and virtually compulsory to make up the wage and the long working hours and what one observer called 'the frenetic pace of the production line' (Britain at Work interview with Jan O'Malley by Dave Welsh, 18 August 2011) led directly to overstrain, stress and exhaustion. Management shifted workers at will from skilled to unskilled work and sackings were common for minor offences, such as being late for work. In 1974 Jan O'Malley was involved with a local community activist group called the Notting Hill People's Association and they tried to assist Fidelity workers to organize and resist what Jan called 'tyrannical management'. There followed a long and bitter struggle for trade union recognition at the factory through 1974 and 1975, with outside community support triggering a surge in union membership and organization within the plant and a series of successes in getting wage rises and improvements in conditions, including an extra week's holiday. The company countered with selective sackings of activists which undermined the nascent shop stewards' organization and ended up moving the factory out to Acton. Fidelity was one example of a wave of union recognition struggles in West London and elsewhere in the 1970s. Jan O'Malley reflected that there were lessons to be learnt from the dispute: 'Community struggles on their own can never win. Industrial struggles are stronger if they have community support.'

The Grunwick dispute provides another example. A mostly female Asian workforce went on strike in the summer of 1976 at this film-processing company in London protesting about unfair dismissals, low wages and grim working conditions. The authoritarian employer (George Ward) rejected all efforts to mediate, refused the arbitration of the government's Arbitration and Conciliation Advisory Service (ACAS) and ignored the results of a Court of Inquiry, whilst the women, with strong support from their trade union and the local trades council, held out on strike for two long years (Reid, 2004, pp. 354–5; Fraser, 1999, p. 232). Grunwick was significant in indicating the persistence of hard-core anti-trade unionism amongst a rump of British employers, though such a position was increasingly viewed as anachronistic. It also indicated the capacity of a politically moderate trade union (the Association of Professional, Executive, Clerical and Computer Staffs) to hold out in defence of workers' rights – though in this case ultimately unsuccessfully.

The building trade was another notoriously poorly organized sector. One London bricklayer described conditions on the sites in the 1960s as 'deplorable', not much better than those famously described by Robert Tressell in the classic novel *Ragged Trousered Philanthropists* before the First World War, with the trade unions having little or no influence outside a minority of unionized sites (Gagg in Fraser, 1969, pp. 134–5). 'The building unions are in a sorry state', he wrote, continuing 'the unions for most bricklayers cease to exist. It is not unusual for men not to know the current union rate of pay... most building workers are selfishly individualistic' (Gagg in Fraser, 1969, p. 136). The situation was particularly bad amongst the building trade subcontractors and smaller sites. A bricklayer, Fred Udell, described a tyrannical subcontractor and appalling conditions working on the new town Stevenage in the 1950s: 'I said, "George, where's the toilet?". He said, "toilet? What do you want a toilet for?". I said, "well, what do you use a toilet for...I need to go". You know what he said: "You shit in your own time, not mine!". That was the atmosphere' (www.buildingworkersstories.com; online booklet, *Building a Community*, 2011, p. 14). Victimization of labour activists was also rife in the building trade, aided by 'vetting' blacklisting organizations such as the Economic League.

Other areas where workers were poorly organized and particularly vulnerable were agriculture, fishing, clerical work, banks and financial services, shops, hotels and catering. The growth of multinational foreign-owned 'branch plant' companies provided another source of difficulty for workers where they were openly anti-union, such as the American-owned IBM plant in Greenock and the US oil companies in the North Sea. As Gregor Gall has shown, the offshore North Sea oil and gas industry was characterized from the 1970s to the 2000s by: 'employer dominance, union marginalisation and limited state regulation in the employment relationship' (Gall, 2006, p. 51). Union recognition was not conceded in the North Sea until the early 2000s, in marked contrast to the well unionized oil and gas sector in Norway (which was largely state owned – Statoil). As noted earlier, this virtually unregulated work regime contributed to the Piper Alpha oil platform disaster where 167 men lost their lives (Gall, 2006, pp. 51–69; Beck et al., 1996; Brotherstone and Manson, 2007; Woolfson and Beck, 2005). Clearly, even in the heyday of trade union power in the UK, many workers remained vulnerable and subject to autocratic management and unilateral employer decision-making.

Underpinning workers' rights in this period was a body of employment law that was relatively favourable to labour. After the repeal of the Trades Disputes and Trade Union Act in 1946, workers had the clear right to organize, to strike and to picket, whilst trade unions had significant immunities in law protecting their funds against sequestration for damages in industrial disputes. A new Factories Act in 1961, the Contract of Employment Act, 1963 (which provided a minimum period of notice when a work contract was being terminated) and the Redundancy Payments Act 1965 (providing minimum financial compensation on termination of contracts) all contributed to improving working conditions and employee rights in the 1960s and 1970s. Unfair dismissal was also made illegal with the Industrial Relations Act 1971 and industrial tribunals set up several years later with the Trade Union and Industrial Relations Act 1974. Such legislation marked a period when heavy state intervention and regulation of labour markets was a central component of policy. The Health and Safety at Work Act, 1974 marked another important watershed for workers and was indicative of a shift in policy on the part of the trade unions towards the greater prioritization of occupational health and safety (see Chapter 5). Workers were reaping the benefits of aggressive campaigning, a strong economy and the growing political influence of the trade unions in the decades immediately following the Second World War. Real wages (that is taking price inflation into account) also almost doubled between 1945 and 1980, whilst non-wage benefits (such as holidays and pensions) also improved substantially, as did the state welfare 'safety net'.

Important advances were also made in addressing unequal opportunities and unequal treatment in the labour market and the workplace. This body of legislation, which included the Disabled Persons (Employment) Act 1944, the Race Relations Act 1965, the Equal Pay Act 1970 and the Sex Discrimination Act 1975) was campaigned for by the trade unions amongst an 'alliance' of progressive groups (including the feminist movement) and agencies. The provisions – or 'benefits'– applied across the labour force for unorganized as well as organized labour. In that respect the influence of the trade union's 'protective' role extended far beyond its membership to shape the experience of work and the employment contract in quite fundamental ways. Writing in 1981, Baker and Caldwell commented that 'unions, through both action and achievement, can justly claim to have become the industrial voice of working people' (Baker and Caldwell, 1981, p. 171).

What is clear is that this was a period when both the trade unions and the state played pivotal roles in structuring and regulating the workplace and that at least up to the 1970s this did impact positively on the sense of respect and dignity in work felt by large segments of the labour force. The statutory Wages Councils, for example, provided a basic minimum wage for considerable numbers of the lowest paid and most marginalized workers in the economy for several decades from the 1940s to the 1980s. The state also implicitly supported voluntary national collective bargaining, which expanded significantly as union membership grew. Concurrently, factory or workplace bargaining expanded, with the growing role of shop stewards, especially in productivity or local piecework wage negotiations. On Clydeside, for example, the coverage of factory bargaining rose by around 350% between 1958 and 1968 (Findlay and McKinlay, 2004, p. 63). From the employers' point of view this represented an erosion of their authority and their right to manage. This was part of an overall very favourable context in which the capacity of workplace resistance and trade union protection of workers' rights was enhanced in the period c1945–75. Crucially, the onus shifted to the workplace, with wide implications, as Findlay and McKinlay have noted: 'This process constituted a major shift in the internal power structure and culture of trade union-ism that elevated the activist over the official, and the workplace over the negotiating chamber' (Findlay and McKinlay, 2004, p. 65).

The power of the trade unions was indicated in the changing nature of strike activity – arguably the primary weapon in the workers' arse-nal of sanctions against unfair work practices and exploitative employ-ers. Studies of strike activity have shown how withdrawing labour was connected to a wider range of issues compared to pre-Second World War – including direct challenges to management authority and con-trol, such as strikes to oppose wrongful sacking of fellow employees, including trade union representatives. Strikes were also widening in intensity and impact, becoming more political (as in the series of one-day TUC initiated 'right to work' strikes: Price, 1986, p. 225). Redundancy was one issue that trade unions were struggling to gain some control over – with limited success with the 1965 Redundancy Payments Act. Struggles over the right to work – such as the campaign to save the Clyde shipyards in the 1971 Upper Clyde Shipbuilders work-in – garnered enormous community support and some (albeit limited) success in delaying and mitigating the pace of job losses across the traditional heavy industries. Discontent with rising prices and taxes eating into real wages from the mid-1960s contributed to a massive spike in working days lost through strikes over 1968–72, and conflict was exacerbated by workers' alienation with government pol-icies, including restrictive incomes policies and the ill-fated and pro-vocative anti-union Industrial Relations Act 1971 (Cronin, 1979, pp. 141–2). The latter was introduced by Edward Heath's Conservative government in an abortive attempt to limit trade union immunities and control strike action and picketing. Workers' outlook shifted from caution to belligerence to protect their living standards and the right to strike. These years witnessed a massive peak in strikes over redundancy, with working days lost through strikes on this issue ris-ing eightfold (Baker and Caldwell, 1981, p. 138). The miners perhaps epitomized this spirit of collective resistance in a series of strikes in the 1970s, expressing their frustrations at the piecemeal contraction of their industry. This phase incorporated Barbara Castle's abortive attempt to tackle strikes with *In Place of Strife* (1969), the defeat of the Heath Conservative government in 1974 and the 'winter of discontent' in 1978–9.

An important new weapon in this period of resistance was the use of mass picketing and the 'flying pickets' moving from place to place to try to neutralize employers' attempts to keep workplaces open and running. Bolstered by a favourable political and economic context, this was a period when unions were regarded as one of the 'estates of the realm'. The negotiation of the 'Social Contract', which provided a raft of benefits to the trade unions in return for a commitment to wage restraint was indicative of trade union influence (Taylor 1978; Fraser, 1999, p. 233). The late 1970s represented the peak of trade union power in post-war history – when membership spiked at over 13 million workers (1979), just a little shy of 60% of the total labour force. Representation had also rocketed in the 1960s and 1970s with the number of shop stewards increasing from 90,000 in 1961, to 175,000 by 1968 and to 250,000 by 1980 (Booth and Melling, 2008, p. 9).

With growing membership and shop steward representation came a heightened commitment to the use of the strike weapon and experimentation with other, more novel forms of industrial action, such as the factory occupation and work-in. The propensity to initiate forms of industrial action varied considerably, however, across industries and regions. Church and Outram (1998), in a wide-ranging analysis of strike activity in UK mining identified a more militant 'Celtic fringe' in Scotland and Wales. Studies of the geography of strikes in the UK have identified west-central Scotland as one of the most strike-prone regions of the UK (Gall and Jackson, 1998, pp. 97–112). John Foster has also shown that Scottish workers had a proportionately greater participation rate in the one-day 'political' strikes that punctuated the period from 1969 to 1984 (Foster, 1998, pp. 230–1). In large part, as Gall and Jackson have persuasively argued, this appears to be a product of differences in industrial/occupational structure between Scotland and England. Other factors which contributed to relatively high levels of strike activity were the persistently authoritarian, inflexible attitudes of many Scottish managers, the insecurity of working in volatile, contracting product markets in the traditional industries, and somewhat poorer working conditions (higher injury rates and poorer standards of occupational health) in Scotland compared to south of the border.

Somewhat belatedly, unionization, conflict and resistance spread to significant groups of non-manual workers – especially in the public sector – and to growing numbers of female workers. At mid-twentieth century the British labour movement remained dominated by the traditional bastions of labour in coal mining and manufacturing – with almost 80% of all trade unionists being manual workers (Bain, 1970, p. 25). Nonetheless there was a long tradition of white-collar unionism stretching back into the nineteenth century in the case of teachers, clerks, shop assistants and post office workers (Reid, 2004, p. 346). However, union densities remained low in most white-collar sectors and non-manual unions tended to refrain from the more militant forms of industrial action, with the exception of some public sector occupations, including local and central government, and the most militant of pre-war white-collar unions, the National Union of Clerks. The Second World War witnessed significant expansion and by the late 1940s there were around two million white-collar trade unionists. Growth was slow over the subsequent two decades – with the trade union movement clearly failing to adapt to the changing labour market and membership haemorrhaging amongst the traditionally well-organized manual sector at a faster rate than the modest growth amongst non-manual workers. Nonetheless, there were important successes amongst the non-manual unions in getting equal pay for women in teaching and the civil service in the 1950s (Reid, 2004, p. 351).

The key phase of growth came in the decade or so from the late 1960s. By 1980, a number of key non-manual unions were amongst the largest in the UK, including the National Association of Local Government Officers (NALGO), the National Union of Public Employees (NUPE) and the Association of Scientific, Technical and Managerial Staff (ASTMS). This contributed to a sharp rise in trade union densities amongst female workers, from around 25% in 1960 to near 40% by 1980. Public sector non-manual workers were particularly well-organized by the 1980s, whilst levels of organization in the private non-manual sector lagged significantly behind (Reid, 2004, pp. 348–9). Still, at the peak of union expansion in the mid–late 1970s only one in five private sector non-manual salaried workers were trade union members (Taylor, 1978, p. 36). Here trade unionism meant little to most workers. Frequently these employees had to take what they were given by way of work contracts and endure whatever work conditions prevailed.

Clearly the trade unions had become more important and influential in working life by the 1960s and the 1970s, but this should not imply that they were omnipotent – as the popular view implies. Power varied considerably across different industries and within different occupations, whilst to some extent the union movement undermined its own influence through internal divisions and internecine squabbles. This reflected workers' complex, intersecting and evolving identities. Unions were divided by politics and by occupation, with inter-union demarcation disputes (disagreements over what jobs should be undertaken by particular trades) especially prevalent in the shipyards and building sites. The traditional male domination of the movement also only eroded very slowly. Consequently, it took time for working women to identify with such institutions, especially when their record on key issues like equal pay was uneven and women had so little representation within positions of power in the labour movement.

As late as 1980, the British Trades Union Congress continued to legitimize traditional gender roles – for example in its recommendation that 'employers recognize that women must work the hours that allow them to fulfil their domestic responsibilities' (Phizacklea and Miles, 1980, p. 97). Few women were represented within the TUC and the higher echelons of the trade unions, which remained dominated by men. One study in 1981 found that female representation above the level of shop steward had hardly changed since a previous TUC survey in 1955 (Ellis, 1988, p. 136). The situation was virtually the same in the Scottish TUC. In 1980, there was only one woman on the General Council of the STUC and only 7 per cent of the delegates to the STUC General Congress were women (McIvor, 1992, pp. 165–7; see also Breitenbach, 1982).

Change, however, did come. The late 1960s and the 1970s witnessed the British trade union movement responding to economic, social and cultural changes in two important and fundamental ways – by refocusing on and prioritizing the rights of minority and under-privileged workers, including women and black and ethnic minorities and significantly shifting strategy on health and safety at work. Belatedly, the worst aspects of sexism were shrugged off – evident in trade union campaigning for the Equal Pay Act 1970 and the Sex Discrimination Act 1975 and in the growth of positive discrimination to ensure female representation in union decision-making. Equal rights and opportunities committees proliferated and the TUC targeted widening female participation. The National Union of Public Employees, for example, created seats on its National Executive for women. Other unions, such as the National Association of Local Government Officers and the National Association of Teachers in Further and Higher Education, campaigned on childcare and nursery provision as key equality issues (Baker and Caldwell, 1981, pp. 47–9), whilst health and safety issues were taken up more vigorously and effectively from mid-1970s (see Eva and Oswald, 1981). Significantly, however, it was not until 2012 that the first female (Frances O'Grady) advanced to the position of TUC General Secretary.

Around the historic peak of trade union power in the UK, Phizacklea and Miles' London based study, *Labour and Racism*, provides a glimpse into the range of attitudes workers themselves exhibited towards collective organization. Most respondents indicated that they joined a union for the representation, support and benefits membership conferred. Most articulated this in terms of what the union could provide for them as individuals in quite an instrumental fashion and saw the core union role as protection and improvement of work conditions (Phizacklea and Miles, 1980, pp. 101–5). In response to being asked why they had become a union member one worker noted: 'You join it because it speaks for you'. Another said: 'If anyone pushes you around they help us'. A further comment was: 'what the management would like to do to the workers is prevented by the unions, so we are protected'. Another said: 'Now I know that personally in the union I am slightly more secure' (Phizacklea and Miles, 1980, pp. 102–3). Respondents articulated a sense that the union enabled them to resist managerial exploitation and control – acting as a buffer between their individual weakness and the power of the employers. 'The importance of unions to a majority of our respondents', Phizacklea and Miles commented, 'is as a means of asserting a degree of autonomy in the work process and obtaining what they regard as an adequate material return... Joining the union is therefore similar to taking out an insurance policy' (Phizacklea and Miles, 1980, pp. 121–2). Despite mostly lacking a trade union tradition before migration, and notwithstanding the prevailing racism within segments of the trade union movement in the 1950s and 1960s, large numbers of BME workers joined unions, a reflection, Phizacklea and Miles assert, of their strong identities as *workers* and members of the (largely manual) working class (Phizacklea and Miles, 1980, p. 104). By the 1970s, as we've seen, BME workers were slightly better organized than white workers.

Were trade unions overly powerful? This was a recurring motif in workers' oral testimonies, undoubtedly much influenced by a powerful discourse within the media from the late 1970s on. An electronic technician who worked in two spells in 1965–70 and 1985–2003 at the US firm Gillette's in London said in an interview in 2009: 'I've never had to be in a trade union. I'm not against trade unions, but some of the things that go on, from what we are shown on the television' (Britain at Work, interview 2009/008; anonymous). However, this notion that unions were omnipotent is a myth – albeit an enduring one. Trade unions fundamentally remained reactive and defensive – responding to changes imposed and pressures generated by market forces and hierarchies of authority on the shop floor. Taylor made the point in his 1978 study of trade union power:

> Far more decisive power rests with the senior civil servants in Whitehall, the financial houses of the City of London, in the boardrooms of the big companies, not in the headquarters of the various unions or even Congress House. (Taylor, 1978, p. 172)

The attitudes and policies of companies continued to exert a powerful influence on whether workers were union members or not. Where unions were unwelcome, by employers and managers with both authoritarian and welfarist attitudes, they rarely thrived. The Gillette factory in London was an example of the latter where a comprehensive welfarist regime, including generous company pensions, extensive medical, physiotheraphy and dental facilities, free protective clothing, a Christmas bonus and a Work Committee, operated to undermine the foundations of collective organization.

However, what was viewed as poor industrial relations and high strike proneness within a section of strategically important industries led to growing claims that productivity – and hence national economic performance – was being compromised by what Booth and Melling refer to as 'business cultures and labour practices' (Booth and Melling, 2008; see also Bufton, 2004). Concerns grew about the impact of strikes on economic performance, resulting upward wage drift from nationally-negotiated wage agreements through local wage bargaining and the 'informal' system of industrial relations as well as the prevalence of what were increasingly being termed 'restrictive practices'. Whatever the reality, public opinion was shifting in the mid–late 1970s towards the view that trade unions had become too powerful (Taylor, 1978, pp. 13–16). Particularly unpopular was the closed shop – something which was seen by some as 'bullying' and an infringement on individual liberty to choose (Fraser, 1999, p. 231). This marked the beginnings of a seismic shift which culminated in the election of a radical-right-wing Conservative government in 1979 and Thatcher's rejection of the post-war policy of maintaining full employment, a liberal pro-union statutory regime and the prioritization of industrial peace. Coinciding with a period of economic recession, partly itself politically generated, this marked a pivotal watershed in industrial relations and the power of workers and their trade unions to resist managerial authority at the point of production and maintain standards of living, job security and the dignity of labour.

Deregulation, power and resistance in the UK workplace since 1980

The political and economic context in which trade unions operated altered quite dramatically with the economic recession of the 1980s and the political assault on the trade unions associated with Thatcherism. Bill Siepmann, a London Transport railway guard and active trade unionist summed up what this meant to him:

> That was the era in which the organized working class as I understood it and knew it, was just completely flattened and defeated. It was the Thatcher era. I can remember in '79 looking at the Conservative manifesto and thinking, 'Nah, they'll never do that!'. Because I'd grown up in the era of what was known as Butskellism, there were certain things that were agreed, there was a consensus between the Labour and the Conservative parties...Thatcher's was an ideological government. They were driven by free market economics...I was just flabbergasted that this could happen. (Britain at Work interview by Dave Welsh, 2 July 2010)

As McInnes' study has shown, Thatcherism seriously undermined the unions and their powers to resist the vagaries of the free market and to uphold the dignity of labour (McInnes, 1987).

Spurred by a radical conservative philosophy the Thatcher administration moved quickly to pass legislation to neuter the power of the unions, targeting their traditional legal immunities. The Employment Act 1982 attacked the closed shop whilst the Trade Union Act, 1984 introduced the pre-strike secret union ballot. The Wages Act 1986 sharply prescribed the work of the Wages Councils in setting minimum wages whilst further Employment Acts in 1988 and 1990 tightened the ballot rules on the trade unions' political levy to the Labour Party, eroded the powers of the industrial tribunals to protect unfairly sacked workers and made unions directly accountable for the unofficial actions of their members. The Trade Union Reform and Employment Rights Act, 1993, further curtailed trade union rights and restrained collective bargaining. It included the introduction of a one-week compulsory prior notice of a strike and the complete abolition of the Wages Councils. This wide-ranging and quite unprecedented spate of vicious anti-trade union legislation seriously undermined the capacity of the labour movement to organize, strike and effectively resist exploitation at the point of production. Concurrently, the Tory governments moved progressively to isolate the trade unions and exclude them from political decision-making, reversing the trend from the Second World War of integrating union officials into government committees and quangos on all matters relating to the economy (see Fraser, 1999, pp. 230–54).

Bolstered by the political turn to neo-liberal policies and encroaching market deregulation, a reinvigorated and more decentralized employers' movement spearheaded a campaign to revive managerial authority, create open shops and force more flexibility on the workforce. Concurrently, employers exploited growing unemployment as a disciplining force. This led to increased workloads and a pervasive intensification of work (see Beynon et al., 2002). This occurred more and more at the plant or firm level as employers' associations (the equivalent of trade unions for employers) atrophied in a period of increasingly decentralized industrial relations and disorganized capital. At peak about half of all British employers were members of employers' associations. By 1990 only 13% of UK companies were members of these bodies (Wrigley, 2007, p. 210; for the earlier period see McIvor, 1996). The Confederation of British Industries (CBI) continued to spearhead the employers' movement, though it operated more as the voice of capital at Westminster and as a figurehead, with the key initiatives being taken across the boardrooms of British companies.

These changes in the market and the political environment shifted power back to employers and management, both encouraging and facilitating experimentation with a series of new strategies to control labour, cut labour costs and maximize capital accumulation. For example, in London Transport management had been threatening to make one driver operation without guards universal since the 1960s. The National Union of Railwaymen (NUR) held out for almost two decades before conceding in the mid-1980s, undermined by support for the change from the other main railway union, the Associated

Society of Locomotive Engineers and Firemen (ASLEF: representing
the train drivers). Despite strike action led by the enigmatic Jimmy
Knapp, thousands of guards lost their jobs in the 'rationalization' that
ensued, whilst train drivers' wages went up. What followed was a managerial assault on the seniority system and an attack on the established
negotiating machinery (Martin Eady, Britain at Work interview by
David Welsh and Roraima Joebear, 20 May 2010). Management could
exploit trade union divisions within the sector and union membership
haemorrhaged in the aftermath as relations between the NUR and
ASLEF (who were accused of 'selling out' the guards) became more
strained.

Other companies sought to exploit the economic recession to
squeeze labour costs and undermine trade unionism. A wood machinist Alan Tyrell recalled how managerial discipline tightened where he
worked in the 1980s in P&O Ferries, with a spate of sackings and
deteriorating health and safety standards. Alan was sacked in 1988
for protesting against the abolition of overtime rates. He recalled one
of the directors saying: ' "Well, I don't think you're a company man.
Get rid of him!" And I was escorted down to my office, told to get
all my papers. I asked if I could speak to my union rep. I was told,
"no". I was escorted out of the building' (Britain at Work interview by
Dave Welsh, 29 June 2010). John Oswell got a job driving tankers for
Esso Petroleum in 1973 and stayed with the company for 24 years. He
described in an oral history interview how it was initially a great job
with good pay and benefits, and how Esso Europe was a closed shop,
much to the chagrin of the parent company Exxon (one of the biggest
corporations in the world) in the USA. The work environment and
labour contract changed though in the later 1980s and into the 1990s.
The closed shop was abolished and Esso cut costs by switching to contract rather than directly employed drivers. By this stage John was a
TGWU shop steward, a health and safety officer and a Labour Party
activist. He recalled the culmination of this managerial offensive was
the scrapping of all trade union collective agreements:

> 1991 we basically were sold out. A directive had come from Exxon in the
> United States that they wanted all...trade union agreements scrapped.
> They didn't want any more trade union movements and activity in their
> terminals and they were instructed to offer us, and the plant operatives,
> staff status...Three years earlier in 1988 they closed our workshops down
> and made all our vehicle fitters redundant and they put it out to contract
> using the same premises. In fact it [the staff status] was a very good deal
> money-wise but I didn't want it and a lot of my comrades didn't want it

either. We didn't want our trade union agreements scrapped. We liked them because they gave us an awful lot of protection. And it meant that we could no longer negotiate anything at all. Anything at all. And they could do exactly what they wanted...They wanted the trade union movement out of the oil industry basically. (Britain at Work interview by Dave Welsh, 19 January 2011)

Whilst the West London depot that John worked from held out for some time, the process of de-recognizing the union and imposing 'staff' working conditions progressed relentlessly. Amongst the changes were a much more pressurized, intense work regime, facilitated by much closer monitoring of the labour process, enhanced by technology such as tachographs, mobile phones and cab computers. Pretty favourable job times negotiated under the union agreements in the 'grey book' were thus 'whittled down'. John left the job a few years after, taking early retirement in 1995 after a car accident left him incapacitated.

Whilst Fordist managerial regimes dominated in the immediate post-war decades (see Melling and Booth, 2008; Wood, 1982; Thompson, 1983), the late twentieth century saw the emergence of new management techniques and adaptations of Taylorism associated with 'lean production' or 'flexible accumulation' – producing goods or services to order (sometimes referred to as 'just in time' production) according to the needs of the market in a flexible, bespoke fashion as distinct from Fordist mass production (Strangleman and Warren, 2008, pp. 129, 194). To some theorists this was simply an adaptation of Taylorism, with heightened levels of work intensification, whilst to others it was qualitatively different (see Beynon et al., 2002; Burchell et al., 2002). One outcome was a sharper focus on the management of human resources (HRM) – referred to by Braverman as 'the maintenance crew' of capitalism (Braverman, 1974, p. 60). Another was more evasive methods of monitoring, supervision and surveillance, ranging from listening in to call centre workers' phone conversations to the annual 'accountability and development' reviews in professions such as teaching and lecturing. In trying to understand such developments some commentators have drawn upon the ideas of Foucault (see his concept of the 'panopticon') – for example see Perchard, 2012 – and how discipline is built into systems to facilitate 'self management' and 'self-exploitation'. Strangleman and Warren argue that these recent developments in labour management are characterized by 'a tendency to individualise the relationships between employer and the employee'. They continue: 'This fragmentation leads to a situation where the employee is potentially more vulnerable in terms of control exercised by the organisation, and this leads to a situation where individuals internalise disciplinary codes' (Strangleman and Warren, 2008, p. 195). Associated with this was the growth of temporary contracts and less job security – non-standard forms of work – a process facilitated by the revival of neo-liberal ideologies within the context of radical Conservative governments from the election of Thatcher in 1979. In employment this frequently translated into companies shedding permanent labour and establishing a two-tier system of core and peripheral labour to give maximum flexibility to respond to markets/consumer demand (Strangleman and Warren, 2008, pp. 130–1). That said, it is also clear that as in the earlier period, older forms of labour control and management overlapped with new forms – and the penetration of 'flexible accumulation' did not go unchallenged and should not be exaggerated. A range of employer attitudes towards trade unions and representation continued to coexist, and hostility to trade unions never reached the levels of the USA (Kochan, 2003, pp. 166–77; Gospel and Wood, 2003, p. 13).

Worker autonomy and control could also be undermined by direct political interference in the workplace. For example, in education the imposition upon teachers of the hugely controversial National Curriculum in 1984–5 was widely resented. Jan Pollock started teaching history in London in 1971, reflecting: 'It was the History Department itself that decided on the curriculum, and that was four of us ... we were left to do what we liked. And I found out very early on that kids respond to history being taught to them when it's angled to the things they know about in the present' (Britain at Work interview by Dave Welsh and Roraima Joebear, 13 May 2010). Jan was amongst those free-spirited teachers pioneering integrated Humanities teaching and new novel approaches to educating in the 1970s and 1980s:

> When I taught in Brixton in '85 and there was the Brixton riots, I chucked all the history we were doing out of the window and we did the history of rioting for a week. And I must say, the kids were most interested and were very good at discussing whilst picking glass out of each others heads and so on.

The introduction of the National Curriculum changed teaching methods and content irrevocably. Jan commented: 'I found it was a terrible straightjacket ... to me it was just a straightjacket imposed by the government, which meant, like I said, so you couldn't mould the curriculum to suit the kids you were teaching'. She left teaching as a consequence, remarking: 'I didn't want to teach in schools if I was going to be dictated to'.

Belligerent employer coercion and unilateralism was also re-energized as the economic recession deepened. Militant shop stewards and convenors were again sacked and victimized, as in the notorious case of Derek Robinson – 'Red Robbo' – at British Leyland in 1980. National collective bargaining was progressively undermined as employers moved increasingly back towards individual and plant-level bargaining, performance-related pay and unilateral imposition of new, less favourable labour contracts. The bonus payments systems in the banks and the financial services sector would be an example – where deskilling through technological change was also much in evidence, as Margaret Taylor (a union activist from the Halifax Bank of Scotland) recently noted (Ellis and Taylor, 2010, pp. 803–12). And the state moved towards administering a lesson to organized labour which would redefine industrial relations for a generation.

The target was what was traditionally the most strike-prone and militant of all the trade unions – the miners. The defeat of the miners in 1984–5 marked a watershed in British industrial relations. Scotland and Yorkshire were the two areas that initially campaigned for wider action to protect miners' jobs in the face of further pit closures, leading to the National Union of Mineworkers calling an all-out strike across the industry, involving some 140,000 miners. The miners exhibited a characteristic display of cameraderie, resilience and courage against massive and insurmountable odds, with the Thatcher government marshalling the full force of the state to crush the strike (though in the event the new anti-picketing legislation was not used). The dispute was characterized by much violence, especially in clashes between pickets and police at Ravenscraig, Hunterston, and at Orgreave, Bilston Glen and Monktonhall collieries. An important supportive role was played in the strike by miners' wives in pit communities up and down the country. The miners held out for a year in one of the most remarkable episodes of trade union solidarity and militancy in British history. They returned, defeated and demoralized, with many activists subsequently sacked by the NCB for their part in the conflict, especially in the more militant areas like Yorkshire and Scotland – including 46 from Monktonhall colliery, the greatest number of victimized men from any single colliery in the UK (see Duncan, 2005, pp. 259–66). Jim Phillips' recent work has added fundamentally to our understanding of this conflict by demonstrating in a very nuanced and sophisticated way the complex array of factors and differing levels of resource which contributed to local and regional levels of support for and solidarity in the strike in Scotland (Phillips, 2009; 2011). The coal industry contracted sharply thereafter to employ just a few thousand underground miners by the 2000s. The defeat sent reverberations across the labour movement, contributing to a sense of powerlessness and demoralization.

In the 1980s union membership declined sharply and strike activity shrunk back as workers and the labour movement adjusted to the new political and market realities. From the late 1970s peak, union membership in the UK fell from more than 13 million to around 7 million over the subsequent 20 years, a drop of almost 40% (Bradley et al., 2000, p. 155). By 2010 there were just 6.3 million trade union members in the UK – at 26% of the labour force this represented the lowest level since the 1930s (Achur, 2010). And membership patterns changed significantly – as Table 6.3 indicates. By the early twenty-first century manual workers were considerably less likely to be union members than professionals.

The decline of the well unionized employment sectors in industry and the public sector and the growth of the least well-organized private service sector jobs, as well as the erosion of working-class identity and changing cultural values have been commonly implicated in the diminishing importance of the trade unions, as has the resurgence of small-scale employment and self-employment (Bradley et al., 2000, pp. 149–5,; 153). The density of union membership fell in manufacturing to below 20% by 2010, and in construction to just 15%. A confident and confrontationist trade movement gave way to a

Table 6.3 Trade union density by major occupational groups, 2010

Managers and senior officials	15.1
Professionals	43.5
Associate professional and technical occupations	40.1
Administrative and secretarial occupations	21.0
Skilled trade occupations	21.9
Personal service occupations	30.7
Sales and customer service occupations	12.9
Process, plant and machine operatives	28.7
Elementary occupations	18.3

Source: Adapted from data from the Office for National Statistics, *Labour Force Survey*. Licensed under the Open Government Licence v.1.0.

weaker, more cooperative and quiescent one. Between 1984 and 1990 the proportion of the labour force covered by collective bargaining agreements fell from 71% to 54% (Fraser, 1999, pp. 248–9) as 'de-recognition' advanced. The employers' open shop offensive was particularly marked in shipping and the newspaper industry (Bradley et al., 2000, pp. 153–4). This impacted particularly adversely upon the weak and the vulnerable in the labour market, who were also hit hard by the abolition of the Wages Councils. Another hugely symbolic defeat came with the abolition of the Dock Labour Scheme in 1989. This had been set up in the aftermath of the Second World War to ban casualization and establish joint regulation of wages and conditions. Its scrapping in 1989 marked a key moment in the shift to deregulation and the pendulum swing towards the empowering of employers, as Jim Phillips has noted:

> Many casual practices were subsequently restored. These included the substitution of basic salaries with hourly wage rates, the disappearance of contracted hours, the frequent re-arrangement of shift patterns at short notice, and considerable uncertainty about bonus, overtime and holiday entitlements. Worse still, there was a reported increase in accidents, including fatalities. (Phillips, 2007, p. 227)

Attitudinal surveys in the 1990s indicated workers becoming more aware of growing job insecurity, poorer industrial relations and the widening wage gap and their lack of power regarding workplace decision-making (Bradley et al., 2000, p. 163). Whilst union membership held up relatively well in the public sector, collective organization remained much weaker amongst private sector workers and young workers. Strike activity reached the lowest figures in recorded history (from 1888) in the 1990s when working days lost averaged less than 5% of the levels recorded in the 1970s (Wrigley, 2007, p. 217). Working days lost from strikes in the 1990s were four times lower than they had been in wartime, when strikes were illegal. In part, this reflected the wider erosion of work and class based collectivism and the growth of individualism across developed capitalist economies, as Bradley et al. argued in 2000:

> The ongoing fall in aggregate trade union membership in many Western economies not only appears to bear out the view that adversarial industrial relations are relatively insignificant now, but it also indicates that the decline of trade unionism may well be the expression of long-term social change. (Bradley et al., 2000, p. 157)

With these changes, the nature of trade unionism was also mutating, especially, perhaps in the industrial heartlands of the movement. As Knox has observed: 'The newly dominant service sector and white-collar unions, with their socially diverse working constituencies, cannot hope to forge such intense solidarities among their members' (Knox, 1999, p. 295). By 2010, trade unionism had a presence predominantly in the public sector, with little representation in the private sector, and female workers were slightly better organized, with about 30% members, than male workers (around 25%). Concurrently, strike activity declined sharply. In the 1970s there were almost 27,000 recorded strikes, with working days lost through strikes averaging 12.8 million per year. By the early 1990s the number of strikes had fallen to 200–300 a year and working days lost to less than a million per annum (Mitchell, 1998, p. 182). By the 2000s, strikes in the private sector were a relatively rare occurrence, as Table 6.4 illustrates:

Amongst the key problems for the trade unions, as the contributors to a comprehensive study into trade union membership and representation by Gospel and Wood in 2003 indicated, were a failure to recruit

Table 6.4 Working days lost due to industrial disputes, 1996–2010 (000s)

	Private sector	Public sector
1996	299	856
1997	163	71
1998	165	117
1999	172	70
2000	136	363
2001	128	397
2002	200	1123
2003	130	369
2004	163	742
2005	59	99
2006	98	656
2007	39	1002
2008	48	711
2009	87	368
2010	56	314

Source: Adapted from data from the Office for National Statistics, *Labour Force Survey*. Licensed under the Open Government Licence v.1.0.

amongst young workers and a failure to get union recognition in new workplaces (see, for example, Machin, 2003, pp. 15–28; Freeman and Diamond, 2003, pp. 29–50).

Whilst resistance to workplace exploitation may have been centred around the trade unions, they were not the exclusive agents of such activity. It would be wrong to assume that there was no workplace resistance where the unions did not have a presence. Moreover, the historical exclusivity and sectionalism of the trade unions left a void that to some extent was filled by other voluntary organizations. Resistance germinated, persisted and developed on an individual and workgroup basis – for example with regulating output, absenteeism, workplace theft, use of the internet for unauthorized purposes, and moving jobs – in an attempt to break monotony, relieve work stress and impose some control over work. Other agencies existed which championed workers' rights on equality and citizenship issues – such as the Equal Opportunities Commission and the Race Relations Board – sometimes working with and sometimes independently from the trade unions. The growth of environmental and occupational health pressure groups are also significant here, such as Nancy Tait's Society for the Prevention of Asbestos and Industrial Related Diseases (SPAID) and local agencies, such as Clydeside Action on Asbestos (CAA). In part, at least, these latter organizations were formed from a nucleus of workers and relatives of workers who felt disgruntled at what they regarded as the failures of the trade union movement to prioritize issues relating to the damage caused to workers' bodies from toxic and carcinogenic substances in the 1970s and 1980s. In the case of SPAID and CAA, they could be extremely effective as Parliamentary lobby groups and as welfare and advice agencies for workers who were victims of work-related diseases (McDougall, 2013).

Did the assault on the trade unions in the 1980s and 1990s result in the capitulation or irrelevance of organized labour? Far from it. Indeed there is a strong argument that the trade unions proved remarkably adaptable and resilient in the face of the multi-faceted offensive against them in the last quarter of the twentieth century. Assertions about the 'death of trade unionism' are premature. The reality is more complex. Bradley et al. have argued persuasively that trade unions should not be written off and that the labour movement retained a powerful presence in the workplace at the turn of the twenty-first century, indicated in examples of successful industrial action and union renewal across a swathe of sectors – including the finance sector, public services (such as the NHS) and car manufacture (e.g. the strikes at Vauxhall Motors, 1995–6) and the London underground (1998) (Bradley et al., 2000, pp. 157–62). NALGO, as Ironside and Seifert have shown, was amongst those unions who battled aggressively to support members and resist public sector cuts, privatization, work intensification, deskilling and degradation in the labour process (Ironside and Seifert, 2000). And whilst representation and collective bargaining eroded, still in 2001 one survey found 36% of UK workers were covered by collective agreements – of which, interestingly, 5.5 million were trade union members and 3.4 million non-members (Wrigley, 2007, p. 220). A decade later in 2010 the proportion of workers covered by collective agreements stood at 30% (Achur, 2010, p. 2). Moreover, the political context changed again with the election of three successive Labour governments from 1997 to 2010. Whilst Blair and New Labour did not remove all the anti-union legislation of the Tory era and remained committed to neo-liberal policies, including a lightly regulated labour market, several modest but significant changes occurred. The legal control of low pay had been undermined in the Thatcher years with the rescinding of the Fair Wages resolution in 1986 and the scrapping of the Wages Councils and the Agricultural Wages Board. Blair reintroduced a degree of regulation, not least with the introduction of the legal minimum wage in 1999, together with improved rights in the case of unfair dismissal and union recognition (enshrined in the Employment Relations Act, 1999). Both helped to underpin dignity at work and stabilize the unions to some extent (slowing down somewhat the rate of membership decline). Together with some improvement in job opportunities and labour markets, these initiatives helped to underpin trade union power in the workplace and sustain new employment rights campaigns in the 2000s, including agitation for equal pay for low paid female public sector workers (fulfilling the promise of the legislation passed three decades previously).

Another important and sometimes neglected factor which helps to explain trade union resilience and the maintenance of employment rights is the influence of the European market and European law. Governments could choose to ignore European Union Directives on labour and employment issues – but political and public pressure frequently had an effect. David Walker, a former shop steward and union activist, observed that European labour directives constituted a vital lever in shop floor negotiations with management in the 1980s and 1990s. European employment directives were influential in a wide range of employment rights issues in the UK, ranging from the revision of the Equal Pay Act in 1984, to parental leave changes in the later 1990s and the outlawing of age discrimination in employment in the 2000s.

What is evident is that there continued to be a strong demand for collective organizations in contemporary Britain, not least in order to protect workers against the worst excesses of hostile authoritarian management. The changes in managerial policies, labour process change, growing job insecurity and work intensification and pressures from globalization which characterized the 1990s and 2000s continued to put pressure upon individual workers and provide the *raison d'etre* for trade unionism. Whilst shorn of some of their power and much of their exclusivity from the 1960s and 1970s, the trade union movement clearly remains a pivotal and necessary protective agency in the contemporary UK workplace. The stabilization of membership in the 2000s suggests that pessimistic prognoses of terminal decline were premature and that the trade unions remain embedded institutions within British society, widely recognized and accepted and still capable of playing a key role in protecting working lives and advancing the dignity of labour in the British workplace. It also paid off financially to be a union member. Trade union members continued to earn a higher wage on average than non-trade unionists, with hourly earnings running at 16% higher in 2009–10 – though this had fallen from a wage premium of 26% in 1995 (Achur, 2010, p. 33).

Conclusion

The workplace was characterized by an adversarial power struggle between capital and labour in the immediate post-war decades. Workers and their organizations actively resisted managerial and corporate exploitation and the initiative ebbed and flowed in an ongoing power struggle, influenced by prevailing economic and political circumstances. Working lives in the UK were intimately affected by the wider industrial relations and political and economic context, and what is clearly evident is that from the 1940s to the 1970s trade unions developed to become powerful institutions and part of the fabric of British society. Workers' collective identities in this period were especially strong, particularly in the proletarian strongholds of coal mining areas and industrial conurbations like Clydeside, Merseyside, Tyneside and South Wales. The trade union *movement* also received strong support in this era from the media and from within their communities. Whilst it has been argued here that it would be erroneous to regard the unions in their heyday as overly powerful and omnipotent (not least because of their own sectionalism and conservatism regarding important segments of the labour force, including the disabled, BME workers and women), clearly collective organization thrived in the three decades or so following the Second World War.

This favourable set of economic, social, cultural and political circumstances unravelled in the 1980s. Trade unions and strike activity came under attack and were critically undermined by the return of mass unemployment and a multi-pronged counter-offensive by big business, Thatcher and successive Tory governments from 1979 to 1997. As a consequence trade unionism atrophied, especially in the private sector. Nonetheless, despite severe setbacks, the trade union movement remained firmly entrenched within British society in the early twenty-first century. Whether the unions ever come to exert as much influence over people's lives as they did in their heyday from the Second World War to the 1970s, however, remains to be seen.

The oral and autobiographical narratives of workers themselves reveal much about what trade unionism signified to workers in this period. What is clear from such testimonies is that historically these institutions have performed a vital role in protecting the interests of the individual in the workplace. Without such collective organizations, individual workers would have been (and would continue to be) subjected without redress to the vicious vagaries of the free, unregulated market. In the UK, most working lives were spent within an exploitative, profit-orientated system, in which labour cost the workers more than their time and exertion – it could also seriously threaten and indeed undermine their health (see Chapter 5). The unions represented workers and played no small part in transforming the deference-based, exploitative master and servant relationship of the Victorian period, creating in its stead communities of workplace citizens with an extensive array of inalienable rights and a reflexive commitment to collective organization and resistance to defend themselves. This was no mean achievement, and one we would do well not to forget in our consumer-orientated, materialist and individualistic age.

7

Loss

Being without work was a horrible experience. It came to me as a complete surprise... After a number of rejections I started to think 'well, whatever's wrong with me?' Your self-confidence goes lower and lower. You
start to think that even applying is a waste of time. You're sure you won't
get it. Then you get diffident and start to avoid people. I felt I was worthless and useless... My finances soon led me to look for any kind of job. I
wasn't choosy... For most people, their job is their main reason for living.
If you can't do that, you feel you're on the scrap-heap; you feel a burden to
society... Even though I've got a job now, I'm not using myself to my full
capacities, nor anywhere near it. This happens to a lot of women. It's being
stretched that gives you satisfaction. Not using the skills you have, you
feel it's such a waste... Here I'm the lowest of the low. (Mrs Tysoe; cited in
Seabrook, 1982, pp. 209–12)

This is how one married woman in her 40s in Bolton described the
experience of losing work in an interview with Jeremy Seabrook in
1981. She was made redundant in 1978 from her non-manual job as an
accounts clerk and later found manual work in a textile factory. Her
evocative narrative oozes with what work signified to her – both in
extrinsic (the money) and intrinsic terms (job satisfaction and independence). One gets an impression of just how central fulfilling work
was to this woman's life and how diminished that life was without it.
Her testimony lends support to the idea that by this time the meaning of employment differed little according to gender. Expressions
such as 'useless', 'burden', 'worthless' and 'waste' combined with the
deployment of the 'scrap-heap' metaphor – commonly recurring in
unemployed workers' narratives – indicate a profound sense of loss of
self-esteem, autonomy and purpose.

This chapter explores the meaning of losing employment in the post-Second World War era. It is built on the premise that understanding the lived experience of being without employment can aid our comprehension of the significance of work. Work was such a common and accepted part of life that it was largely taken for granted and its importance in people's lives was sharply exposed when work was lost. The growth of mass and long-term unemployment from the late 1970s led some commentators to argue that this enforced 'idleness' eroded the will to work, whilst others, such as Jahoda (1982) argued quite the opposite – that the experience demonstrated the significance of employment and its centrality in people's lives (see Russell, in Jowell, 1998, pp. 77–9). This chapter provides a review of the literature and the data, a synthesis of the core studies of unemployment and draws upon some of the ethnographic studies and the personal accounts of those without work, including oral testimonies, to explore how being without employment in modern society affected people's lives.

Measuring unemployment

Calculating unemployment rates accurately are notoriously difficult, not least because the numbers of people *registered* as unemployed or those getting state benefits for unemployment significantly under-represent those actually out of work and seeking employment. To at least the 1980s female unemployment rates were seriously under-counted because of prevailing attitudes about domestic roles and the sexual division of labour, as well as restrictions on married women's right to claim benefit. (*Labour Research*, September 1981, 70(9), p. 189). Moreover, governments have had a political incentive to try to minimize unemployment levels and so have massaged the figures downward. This happened most blatantly with the Thatcher administrations – there were 30 such 'adjustments' in the way unemployment was measured between 1979 and 1989 (Edgell, 2006, p. 104). *Labour Research* estimated that in the mid-1990s the official figures represented only about half of those out of work and wanting employment (*Labour Research*, May 1997, 21). Unemployment in mining communities, for example, was seriously underestimated in official figures because of an increasing tendency to classify those out of work and economically 'inactive' as permanently sick, disabled and early retired (Fieldhouse and Hollywood, 1999; Coates and Barratt Brown, 1997, pp. 30–3; Strangleman, 2001, p. 261). Actual unemployment rates in coalfield communities were in the region of double the official 'claimant count'. Latterly, whilst continuing to use the more restrictive 'claimant count' statistics, the UK government has also recognized (from the late 1990s) the more widely accepted ILO definition of unemployment and collected this data. The latter counts those who are not just registered and on benefits, but all those who are out of work, available for work and actively seeking paid employment (see Gazeley and Newell, 2007, p. 226; Gallie and Alm, 2000, p. 111).

Even making some allowances for reporting discrepancies, it is evident that for three decades or so from 1940 Britain experienced virtual full *male* employment (it was never the policy to have full *female* employment in the UK at this time – unlike, for example, in Sweden: Bellaby and Bellaby, 1999, p. 463). Unemployment from 1945–70 averaged around 2% (by claimant count; perhaps around 3% by the ILO criteria). This was sustained by macro-economic policies informed by Keynesian ideas and a political consensus not to return to the high unemployment levels of the 1930s. Unemployment rates began to edge up in the 1960s, rose at a higher rate in the 1970s and in the 1980s the UK witnessed a return to mass unemployment levels similar to the 1930s, with over three million out of work. The unemployment rate never fell below 7% between 1980 and 1996, peaking at 10–12% (by the ILO measure) for several years from 1980–1987 and again over 1992–4.

Like during the interwar Depression, the incidence of unemployment varied widely by class and occupation, age, gender, race and place. There were geographical pockets of very high unemployment, linked to the collapse of particular industries such as coal mining, textiles, iron and steel and shipbuilding. This could push unemployment levels in particular communities up to 30, 40, 50 per cent and even higher. With the closure of all underground mining operations, the Wingate area of Sedgefield in Tony Blair's constituency in Durham had an unemployment rate in excess of 40% in 1983 (Coates and Barratt Brown, 1997, p. 15). Between 1981 and 1994, 216,000 jobs were lost in British collieries and the labour force contracted to just 8,518 miners in 17 collieries (Fieldhouse and Hollywood, 1999, pp. 483–4). One study which examined the position of former miners in 1991 found that of those who were miners a decade before in 1981, just one in four had a full-time job (Fieldhouse and Hollywood, 1999, p. 487). Their chances of obtaining alternative work was constrained by a whole raft of factors, including the lack of local alternative job opportunities and, importantly, high levels of ill-health and disability – a cumulative legacy of working underground (McIvor and Johnston, 2007;

and see Chapter 5). Place was important, as Strangleman has shown, with local support networks vital in the search for work and the provision of childcare (Strangleman, 2001). Pessimism over job opportunities drew large numbers of miners over the age of 50 into premature retirement – the retiral rate of miners under age 65 was three times higher than the national average (Fieldhouse and Hollywood, 1999, p. 490). Of the minority of ex-miners that found work, moreover, there was marked downgrading of occupational status and a sharp fall in income (Strangleman, 2001, pp. 259–60).

According to official figures, unskilled labourers represented over half of all the unemployed in the early 1970s, and 65% of all the unemployed in North England. Less than 2% of employers, managers, professionals, foremen, supervisors and farmers were recorded as unemployed in 1970, compared to 9.3% of unskilled workers (Hill et al., 1973). Class and occupation continued to influence levels of vulnerability, with markedly lower levels of non-manual unemployment in the 1980s recession than manual workers and education levels correlating closely to unemployment rates. In the early 1980s, unemployment levels of skilled manual workers were more than twice the rate of non-manual workers, whilst unemployment rates for unskilled manual workers were double the rate of skilled manual workers and almost five times the rate of the non-manual (Burnett, 1994, p. 275). Youth unemployment rocketed to over 25% in the 1980s and a key problem emerged as the inability to get in to the labour market for these marginalized young people. This was exacerbated by a sharp contraction in unskilled jobs and apprenticeships (Burnett, 1994, p. 272; Pollock, 1997, pp. 617–18).

Older workers, over 50, were also disproportionately represented amongst the unemployed. Frequently the first to be selected for redundancy, older workers found it difficult thereafter to be re-employed, especially as manufacturing jobs atrophied and deindustrialization accelerated from the 1970s. Ageism was rife within many economic sectors, forcing older people into early retirement (see Casey and Laczko, 1989). By 1987, the economic activity rate of men aged 55–64 was down to just 67% (Johnston, 1989, p. 352 and see Johnston, 1989, pp. 64–5) and it continued to fall to the early 2000s, when the rates were 75% for 55–9 year olds and just 50% for 60–64 year olds (Duncan, 2003, pp. 101–2). The pattern for women was somewhat different, with participation rates continuing to rise sharply for those aged 55–9 in the second half of the twentieth century (Duncan, 2003, pp. 101–2).

Whilst reasons for early retirement from paid work are complex, involving both 'push' and 'pull' factors, as Duncan and Johnston have shown, it does appear that the larger share of this is the consequence of involuntary, forced redundancy and ageism, rather than personal choice (Duncan, 2003, pp. 103–5; see also Jefferys, 1989, pp. 64–7). This view has largely been supported by qualitative, interview-based research on the constraints operating on older folk in relation to employment and re-employment (Porcellato et al., 2010). Ageism has recently been embraced as part of the employment equal rights agenda, with age discrimination officially outlawed under the Employment Equality (Age) Regulations, 2006 (which enforced EU Directives from 2000) and the Equality Act (2010).

Burnett has shown the occupational and geographical differences in unemployment rates had narrowed somewhat by the 1980s depression, whilst the proportion of the jobless who were *long-term*

Table 7.1 Regional unemployment rates (percentages), 1966–2010

	1966	*1986*	*2010*
United Kingdom		11.2	7.8
England		11.3	7.7
North East	2.4	15.4	9.4
North West	1.4	13.8	8.1
Yorkshire and The Humber	1.1	12.6	9.1
East Midlands	1.0	9.9	7.4
West Midlands	0.8	12.6	8.3
East	1.4	8.1	6.8
London			9.3
South East	0.9	8.3	6.1
South West	1.7	9.5	6.1
Wales	2.7	13.9	9.0
Scotland	2.7	13.4	8.4
Northern Ireland		17.4	6.6
Britain	1.4		

Note: Unemployed as a percentage of all economically active people aged 16 and over (seasonally adjusted).

Sources: 1966 and 1986 from Burnett, 1994, p. 276; 2010: adapted from data from the Office for National Statistics, *Labour Force Survey*. Licensed under the Open Government Licence v.1.0. Figures are for second quarter 2010.

Table 7.2 Unemployment rates (%) and long-term unemployment (over one year), 2010 (by Standard Occupational Classification)

	Unemployment rates	Long-term unemployment
Managers and senior officials	3.5	8.5
Professionals	2.2	3.7
Associate professionals and technical	3.6	6.9
Admin and secretarial	5.5	9.1
Skilled trades	7.9	13.8
Personal services	4.6	5.1
Sales and customer services	9.4	8.0
Process, plant and machine operatives	9.3	14.0
Elementary occupations	13.3	30.9

Notes: Figures for first quarter 2010. See Table 1.5 for a definition of elementary occupations.

Source: Adapted from data from the Office for National Statistics, *Labour Force Survey*. Licensed under the Open Government Licence v.1.0.

unemployed was markedly higher. In the mid-1980s every four out of ten unemployed people had been jobless for more than a year (Burnett, 1994, p. 276). Geographical divergence had narrowed even further by 2010 (see Table 7.1), with a much more even distribution of the unemployed, at least at the regional level.

Vulnerability in the labour market and susceptibility to job loss varied widely across socio-economic groups right up to the present, with manual workers – both skilled and unskilled – hit hardest, as Table 7.2 indicates.

Jobless in the era of 'full employment', 1945–75

The lived experience of unemployment first became a focus of serious investigation in the economic slump of the 1930s when at peak over three million were out of work – around 15–20% of the total workforce (Gazeley and Newell, 2007, p. 225). These early studies in a period of mass unemployment across developed economies in Europe and the USA established a basic framework for understanding what loss of paid employment meant for those affected. A classic

study (published 1933) of a small single industry town in Marienthal
in Austria (where the closure of the works in 1929 led to virtually all
adult men in the community being made unemployed) by several psychologists defined a series of impacts of losing work – financial, social
and psychological. They linked loss of employment to material deprivation and poverty, but also identified a series of psychological effects
of losing of work – loss of purpose, erosion of status, identity and dignity, and corrosion of routines and personal time structure. The latter
were a legacy of the regularization of work that came with industrialization and had been inculcated first in school and cemented on the
job, not least with the process of clocking in and out. These impacts
were most pronounced where individuals were unemployed for long
periods (Jahoda, 1982, pp. 21–2).

Studies in the UK, such as Bakke (1933), Caradog Jones (1934),
the Pilgrim Trust (1938), those of political activists, such as Wal
Hannington's *The Problem of the Depressed Areas* (1936) and Ellen
Wilkinson's *The Town that Was Murdered* (1936), as well as investigative journalists and novelists from George Orwell to Edwin Muir,
provided broadly similar representations of the social disintegration,
personal degradation, humiliation and physical and mental deterioration of those without work. What was also evident from these
investigations were the wide *range* of responses, coping strategies and
different degrees of adaptation, depending, in part, upon individual,
family and community resources, as well as age, social class and gender. Reactions to unemployment included despair, a sense of release,
resignation, apathy and those who coped without their mental health
being undermined at all. At the extreme, this coalesced into a sense
of personal worthlessness, powerlessness and increasing isolation
from society. The 1930s studies defined a common 'phased' response
as individuals made the forced transition from work to unemployment. This consisted of the initial shock of losing work, followed by a
period of optimism that they would be re-employed; then pessimism
as the job search persisted; and finally fatalism and depression associated with the realisation that their situation had altered irrevocably
(Jahoda, 1982, pp. 21–2; Ashton, 1986, pp. 140–3). This was deemed
to be at least as traumatic as other life transitions, such as school to
work and work to retirement. The 'phased model' was to dominate
the thinking on the social and psychological consequences of job loss
for several decades.

Many, perhaps most, blamed themselves, influenced by a pervasive
notion, especially amongst the older generation, that the responsibility

lay with the individual, not the economic system or the state. This experience was capable of radicalizing and politicizing some (see, for example, the National Unemployed Workers Movement in the UK), though for most the effects appear to have been constraining, resulting more frequently in political indifference and social isolation (Bakke, 1933; Jahoda, 1982, p. 27). William Beveridge summed up the position of someone who had been deprived of their capacity to sell their labour in his famous bestselling report on the shape of future social services in the UK in 1942 as 'a personal catastrophe'. This was not just because of the financial implications of job loss. Beveridge understood the moral dimensions of work, seeing employment as something which not only provided personal and family economic security but also a sense of worth and value in society central to full citizenship (Sinfield, 1981, pp. 128–30).

In the main, the period from 1945 to 1975 saw the availability of jobs persistently outstripping labour supply, so there was virtually full male employment. School leavers were usually funnelled into employment or – for the privileged minority – into higher education. When jobs were lost, alternative employment was invariably found in a relatively short period. John Oswell, a lathe operator in London who started work in 1962 commented: 'You could leave one job in the morning and get another one in the afternoon. And that's exactly what I did [in 1966]' (Britain at Work interview, by Dave Welsh, 19 January 2011). Reflecting back on the 1960s, a London typist Pam Osborne noted:

> I think it was a good time to be in work, because most people then, it was a job for life. I flitted about a bit, but most people would have started a job and expected to stay there. Well, men, in particular, for life. The turnover of staff was negligible. And also, if you did leave, getting another job was not a problem. There was plenty of jobs out there, not like now. (Britain at Work interview, by Ruth Sheldon, 12 June 2009)

Nonetheless, there were *some* who experienced long-term unemployment (over one year). By the late 1960s there were over 70,000 long-term unemployed; more than double the number of a decade before (Department of Employment and Productivity, *British Labour Statistics: Historical Abstract, 1886–1968*, pp. 360–2). The impact of unemployment was the focus of Wedderburn's work on redundancy in the 1960s and Hill et al.'s study which contrasted experience in three communities in the early 1970s – Coventry, Newcastle and Hammersmith, London (Hill et al., 1973; see also Gazeley and

Newell, 2007, pp. 230–8). Both studies showed marked differences in
the duration and experience of unemployment for non-manual compared to manual workers. Non-manual workers, including technicians
and engineers, would be reabsorbed quickly, as Wedderburn's 1964
study indicated – with 'negligible financial hardship' (Wedderburn,
1964, pp. 19–20, 37–40).

Older, unskilled workers in the traditional manual sectors of
the economy located in the north of England, Scotland, Wales and
especially Northern Ireland remained particularly vulnerable. Jock
Keenan a Scottish (Fife) miner (born 1916) eloquently described his
experience of being unemployed for ten months in the mid-1960s:

> ...It can all be summed up in one word – redundancy. How beautifully
> it rolls off the tongue! This means, if it means anything, superfluous to
> industry... Most men can learn to live with most forms of adversity. But
> what scarcely any man can bear with any degree of equanimity is to be
> undermined in his natural pride; to be stripped of his native dignity; to be
> left naked and defenceless, beaten and broken, a fit object for little more
> than charity. That is when the cold winds blow. (Keenan in Fraser, 1968,
> pp. 271–2)

Keenan's commentary eloquently evokes the depth of loss (which
extended way beyond the wage packet) associated with being deprived
of employment in a work-oriented society in the 1960s. It speaks volumes about the meaning of work in post-war Britain as a source of
identity, esteem, dignity and independence. He also reflected on a
'normal' day on the dole, commenting: 'Lovely life if you happen to
be a turnip. But I am not a turnip, mate. I am a thoughtful, sensitive,
widely read man'. He regarded unemployment as 'a bloody pointless
waste of a good citizen' (Keenan in Fraser, 1968, pp. 274–5).

Around the same time, there were a clutch of studies of unemployment and redundancy, including Wedderburn's investigation of the
impact of the closure of Rolls-Royce in Glasgow and Derby and railway workshops in Manchester and Darlington in 1963 (Wedderburn,
1965; Wedderburn, 1973, pp. 419–20). In both cases the most vulnerable
were older workers over 50 and those who were unhealthy or disabled.
Ageism was rife: 'Where he has a choice', Wedderburn commented,
'the employer will nearly always take the younger man' (Wedderburn,
1965, p. 85). In their personal testimonies these workers frequently
used the 'scrap-heap' metaphor, describing their experiences with a
mixture of shock, sadness, anxiety and disappointment: 'my world

had been shattered' one railway worker commented, 'we had been thrown on the scrap-heap' (Wedderburn, 1965, p. 62). Wedderburn defined these as 'personal trauma' narratives (Wedderburn, 1973, pp. 419–20). Whilst some alienated car workers and unskilled workers welcomed early retirement as a release from drudgery if they had an adequate pension to get by on, the prevailing sense was of the premature loss of something fundamental to their very existence (Hill et al., 1973, p. 5; Fineman, 1987, p. 87). Workers, Wedderburn reflected: 'squeeze satisfaction from the most improbable work situations' (Wedderburn, 1973, p. 424). Whilst financial hardship was evident, the emotional shock waves reverberated through unemployed workers' personal accounts which were punctuated with a sense of shame, loss of self-confidence, erosion of identity, loneliness and stress. There was a poignant grieving for the loss of purpose and social contacts that went along with work. Those out of work talked of feeling 'infirm' and 'incompetent' (Wedderburn, 1965, pp. 90–1). Clearly this hit at the very heart of masculine values, corroding the capability to act as the 'breadwinner' in what was still a very patriarchal, sexist society.

Tunstall's pioneering study of fishermen in the 1960s threw up similar descriptions of lost identities, nicely encapsulated in the expression 'being beached' (like a whale out of the water). Encroaching age and declining physical capacity led to older fishermen being laid off. Some found a lighter job as a trawler watchman or casual labourer for a while. Loss of work for these men meant a reorientation from a male-dominated environment to the female-dominated sphere, forging new relationships in different environments and at the extreme to dependence on family and charity (Tunstall, 1973, pp. 430–1). This was new territory for many to adjust to, and some coped better than others. As one retired fisherman noted: 'Wife and I just getting to know one another' (Tunstall, 1973, p. 431).

Many post-war studies of unemployment focused directly on the lived experience of the jobless, including the early accounts of Gould and Kenyon, *Stories from the Dole Queue* (1972) and Marsden and Duff's, *Workless* (1975). Joe Kenyon was well placed to comment as he had been unemployed as a young man in the 1930s and an organizer in the National Unemployed Workers' Movement, then out of work again for six years from the mid-1960s (laid off from the pits), when he formed the Claimants and Unemployed Workers' Union. He noted the financial hardships, but also the negative social attitudes and pervasive belief that the unemployed were feckless, were doing well on the dole and could get a job if they only tried. This made matters worse. A common reaction was to withdraw from society:

> What happens is, after they've been on the dole for a long time they lose their spirit, they've got no fight in them, they crawl into their bloody holes, they sit around the fire, they get used to doing nothing, they stand at the bloody window watching the world pass them by, sort of, and then they begin to feel resentful, they get depressed and they lose all their will to want to do anything again... The attitude now to a man on the dole is that his place is in the house: 'If you're not working then you sit up home, boy, and be thankful that we're feeding you'. (Gould and Kenyon, 1972, p. 175)

Keith Birch, an unemployed labourer in Hull in the early 1970s, articulated his loss in these terms:

> Absolute boredom. This comes before the financial position, I think, for the man and the woman. Financially it's terrifically hard... but the boredom affects you more than anything. You have to really try hard to stop yourself going downhill. (Gould and Kenyon, 1972, p. 41)

The return to mass unemployment

Rising levels of joblessness in the 1970s and a return in the 1980s to levels of mass unemployment comparable to the 1930s produced a plethora of studies focusing on the social impact of unemployment which further developed understanding of the meaning of work (see Febre, 2011). A debate simmered over whether state benefits insulated those affected from the worst consequences of joblessness, or whether the situation was worse in the 1980s compared to the 1930s. Because of rising expectations and full employment in the interim, Burnett, for example, argued in his historical survey of unemployment in 1991: 'the emotional impact of loss of work now seems greater' (Burnett, 1994, p. 312). The effects of unemployment could be more devastating because the support networks of tight-knit working-class communities had atrophied – there was less sympathy, understanding, tolerance and more accusations of being lazy, 'work-shy' or 'benefit scroungers' (Seabrook, 1982, pp. 3–5, 31). As the post-war consensus unravelled, the trade unions and the unemployed became scapegoats for Britain's economic ills. One argument was that the work ethic had been seriously eroded by generous state benefits which discouraged people from working for a living. Welfare spending was something that the Thatcherite government were determined to control, together with price inflation. Rising unemployment was part of a political agenda to reassert control over labour, as one member of Thatcher's cabinet, Nicholas Ridley, tactlessly admitted in March 1981: 'the high level of unemployment is evidence of the progress we are making' (McInnes, 1987, p. 57).

New studies challenged the influential 'stages of demoralisation' thesis of Jahoda and her co-investigators at Marienthal in the 1930s. It was argued that the earlier accounts had failed to differentiate experience enough by social class, had neglected the experience of women and not fully distinguished the financial implications of job loss from the impact on identities (Ashton, 1986, pp. 143–4). Sinfield, in *What Unemployment Means* (1981) argued that the phased 'shock – optimism – pessimism – fatalism' thesis failed to account for a wide range of experience; that nothing was inevitable or predictable and much depended upon 'age, health and level of resources', whilst outrage, anger, bitterness and a sense of injustice were amongst the range of emotional responses to job loss (Sinfield, 1981, pp. 37–8). To Sinfield, work provided a purpose and sense of value to individuals – something central to humanity and to citizenship in a modern society (Sinfield, 1981, pp. 129–30). Its loss had deep ramifications in a society which held work in such high esteem. Others, such as Seabrook (1982) eloquently drew upon the narratives of the unemployed to provide insights into what he perceived as a fundamental 'violence' and waste of potential: 'skills, strengths, powers and possibilities lie choked and unused' (Seabrook, 1982, p. 10). An unemployed cabinet-maker reflected: 'The same things happen every day. Bugger-all' (in Seabrook, 1982, p. 109). The sheer boredom and monotony of life on the dole also came through strongly as the 'predominant experience' in the central Scotland coal mining community that Daniel Wight studied in *Workers not Wasters* – a seminal piece of anthropological research in the period (Wight, 1993, p. 199).

The unemployed were not just victims, however, but active participants in this story. Loss of work could provoke deep emotions and redundancies were frequently opposed and resisted. Studies have highlighted how unemployment fuelled social tension – including sectarianism in Northern Ireland and the British race riots of 1981 (for which the Coventry-based multi-cultural ska band *The Specials* haunting track 'Ghost Town' provided the anthem) – and incubated collective responses and resistance (Ashton, 1986, pp. 143–4, 155–61). The latter included the formation of unemployed workers' pressure groups (see Gould and Kenyon, 1972), the creation of workers' cooperatives to preserve jobs, trade union campaigns on the 'right to work' issue and industrial action to fight closures – the most significant of which was undoubtedly the British miners' strike of 1984–5. There were also individual plant-level struggles to preserve jobs such as in the UCS work-in (1971) and the Lee Jeans occupation in 1981 (see, for example, Foster and Woolfson, 1986). Strangleman has persuasively argued that we need to get beyond the overgeneralizations of theorists (such as Beck, Cassells and Bauman) who see unemployed workers as 'mute victims' of globalization, positing: 'agency is exercised even within a restricted menu of options' (Strangleman, 2001, p. 266). For Strangleman, the impacts of job loss were mediated through intermeshing networks of family, class, work and place.

The poverty of unemployment: financial impacts

Those who lost their jobs in Britain in the last quarter of the twentieth century were supported through a state welfare regime that was generous by international standards, though by no means the most progressive. What Gallie and Paugam have defined as the UK's 'liberal/minimal' unemployment welfare regime was positioned somewhere between the 'universalistic' welfare regimes of Denmark and Sweden, the 'employment centred' ones (of Germany, France, The Netherlands and Belgium) and the weaker 'sub-protective' welfare regimes of southern European countries such as Greece, Italy and Spain (Gallie and Paugam, 2000, pp. 9–11). Whatever its nominal 'ranking', the UK's welfare state could not prevent unemployment being clearly associated with poverty in the post-war period, much as it had been in the 1930s. Paid work remained the most important determinant of living standards and the loss of employment – especially over the long term – continued to have drastic economic and social effects on individuals, families and communities.

In the post-war period, Britain had a dual system of assistance for those who lost their jobs: an insurance benefit scheme and a means-tested supplementary benefits scheme. The National Insurance Act 1946 provided a system where those in work paid into an insurance scheme (with 'stamps') and drew benefits from this when unemployed. How long unemployment benefits lasted depended on the period a worker paid into the system. When insurance benefits ran out (frequently between six months and a year), the unemployed were supported through the second tier of support: means-tested supplementary benefits (plus some discretionary one-off payments, for example for clothes and shoes). Supplementary benefits provided an income of around half the average manual worker's wage. Most long-term unemployed people – out of work for more than a year – were surviving on supplementary benefits. These were subject to varying levels of means-testing against savings and any earnings. For example, in the 1970s only £2 per week was allowed in additional family earnings before the balance was deducted from benefits. This constituted a major disincentive on wives of unemployed men to take on full-time employment (Marsden and Duff, 1975, p. 136). From 1965, the impact of job loss was cushioned somewhat by the passage of the Redundancy Payments Act, which provided for variable lump sum payments to be made by employers to those they laid off, with amounts linked to the number of years employed in the firm. In practice, however, the statutory redundancy payments were limited. In the early 1970s, less than one in ten of the unemployed had received any redundancy pay and only 21% by the late 1980s (Sinfield, 1981, p. 51; Burnett, 1994, p. 283).

How did this welfare regime affect the experience of job loss? Interpretations differ. To some commentators, theorists and politicians, unemployment benefits were so generous they not only insulated those affected from deprivation but also represented a disincentive to work – so-called 'benefit-induced unemployment' (Edgell, 2006, p. 104; Burnett, 1994, p. 279). In a critical commentary on 'Life on the Dole' in 1977, the Labour Research Department asserted:

> There is nothing new about this attempt to smear the unemployed. The Tories invariably mount such a campaign when unemployment is high. We saw it between the wars when they were obsessed with what they called 'malingerers', and persecuted them for 'not genuinely seeking work'. At times of full employment malingerers are hard to find: they only appear, it seems, when there are no jobs to be had. (*Labour Research*, 66(1), January 1977, 3)

In the early 1970s Kenyon made the point that with post-war improvements in social security and earnings-related benefits the financial impact was only 'cushioned' temporarily, for six months or so, but thereafter real hardship intensified:

> Once you've been on the dole for a year and your dole has stopped completely, you're drawing supplementary benefits, then the harsh reality of unemployment hits you smack in the bloody face. Clothes are beginning to wear out; things need replacing in the house; and then your income is drastically reduced and it's subject to a mean test. (Gould and Kenyon, 1972, p. 174; see also Ashton, 1986)

Marsden and Duff's authoritative 1975 study confirmed this general picture, demonstrating that whilst it was possible under certain exceptional circumstances (for example those with substantial redundancy pay, insurance benefits and earnings-related benefits) 'over a short period of time' to be getting more money on the dole than from paid work, this was very unusual (Marsden and Duff, 1975, pp. 133–4). Peter Townsend was amongst those who pioneered the concept of *relative* poverty in the 1960s and his seminal study of deprivation in Britain published in 1979 found a clear correlation between being without work or underemployed and poverty (Townsend, 1979, p. 589). Burnett examined the complex benefit system in the early 1980s, argued few individuals or families were financially better off on benefits than in work and estimated that: 'for almost all, therefore, unemployment means a substantial fall in disposable income, often up to half' (Burnett, 1994, pp. 280–1; see also Fryer, 1992, p. 116).

There was consequently a close association between unemployment and poverty. The narratives of the unemployed commonly focus on such financial hardship and flesh out what unemployment poverty actually meant on a day to day basis. For some, working 'on the side' for cash in hand whilst drawing the dole – 'fiddling' – could soften the financial impact of job loss (Wight, 1993, pp. 219–22). Others turned to different illegal activities as survival strategies – petty theft; fiddling the electric and gas meters; anything to get by (Seabrook in Fineman, 1987, pp. 13–19; Burnett, 1994, pp. 294–5; Ashton, 1986, p. 154). Financial hardship and material deprivation was widespread, with the long-term unemployed and those with families particularly badly hit (Sinfield, 1981, pp. 51–2). In relation to other European countries, moreover, unemployment poverty and financial hardship worsened in the UK in this period (Hauser and Nolan, 2000, pp. 37, 46; Gallie et al., 2000, p. 67). According to Hauser and Nolan, in the mid-1990s almost 50% of those unemployed were defined as living below the poverty line (at a time when the average figure for those in poverty was around 15% of the UK population; Hauser and Nolan, 2000, p. 42). Nor was this just the outcome of the male 'breadwinner' being out of work. By the end of the century, the association between female unemployment and poverty was well established (see Russell and Barbieri in Gallie and Paugam, 2000, p. 332). As Coyle's work has shown, amongst the groups most susceptible to poverty as a consequence of job loss were single-parent mothers (Coyle, 1984, p. 105).

Status and identity

Unemployment had fundamental impacts upon status and identities. A sense of this was conveyed poignantly in the acclaimed 1982 TV drama series *Boys from the Blackstuff* which followed the struggles of several characters faced by unemployment and labour market insecurity. The desperation of Yosser was encapsulated in his insistent demand: 'gizza job'. A decade or so before, Kenyon reflected on the corrosion of 'self-respect and pride' that went with the loss of work and the income that went along with it. Professionals, managers and white collar workers may have been markedly less likely to have experienced long-term unemployment, but they were not immune and felt such identity mutations acutely (Townsend, 1979, pp. 601–2). The sense of loss was tangible, whatever one's occupation. Fineman's interviews with 100 middle-class men made unemployed in the early 1980s found a wide range of reactions, from a sense of relief to intense trauma. One 46-year-old unemployed finance manager commented:

> I've run into deep financial problems which have pushed me on to tranquillizers. I've become very worried about spending my money with little coming in. I haven't told many people that I'm unemployed. Should I go back to finance? Or change my past completely? Self-employable? I'm beginning to think I've wasted my life up to date. (Fineman, 1987, p. 86)

'Rejection and failure are dominant themes in these accounts', Fineman commented, adding, 'Unemployment was a dramatic vote of no confidence... they frequently mourned their loss' (Fineman, 1987, p. 86).

The coal miners that Strangleman interviewed in North-East England associated this sense of loss with the physical places they occupied in their working lives and many expressed deep shock at losing their work. One young miner reflected:

> When they shut it was sheer devastation, hard, tough lads in tears. We knew they'd close it, we didn't want it closing...Nobody down there, my age, wanted the pits to shut. Lads, 50, you can understand it. Nice age to say you want to retire. But 32 year olds, we didn't want it. Conditions were bad, but you didn't want it to close...Then the penny dropped. You thought what am I going to do now? It was the way you used to think – emptiness. They counselled the lads at the colliery, but this was all they knew, pit work. We didn't know other jobs. (Phil, 37, redundant miner, interviewed in 1999, cited in Strangleman, 2001, pp. 258–9)

Much depended upon how much intrinsic satisfaction an individual drew from their occupation. Blue collar workers frequently developed very strong attachments to their work and well defined occupational identities and hence felt such losses deeply when unemployed, as well as the pecuniary impacts. As an unemployed Sunderland cabinet-maker put it: 'we were raised on work up here' (in Seabrook, 1982, p. 109). Whether the impact of job loss differed according to social class continues to be a subject of debate in the sociology of unemployment (Strangleman and Warren, 2008, p. 261). The evidence for suicide and parasuicide (attempted suicide) rates associated with loss of work perhaps supports the view that those with highest status jobs had farther to fall and the emotional impact could cut deeply and tragically (Grint, 1991, p. 109; Platt, 1986, p. 165). The empirical evidence suggests, however, deep cultural and psychological effects when work is lost, irrespective of social class.

Amongst the emotional responses were humiliation, embarrassment and a sense of degradation. Motivation eroded and confidence could collapse (Sinfield, 1981, pp. 91–2). One unemployed clerical worker aged 60 commented in 1968: 'It's not living. It's no joke to know you're no use' (in Townsend, 1979, p. 607). A Jamaican immigrant who came to Birmingham to work in 1956 reflected in an interview in the early 1980s on his subsequent experience of redundancy and unemployment: 'Now I wake up, and I sometimes think I must jump out of bed. But what for? I might as well be dead. How do I know I'm not dead? You feel worthless, nobody wants you...' (in Seabrook, 1982, p. 70). Another unemployed man in the early 1970s commented on becoming 'like a bloody hermit', continuing: 'All I wanted was a job, so that I could hold my bloody head up ... I think you start to lose your identity in yourself ... there's times when, well ... what am I?' (Marsden and Duff, 1975, p. 202). When asked in an interview how unemployment affected her father a Newcastle woman commented:

> He stopped going out of the house a lot. There was one point where he wouldn't even go down to the paper shop for a paper. He used to stay in quite a lot. I think he ... you tend to lose your confidence as well, you know, sort of if you ... lost your job. (Jacqueline Robbins, interview 121, 100 Families Project SN4938, ESDS Archive)

An unemployed semi-skilled machinist who had worked in an engineering firm in Coventry for twenty-years commented:

> My confidence is going. When people ask me how long I've been out of work, I think, shall I lie? When you're unemployed, you feel like you've

committed a crime somewhere, but nobody tells you what you've done. (Cited in Campbell, 1984, p. 179)

This sense of worthlessness, loss of identity and isolation pervades more contemporary oral testimonies of the impact of unemployment. One 40-year-old out of work for five years and homeless reflected in an interview in 2001:

> It's rubbish. It's awful now because there doesn't seem to be an end to it ... The money never bothers me, unless it's like feasibly unworkable. It's just that the whole structure of your life is (inaudible) ... You're the bottom of the bottom. It's been so long now, I just don't care ... And that's the worst thing, when you do get complacent ... When you're unemployed, you're not working, you're not socializing ... And I get upset quite a lot about stuff. (Interview 01/ESDS Archive/Project 4739)

He went on to comment on how unemployment was stigmatized: 'I was talking to this barmaid last night and she was saying "how come you're unemployed, because you seem quite nice, you seem reasonably intelligent. I can't believe you're not working".' Another 39-year-old (with learning difficulties) commented in an interview in 2001 on his perception of the loss of self esteem on the dole:

> At least if you're working your mind's clear, you've got your dignity, you've got your pride, nobody can come along and say, 'Look at that bum, he's sitting on the state and I'm paying for him.' Whether he's disabled or what, he's got his pride, he's got his dignity. (Interview 01/ESDS Archive/Project 4739)

Another unemployed man in 2001 reflected on the loss of structure to his day. When asked 'So how have you felt in yourself, while you've been unemployed?' he responded: 'I feel lost, I feel crap... Cos I've been like working since I was about sixteen ... I just like feel low ... That's how, I mean, I've been like ever since looking for a job' (Interview 02/ESDS Archive/Project 4739).

Much depended upon individuals' relationship with work and the evidence indicates that this could differ across a wide spectrum. For some, loss of work represented 'personal liberation' from deskilled and monotonous work that had lost all meaning beyond the wage packet (Seabrook, 1982, p. 12). Most, however, felt the loss acutely. As Fineman put it: 'Employment acts so powerfully as a psychic glue, holding people together in aim, purpose and time' (Fineman, 1987, p. 247). An unemployed Sunderland man, Harry King reflected: 'You feel as if your whole world is crumbling... Our lives become narrower through the loss of work' (in Seabrook, 1982, p. 123). The losses went beyond the labour process and skills to relationships, as King commented: 'Being out of work is a lonely experience... work is collective; unemployment is solitary' (Seabrook, 1982, p. 142). This has been aptly described as 'social disqualification' (Gallie and Paugam, 2000, p. 1).

Did this experience loosen attachment to work? *Social Attitudes* evidence in the 1980s and 1990s tended to confirm that unemployment did not erode the work ethic – rather the opposite, as Russell argued:

> Our data suggest that high levels of unemployment in society are linked to a *stronger* belief in the importance of work. It would seem that job scarcity apparently highlights the importance of having a job to the workforce in general. A similar process is also evident among individual workers. (Russell, 1998, p. 93)

The impact of job loss on male identity was invariably profound, because employment was socially constructed as central to men's lives – a core element of masculinity (see Chapter 3). Unemployment hit at the very essence of masculinity: the capacity to deliver in the 'provider' or 'breadwinner' role. Coyle has commented:

> Unemployment is not just the loss of a wage, it is the loss of a breadwinner's wage and a place amongst men. Work and masculinity are so entangled that in unemployment men are not only workless, they are seemingly unsexed. They have lost the very point of their existence as men, to work to support a family. (Coyle, 1984, p. 94)

A young unemployed father commented in an interview with Jeremy Seabrook in 1980: 'I'm ashamed I can't provide them [the children] with everything they need. What kind of father is that?... I feel like topping myself and taking them with me' (Seabrook, 1982, p. 3). Work and the earnings that went along with it conferred status, whilst the 'sacrifice' inherent in personal commitment to work could constitute the basis for male power and dominance within the home (see Chapter 3). This was fractured by unemployment. Masculinity was also challenged by the shift from independent earner to dependence – upon the state and family – and from a male-dominated physical space at work to a female-dominated one in the home. An unemployed joiner in Sunderland commented:

> Socially, not having work is upsetting, especially if you've been a fairly tough sort of bloke. You lose something of your self-respect in the company

of people who are working. You go into a pub, people look at you critically. They say 'I'd die of boredom if I was at home all day'... There is a stigma, even where a lot of people are out of work. You're almost an affront to people who are working. (Cited in Seabrook, 1982, p. 136)

This blurring of gender boundaries could be threatening to men and create tensions, exacerbated by financial pressures. McKee and Bell in their study of Kidderminster saw this as a 'collision' between male and female social worlds, rather than 'harmonisation' (see McKee and Bell, 1986, pp. 142–4). At the very least it involved painful adjustment to a new set of social relations, and some coped easier with this transition than did others. The wife of the joiner cited above touched on this:

A lot of men see their role as being attacked, and they can't cope with it. Being out of work, it finds them. If a man is used to being his own man, he doesn't believe in equality, he has been the master really, so when he falls out of work it can be traumatic. They're the ones that fall apart, get violent, just go on the tramp. (Cited in Seabrook, 1982, p. 137)

What doesn't appear to have happened to any systematic extent is a redrawing of the sexual division of labour within the home as a consequence of male job loss (Wight, 1993, pp. 199–200; Coyle, 1984, pp. 113–20; McKee and Bell, 1986; Marsden and Duff, 1975). Studies of the impact of unemployment on family life in the 1970s and 1980s largely concur that the opportunity was rarely taken by unemployed men to re-orientate their lives to become more active fathers and play an equal role in domestic work and responsibilities and fully share household tasks. An unemployed Yorkshire male clothing worker commented: 'I'd go to the Job Centre, come home, do nothing much. I lost interest in a lot of things. I didn't do anything around the house. I just hated it, it was degrading, it was a nightmare' (Coyle, 1984, p. 113). For men, perhaps this was tantamount to admitting that their primary role as breadwinner was over (McKee and Bell, 1986, p. 145). As one unemployed man's wife noted in the mid 1980s:

...the man he is, is like a he-man. 'I'll keep my family and nobody else'. That's Bill's attitude anyway... He says women are equal to men in some ways, but he says men will always be the breadwinners. (McKee and Bell, 1986, p. 141)

This challenge to masculinity could create tensions. A woman living in a refuge in the early 1980s commented on her husband, a carpenter who had lost his job:

He very rarely helped around the house, because he felt we had different jobs. I'd ask him to clean the bath when he got up or occasionally hoover, but he wouldn't so we rowed about that, especially after he got made redundant. I'd be working away while he was just sitting... I got several black eyes during the rows and eventually I left – I left several times and always went back. (Cited in Cambell, 1984, p. 89)

A somewhat different set of problems faced the sharply growing pool of young unemployed in the 1980s and 1990s. They encountered never having experienced work, uncertainty and a more marginal relationship with the labour market; being underemployed; part-time working and temporary contracts, with few job rights (such as sick pay and paid holidays; Pollock, 1997, p. 630). In his maiden speech in Parliament in July 1983 the young socialist MP Tony Blair referred to such experience in his coal mining constituency of Sedgefield:

Those young people are not merely faced with a temporary inability to find work. For many, the dole queue is their first experience of adult life. For some, it will be their most significant experience. Without work, they do not merely suffer the indignity of enforced idleness – they wonder how they can afford to get married, to start a family, and to have access to all the benefits of society that they should be able to take for granted. Leisure is not something they enjoy, but something that imprisons them. (Cited in Coates and Barratt Brown, 1997, p. 15)

The failure to find permanent work on leaving school, college and higher education was a feature of the 1980s recession and the ramifications of this denial of employment experience became a focus of research. Pollock stressed the growing uncertainty associated with the transition from school to work and the increasing variety of trajectories, in marked contrast to the relative certainty of the move from school to work from the 1940s to the 1970s. Government youth training schemes (YTS) were one attempt to address the problem, but arguably with little sustained success (*Labour Research*, Jan 1979, 5). One estimate suggests around 50% of 16–18 year olds in the UK were either unemployed or on YTS schemes in the late 1980s (Hart, 1988, p. 1). A common effect was the delaying of financial independence that was associated with attaining the status of full adulthood. Some studies also associated youth unemployment with crime and anti-social behaviour. Whether such experiences and the disillusionment and alienation that went along with them had any lasting effects on attachment to and orientation towards work is less certain.

Women and unemployment

Most of the early studies of the impact of unemployment focused upon the experience of men. This perhaps reflected the dominant view into the late twentieth century of male centrality in employment as the 'breadwinners' and women as supplementary earners. As Sinfield noted in 1981: 'Britain still does not view married women in particular as full members of the labour force' (Sinfield, 1981, p. 89). We have seen how a sexual division of labour persisted in post-war British society and how labour market participation was gendered. Was women's experience of unemployment different from men?

Women had a varied and changing relationship with the post-war labour market; one that could be different but also similar in many respects to men. Whereas men typically had a full-time, continuous relationship with paid work, women were divided into a segment with similar experience and those whose participation was discontinuous (broken by marriage or childbirth) and part-time (Edgell, 2006, pp. 112–4; Cragg and Dawson, 1984; Ashton, 1986). Where women had a family and home-centred identity, rather than a clear occupational identity, the deleterious impact of job loss was likely to be less significant. As the economic recession deepened in the 1980s, some out of work married women continued to view themselves as not unemployed because of their primary domestic role (Hurstfield, 1986, pp. 42–3; Callender, 1987, p. 26; Wight, 1993, p. 212). One woman commented in the early 1980s:

> I think women are silly to think of themselves as unemployed because running a home is a job. In fact it's a full-time job. It's a job that's unpaid but I still don't see that I'm unemployed. (Cragg and Dawson, 1984, p. 18; cited by Hurstfield, 1986, p. 43)

Some studies have also suggested that women's social networks may have survived unemployment rather better than male social networks. Hence unemployed women may have experienced less social exclusion than men. This appears to be the case, however, only for previously employed female part-time workers, rather than for female full-time workers (Russell, 1999).

For many women, however, the impact of unemployment was broadly similar to that of men. Misunderstandings emerged, partly because of the marginalization of women in research on the social impact of unemployment. Those studies that did focus specifically on women's experiences of unemployment – such as Martin and Wallace (1984), Coyle (1984), and Cragg and Dawson (1984) – demonstrated how women acutely felt both the financial and the social/psychological impacts of job losses. When Martin and Wallace were interviewing women made redundant and unemployed in five factories in the early 1980s they found that despite the typical experience of discontinuous work histories (69 per cent had a break in their employment) women worked for very similar reasons to men – for the money *and* for social aspects of the work, such as companionship, *and* for the intrinsic interest in the work – and had similar levels of job satisfaction to men (Martin and Wallace, 1984, pp. 81–96, 281–3). Like men, the majority of women experienced unemployment as a 'personal deprivation', feeling the financial loss acutely as well as the boredom and isolation of unemployment. (Martin and Wallace, 1984, p. 287). Coyle's study of unemployed women from two Yorkshire clothing factories which closed in 1980 largely concurred with this view. 'What emerges from these women's accounts', Coyle noted, 'is the extraordinary attachment women have to their paid employment' (Coyle, 1984, p. 121). A skilled female electrical engineer reflected:

> I got £3000 redundancy money, for thirty-one years! When I left I was shocked, and I felt very bitter, so mad about the whole thing. For six months, till I got another job, much lower paid, I was crawling up the wall. I wasn't used to being at home, I'd been a career girl, you see. That was my life. (Cited in Campbell, 2000, p. 188)

Mrs Tysoe, a Bolton woman made unemployed in 1978, provides another example. Her experience followed the pattern of many women: occupational demotion on re-entry to the labour market after marriage (from nursery teacher to accounts clerk) and demotion again after a long spell (18 months) of unemployment (taking a job eventually as a textile machinist). An extract from her evocative narration of what work and its loss in the early 1980s signified to her is cited at the beginning of this chapter. Roughly twenty years later this is how another woman – an ex-civil servant – narrated her experience of unemployment:

> I'm very depressed because I'm unemployed... And nobody really takes very much notice of me, you know, when you're unemployed nobody wants to know you, it's like a disease... Because you've got no money to do anything, all you can do is just pay, just about pay your telephone bill, your gas bill, your 'lectric bill, you know, that kind of thing and nobody really wants to know you, and not only that, plus I live in a high rise flat, and most of

my friends they've all branched out and doing well for themselves, and I'm
the one that's fallen right down, right deep down in a pit really. That's sort
of how I look at it, I'm in a pit which I can't drag myself out of, you know.
(Interview 23/ESDS Archive/Project 4739)

A key feature of paid work for many women was how it facilitated
their independence, giving them a separate income. Coyle argued
that this meant that for women unemployment implied more of
a 'crisis of autonomy' and less a 'crisis of gender identity', as with
men (Edgell, 2006, p. 114; Coyle, 1984, p. 121). As one unemployed
woman related: 'For once in my life I feel as though I'm being kept
and I've never had that feeling. I've always been very independent...
I've felt it terribly, that loss of independence (Coyle, 1984, p. 107).
Amongst the emotional responses indicated by unemployed women
were 'feeling less independent, feeling frustrated, insecure, worthless, isolated, and experiencing changing sleep patterns' (Martin and
Wallace, 1984, p. 265).

Over time, women's relationship with the labour market was changing, becoming more like that of men. In the 1950s and 1960s most
female workers may well have experienced unemployment differently
to men because of the deeply entrenched societal values that meant
most women still expected not to work continuously and derived their
identities primarily from home and family. Gender roles were sharply
defined and the expectations of post-war femininity combined with
structural discrimination and segregation in labour markets coloured
women's experience of paid employment and in turn shaped what work
meant to them. Fifty years later, by the early twenty-first century, the
labour market was considerably less gendered; convergence was well
advanced and undoubtedly one consequence was a blurring of gender difference in work identities and, thus, how job loss was felt and
experienced in economic, social and psychological terms. There were
also smaller families with a reduction in the duration of child-rearing,
more single mother families (without a male 'breadwinner') and the
increasing fragility of marriage may well have contributed to a deepening attachment by women to employment. Research on the work
identities of unemployed men and women in the late 1990s suggested,
if anything, that women had a stronger, not a weaker attachment to
paid employment. When asked if they would want employment even
if they did not need the income, 87% of a sample of women in the UK
answered in the affirmative, compared to 72% of men (Gallie and
Alm, 2000, p. 119).

Unemployment and health

The impact of job loss on health is a controversial topic and has been debated intensely since at least the interwar depression. Mel Bartley has argued that this discussion was characterized by 'a loop of claim and counter-claim' (Bartley, 1992, p. 57). Whilst the evidence strongly indicates a clear correlation between high unemployment levels and ill-health, the case for unemployment as a *direct* cause is more contested. Region and environment are important variables (as there are long-standing regional differences in health standards) whilst a primary complicating factor lies with 'the healthy worker effect – the tendency of healthy workers to survive in employment while the unhealthy lose their jobs' (Bellaby and Bellaby, 1999, p. 463). It has also been argued that sickness rates in areas of high unemployment have been artificially inflated by the benefits regime which provides a premium for those claiming for long-term sickness as opposed to the dole.

Nonetheless, because health standards correlate directly with income levels and social class, loss of work and falling income inevitably impacted adversely on morbidity and mortality. Studies of the mortality rates of the employed and unemployed have demonstrated reduced life expectancy with long-term unemployment, even when behaviour (such as alcohol consumption and smoking) and social class have been allowed for (Shaw et al., 1999, p. 45; Brenner and Mooney, 2003). A *British Medical Journal* editorial in August 1992 stated categorically: 'Unemployment begets poverty, which begets ill-health and premature death' (cited in Coates and Barratt Brown, 1997, p. 45). Morbidity was also clearly associated with unemployment and labour market insecurity – with symptoms including high blood pressure, ulcers, weight loss, weight gain, heart disease and alcoholism (Burnett, 1994, p. 293; Ashton, 1986, pp. 150–1; Bellaby and Bellaby, 1999, pp. 464–5). Periods of sustained economic recession and high levels of unemployment could also impact adversely upon the health and well-being of those holding down jobs, increasing their insecurity and contributing to work intensification, fatigue and overwork, and heightened levels of stress (Ferrie et al., 1995). As Shaw et al.'s study demonstrates, places with the highest levels of unemployment also had the highest recorded levels of ill-health (measured by those on permanent incapacity and sickness benefits). In some districts of Glasgow, for example, male unemployment rates in 1991 ranged between 20–25% and in the same areas those on incapacity benefits reached 12–16%.

In more affluent areas of the UK – such as Buckingham, Wokingham, Chesham and Amersham there was less than 5% unemployment and less than 2% permanently sick on incapacity benefits (Shaw et al., 1999, p. 47). 'Clearly', Shaw and her colleagues asserted, 'being out of work in such large numbers damages the health of men of working age in these places' (Shaw et al., 1999, p. 46). The same was the case for women, though the relationship was not quite so clearly defined (Shaw et al., 1999, p. 49). The coalfields exhibited similar patterns. Around 750,000 people of working age in the coalfields self-reported as having 'a limiting long-term illness' to the 1991 Census. Losing work clearly impacted upon ex-miners' bodies, resulting, for example, in higher levels of obesity due to inactivity and higher rates of smoking and drinking (Coates and Barratt Brown, 1997, pp. 47–9).

Sociological, ethnographic and psychological studies have also clearly identified a range of mental ill-health consequences of job loss, including depression, anxiety, negative self-esteem, eroded self-confidence and insomnia (Strangleman and Warren, 2008, p. 256; Martin and Wallace, 1984, pp. 260–7; Bartley, 1992 Shaw et al., 1999, p. 45). Studies have also shown suicide and attempted suicide rates are higher amongst the unemployed compared to those in employment (Lewis and Sloggett, 1998; Platt, 1986). Two studies put suicide rates amongst unemployed men at double the rate of the general population. One was based on a very large sample of 500,000 from the 1971 Census which tracked morbidity and mortality over the subsequent five years, 1971–76, and the other appeared in the *British Medical Journal* in August 1992 (Bartley, 1992, p. 58; Coates and Barratt Brown, 1997, p. 46). Where there was considerable debate, however, was over whether mental ill-health was the consequence of poverty (as studies of the 1930s had tended to stress) or the result of the loss of the cluster of intrinsic rewards which employment provided, such as status, identity, time structure, esteem, social contact, control and power. Much of the research in the 1980s stressed the latter (some thus implying that benefit levels were adequate, or even generous and representing a disincentive to work), whilst Fryer has argued a strong case for connecting the two, identifying 'unemployment poverty' as the primary stressor and cause of mental ill-health, suggesting scholarship failed to recognize 'that poverty is a social psychological as well as an economic state' (Fryer, 1992, p. 119).

Precise triggers are often difficult to identify. Unemployment is likely to be one of a number of contributory factors in both mental and physical ill-health. Given the arguments made in Chapter 5, moreover, there were some positive health benefits to leaving some types of employment for some people – including relief from work pressure, exposure to toxins and carcinogens, fatigue and stress. Interestingly, in Martin and Wallace's study of unemployed women, more of those interviewed self-reported that their physical health had *improved* since leaving work than those who reported a deterioration (see Martin and Wallace, 1984, pp. 260–2, 286). However, the same study found unemployment caused a range of mental health problems. Other work has suggested that 'psychological distress' was worse amongst unemployed single and childless married women than unemployed married mothers (Fryer, 1992, p. 107). The impact on men was wrapped up in deeply entrenched notions of masculinity, including the need to fulfil the breadwinner role. Goodwin's quantitative analysis (of a 1991 data cohort) supports the view that unemployment caused emotional problems and mental ill-health amongst male workers because: 'there is a societal mis-match between men who do not work and the masculine ideal' (Goodwin, 1999, p. 192).

The argument that loss of work is detrimental to health and wellbeing is irrefutable and strongly supported by the empirical evidence, both quantitative and qualitative. Ill-health is a recurring theme in unemployed workers' own narratives, as we have already seen, and depression is a common outcome of job loss. In Martin and Wallace's study almost half of the unemployed women reported being depressed as a result of losing their jobs, with loneliness a recurring trigger (Martin and Wallace, 1984, pp. 263–5). It might be argued that unemployed people might 'self-assess' as more unhealthy because they wished to avoid the stigma of being unemployed. This was discounted by Bellaby and Bellaby in their study of unemployment and health in the period 1984–1991. They found a strong association between loss of work and ill-health even when allowances had been made for 'the unhealthy worker' effect. They concluded that 'high levels of unemployment generate ill health that leads to more irregular employment and more frequent early exit from the labour market', whilst 'rising rates of unemployment adversely affect job stress' (Bellaby and Bellaby, p. 479).

Retirement

Thane has argued that the post-Second World War era was characterized by 'the emergence of mass retirement' (Thane, 2000, p. 385). For most workers of the post-war generation, the end of employment in

Britain was marked by compulsory retirement, at aged 60 for women and 65 for men. The two decades following the Second World War were characterized by a wide-ranging 'retirement debate' in which it was popularly believed that forced and sudden exit from work was detrimental to health and well-being (Harper and Thane, 1989, pp. 43–61; Thane, 2000, pp. 364–84). The evidence, however, of an 'ill-health effect' of retirement remains ambiguous, anecdotal and contested. Nonetheless, this period saw a proliferation of schemes by welfare groups and voluntary associations established to try to find job opportunities beyond retirement age, though with little overall success. A key problem was that there was little planning for a life without work in retirement and, as Townsend's work indicated, there continued to be a clear association between retirement and poverty (Townsend, 1979, pp. 310–11, 333–4). All this occurred in a context of demographic change, with the numbers of over 65-year-olds more than doubling between the mid-1930s (3.9 million) and the late 1970s (over 8 million) (Hannah, 1986, p. 125).

Responses to enforced retirement varied widely. Hill argued that middle-class workers welcomed retirement and some groups, such as male civil servants, frequently voluntarily retired early at 60 (Hill et al., 1973, pp. 144–5). Attitudes were linked to an individual's state of health and whether or not pension income could support living standards in retirement. Clearly those with occupational pensions were at a distinct advantage here (see Thane, 2000, pp. 236–56). Amongst all workers' reactions to retirement ranged from those relieved to be released from the burden and pressure of work as their health and capacities deteriorated, to those frustrated and deprived by the loss of identity, status and the social contacts which came with employment. Beveridge's 1968 investigation of retirement found a large proportion of industrial workers in London (40% of the sample) associated retirement with more 'freedom' and 'independence' to do what they wanted with their time. Beveridge also found, however, that retired workers articulated a deep sense of loss of occupational identity, respect, status, income and, most important of all, that they missed the companionship of people at work (Beveridge, 1968). To some post-war commentators, enforced exit from work at any age was 'arbitrary and unscientific' (Parkinson's Law, 1958, cited in Thomas, 1999, p. 591).

Parker's wide-ranging 1982 study, *Work and Retirement*, indicated a broad spectrum of responses to the termination of employment. A labourer aged 62 reflected: 'I shall be able to please myself what I do and where I go', whilst a fitter's mate (aged 64) commented: 'It means escape from work. I think I've done enough work' (Parker, 1982, p. 105). As we've seen (Chapter 5) industrial work was capable of consuming workers' bodies and for many such workers retirement marked a welcome and necessary relief from hard graft which exacted a heavy toll upon the body. A key finding of Parker's investigation, however, was that on balance the negative impacts outweighed the positive. An ex-salesman aged 72 recalled: 'I hate it because I was never an idle person in my life – I've taken it badly being at home' (Parker, 1982, p. 109), whilst a 70-year-old pensioner stated:

> I think they treat the old folk very shabbily. Until they told me I had reached the age when I had to retire I had worked all my years in a useful occupation. Then they threw me on the scrap heap. I looked around for another job but there just weren't any to be had. I had always been used to going out every day and not having a job to go to hit me very hard ... Leisure? I've never known what leisure is ... It's a lousy system that takes people's jobs away from them. (Parker, 1982, p. 47)

Given the deeply ingrained work ethic and the central role work played in people's lives, Parker asserted: 'the gains of retirement – freedom, getting rid of undesired work and its consequences – are balanced by losses of valued work experiences and the feeling of being useful' (Parker, 1982, p. 121). The effects were equated to bereavement and were not unlike those felt by the long-term unemployed and those made redundant during their working lives (Parker, 1982, p. 115). A few years later (1991) a retired woman (Mrs Bruce) expressed her resentment at being forced to retire, commenting: 'Going out to work is much easier than staying at home. Your life is far more clearly defined and you're not so much at everyone's beck and call' (cited in Thomas, 1999, p. 591). Such reactions again serve to signify the meaning of work to this generation, the pervasiveness of the work ethic and the centrality of employment in people's lives.

As noted in Chapter 1, policy on retirement shifted significantly in the early twenty-first century, with the scrapping of forced retirement, removal of the default retirement age and raising of the state pension age. These changes were responses to sharply rising life expectancy, improved health standards in older age, the pensions funding crisis and the inequalities associated with age discrimination. It provided workers who wished to continue in employment the statutory right to do so. The implications are wide-ranging and difficult to assess at this early juncture. However, it does mean a reversal of trends since the 1930s of earlier retirement, more flexibility in how people negotiate their disengagement from work, and a steadily rising exit age from employment in the future. According to data compiled by the Office of National Statistics, the latter reached its lowest point in the early–mid 1990s and from then exit ages rose by 3–4 years for men and women, to average 64 for women and 66 for men in 2010.

Conclusion

Losing employment – especially if unemployment was sustained over the long term – was invariably a traumatic and deeply disturbing experience, and some coped better with this than others. This is a deeply contested terrain and interpretations of the impact of losing employment range widely. Whilst unemployment affected living standards, impacted on identities and undermined health and well-being, studies of unemployment and the narratives of those who lost jobs indicate, however, that experience varied widely. Impacts differed across a wide spectrum from those who welcomed the release from the drudgery and violence of exploitative and alienating paid employment to those whose lives were shattered from the loss of a role that was central to their lives.

Much depended upon what work signified to people on an individual basis and on the duration of unemployment, which was experienced differently depending upon resources, social class, gender, race, age and place. For youths not yet in the labour market, unemployment delayed their transition to adulthood and could destabilize their relationship with society, sharpening a sense of alienation and contributing to anti-social behaviour and crime. For older men, job loss frequently challenged their masculinity. For men this could constitute a fundamental 'crisis of gender identity'; for women a traumatic 'crisis of autonomy' linked to the loss of independence (Coyle, 1984). Moreover, as women's relationship with the labour market changed from the 1950s to the present, the effects of losing employment became more significant to them. Paid work was a key determinant of living standards and whilst other factors contributed to deprivation and illness, unemployment was a primary cause of poverty and ill-health. Much depended, however, on an individual's orientation to work; the more intense the meaning of work and the *intrinsic* rewards derived from it, then the deeper its loss was felt. The deleterious effects of losing work indicate much about the persistence of a deeply ingrained work ethic and the significance and meaning of employment in modern society.

Conclusion

This book explores the history of work, the changing shape of employment and meaning of work in Britain from 1945 to the present. It has drawn heavily upon workers' own narratives of their working lives to present a re-focused history of the workplace, engaging along the way with the debates and historiographies of work. What conclusions can be drawn from this exercise? What did work signify and how did it change over this period of almost seventy years since the Second World War?

Working lives, 1945–1970s

One thing that is clear is the centrality of work in people's lives when we pick up the story in the middle of the twentieth century in the aftermath of the Second World War. To be sure, already things had changed to the extent that paid employment was no longer a *necessity* to exist and avoid starvation, as it had been in the Victorian period. The coming of the Welfare State changed that. Nonetheless, whilst employment may not have been as important to people's survival, at a material level it provided the means to participate in an increasingly consumer-oriented society. The alternative for those without employment on state benefits or on the margin of the labour market in casual, irregular, low paid work was relative poverty and degrees of social exclusion.

But work meant so much more than just the wage packet, and not just to those in professional and creative jobs – like the University academic main character in David Lodge's novel *Nice Work* (1989) who said: 'It's nice work. It's meaningful. It's rewarding. I don't mean in money terms. It would be worth doing even if it wasn't paid anything at all'. This reflection was in response to Lodge's fictional factory managing director who had made the point:

> Men like to work. It's a funny thing but they do. They may moan about it every Monday morning and they may agitate for shorter hours and longer

holidays, but they need to work for their self-respect. (Lodge, 1989, pp. 126–7)

Post-war Britain was a nation of *grafters* where a powerful work ethic prevailed and people worked for the intrinsic rewards as well as the extrinsic material benefits. And work still dominated most ordinary folks' adult lives, usually from leaving school until virtually the end of the life span (given that average life expectancy in 1950 was 68 years).

The meaning of employment was signified by workers themselves, in memoirs, interviews, in work-life narratives and autobiographies. Hence, men frequently celebrated 'never having lost a day's work in their lives', whilst women recalled in their narrative accounts a lifetime of activity, of never having a moment to themselves whether in paid employment, in unpaid domestic labour or, as was becoming more frequent, a combination of market and non-market activity. Within this context, workers and their families bore the brunt of work deprivations, insecurity, hardship, inequalities, lack of opportunities, danger and risk invariably with stoicism and dignity. People identified closely with their work and were defined by it. Oral testimonies and autobiographical work narratives capture the essential dualism of work – the joy, pride and sense of achievement together with the frustrations, the alienation and the degradation.

Work opportunities, however, were distributed very unevenly in post-war Britain, following and reproducing the patterns of power and social divisions within society. Class, gender, race and disability patterned employment opportunities and hence income and wealth. This was a society deeply divided by class and one where employment opportunities in the 1950s and 1960s depended to a large extent upon education and qualifications. Hence the top jobs were monopolized by the middle and upper classes – the 'toffs' – whilst the working classes (easily enough identified from their spoken voice, accent and clothing) provided the labour for the farms, factories, mines, building sites, transporting of goods and routine clerical, personal service and shop jobs. Social mobility across the manual/non-manual divide was possible, but still extremely limited. Transgressions there were, but these were still unusual and the norm remained for the sons of working-class fathers to follow into manual jobs and daughters to replicate the pattern of their mothers' bi-modal working lives. Still, in the 1950s and 1960s, women were predominantly taking paid employment until marriage and the birth of their children, then withdrawing from the formal economy to continue their working lives in the home in unpaid domestic labour pivoting around the family's needs until the children were grown up.

This shared experience of wage labour and hardship gave working-class communities their cohesion and cemented a working-class camaraderie and solidarity, reflected, not least, through a strong affiliation by manual workers and public sector workers to their trade unions in the 1950s, 1960s and into the 1970s – and, though perhaps less assuredly so, to the Labour Party, widely regarded as the party of the working class. The unions were workers' protective shield against exploitation in the labour market and they fulfilled a vital function in defending employees' rights and maintaining living standards. And they were desperately needed because workers experienced a daily assault on their bodies and minds in the workplace – where they faced an uphill struggle in an unequal power relationship against varying types of exploitative employers and styles of management energized by the profit motive within what was an economy dominated by competitive market forces. Whilst the power of the trade union movement in this period has been exaggerated and the idea of a 'golden age' over-egged (another product of a Thatcherite discourse), membership did reach a peak in the 1970s and the unions did flourish in the post-war decades of (virtual) full male employment in a favourable social and political context, bolstered by extensive statutory rights.

At mid-twentieth century most people felt their work resonating through their bodies, in their flesh and bones. The body was positioned, as McEvoy (1997) has commented, at the 'ecological core of the workplace'. Manual labour was capable of forging a fit and honed body, and employment has been positively associated with health and well-being. However, workers were also exposed to overwork, fatiguing and dangerous work practices, high injury, disease and disability rates, especially, though not exclusively, in heavy manual work including in coal mines, steel works, construction, shipbuilding, chemical works and heavy engineering. The asbestos-related diseases and coal miners' respiratory diseases which ravaged working-class communities in the second half of the twentieth century are testament to the deleterious impact work could have on the body. Masculinity was forged in such dangerous work environments – where risk-taking was encouraged by peer pressure to 'act as real men' and this in turn enabled men to claim such sacrifice as a 'justification' for privileged treatment in the home. For married women at mid-twentieth century, the 'dual burden' of paid and unpaid work could lead to endemic overstrain, stress and prescribed lives. These were lives bounded by the drudgery, monotony and sheer hard graft of household duties and childcare that Oakley's respondents recounted so evocatively in *Housewife* (1974). Whether in unpaid work in the home or in the market economy, bodies were vulnerable and, as Wolkowitz (2006) put it so neatly, 'felt the pinch'.

This was, however, a dynamic process and relationships with work were complex. Workers rarely passively accepted prevailing employment conditions, rather they negotiated and mediated them utilizing a wide array of individual tactics and collective strategies. There was a long tradition of labour organization and resistance in the UK and employees challenged social and cultural norms and responded to their work in a myriad of ways in the immediate post-war context. Structuralist or modernist interpretations, with meta-narratives of omnipotent capital versus labour, the rapacious exploitation of workers and degradation of work, encroaching proletarianization and conflictual, adversarial industrial relations within capitalist societies, are no longer tenable – at least without serious qualification. Whilst workers' relationships to the means of production may have provided a fundamental point of common interest, in reality individuals' interactions with work varied widely as work signified many different things to different people. The labour force was fractured and class identities rooted in economic relationships and material circumstances were blurred by their intersection with other divisions and identities associated with gender and sexuality, age, disability, race and ethnicity. Work cultures embraced competition, sexism and racism and were as likely to be exclusionist as all-embracing, individualist as collective, cooperative and consensual, as much as conflictual. In part, this reflected a defensive post-war work culture on the part of a generation deeply affected by the insecurities of the 1930s Slump, which was seared into popular consciousness.

Deeply entrenched notions of the masculine 'breadwinner' or provider role perpetuated the exclusion of married women from full-time employment, legitimized low pay for women workers and shaped their entry (and re-entry) into the formal economy – hence the post-war proliferation of part-time work for women. Wide inequalities existed and persisted, not least based on social class and linked to the restriction of educational opportunities for working-class children and a privileged education, leading to the top jobs and the highest earnings, for the elites and the middle classes. Social class, gender, disability, race and ethnicity all denoted advantage and disadvantage in the mid-twentieth-century workplace – and the labour market was deeply segmented with varying levels of access and reward. Work identities were refracted through this. And to some extent this gender and racial apartheid was policed by the white male working-class majority and its organizations – including the trade unions – at least up until the 1970s.

Moreover, capitalism was no monolithic entity at mid-twentieth century. Employers were divided by product markets, company structures and 'strategic choices' (Zeitlin, 2004), whilst managers could be autonomous and complex actors, as Perchard (2007a) has argued, and not necessarily the uncritical and robotic mouthpieces of their bosses and the boardroom. Labour management methods were in flux and varied widely across a spectrum from the more benign public sector, to the paternalist and welfarist companies, to socially irresponsible exploitative multi-national corporations who blatantly abused the bodies of their workers to maximize profits. Workers' relationships with capitalism were thus complex and this shaped attitudes and behaviour, contributing to the persistence of a large segment of non-unionized and politically deferential conservative labour, especially, though not exclusively, in London and the South.

At least in the years of tight labour markets post-war until the mid-1970s workers could deploy their trade unions to fight to improve conditions and could ultimately vote with their feet, hence contributing to a general uplifting of employment conditions, rights and real wages. There was also a sustained assault on the inequalities, discrimination and restricted opportunities that characterized the mid-twentieth-century labour market. This reflected a tension within working-class communities between defensive conservatism (embracing jingoism, sexism and racism) and recognition that fighting for the rights of all workers irrespective of gender, race and disability would be the most effective way of raising standards of living, the dignity of labour and the quality of life. Amongst the outcomes in this period were the evaporation of the marriage bar, statutory protections against unfair dismissal and redundancy, the reforming of casualization (as on the docks), legal control of low pay through the Wages Boards and legislation directed at addressing unequal treatment on the basis of disability (1944), race (1965; 1968) and gender (1970; 1975). Undoubtedly, citizenship in the workplace was enhanced in the process, and workers' own personal testimonies from the period provide much evidence of this incremental emancipation.

The 'end of work'? Continuity and change since mid-twentieth century

Behind the rhetoric and the contrasting, contradictory and competing discourses around the workplace there were multiple, diverse, complex and many layered experiences that coagulated into the material reality of everyday working lives. Is it possible to say what had fundamentally changed in the world of work between 1945 and the present? How do the key theories of the changing nature of work stand up to critical review? Are we living through a profound degradation of work brought on by global capitalism – or the 'end of work' with the erosion of the idea of a lifetime career, the growth of 'non-standard' employment, part-time work and risky, insecure jobs? Or, alternatively, are we witnessing widespread re-skilling and 'upgrading' of work, the end of drudgery and the advent of more creative, autonomous and meaningful labour?

This period since the Second World War undeniably witnessed unprecedentedly rapid and profound changes in our relationship with work. In terms of the type of jobs people do, there has been a fundamental transformation from manual to non-manual labour – with nine out of ten female employees and more than seven out of ten male employees in non-manual employment in the early 2010s. In this contemporary knowledge and service sector based economy people now work more with their heads than with their hands, with sophisticated electronic equipment on computers and the web in offices rather than in factories, mines or workshops. The labour processes, spaces and physical environments in which most workers toil have also changed dramatically and this has had wide-ranging ramifications, not least on the body as more sedentary work has replaced physical labour and people are funneled into more benign and less dangerous workplaces. Labour processes and the organization of work have been transformed accordingly with the shift associated with the demise of Fordist styles of production, towards more flexible, 'lean production' and 'human factor' styles of management. All this has had enormous ramifications, including being implicated in a shift towards more 'middle-class' occupations and the fracturing of traditional working-class consciousness, solidarities and culture. The manual craft artisanal ethos, so important in the shaping of working-class culture and communities in Britain, has atrophied as apprenticeships and skilled jobs sharply declined and the moral economy of the skilled manual worker was put under pressure from technological change, deskilling and market forces.

But the process of change has been contradictory, complex and multi-layered. On the one hand, there has been a marked tendency for labour processes to be deskilled with technological and organizational change, and this can be seen across manufacturing, mining and in clerical work and the service sector. Workers lost jobs, cherished skills were no longer needed and redundancies followed with all the loss of self-esteem, the trauma and disruption to the community that entailed. This was captured in some of the social realist fiction, and acclaimed drama and movies, such as *Brassed Off* and Alan Bleasdale's *Boys from the Black Stuff*. Technological change with automation, information technology and computer systems were also responsible for both extending managerial monitoring, surveillance and control, and creating drudgery – epitomized perhaps by jobs in McDonald's and the call centres. Concurrently, the transformation of work relieved the heavy physical toll upon the body that characterized the traditional 'heavy' industries and the labour-intensive, pre-mechanized household.

What is undeniable is that a significantly larger proportion of the labour force overall were employed in the rapidly expanding managerial, creative and professional sectors – what Reich has termed 'symbolic analysts' – whilst unskilled manual jobs in manufacturing declined. And, as a whole, the labour force was much better educated in the early twenty-first century, with the massive rise in the proportion of school leavers going on to further and higher education. This has all had something of a polarizing effect, sharpening the two-tier nature of the labour market and reconfiguring the basis of privilege and disadvantage in employment. All this cannot be disconnected from the wider world, where the globalizing economy has increasingly seen the 'bad jobs' (including the dangerous manual ones) located in underdeveloped and developing countries – such as India – where multi-national companies can exploit cheap labour and benefit from tax breaks and little or no statutory regulation of work conditions. Meanwhile, the 'good jobs' – or at least the better ones in the tertiary and knowledge-based sector – are becoming increasingly concentrated in developed richer nations like the UK.

Whilst British society as a whole may have gained in material terms from all these changes, with real wages more than doubling in the second half of the twentieth century and significant improvement in employment rights and non-wage benefits (such as holidays and pensions), nonetheless deep inequalities persisted or re-emerged in new configurations as the economy metamorphized into its present form. We see this in the unprecedented (and quite obscene) wage gap between the highest and lowest earners, in the continuing degradation of casual, migrant labour, the persisting disadvantages of BME and disabled workers, and in the emergence of a two-tier labour market distinguished by those with job security and those without. The return of mass unemployment and revival of neo-liberal economics in the late twentieth century posed a fundamental challenge. This precipitated a fundamental shift in the balance of power in the UK workplace, characterized by a resurgence of managerial authority and a withering of workers' power and erosion of trade unionism in the face of job losses, anti-labour legislation, deregulation and exposure to the globalized market. The labour movement suffered a deeply symbolic defeat in the miners' strike of 1984–5. What followed reaffirmed the lessons of the past – that trade unions play a vitally important role in protecting workers from the vagaries of the competitive market place and are needed more than ever in contemporary society.

The 1980s marked a watershed in many respects, witnessing a sharp deterioration in work conditions as mass unemployment acted as a disciplining force on those in jobs, leading to a tightening of managerial control and work intensification, delivered through a myriad of ways in the workplace. Manifestations of this are the shift towards an 'overwork culture' (Bunting, 2004) and the modern-day workplace stress epidemic – the latter an indication that work does still continue to impact adversely upon the body, though in very different ways to the trauma, chronic disease, disability and premature mortality associated with the heavy industry workplace in the heyday of Fordist production. Increasingly, job security has eroded with the proliferation of non-standard, temporary, part-time job contracts and under-employment. The proportion of workers on secure, full-time and 'lifetime' tenured contracts is dwindling. The 'career' worker is fast becoming a thing of the past, with young people entering the labour market now more likely to combine a series of part-time jobs and have several career changes over their lifetimes. Inequality and polarization in the labour market is intensifying, between those whose employment security and work experience is being enhanced and real wages are rising, and those experiencing stagnating real wages, uncertain employment and degradation in the nature of their work.

This transformation has been associated with the idea of 'the end of work'. It has been posited that with more risky and insecure work

contracts and labour market experiences work identities are meta-
morphizing and the 'work ethic' dissolving. People's relationship to
work is in flux. In this new world, attachments to work are deemed
to be tenuous, work identities to be less certain and the moral dimensions of work – its intrinsic value and significance – to no longer be
central in people's lives. The argument being developed here is that
these claims need to be kept in perspective. At the very least the
collapse of work thesis requires refinement and qualification. The
idea of the 'end of work' applies more to male white workers than
other groups. As we have seen, the labour market at mid-twentieth
century was characterized by much insecurity and deep inequalities,
with female workers, the disabled and BME workers subordinated
and disadvantaged. The trajectory for such marginalized workers has
been towards more job security and a larger proportion in full-time
career employment, so the 'end of work' thesis hardly fits their experience. Moreover, the majority of adult men are still on full-time career
labour contracts as we enter the second decade of the twenty-first
century and the tendency towards casualization and insecurity may
yet be reversed if, for example, economic and political circumstances
change. Whilst the Labour administrations from 1997–2010 remained
committed to most aspects of a deregulated market (with disastrous
consequences in relation to the banking and financial sector, and, ultimately, the economy when the bubble burst in 2008), there were significant policy shifts designed to address issues of fairness and dignity
at work, including the statutory minimum wage from 1999. European
Union Labour Directives have provided another important mecha-
nism through which a floor has been placed on the downward pressures of the open market. Moreover, there remains much evidence to
contest the view that paid work diminished in importance in people's
lives, not least in workers' own voices and narratives.

A key change since the Second World War has been in the relationship of women to the labour market. Work has always been gendered and quite fundamental changes have occurred since the 1940s
regarding the relationship of both men and women to work. The
traditional boundaries and gendered roles which positioned men as
'breadwinners' and providers and women as homemakers and child
nurturers have dissolved in the face of a sharp rise in the participation of married and cohabiting women in paid employment. There has
been a converging effect in work identities and a blurring of dominant or hegemonic modes of masculinity and femininity associated
with the 'separate spheres' ideology. Traditional working-class styles

of masculinity, including the hegemonic 'hard man' mode characteristic of (though never completely dominant in) urban working-class
communities and the mining villages has atrophied. Office work –
'pen-pushing' – might have been widely regarded in working-class
communities as emasculating, but a tsunami of such jobs submerged
the manufacturing heartlands nonetheless. Whilst providing more
choice and opportunity for women and ultimately liberating, the
changing shape of the labour market has precipitated something of
a crisis of masculinity to which men were (and continue to be) forced
to adapt. Whilst this may be perceived by some men – almost instinc-
tively in some cases – as a challenge and a threat, the positive outcome
is the potential for a more rewarding work-life and family-employ-
ment balance as masculinities and femininities are renegotiated and
reconfigured in modern society.

Privileging the narrative voices of the workers

The meaning of work and the changes that have occurred in it have
been felt by workers themselves and articulated through their voices
and narratives in autobiographies and work-life oral history testimonies. Such material needs to be treated sensitively, given the issues
relating to memory, intersubjectivity and narrative construction that
oral historians and others have identified in their studies. None the
less, working with personal narratives gets us closer to everyday lived
experience and what work *signified* to those who were directly involved
in it. The discourses embedded within such narratives act as a barometer of shifting workplace culture, elucidating mutating work identities
and signifying the degree and limits of erosion of the work ethic – of
attachment and commitment to work. This provides the potential for
a focus not just on human experience, but also on feelings, the body
and on emotions. In such accounts nostalgia for a lost 'golden' past
of more meaningful and secure work, of camaraderie and a 'job for
life' intermingles with a sense of progress and positive change – more
opportunities, less hard physical labour, more education, more choice.
Orientations to work vary across a wide spectrum from the alienation
narratives of call centre workers and casual labour to those who felt a
deep connection with and drew substantial satisfaction and even joy
from their work, as with most skilled manual work and creative professions. What is also evident in such narratives is a lingering sense of loss
of power and autonomy at work, linked to a series of changes in labour
markets since the 1980s. It appears, nonetheless, that work retained

a deep and elemental meaning in most people's everyday lives, providing structure to the day, purpose and much intrinsic satisfaction.
Understandably earnings remained of pivotal importance, but workers were motivated by intrinsic rewards too and frequently blended
economic and cultural motivations into their responses and narratives
when asked to explain why they work or what work meant to them
(Bradley et al., 2000, pp. 169–86). When employment was lost, this
could be felt like bereavement. The impacts of unemployment starkly
elucidate the meanings of work. Assertions that people only work for
the money as well as claims of the 'abandonment' of the commitment
to work do not stand up to closer scrutiny. In large part these have
been a fabrication of the carefully remobilized notion of the Victorian
work ethic within Thatcherism.

At present, work-life oral history approaches are still in their
infancy in relation to the reconstruction of *work identities* in the UK.
Clearly, there is much potential here to develop a re-focused history
of the meaning of work in everyday lives. Seminal studies such as
those of Tim Strangleman, John Kirk and Christine Wall for the UK,
and Alessandro Portelli and Steve High in relation to the USA and
Canada point the way, showing the promise of a focus upon work–life
oral histories to understand the meaning of work and its loss, and
to comprehend work cultures in different contexts and the ways in
which people's relationship to work is changing. The dignity of human
toil in the face of hardship, injustice and insecurity oozes from such
well-crafted oral history-based scholarship. These researchers demonstrate that emotional attachments to employment in occupational
communities as diverse as banking, teaching and the railways in the
UK, coal mining in Harlan County USA and metal working, paper
making and car manufacture in Michigan and Ontario were intense
but also complex. What is also apparent is that a range of work orientations and identities existed and continue to coexist, whilst even in the
less secure, precarious and risky modern-day workplace identification
with work remains of fundamental importance and the moral dimensions of work of deep significance in many people's lives. We urgently
require more such studies deploying work-life oral testimonies, ethnographic approaches and the study of workers' autobiographical and
personal accounts to deepen our understanding of what both paid and
unpaid work denoted in the past and continues to mean in the present.
If this book plays a part in stimulating such a re-focused study of the
meaning of work in modern society and encourages critical reflection
and debate on what work has signified in the past and continues to
denote in our lives it will have achieved its aim.

Bibliography

Primary Sources

Archived Oral Testimonies and Fieldwork

Britain at Work: Voices from the Workplace, 1945–1995

Accessed at http://www.unionhistory.info/britainatwork/resources/audio.php (2012). 25 work-life interviews of London workers. Website hosted by the TUC (Chris Coates). Project leaders: Stefan Dickers and David Welsh.

British Library Sound Archive National Life Stories

Lives in the Oil Industry. Project leaders: Terry Brotherstone and Hugo Manson.

Constructing Post-War Britain: Building Workers' Stories, 1950–1970

Accessed at http://www.buildingworkersstories.com/
Project run by the University of Westminster in the Centre for the Study of the Production of the Built Environment. Currently comprises 50 construction workers work-life interviews. Project leaders: Christine Wall and Linda Clarke.

Economic and Social Data Service

Accessed at: http://www.esds.ac.uk/qualidata/online
Archive Project SN4938: 100 Families (Social Mobility and Ageing), 1985–6.
Archive Project SN 4815: Employment and Working Life Beyond the Year 2000: Employee Attitudes to Work in Call Centres and Software Development, 1999–2001.
Archive Project SN 4739: Qualitative Investigation of Living and Labour Market Experiences of Persons with Multiple Problems and Needs, 2001–2.

Glasgow Museums Oral History Collection

Springburn Oral History Project (1983–5).
Glasgow 2000 Lives Project (1995–9).
Glasgow Dock Workers (Project leader: David Walker, 2009).

Glasgow Working Lives (Project leaders: David Walker and Arthur McIvor, 2010–).

London Dockers Memoryscape

Lovell's Wharf excerpt: A.S. Ellis.
Accessed at http://www.memoryscape.org.uk/Dockers%20transcript.htm
Project leader: Toby Butler.

Scottish Oral History Centre (SOHC) Archive

SOHCA/010: Women in the Scottish Communist Party (Neil Rafeek).
SOHCA/016: Occupational Health Oral History Project 1: Asbestos (Ronnie Johnston and Arthur McIvor; with some interviewing by Neil Rafeek and Hilary Young). Note: Narrators all anonymized.
SOHCA/017: Occupational Health Oral History Project 2: Coal mining (Ronnie Johnston and Arthur McIvor; with some interviewing by Neil Rafeek, Hilary Young and Susan Morrison).
SOHCA/018: Occupational Health Oral History Project 3: Medical professionals; industrial hygienists; nurses (Ronnie Johnston and Arthur McIvor; with some interviewing by Neil Rafeek, Hilary Young and Susan Morrison).
SOHCA/019: University of Strathclyde Oral History Project (Callum Brown, Arthur McIvor, Neil Rafeek, Hilary Young).
SOHCA/022: British Chemical Industry Workers (David Walker).
SOHCA/023: M74 Glasgow Oral History Project (David Walker).
SOHCA/032: Reserved Occupations in the UK, 1939–45 (Juliette Pattinson, Arthur McIvor, Wendy Ugolini, Alison Chand, Linsey Robb).
SOHCA/042: Glasgow Working Lives Project (David Walker and Arthur McIvor)

Scottish Working People's History Trust (SWPHT)

A substantial collection of oral interviews (with full transcriptions) of journalists, librarians, seamen, shipyard workers, miners, textile workers, dockers and others archived in the SOHC Archive /030 and in the School of Scottish Studies Archive, University of Edinburgh. Project leader: Ian MacDougall.

South Wales Coalfield Collection, Miners' Library, University of Swansea

Interview with John Evans, 13 June 1973, AUD/84.
Interview with Dr Thomas, n.d., AUD/374.
Interview with M. Morris, n.d., AUD/389.
'The Big Hewer', n.d., AUD/580.

Stirling Women's Oral History Project

Smith Library, Stirling. Copies of 80 interviews archived in the Scottish Oral History Centre, SOHCA/05. Project leader: Jayne Stephenson

Autobiographies and Ethnographies

Ashley, J. (1992) *Acts of Defiance* (London).
Beattie, G. (1998) *Hard Lines: Voices From Deep Within a Recession* (Manchester).
Cavendish, R. (1982) *Women on the Line* (London).
Collins, W. (1965) *Jamaican Migrant* (London).
Coombes, B. (1939) *These Poor Hands* (London).
Ellis, T. (2004) *After the Dust has Settled* (Wrexham).
Ellis, V. and Taylor, M. (2010) 'Banks, Bailouts and Bonuses: A Personal Account of Working in Halifax Bank of Scotland During the Financial Crisis', *Work, Employment & Society*, 24(4), December, 803–12.
Fraser, R. (ed.) (1968) *Work: Twenty Personal Accounts* (Harmondsworth).
Fraser, R. (ed.) (1969) *Work 2: Twenty Personal Accounts* (Harmondsworth).
Glasser, R. (1987) *Growing Up in the Gorbals* (London).
Gould, T. and Kenyon, J. (1972) *Stories from the Dole Queue* (London).
Kenyon, J. (2003) *A Passion for Justice* (Nottingham).
Marsden, D. and Duff, E. (1975) *Workless: Some Unemployed Men and their Families* (Harmondsworth).
McGeown, P. (1967) *Heat the Furnace Seven Times More* (London).
McKessock, B. (1995) *Mesothelioma: the Story of an Illness* (Argyll).
Moffat, A. (1965) *My Life with the Miners* (London).
Sirs, B. (1985) *Hard Labour* (London).
Smith, B. (1991) *Seven Steps in the Dark: A Miner's Life*, Barr, (Scotland).
Toynbee, P. (1971) *A Working Life* (London).
Toynbee, P. (2003) *Life in Low-Pay Britain* (London).
Westwood, S. (1984) *All Day, Every Day: Factory and Family in the Making of Women's Lives* (London).
Wight, D. (1993) *Workers not Wasters: Masculine Respectability, Consumption and Employment in Central Scotland* (Edinburgh).

Government Publications, Journals and Reports

Achur, J. and the Department for Business, Innovation and Skills (2010) *Trade Union Membership* (London), accessed at http://stats.bis.gov.uk/UKSA/tu/sa20100430.htm
Annual Reports of HM Chief Inspector of Factories (HMSO, London).

Department of Employment and Productivity (1971) *British Labour Statistics: Historical Abstract, 1886–1968,* London: HMSO.

Department of Enterprise, Trade and Investment, Labour Force Survey, Historical Supplement, Oct 2008, accessed at http://www.detini.gov.uk/lfs_historical_supplement_2008.pdf.

Health and Safety Executive (1998) *The Stress and Health at Work Study*(London).

Health and Safety Executive (2001) *Tackling Work Related Stress: A Managers' Guide to Improving and Maintaining Employee Health and Wellbeing* (Sudbury).

Health and Safety Executive (2006) *British Partnership in Health and Safety* (London).

Health and Safety Executive (1993) *Annual Report*, Statistical Supplement (London).

Health and Safety Executive: http://www.hse.gov.uk/statistics/history/fatal.htm

Labour Research, 1970–1985

Life Opportunities Survey, 2009–10 (2010) Interim Results. Consulted at http://www.statistics.gov.uk/pdfdir/los1210.pdf

Office for National Statistics, *Labour Market,* consulted at *http://www.statistics.gov.uk/hub/labour-market/index.html*

Office of Population Censuses and Surveys (Health and Safety Executive), *Occupational Health Decennial Supplement* (London, 1995).

Registrar General's Decennial Supplement on Occupational Mortality, England and Wales, 1951, Pt 2, Vol 1, London, 1958.

Reports of HM Inspector of Mines (Scottish Division), London, 1949–1955.

Royal Commission on Trade Unions and Industrial Relations (Donovan), Report (London, 1968).

Secondary Sources

Abbotts, J., Williams, R., West, P., Hunt, K. and Ford, G. (2004) 'Catholic Socio-Economic Disadvantage in The West of Scotland: A Narrowing of Inequality', *Scottish Affairs*, 49.

Abrams, L. (1999) '"There Was Nobody Like My Daddy": Fathers, The Family and the Marginalisation of Men in Modern Scotland', *Scottish Historical Review*, LXXVII, 2, pp. 219–42.

Abrams, L. (2010) *Oral History Theory* (London).

Abrams, L. and Brown, C. G. (eds) (2010) *A History of Everyday Life in Twentieth Century Scotland* (Edinburgh).

Airey, C. A. (1984) 'Social and Moral Values' in R. Jowell and C. Airey *British Social Attitudes: The 1984 Report* (Aldershot), pp. 121–56.

Aldred, C. (1981) *Women at Work* (London).

Allen, S., Waton, A., Purcell, F. and Wood, S. (eds) (1986) *The Experience of Unemployment* (Basingstoke).

Anderson, J. (2011) *War, Disability and Rehabilitation in Britain* (Manchester).

Ashton, D. N. (1986) *Unemployment Under Capitalism* (Brighton).

Ashton, D. (1988) 'Educational Institutions, Youth and the Labour Market' in D. Gallie (ed.) *Employment in Britain* (Oxford), pp. 406–36.

Ashworth, W. (1986) *The History of the British Coal Industry, vol 5, 1946–1982: The Nationalised Industry* (Oxford).

Ayers, P. (2004) 'Work Culture and Gender: The Making of Masculinities in Post-War Liverpool' in E. Yeo (ed.) *Working Class Masculinities in Britain, 1850 to the Present*, special edition, *Labour History Review*, 69(2), August, pp. 153–68.

Bain, G. S. (1970) *The Growth of White Collar Unionism* (Oxford).

Bain, G. S. and Price, R. (1980) *Profiles of Union Growth* (Oxford).

Baines, D. (2007) 'Immigration and the Labour Market' in N. Crafts, I. Gazeley and A. Newall *Work and Pay in Twentieth Century Britain* (Oxford), pp. 330–52.

Baker, C. and Caldwell, P. (1981) *Unions and Change Since 1945* (London).

Bakke, E. W. (1933) *The Unemployed Man* (London).

Baldry, C., Bain, P. and Taylor, P. (1997) 'Sick and Tired: Working in the Modern Office', *Work, Employment and Society*, 11(3), September, pp. 519–39.

Ballard, R. and Holden, B. (1981) 'The Employment of Coloured Graduates in Britain' in P. Braham, E. Rhodes and M. Pearn (eds) *Discrimination and Disadvantage in Employment: The Experience of Black Workers* (London), pp. 163–76.

Barke, J.(1936) *Major Operation* (London).

Barnes, C, and Mercer, G. (2003) *Disability* (Cambridge).

Barnes, H. (2000) *Working for a Living? Employment, Benefits and the Living Standards of Disabled People* (Bristol).

Barnes, H., Thornton, C. and Campbell, S. M. (1998) *Disabled People and Employment* (Bristol).

Bartie, A. (2010) 'Moral Panics and Glasgow Gangs: Exploring "the New Wave of Glasgow Hooliganism", 1965–1970', *Contemporary British History*, 24(3), pp. 385–408.

Bartley, M. (1985) 'Coronary Heart Disease' in P. Weindling (ed.) *The Social History of Occupational Health* (London).

Bartley, M. (1992) *Authorities and Partisans: The Debate on Unemployment and Health* (Edinburgh).

Bartrip, P. W. J. (1987) *Workmen's Compensation in Twentieth Century Britain: Law, History and Social Policy* (Aldershot).

Bartrip, P. W. J. (2001) *The Way from Dusty Death: Turner and Newall and the Regulation of the British Asbestos Industry 1890s-1970* (London).

Bartrip, P. W. J. (2005) *Beyond the Factory Gates: Asbestos and Health in Twentieth Century America* (London).

Bauman, Z. (1998) *Work, Consumerism and the New Poor* (Buckingham).

Beaumont, P. B. (1983) *Safety at Work and the Unions* (Beckenham).

Beck, M., Foster, J. and Woolfson, C. (1996) *Paying for the Piper: Capital and Labour in Britain's Offshore Oil Industry* (London).

Beck, U. (1992), *Risk Society: Towards a New Modernity* (London).

Beck, U. (2000) *The Brave New World of Work* (Cambridge).

Bell, D. (1973) *The Coming of the Post-Industrial Society* (London).

Bellaby, P. and Bellaby, F. (1999) 'Unemployment and Ill Health: Local Labour Markets and Ill Health in Britain, 1984–1991', *Work, Employment and Society*, 13(3), pp. 461–82.

Bellamy, M. (2001) *The Shipbuilders* (Edinburgh).

Beveridge, W. E. (1968) 'Problems in Preparing for Retirement' in H. B. Wright (ed.) *Solving the Problems of Retirement* (London).

Beynon, H. (1973) *Working for Ford* (London).

Beynon, H. and Blackburn, R.M. (1972) *Perceptions of Work: Variations within a Factory* (London).

Beynon, H., Grimshaw, D., Rubery, J. and Ward, K. (2002) *Managing Employment Change: The New Realities of Work* (Oxford).

Bhat, A., Carr-Hill, R. and Ohri, S (eds) (1988) *Britain's Black Population: A New Perspective* (Aldershot).

Blackburn, R. and Mann, M. (1979) *The Working Class in the Labour Market* (London).

Blackburn, R. and Mann, M. (1981) 'Ethnic Stratification in an Industrial City' in P. Braham, E. Rhodes and M. Pearn, M. (eds) *Discrimination and Disadvantage in Employment: The Experience of Black Workers* (London), pp. 138–49.

Blackwell, T. and Seabrook, J. (1996) *Talking Work: An Oral History* (London).

Blake, G. (1935; 1993) *The Shipbuilders* (Edinburgh).

Blakemore, K. and Drake, R. (1996) *Understanding Equal Opportunity Policies* (London).

Blaxter, M. (1976) *The Meaning of Disability: A Sociological Study of Impairment* (London).

Boardman, J. (2003), 'Work, Employment and Psychiatric Disability', *Advances in Psychiatric Treatment*, 9, pp. 327–334.

Bolton, S. and Boyd, C. (2003) 'Trolley Dolly or Skilled Emotion Manager? Moving on From Hochschild's Managed Heart', *Work, Employment and Society*, 17(2), June, pp. 289–308.

Booth, A. and Melling, J. (2008) 'Workplace Cultures and Business Performance' in J. Melling and A. Booth (eds) *Managing the Modern Workplace: Productivity, Politics and Workplace Culture in Postwar Britain* (Aldershot), pp. 1–26.

Borsay, A. (2005) *Disability and Social Policy in Britain since 1750: A History of Exclusion* (Basingstoke).

Bourdieu, P. (1999; first published 1993) *The Weight of the World: Social Suffering in Contemporary Society* (Cambridge).

Bourke, J. (1994) *Working Class Cultures* (London).

Bowden, S. and Tweedale, G. (2003) 'Mondays without Dread: The Trade Union Response to Byssinosis in the Lancashire Cotton Industry in the Twentieth Century', *Social History of Medicine*, 16(1), pp. 79–95.

Boyd, C. (2002) 'Customer Violence and Employee Health and Safety', *Work, Employment and Society*, 16(1), March, pp. 151–69.

Boyle, M. (2011) *Metropolitan Anxieties: On the Meaning of the Irish Catholic Adventure in Scotland* (Farnham).

Bradley, D. (2011) 'Oral History, Occupational Health and Safety and Scottish Steel, c1930–1988', *Scottish Labour History*, 46, pp. 86–101.

Bradley, H., Erickson, M., Stephenson, C. and Williams, S. (2000) *Myths at Work* (Cambridge).

Braham, P., Rhodes, E. and Pearn, M. (eds) (1981) *Discrimination and Disadvantage in Employment: The Experience of Black Workers* (London).

Braverman, H. (1974; 25th anniversary edition 1999) *Labor and Monopoly Capital* (New York).

Braybon, G. and Summerfield, P. (1987) *Out of the Cage* (London).

Brenner, M. H. and Mooney, A. (2003) 'Unemployment and Health in the Context of Economic Change', *Social Science and Medicine*, 17, pp. 1125–38.

Breitenbach, E. (1982) *Women Workers in Scotland* (Edinburgh).

British Safety Council (n.d., c1970) *Common Causes of Factory Accidents* (London).

Brooke, S. (2001) 'Gender and Working Class Identity in Britain During the 1950s', *Journal of Social History*, 34(4), Summer, pp. 773–95.

Brooks, A. (1975) *Academic Women* (London).

Brooks, D. (1975) *Race and Labour in London Transport* (London).

Brooks, D. (1981) 'Race and Labour in London Transport: Some Conclusions' in P. Braham, E. Rhodes and M. Pearn (eds) *Discrimination and Disadvantage in Employment: The Experience of Black Workers* (London), pp. 126–37.

Brotherstone, T. and Manson, H. (2007) 'North Sea Oil, its Narratives and its History', *Northern Scotland*, 27, pp. 15–41.

Brotherstone, T. and Manson, H. (2011) 'Voices of Piper Alpha: Enduring Injury in Private Memory, Oral Representation and Labour History', *Scottish Labour History*, 46, pp. 71–85.

Brown, C. (2000) *The Death of Christian Britain* (London).

Brown, C., McIvor, A. and Rafeek, N. (2004) *The University Experience, 1945–1975: An Oral History of the University of Strathclyde* (Edinburgh).

Brown, J. C. (1982) *Disability Income Part 1: Industrial Injuries* (London).
Brown, M. (ed.) (1983) *The Structure of Disadvantage* (London).
Bruley, S. (1999) *Women in Britain since 1900* (Basingstoke).
Bufton, M. (2004) *Britain's Productivity Problem, 1948–1990* (Basingstoke).
Bunting, M. (2004) *Willing Slaves: How the Overwork Culture is Ruining our Lives* (London).
Burchell, B., Ladipo, D. and Wilkinson, F. (eds) (2002) *Job Insecurity and Work Intensification* (London).
Burnett, J. (1994) *Idle Hands: The Experience of Unemployment, 1790–1990* (London).
Burton, D. (1997) 'Ethnicity and Occupational Welfare: A Study of Pension Scheme Membership in Britain', *Work, Employment and Society*, 11, pp. 505–18.
Callender, C. (1987) 'Women Seeking Work' in S. Fineman (ed.) *Unemployment: Personal and Social Consequences* (London), pp. 22–46.
Campbell, A. (2000) *The Scottish Miners 1874–1939, volume 1: Industry, Work and Community* (Aldershot).
Campbell, B. (1984) *Wigan Pier Revisited, Poverty and Politics in the 80s* (London).
Caradog Jones, D. (1934) *The Social Survey of Merseyside* (Liverpool).
Casey, B, and Laczko, F. (1989) 'Early Retired or Long-Term Unemployed? The Situation of Non-Working Men Aged 55–64 from 1979 to 1986', *Work, Employment and Society*, 3(4), pp. 509–26.
Casey, C. (2003) *Work, Self and Society After Industrialism* (London).
Cassells, M. (1997) *The Power of Identity* (Oxford).
Chand, A. (forthcoming 2013) *The Second World War in Glasgow and Clydeside: Men in Reserved Occupations 1939–1945*, PhD thesis, University of Strathclyde.
Chappell, H. (1983) 'Fighting Each Other Over Asbestos', *New Society*, 29, September, pp. 471–3.
Cheshire, P. C. (1973) *Regional Unemployment Differences in Great Britain* (London).
Church, R. and Outram, Q. (1998) *Strikes and Solidarity: Coalfield Conflict in Britain, 1889–1966* (Cambridge).
Clarke, J. S. (1951) *Disabled Citizens* (London).
Clarke, L. and Wall, C. (2009) ' "A Woman's Place is Where She Wants to Work": Barriers to the Entry and Retention of Women into the Skilled Building Trades', *Scottish Labour History*, 44, pp. 16–39.
Clarke, R. (1982) *Work in Crisis* (Edinburgh).
Coates, K. (1982) 'The vagaries of Participation' in B. Pimlott, and C. Cook (eds) *Trade Unions in British Politics* (London).

Coates, K. and Barratt Brown, M. (1997) *Community Under Attack: The Struggle for Survival in the Coalfield Communities of Britain* (Nottingham).

Cockburn, C. (1983) *Brothers: Male Dominance and Technological Change* (London).

Collinson, D. and Hearn, J. (1996a) 'Men at "Work": Multiple Masculinities/ Multiple Workplaces' in M. Mac an Ghail (ed.) *Understanding Masculinities* (Buckingham), pp. 61–76.

Collinson, D. and Hearn, J. (eds) (1996b) *Men as Managers; Managers as Men*, London: Sage.

Collinson, D. and Hearn, J. (2001) 'Naming Men as Men: Implications for Work, Organisation and Management' in S. M. Whitehead, and F. J. Barrett (eds) *The Masculinities Reader* (Cambridge).

Connell, R. and Messerschmidt, J. (2005) 'Hegemonic Masculinity: Rethinking the Concept', *Gender and Society*, 19(6), pp. 829–59.

Connell, R.W. (2000) *The Men and the Boys* (Oxford).

Connolly, S. and Gregory, M. (2007) 'Women and Work since 1970' in N. Crafts, I. Gazeley and A. Newall (eds) *Work and Pay in Twentieth Century Britain* (Oxford).

Cornwell, J. (1984) *Hard Earned Lives* (London).

Cowan, R. S. (1989) *More Work for Mother* (London).

Cowley, U. (2001) *The Men Who Built Britain: A History of the Irish Navvy* (Merlin).

Coyle, A. (1984) *Redundant Women* (London).

Crafts, N., Gazeley, I. and Newall, A. (eds) (2007) *Work and Pay in Twentieth Century* Britain (Oxford).

Cragg, A. and Dawson, T. (1984) *Unemployed Women: A Study of Attitudes and Experiences*, Research Paper 47, Department of Employment (London).

Crick, B. (ed.) (1981) *Unemployment* (London).

Crompton, R. (1994) 'Non-Manual Labour' in J. Obelkevich and P. Catterall, P. (eds) *Understanding Post-War British Society* (London), pp. 99–115.

Crompton, R. (1997) *Women and Work in Modern Britain* (Oxford).

Cronin, J. E. (1979) *Industrial Conflict in Modern Britain* (London).

Cunningham, H. (1995) *Children and Childhood in Western Society since 1500* (Harlow).

Dale, A, Fieldhouse, E., Shaheen, N. and Kalra, V. (2002) 'The Labour Market Prospects for Pakistani and Bangladeshi Women', *Work, Employment and Society*, 16, pp. 5–25.

Dalton, A. (1998) *Safety, Health and Environmental Hazards at the Workplace* (London).

Daniel, W. W. (1968) *Racial Discrimination in England* (Harmondsworth).

Daniels, S. and Rycroft, S. (1993) 'Mapping the Modern City: Alan Sillitoe's Nottingham Novels', *Transactions of the Institute of British Geographers*, New Series, 18(4), pp. 460–80.

Darby, J. (1987) 'Religious Discrimination and Differentiation in Northern Ireland: The Case of the Fair Employment Agency' in R. Jenkins and J. Solomos (eds) *Racism and Equal Opportunity Policies in the 1980s* (Cambridge), pp. 54–72.

Daykin, N. and Doyal, L. (eds) (1999) *Health and Work: Critical Perspectives* (Basingstoke).

Deakin, N. (1969) *Colour, Citizenship and British Society* (London).

Dembe, A. (1996) *Occupation and Disease* (New Haven).

Dennis, N., Henriques, F. and Slaughter, C. (1956; second edition 1969) *Coal is Our Life* (London).

Devine, T. (ed.) (2000) *Scotland's Shame? Bigotry and Sectarianism in Modern Scotland* (Edinburgh).

Donkin, R. (2001) *The History of Work* (Basingstoke).

Dougall, R. (2008) 'Being the Queen's Nurse: Work and Identity as a Queen's Nurse' in M. A. Mulhern, J. Beech, and E. Thompson (eds), *The Working Life of the Scots: A Compendium of Scottish Ethnology, vol 7* (Edinburgh), pp. 334–47.

Doyal, L. (1999) 'Women and Domestic Labour: Setting the Research Agenda' in N. Daykin and L. Doyal (eds) *Health and Work: Critical Perspectives* (Basingstoke).

Draper, J. (2008) 'The Working Lives of Scottish Schoolteachers' in M. A. Mulhern, J. Beech and E. Thompson (eds) *The Working Life of the Scots: A Compendium of Scottish Ethnology, vol 7* (Edinburgh), pp. 525–40.

Dresser, M. (1986) *Black and White on the Buses: The 1963 Colour Bar Dispute in Bristol* (Bristol).

Drever, F. (ed.) (1995) *Occupational Health: Decennial Supplement* (London).

Duffield, M. (1985) 'Rationalisation and the Politics of Segregation: Indian Workers in Britain's Foundry Industry, 1945–62' in K. Lunn (ed.) *Race and Labour in Twentieth Century Britain*, special issue, *Immigrants and Minorities*, 4(2), July, pp. 142–72.

Duncan, C. (2003) 'Assessing Anti-Ageism Routes to Older Worker Re-engagement', *Work, Employment and Society*, 17(1), March, pp. 102–20.

Duncan, R. (2005) *The Mineworkers* (Edinburgh).

Edgell, S. (2006) *The Sociology of Work* (London).

Ellis, V. (1988) 'Current Trade Union Attempts to Remove Occupational Segregation in the Employment of Women' in S. Walby (ed.) *Gender Segregation at Work* (Milton Keynes).

Ellis, V. and Taylor, M. (2010) 'Banks, Bailouts and Bonuses: A Personal Account of Working in Halifax Bank of Scotland During the Financial Crisis', *Work, Employment and Society*, 24(4), December, pp. 803–12.

Esland, G. and Salaman, G. (eds) (1980) *The Politics of Work and Occupations* (Milton Keynes).

Esland, G., Salaman, G. and Speakman, M.-A. (eds) (1975) *People and Work* (Milton Keynes).

Eva, D. and Oswald, R. (1981) *Health and Safety at Work* (London).

Febre, R. (2011) 'Still on the Scrapheap? The Meaning and Characteristics of Unemployment in Prosperous Welfare States', *Work, Employment and Society*, 25(1), pp. 1–9.

Fernie, S. and Metcalf, D. (1998) '(Not) Hanging on the Telephone: Payment Systems in the New Sweatshops', Centre for Economic Performance, LSE, May.

Ferrie J. E., Shipley M. J., Marmot M. G., Stansfeld S. and Smith G. D. (1995) 'Health Effects of Anticipation of Job Change and Non-Employment: Longitudinal Data from the Whitehall II Study', *British Medical Journal*, 311(7015), November 11, pp. 1264–9.

Fieldhouse, E. and Hollywood, E. (1999) 'Life after Mining: Hidden Unemployment and Changing Patterns of Economic Activity amongst Miners in England and Wales, 1981–1991', *Work, Employment and Society*, 13(3), September, pp. 483–502.

Findlay, P. and McKinlay, A. (2004) '"Restless Factories": Shop Steward Organisation on Clydeside, c1945–70', *Scottish Labour History*, 39, pp. 50–69.

Fineman, S. (ed.) (1987) *Unemployment: Personal and Social Consequences* (London).

Finkelstein, V. (1980) *Attitudes and Disabled People: Issues for Discussion* (New York).

Fletcher, B. C. (1991) *Work, Stress, Disease and Life Expectancy* (Chichester).

Fleming, L. (2005) 'Jewish Women in Glasgow c1880–1950: Gender, Ethnicity and the Immigrant Experience', PhD thesis, University of Glasgow.

Foster, J. (1998) 'Class' in A. Cooke, A. Donnachie, A. MacSween and C. A. Whatley (eds) *Modern Scottish History 1707 to the Present, vol 2* (East Linton), pp. 210–34.

Foster, J. and Woolfson, C. (1986), *The Politics of the UCS Work-In* (London).

Francis, H. and Smith, D. (1980) *The Fed: A History of the South Wales Miners in the Twentieth Century* (London).

Fraser, W.H.(1999) *A History of British Trade Unionism, 1700–1998* (Basingstoke).

Freeman, R. and Diamond, W. (2003) 'Young Workers and Trade Unions' in H. Gospel and S. Wood (eds) *Representing Workers: Union Recognition and Membership in Britain* (London), pp. 29–50.

Fryer, D. (1992) 'Psychological or Material Deprivation: Why Does Unemployment Have Mental Health Consequences' in E. McLaughlin (ed.) *Understanding Unemployment* (London), pp. 103–25.

Fryer, P. (1984) *Staying Power: The History of Black People in Britain: Black People in Britain Since 1504* (London).

Furlong, A. (1992) *Growing up in a Classless Society? School to Work Transitions* (Edinburgh).

Gaitens, E. (1942) *Growing Up* (London).

Gaitens, E. (1948; 2001) *Dance of the Apprentices* (Edinburgh).

Gall, G. (2006) 'Union Organising in the North Sea Oil and Gas Industry', *Scottish Labour History*, 41, pp. 51–69.

Gall, G. and Jackson, M. (1998) 'Strike Activity in Scotland', *Scottish Labour History*, 33, pp. 97–112.

Gallie, D. (ed.) (1988) *Employment in Britain* (Oxford).

Gallie, D. (2000) 'The Labour Force' in A. H. Halsey and J. Webb (eds) *Twentieth Century British Social Trends* (Basingstoke), pp. 281–323.

Gallie, D. and Alm, S. (2000) 'Unemployment, Gender and Attitudes to Work' in D. Gallie and S. Paugam (eds) *Welfare Regimes and the Experience of Unemployment in Europe* (Oxford), pp. 109–33.

Gallie, D., Jacobs, S. and Paugam, S. (2000) 'Poverty and Financial Hardship Amongst the Unemployed' in D. Gallie and S. Paugam (eds) *Welfare Regimes and the Experience of Unemployment in Europe* (Oxford), pp. 47–68.

Gallie, D. and Paugam, S. (eds) (2000) *Welfare Regimes and the Experience of Unemployment in Europe* (Oxford).

Gazeley, I. and Newell, A. (2007) 'Unemployment' in N. Crafts, I. Gazeley and A. Newall (eds) *Work and Pay in Twentieth Century Britain* (Oxford).

Geiser, K. (1986) 'Health Hazards in the Microelectronics Industry', *International Journal of Health Services*, 16(1), pp. 105–20.

Gersuny, J. (2000) *Changing Times: Work and Leisure in Post Industrial Society* (Oxford).

Glass, D. V. (ed.) (1954) *Social Mobility in Britain* (London).

Glass, D. V. and Hall, J. R. (1954) 'Social Mobility in Great Britain: A Study of Intergeneration Changes in Status' in A. P. M. Coxon and C. L. Jones (eds) *Social Mobility* (Harmondsworth).

Glasser, R. (1987) *Growing Up in the Gorbals* (London).

Glucksmann, M. (2006) 'The Total Social Organisation of Labour' in L. Pettinger, J. Perry, R. Taylor and M. Glucksmann (eds) *A New Sociology of Work* (Oxford).

Glynn, S. (1991) *No Alternative? Unemployment in Britain* (London).

Goldthorpe, J., Lockwood, D., Bechhofer, F. and Platt, J. (1968) *The Affluent Worker: Industrial Attitudes and Behaviour* (Cambridge).

Goldthorpe, J. H. (1980) *Social Mobility and Class Structure* (Oxford).

Gooding, C. (1994) *Disabling Laws, Enabling Acts: Disability Rights in Britain and America* (London).

Gooding, C. (1996) *Disability Discrimination Act, 1995* (London).

Goodwin, J. (1999) *Men's Work and Male Lives: Men and Work in Britain* (Aldershot).

Goos, M. and Manning A. (2007) 'Lousy and Lovely Jobs: The Rising Polarization of Work in Britain', *The Review of Economics and Statistics*, 89(1), pp. 118–33.

Gorman, E. H. and Kmec, J. A. (2007) 'We (have to) Try Harder: Gender and Required Work Effort in Britain and the United States', *Gender and Society*, 21(6), December, pp. 828–56.

Gorz, A. (1999) *Reclaiming Work: Beyond the Wage-Based Society*, (Cambridge).

Gospel, H. and Wood, S. (2003), *Representing Workers: Union Recognition and Membership in Britain*, London: Routledge.

Gray, A. (2004), *Unsocial Europe: Social Protection or Flexploitation?* London: Pluto Press.

Greenwood, W. (1933) *Love on the Dole* (Harmondsworth).

Gregson, N. and Lowe, M. (1994) *Servicing the Middle Classes: Class, Gender and Waged Domestic Labour in Contemporary Britain* (London).

Grint, K. (1991) *The Sociology of Work: An Introduction* (Cambridge).

Grint, K. (ed.) (2000) *Work and Society: A Reader* (Cambridge).

Hakim, C. (1991) 'Grateful Slaves and Self-Made Women: Fact and Fantasy in Women's Work Orientations', *European Sociological Review*, 7, pp. 101–21.

Hakim, C. (1998) *Social Change and Innovation in the Labour Market* (Oxford).

Hammond, E. (1968) *An Analysis of Regional Economic and Social Statistics* (London).

Hannah, L. (1986) *Inventing Retirement: The Development of Occupational Pensions in Britain* (London).

Harper, S. and Thane, P. (1989) 'The Consolidation of "Old Age" as a Phase of Life' in M. Jeffreys (ed.) *Growing Old in the Twentieth Century* (London).

Hart, P.E. (1988) *Youth Unemployment in Great Britain* (London).

Hauser, R. and Nolan, B. (2000) 'Unemployment and Poverty: Change Over Time' in D. Gallie and S. Paugam (eds) *Welfare Regimes and the Experience of Unemployment in Europe* (Oxford), pp. 25–46.

Health and Safety Executive (1998) *The Stress and Health at Work Study* (London).

Health and Safety Executive (2001) *Tackling Work Related Stress: A Managers' Guide To Improving And Maintaining Employee Health And Well-Being* (Sudbery).

Health and Safety Executive (2006) *British Partnership in Health and Safety* (London).

Higgison, A. (2005) 'Asbestos and British Trade Unions, 1960s and 1970s', *Scottish Labour History*, 40, pp. 70–86.

Hill, M. J., Harrison, R. M., Sargeant, A. V. and Talbot, V. (1973) *Men out of Work: A Study of Unemployment in Three English Towns* (London).

Hill, S. (1976) *The Dockers: Class and Tradition in London* (London).

Hinds, K. and Jarvis, L. (2000) 'The Gender Gap' in R. Jowell et al. (eds) *British Social Attitudes: The 17th Report. Focusing on Diversity* (London), pp. 101–18.

Hinton, J. (1994) *Shop Floor Citizens: Engineering Democracy in 1940s Britain* (Aldershot).

Hobbs, S., Lindsay, S. and McKechnie, J. (1996) 'The Extent of Child Employment in Britain', *British Journal of Education and Work*, 9, pp. 5–18.

Hobbs, S. and McKechnie, J. (1998) 'Children and Work in the UK: The Evidence' in B. Pettitt (ed.) *Children and Work in the UK* (London), pp. 8–21.

Hochschild, A. (1990) *The Second Shift: Working Parents and the Revolution in the Home* (London).

Hodson, R. (2001) *Dignity at Work* (Cambridge).

Hoggart, R. (1957) *The Uses of Literacy* (London).

Holgate, J. (2005) 'Organizing Migrant Workers : A Case Study Of Working Conditions And Unionization In A London Sandwich Factory', *Work, Employment and Society*, 19, pp. 463–80.

Horrell, S. (2007) 'The Household and the Labour Market' in N. Crafts, I. Gazeley and A. Newall (eds) *Work and Pay in Twentieth Century* Britain (Oxford), pp. 117–41.

Hughes, B. (2002) 'Bauman's Strangers: Impairment and the Invalidation of Disabled People in Modern and Post–Modern Cultures', *Disability and Society*, 17(5), pp. 571–84.

Humphries, S. and Gordon, P. (1992) *Out of Sight: The Experience of Disability, 1900–1950* (Plymouth).

Hunter, D. (1959) *Health in Industry* (Harmondsworth).

Hurstfield, J. (1986) 'Women's Unemployment in the 1930s: Some Comparison with the 1980s' in S. Allen, A. Waton, F. Purcell and S. Wood (eds) *The Experience of Unemployment* (Basingstoke), pp. 29–44.

Hyman, R. (1972) *Strikes* (London).

Hyman, R. (1989) *The Political Economy of Industrial Relations, Theory and Practice in a Cold Climate* (London).

Ignaski, P. and Payne, G. (1996) 'Declining Racial Disadvantage in the British Labour Market', *Ethnic and Racial Studies*, 19(1), pp. 113–34.

Ironside, M. and Seifert, R. (2000) *Facing Up to Thatcherism: The History of NALGO, 1979–93* (Oxford).

Jackson, B. (1968) *Working Class Community* (London).

Jahoda, M. (1982) *Employment and Unemployment* (Cambridge).

Jefferys, M. (ed.) (1989) *Growing Old in the Twentieth Century* (London).

Jenkins, C. and Sherman, B. (1979) *White Collar Unionism, The Rebellious Salariat* (London).

Jenkins, C. and Sherman, B. (1979) *The Collapse of Work* (London).

Jenkins, R. and Solomos, J. (1987) *Racism and Equal Opportunity Policies in the 1980s* (Cambridge).

Jenkins, R. (1988) 'Discrimination and Equal Opportunity in Employment: Ethnicity and "Race" in the UK' in D. Gallie (ed.) *Employment in Britain* (Oxford), pp. 310–43.

Johnston, P. (1989) 'The Structured Dependency of the Elderly' in M. Jefferys (ed.) *Growing Old in the Twentieth Century* (London), pp. 62–72.

Johnston, P. (1989) 'The Labour Force Participation of Older Men in Britain, 1951–81', *Work, Employment and Society*, 3(3), pp. 351–68.

Johnston P. and Zaidi, A. (2007) 'Work over the Life Course' in N. Crafts, I. Gazeley and A. Newall (eds) *Work and Pay in Twentieth Century* Britain (Oxford), pp. 98–116.

Johnston, R. and McIvor, A. (2000a) *Lethal Work* (East Linton).

Johnston, R. and McIvor, A. (2000b) 'Whatever Happened to the Occupational Health Service?' in C. Nottingham (ed.) *The NHS in Scotland* (Aldershot), pp. 79–105.

Johnston, R. and McIvor, A. (2004) 'Dangerous Work, Hard Men and Broken Bodies: Masculinity in the Clydeside Heavy Industries, c1930–1970s' in E. Yeo (ed.) *Working Class Masculinities in Britain, 1850 to the Present*, special edition, *Labour History Review*, 69(2), August, pp. 135–52.

Johnston, R. and McIvor, A. (2005) 'The War At Work: Occupational Health and Safety in Scottish Industry, 1939–1945', *Journal of Scottish Historical Studies*, 2, pp. 113–36.

Johnston, R. and McIvor, A. (2008), 'Marginalising the Body at Work? Employers' Occupational Health Strategies and Occupational Medicine in Scotland c. 1930–1974', *Social History of Medicine*, 21, 1, pp. 127–44.

Jones, C. (2002) *Grafters* (London).

Jones, E. L. and Snow, S. J. (2010) *Against the Odds: Black and Minority Ethnic Clinicians in Manchester, 1948–2009* (Manchester).

Jones, H. (1985) 'An Inspector Calls' in P. Weindling (ed.) *The Social History of Occupational Health* (London).

Jones, T. (1993) *Britain's Ethnic Minorities: An Analysis of the Labour Force Survey* (London).

Joshi, H. and Paci, P. (1998) *Unequal Pay for Women and Men* (Cambridge, Mass).

Kay, D. and Miles, R. (1992) *Refugees or Migrant Workers? European Volunteer Workers in Britain, 1946–1951* (London).

Kenyon, J. (2003) *A Passion for Justice* (Nottingham).

Kiernan, K. (1992) 'Men and Women at Work and at Home' in R. Jowell et al. (eds) *British Social Attitudes: The Ninth Report* (Aldershot), pp. 89–112.

Kinnersley, P. (1973) *The Hazards of Work: How to Fight Them* (London).

Kirk, J. (2008) 'Coming to the End of the Line? Identity, Work and Structures of Feeling', *Oral History*, 36(2), Autumn, pp. 44–53.

Kirk, J. and Wall, C. (2010) *Work and Identity* (Basingstoke).

Kirkpatrick, I. and Hoque, K. (2006) 'A Retreat From Permanent Employment? Accounting for the Rise of Professional Agency Work in UK Public Services', *Work, Employment and Society*, 20(4), December, pp. 649–66.

Kirkwood, D. (1935) *My Life of Revolt* (London).

Knox, W. (1999) *Industrial Nation: Work, Culture and Society in Scotland, 1800–Present* (Edinburgh).

Knox, W. and McKinlay, A. (2008) 'Work in Twentieth Century Scotland' in M. A. Mulhern, J. Beech and E. Thompson (eds) *The Working Life of the Scots: A Compendium of Scottish Ethnology, vol 7* (Edinburgh), pp. 48–66.

Kochan, T.A. (2003) 'A US Perspective on the Future of Trade Unions in Britain' in H.Gospel and S. Wood (eds) *Representing Workers: Union Recognition and Membership in Britain* (London), pp. 166–77.

Kondylis, F. and Wadsworth, J. (2007) 'Wages and Wage Inequality 1970–2000' in N. Crafts, I. Gazeley and A. Newall (eds) *Work and Pay in Twentieth Century* Britain (Oxford), pp. 80–97.

Kosmin, B. (1979) 'Traditions of Work Amongst British Jews' in S. Wallman (ed.) *Ethnicity at Work* (London), pp. 37–70.

Kynaston, D. (2007) *Austerity Britain, 1945–51* (London).

Kynaston, D. (2009) *Family Britain, 1951–57* (London).

Lavalette, M. (1998) 'Child Labour: Historical, Legislative and Policy Context' in B. Pettitt (ed.) *Children and Work in the UK* (London), pp. 22–40.

Law, C. M. (1994) 'Employment and Industrial Structure' in J. Obelkevich and P. Catterall (eds) *Understanding Post-War British Society* (London), pp. 85–98.

Lee. C. R. (1979) *British Regional Employment Statistics, 1841–1971* (Cambridge).

Lee, G. and Wrench, J. (1980) 'Accident Prone Immigrants: An Assumption Challenged', *Sociology*, 14(4), pp. 551–66.

Leicester, L. (2009) 'The 1970 Leeds Clothing Workers' Strike: Representations and Refractions', *Scottish Labour History*, 44, pp. 40–55.

Lewis, G. and Sloggett, A. (1998) 'Suicide, Deprivation and Unemployment: Record Linkage Study', *British Medical Journal*, 317(1283), 7 November, accessed at http://www.bmj.com/content/317/7168/1283.full.

Lewis, J. (1992) *Women in Britain since 1945* (Oxford).

Life Opportunities Survey, 2009–10 (9 Dec 2010) *Interim Results*, accessed at http://www.statistics.gov.uk/pdfdir/los1210.pdf.

Littler, C. (ed.) (1985) *The Experience of Work* (Aldershot).

Lockwood, D. (1958) *The Blackcoated Worker* (London).

Lodge, D.(1989) *Nice Work* (Harmondswort).

Long, V. (2006) ' "A Satisfactory Job is the Best Psychotherapist": Employment and Mental Health, 1939–60' in P. Dale and J. Melling (eds) *Mental Illness and Learning Disability Since 1850* (Abingdon).

Long, V. (2011) *The Rise and Fall of the Healthy Factory: The Politics of Industrial Health in Britain, 1914–60* (Basingstoke).

Lunn, K. (1985) 'Race Relations or Industrial Relations? Race and Labour in Britain, 1880–1950' in K. Lunn (ed.) *Race and Labour in Twentieth-Century Britain*, Special edition, *Immigrants and Minorities*, 4(2), July, pp. 1–29.

Lunn, K. (1999) 'Complex Encounters: Trade Unions, Immigration and Racism' in J. McIllroy, N. Fishman and A. Campbell (eds) *British Trade Unionism and Industrial Politics, vol. 2, The High Tide of Trade Unionism, 1964–79* (Aldershot), pp. 70–92.

Luthra, M. (1997) *Britain's Black Population* (Aldershot).

MacDougall, I. (2000) *Voices from Work and Home* (Edinburgh).

Machin, S. (2003) 'Trade Union Decline, New Workplaces and New Workers' in H. Gospel and S. Wood (eds) *Representing Workers: Union Recognition and Membership in Britain* (London), pp. 15–28.

Martin, R. and Wallace, J. (1984) *Working Women in Recession: Employment, Redundancy and Unemployment* (Oxford).

Mason, D. (2000) 'Ethnicity' in G. Payne (ed.) *Social Divisions* (Basingstoke).

Mass Observation (1942) *People in Production* (Harmondsworth).

Maume, D. J., Sebastian, A. R. and Bardo, A. R. (2010) 'Gender, Work-Family Responsibilities and Sleep', *Gender and Society*, 24, December, pp. 746–68.

McCallum, R. I. (1953–4) 'Pneumoconiosis and the Coalfields of Durham and Northumberland', *Transactions of the Institute of Mining Engineers*, 113.

McCulloch, J. and Tweedale, G. (2008) *Defending the Indefensible* (London).

McDougall, W. (forthcoming, 2013) 'Pressure Group Influence and Occupational Health: SPAID/OEDA, 1978–2008', PhD thesis, Glasgow Caledonian University.

McDowell, L. (2003) *Redundant Masculinities: Employment Change and White Working Class Youth* (Oxford).

McEvoy, A. F. (1997) 'Working Environments: An Ecological Approach to Industrial Health and Safety' in R. Cooter and B. Luckin (eds) *Accidents in History: Injuries, Fatalities and Social Relations* (Amsterdam).

McIllroy, J., Fishman, N. and Campbell, A. (eds) (1999) *British Trade Unionism and Industrial Politics. Volume 1: The Post-War Compromise, 1945–64* (Aldershot).

McIllroy, J., Fishman, N. and Campbell, A. (eds) (1999) *British Trade Unionism and Industrial Politics. Volume 2: The High Tide of Trade Unionism, 1964–79* (Aldershot).

McIlvanney, W. (1996) *The Kiln* (London).

McInnes, J. (1987) *Thatcherism at Work* (Milton Keynes).

McIvor, A. (1992) 'Gender Apartheid' in A. Dickson and J. Treble (eds) *People and Society in Scotland*, vol. 3, *1914–1990* (Edinburgh).

McIvor, A. (1996) *Organised Capital* (Cambridge).

McIvor, A. (2001) *A History of Work in Britain, 1880–1950* (Basingstoke).

McIvor, A. (2010) 'The Realities and Narratives of Paid Work: The Scottish Workplace' in L. Abrams and C. G. Brown (eds) *A History of Everyday Life in Twentieth Century Scotland* (Edinburgh), pp. 103–30.

McIvor, A. (2012) 'Germs at Work: Establishing Tuberculosis as an Occupational Disease in Britain, c1900–1951', *Social History of Medicine*, 25(4), pp. 812–29.

McIvor, A. and Johnston, R. (2007) *Miners' Lung* (Ashgate).

McKechnie, J., Lavalette, M. and Hobbs, S. (2000) 'Child Employment Research in Britain', *Work, Employment and Society*, 14(3), September, pp. 573–80.

McKee, L. and Bell, C. (1986) 'His Unemployment, Her Problem: The Domestic and Marital Consequences of Unemployment' in S. Allen, A. Waton, F. Purcell and S. Wood (eds) *The Experience of Unemployment* (Basingstoke), pp. 134–49.

McKenna, F. (1980) *The Railwaymen* (London).

McKibbin, R. (1998) *Classes and Cultures: England, 1918–1951* (Oxford).

McKinlay, A. (1991) *Making Ships, Making Men* (Clydebank).

McLaughlin, E. (ed.) (1992) *Understanding Unemployment* (London).

Melling, J. (2003) 'The Risks of Working and the Risks of Not Working: Trade Unions, Employers and Responses to the Risk of Occupational Illness in British Industry, c1890–1940s', *ESRC Centre for Analysis of Risk and Regulation Discussion Paper 12*, pp. 14–34.

Melling, J. and Booth, A. (eds) (2008) *Managing the Modern Workplace: Productivity, Politics and Workplace Culture in Postwar Britain* (Aldershot).

Mitchell, B. R. (1998) *International Historical Statistics: Europe, 1750–1993*, (4th ed.).

Modood, T., Berthoud, R., Lakey, J., Nazroo, J., Smith, P., Virdee, S. and Beishon, S. (1997) *Ethnic Minorities in Britain: Diversity and Disadvantage* (London).

Modood, T. (1997) 'Employment' in T. Modood, R. Berthoud, J. Lakey, J. Nazroo, P. Smith, S. Virdee and S. Beishon (eds) (1997) *Ethnic Minorities in Britain: Diversity and Disadvantage* (London).

Moffat, A. (1965) *My Life with the Miners* (London).

Morris, A. and Butler, A. (1972) *No Feet to Drag: Report on the Disabled* (London).

Morrison, S. (2005) 'The Factory Inspectorate and the Silica Dust Problem in UK Foundries, 1930–1970', *Scottish Labour History*, 40, pp. 31–49.

Morrison, S. (2010) *The Silicosis Experience in Scotland* (Saarbrucken).

Mort, F. (1999) 'Fathers and Sons in Postwar Britain', *Journal of British Studies*, 38(3), July, pp. 353–84.

Mukherjee, S. (2010) *Surviving Bhopal* (New York).

Muldowney, M. S. (2007) *The Second World War and Irish Women: An Oral History* (Dublin).

Mullen, K. (1993) *A Healthy Balance: Glaswegian Men Talk about Health, Tobacco and Alcohol* (Aldershot).

Mulhern, M. A., Beech, J. and Thompson, E. (eds) (2008) *The Working Life of the Scots: A Compendium of Scottish Ethnology, vol 7* (Edinburgh).

Munro, H. (1961) *The Clydesiders* (Edinburgh).

Murphy, M. (2006) *Sick Building Syndrome and the Problem of Uncertainty*, Durham (N Carolina).

Myrdal, A. and Klein, V. (1956) *Women's Two Roles* (London).

National Institute of Industrial Psychology (1971) *200 Accidents A Shop Floor Study of their Causes* (London).

Navarro, V. and Berman, D. (eds) (1983) *Health and Work Under Capitalism: An International Perspective*, Farmington (New York).

Newby, H. (1977) *The Deferential Worker* (London).

Newell, A. (2007) 'Structural Change' in N. Crafts, I. Gazeley and A. Newall (eds) *Work and Pay in Twentieth Century Britain* (Oxford), pp. 35–54.

Nichols, T. (1975) 'The Sociology of Accidents and the Social Production of Industrial Injury' in G. Esland, G. Salaman and M.-A. Speakman (eds) *People and Work* (Milton Keynes), pp. 217–29.

Nichols, T. (1997) *The Sociology of Industrial Injury* (London).

Nichols, T. (1999) 'Death and Injury at Work: A Sociological Approach' in N. Daykin and L. Doyal (eds) *Health and Work: Critical Perspectives* (Basingstoke).

Nichols, T. and Beynon, H. (1977) *Living with Capitalism: Class Relations and the Modern Factory* (Henley on Thames).

Nichols, T. and Beynon, H. (1981) 'Black Worker, White Foreman' in P. Braham, E. Rhodes and M. Pearn (eds) *Discrimination and Disadvantage in Employment: The Experience of Black Workers* (London), pp. 155–62.

Noon, M. and Blyton, P. (2002) *The Realities of Work* (Basingstoke).

Oakley, A. (1974) *Housewife* (London).

Oakley, C.A. (1975) *Men at Work* (London).

Obelkevich, J. and Catterall, P. (eds) (1994) *Understanding Post-War British Society* (London).

Ohri, S. and Faruqi, S. (1988) 'Racism, Employment and Unemployment' in A. Bhat, R. Carr-Hill and S. Ohri (eds) *Britain's Black Population: A New Perspective* (Aldershot), pp. 61–102.

Oliver, M. (1990) *The Politics of Disablement* (Basingstoke).

Osnowitz, D. (2005) 'Managing Time in Domestic Space: Home-Based Contractors and Household Work', *Gender and Society*, 19(1), February, pp. 83–103.

Packman, R. (1968) *A Guide to Industrial Safety and Health* (London).

Pagnamenta, P. and Overy, R. (1984) *All our Working Lives* (London).

Pahl, R. (1995) *After Success* (Cambridge).

Parker, S. (1982) *Work and Retirement* (London).

Patterson, S. (1963) *Dark Strangers: A Study of West Indians in London* (Harmondsworth).

Pattinson, J. (2007) *Behind Enemy Lines: Gender Passing and the Special Operations Executive in the Second World War* (Manchester).

Payne, G. (ed.) (2000) *Social Divisions* (Basingstoke).

Payne, J. and Payne, C. (1993) 'Unemployment and Peripheral Work', *Work, Employment and Society*, 7(4), December, pp. 513–34.

Penn, R. (1982) 'Skilled Manual Workers and the Labour Process, 1856–1964' in S. Wood (ed.) *The Degradation of Work?* (London).

Penn, R. (1985) *Skilled Manual Workers in the Class Structure* (London).

Perchard, A. (2005) 'The Mine Management Professions and the Dust Problem in the Scottish Coal Mining Industry, c1930–1966', *Scottish Labour History*, 40, pp. 87–109.

Perchard, A. (2007a) *The Mine Management Professions in the Twentieth Century Scottish Coal Mining Industry* (Lampeter).

Perchard, A. (2007b) 'Sculpting the "Garden of Eden": Patronage, Community and the British Aluminium Company in the Scottish Highlands, 1895–1982', *Scottish Labour History*, 42, pp. 49–69.

Perchard, A. (2012) *Aluminiumville* (Lancaster).

Perchard, A. and Phillips, J. (2011) 'Transgressing the Moral Economy: Wheelerism and Management of the Nationalised Coal Industry in Scotland', *Contemporary British History*, pp. 1–19.

Perks, R. and Thomson, A. (eds) (2006) *The Oral History Reader*, second edition (London).

Pettitt, B. (ed.) (1998) *Children and Work in the UK* (London).

Phillips, J. (2005) 'Class and Industrial Relations in Britain: The "Long" Mid-Century and the Case of Port Transport, c1920–1970', *Twentieth Century British History*, 16(1), pp. 52–73.

Phillips, J. (2007) 'Industrial Relations, Historical Contingencies and Political Economy: Britain in the 1960s and 1970s', *Labour History Review*, 3(72), December, pp. 215–34.

Phillips, J. (2009) 'Workplace Conflict and the Origins of the 1984–85 Miners' Strike in Scotland', *Twentieth Century British History*, 20, pp. 152–72.

Phillips, J. (2011) 'Material and Moral Resources: the 1984–5 Miners' Strike in Scotland', *Economic History Review*, 65(1), pp. 256–76.

Phillips, S., Hallett, C. and Abendstern, M. (2007) ' "If we Depart From These Conditions...". Trade Union Reactions to European Immigrant Workers in the Textile Industry, c1946–1952', *Labour History Review*, 72(2), August, pp. 135–54.

Phillipson, C. (1998) *Reconstructing Old Age* (London).

Phizacklea, A. (1988) 'Gender, Racism and Occupational Segregation' in S. Walby (ed.) *Gender Segregation at Work* (Milton Keynes).

Phizacklea, A. and Miles, R. (1980) *Labour and Racism* (London).

Phizacklea, A. and Wolkowitz, C. (1995) *Homeworking Women: Gender, Racism and Class at Work* (London).

Pilgrim Trust (1938) *Men Without Work* (Cambridge).

Platt, S. (1986) 'Recent Trends in Parasuicide ("Attempted Suicide") and Unemployment Amongst Men in Edinburgh' in S. Allen, A. Waton, F. Purcell and S. Wood (eds) *The Experience of Unemployment* (Basingstoke), pp. 150–67.

Pollock, G. (1997) 'Uncertain Futures: Young People in and out of Employment since 1940', *Work, Employment and Society*, 11(4), pp. 615–38.

Pollert, A. (1981) *Girls, Wives, Factory Lives* (London).

Porcellato, L., Carmichael, F., Hulme, C., Ingram, B. and Prashar, A. (2010), 'Giving Older Workers a Voice: Constraints on the Employment of Older people in the North West of England', *Work, Employment and Society*, 24 (1), pp. 85–103.

Portelli, A. (1991) *The Death of Luigi Trastulli and Other Stories: Form and Meaning in Oral History* (New York).

Portelli, A. (2011) *They Say in Harlan County: An Oral History* (New York).

Price, R. (1986) *Labour in British Society* (London).

Pringle, R. (1988) *Secretaries Talk: Sexuality, Power and Work* (London).

Rahikainen, M. (2004) *Centuries of Child Labour: European Experiences from the Seventeenth to the Twentieth Century* (Aldershot).

Ramdin, R. (1987) *The Making of the Black Working Class in (Britain)*.

Reich, R. B. (1992) *The Work of Nations* (New York).

Reid, A. (2004) *United We Stand: A History of Britain's Trade Unions* (London).

Reid, I. (1989) *Social Class Differences in Britain* (Glasgow).

Reilly, E. (2010) *Civilians into Soldiers: The British Male Military Body in the Second World War*, PhD thesis, University of Strathclyde.

Riach, K. and Lorretto, W. (2009) 'Identity Work and the "Unemployed" Worker: Age, Disability and the Lived Experience of the Older Unemployed', *Work, Employment and Society*, 23(1), pp. 102–19.

Richmond, A.H. (1954) *Colour Prejudice in Britain: A Study of West Indian Workers in Liverpool, 1941–1951* (London).

Robb, L. (forthcoming, 2013) ' "Fighting In Their Ways"? The Working Man in British Culture, 1939–1945', PhD thesis, University of Strathclyde.

Roberts, E. (1995) *Women and Families: An Oral History, 1940–1970* (Oxford).

Robinson, A. M. and Smallman, C. (2006) 'The Contemporary British Workplace: A Safer and Healthier Place?', *Work, Employment and Society*, 20, pp. 87–107.

Roper, M. (1994) *Masculinity and the British Organisation Man Since 1945* Oxford).

Roper, M. and Tosh, J. (eds) (1991) *Manful Assertions* (London).

Rose, M. (1988) 'Attachment to Work and Social Values' in D. Gallie (ed.), *Employment in Britain* (Oxford), pp. 128–56.

Rose, S. O. (2004) *Which People's War? National Identity and Citizenship in Wartime Britain 1939–1945* (Oxford).

Rowbotham, S. and Beynon, H. (2001) *Looking at Class: Film, Television and the Working Class in Britain* (London).

Runnymede Trust and the Radical Statistics Group (1980) *Britain's Black Population* (London).

Runnymede Trust and the Radical Statistics Group (1981) 'A Profile of Black Employment' in P. Braham, E. Rhodes and M. Pearn (eds) *Discrimination and Disadvantage in Employment: The Experience of Black Workers* (London), pp. 96–108.

Russell, A. (1998) *The Harmonisation of Employment Conditions in Britain* (Basingstoke).

Russell, H. (1998) 'The Rewards of Work' in R. Jowell et al. (eds) *British – and European – Social Attitudes: the 15th Report. How Britain Differs* (Aldershot), pp. 77–97.

Russell, H. (1999) 'Friends in Low Places: Gender, Unemployment and Sociability', *Work, Employment and Society*, 13(2), June, pp. 205–24.

Russell, H. and Barbieri, P. (2000), 'Gender and the Experience of Unemployment', in D. Gallie and S. Paugam (eds), *Welfare Regimes and the Experience of Unemployment in Europe* (Oxford), pp. 307–333.

Sabo, D. and Gordon, D. F. (1995) *Men's Health and Illness: Gender, Power and the Body* (London).

Sanderson, M. (2007) 'Education and the Labour Market' in N. Crafts, I. Gazeley and A. Newall (eds) *Work and Pay in Twentieth Century Britain* (Oxford), pp. 264–300.

Sapey, B. (2000), 'Disablement in the Informational Age', *Disability and Society*, 15 (4), pp. 619–36.

Savage, M. (1999) 'Sociology, Class and Male Manual Work Cultures' in J. McIllroy, N. Fishman and A. Campbell (eds) *British Trade Unionism and Industrial Politics. Volume 2: The High Tide of Trade Unionism, 1964–79* (Aldershot), pp. 23–42.

Sayce, S., Ackers, P. and Greene, A-M. (2007) 'Work Restructuring and Changing Craft Identity: The Tale of the Disaffected Weavers (or What Happens When the Rug is Pulled From Under Your Feet)', *Work, Employment and Society*, 21, pp. 85–101.

Scambler, G. and Scambler, A. (1999) 'Health and Work in the Sex Industry' in N. Daykin and L. Doyal (eds) *Health and Work: Critical Perspectives* (Basingstoke), pp. 71–85.

Schwartz, H. S. (1995) 'Masculinity and the Meaning of Work: A Response to Manichean Feminism', *Administration and Society*, 27, August.

Scott, J., Dex, S. and Joshi, H. (2008) *Women and Employment: Changing Lives and New Challenges* (Cheltenham).

Scott, J., Braun, M. and Alwin, D. (1998) 'Partner, Parent, Worker: Family and Gender Roles' in R. Jowell et al. (eds), *British and European Social Attitudes: The 15th Report. How Britain Differs* (Aldershot), pp. 19–38.

Seabrook, J. (1982) *Unemployment* (London).

Seabrook, J., 'Surviving' in Fineman, S. (ed.) (1987) *Unemployment: Personal and Social Consequences* (London), pp. 7–21.

Searle, K. (2010) *From Farms to Foundries: An Arab Community in Industrial Britain* (Bern).

Seaton, A., Agius, R., McCloy, E. and D'Auria, D. (1994) *Practical Occupational Medicine* (London).

Segal, L. (1997) *Slow Motion: Changing Masculinities, Changing Men* (London).

Sennett, R. (1999) *The Corrosion of Character: The Personal Consequences of Work in the New Capitalism* (New York).

Shaw, M., Dorling, D., Gordon, D. and Smith, G. D. (1999) *The Widening Gap: Health Inequalities and Policy in Britain* (Bristol).

Sherwood, M. (1985) ' "It is not a Case of Numbers": A Case Study of Institutional Racism in Britain, 1941–3' in K. Lunn (ed.) *Race and Labour in Twentieth-Century Britain*, special edition, *Immigrants and Minorities*, 4(2), July, pp. 116–41.

Sherwood, M. (2003) 'Lascars in Glasgow and the West of Scotland during World War Two', *Scottish Labour History*, 38, pp. 37–50.

Shrivastava, P. (1992) *Bhopal, Anatomy of a Crisis* (London).

Sillitoe, A. (1958) *Saturday Night, Sunday Morning* (London).

Siltanen, J. M. (1994) *Locating Gender: Occupational Segregation, Wages and Domestic Responsibilities* (London).

Simpson, R. (2004) 'Masculinity at Work: The Experience of Men in Female Dominated Occupations', *Work, Employment and Society*, 18, pp. 349–68.

Sinfield, A. (1970) 'Poor and Out of Work in Shields' in P. Townsend (ed.) *The Concept of Poverty* (London).

Sinfield, A. (1981) *What Unemployment Means* (Oxford).

Sly, F. (1994) 'Ethnic Groups and the Labour Market', *Employment Gazette*, May, pp. 147–59.

Smith, D. (1981) 'Discrimination Against Applicants for White Collar Jobs' in P. Braham, E. Rhodes and M. Pearn (eds) *Discrimination and Disadvantage in Employment: The Experience of Black Workers* (London), pp. 177–84.

Smith, D. J. (1974) *Racial Disadvantage in Employment* (London).

Smith, R. (1987) *Unemployment and Health* (Oxford).

Snashall, D. (1999) *ABC of Work-Related Disorders* (London).

Stanley, K. and Regan, S. (2003), *The Missing Million: Supporting Disabled People into Work* (London).

Stephenson, J. and Brown, C. (1990) 'The View from the Workplace' in E. Gordon and E. Breitenbach (eds) *The World is Ill-Divided* (Edinburgh).

Strangleman, T. (2001) 'Networks, Place and Identities in Post- Industrial Mining Communities', *International Journal of Urban and Regional Research*, 25(2), June, pp. 253–67.

Strangleman,T. (2002) 'Nostalgia for Nationalisation – the Politics of Privatisation' *Sociological Research Online*, 7(1). <http://www.socresonline.org. uk/7/1/strangleman.html>

Strangleman, T. (2004) *Work Identity at the End of the Line? Privatisation and Culture Change in the UK Rail Industry* (Basingstoke).

Strangleman, T. (2007) 'The Nostalgia for Permanence at Work: The End of Work and its Commentators', *Sociological Review*, 55(1), pp. 81–103.

Strangleman, T. and Warren, T. (2008) *Work and Society: Sociological Approaches, Themes and Methods* (Abingdon).

Strangleman, T. (2011) 'Writing Workers: Re-reading Workplace Autobiography', *Scottish Labour History*, 46, pp. 26–37.

Stanley, K. and Regan, S. (2003) *The Missing Million: Supporting Disabled People into Work* (London).

Summerfield, P. (1998) *Reconstructing Women's Wartime Lives*, (Manchester).

Summerfield, P. and Peniston-Bird, C. (2007) *Contesting Home Defence: Men, Women and the Home Guard in the Second World War* (Manchester).

Sykes, A. J. M. (1973) 'Attitudes of Navvies' in D. Weir (ed.) *Men and Work in Modern Britain* (London).

Taylor, P., Mulvey, G., Hyman, J. and Bain, P. (2002) 'Work Organisation, Control and the Experience of Work in Call Centres', *Work, Employment and Society*, 16(1), March, pp. 133–50.

Taylor, P., Baldry, C., Bain, P. and Ellis, V. (2003) 'A Unique Working Environment': Health, Sickness and Absence Management in UK Call Centres', *Work, Employment and Society*, 17(3), September, pp. 435–58.

Taylor, P. and Connelly, L. (2009) 'Before the Disaster: Health, Safety and Working Conditions at a Plastics Factory', *Work, Employment and Society*, 23(1), March, pp. 160–8.

Taylor, R. (1978) *The Fifth Estate: Britain's Unions in the Modern World* (London).

Taylor, R. and Steele, T. (2011) *British Labour and Higher Education, 1945–2000* (London).

Terkel, S. (1972) *Working* (New York).

Thane, P. (1994) 'Women since 1945' in P. Johnston (ed.) *Twentieth Century Britain* (London), pp. 392–410.

Thane, P. (2000) *Old Age in English History* (Oxford).

Thomas, K. (ed.) (1999) *The Oxford Book of Work* (Oxford).

Thompson, P. (1983) *The Nature of Work* (Basingstoke).

Thompson, P. (2000) *The Voice of the Past*, third edition (Oxford).

Thomson, A. (1994) *Anzac Memories: Living with the Legend* (Oxford).

Thomson, A. (2007) 'The Four Paradigm Transformations in Oral History', *Oral History Review*, 34(1).

Thornton, P. (2005) 'Disabled People, Employment and Social Justice', *Social Policy & Society*, 4(1), pp. 65–73.

Tiratsoo, N. (1999) 'Cinderellas at the Ball: Production Managers in British Manufacturing, 1945–80', *Contemporary British History*, 13(3). Special Issue: *Management in Post War Britain*, pp. 105–120.

Topliss, E. (1979) *Provision for the Disabled* (Oxford).

Townsend, P. (1979) *Poverty in the United Kingdom* (Harmondsworth).

Tucker, R. C. (ed.) (1978) *The Marx–Engels Reader* (2nd ed.) (London).

Tunstall, J. (1973) 'Fishermen on the Beach' in D. Weir (ed.) *Men and Work in Modern Britain* (London).

Turner, A. (2010) 'From Institutions to Community Care? Learning Disability in Glasgow from c1945', PhD thesis, University of Strathclyde.

Tweedale, G. (2000) *Magic Mineral to Killer Dust: Turner and Newall and the Asbestos Hazard* (Oxford).

Tweedale, G. and Hansen, P. (1998) 'Protecting the Workers: The Medical Board and the Asbestos Industry, 1930s-1960s', *Medical History*, 42, pp. 439–57.

Virdee, P. (2006) *Coming to Coventry* (Coventry).

Wainwright, D. and Calnan, M. (2002) *Work Stress: The Making of a Modern Epidemic* (Buckingham).

Walby, S. (1986) *Patriarchy at Work* (Cambridge).

Walby, S. (ed.) (1988) *Gender Segregation at Work* (Milton Keynes).

Walby, S. (1997) *Gender Transformations* (London).

Walker, A. (1982) *Unqualified and Underemployed: Handicapped Young People and the Labour Market* (London).

Walker, D. (2005) '"Working in it, Through it, and Among it all Day": Chrome Dust at J & J White of Rutherglen, 1893–1967', *Scottish Labour History*, 40, pp. 50–69.

Walker, D. (2007) *Occupational Health and Safety in the British Chemical Industry, 1914–1974*, PhD thesis, University of Strathclyde. Downloadable at http://strathprints.strath.ac.uk/6429/.

Walker, D. (2011) '"Danger was Something you were Brought up with": Workers' Narratives on Occupational Health and Safety in the Workplace', *Scottish Labour History*, 46, pp. 54–70.

Wallman, S. (ed.) (1979) *Ethnicity at Work* (London).

Warr, P. and Wall, T. (1975) *Work and Well-Being* (Harmondsworth).

Watson, W. G. D. (2008) 'Printing in Scotland' in M. A. Mulhern, J. Beech and E. Thompson (eds) *The Working Life of the Scots: A Compendium of Scottish Ethnology, vol. 7* (Edinburgh), pp. 402–18.

Watson, J. (2000) *Male Bodies: Health, Culture and Identity* (Buckingham).

Watson, N. and Woods, B. (2005) 'No Wheelchairs Beyond this Point: A Historical Examination of Wheelchair Access in the Twentieth Century in Britain and America', *Social Policy and Society*, 4(1), pp. 97–105.

Watson, T. J. (1980) *Sociology, Work and Industry* (London).

Watterson, A. (1999) 'Why we Still have "Old" Epidemics and "Endemics" in Occupational Health: Policy and Practice Failures and Some Possible Solutions' in N. Daykin and L. Doyal (eds) *Health and Work: Critical Perspectives* (Basingstoke), pp. 107–26.

Webster, W. (2000) 'Defining Boundaries: European Volunteer Worker Women in Britain and Narratives of Community', *Women's History Review*, 9(2), pp. 257–76.

Wedderburn, D. (1964) *White Collar Redundancy: A Case Study* (London).

Wedderburn, D. (1965) *Redundancy and the Railwaymen* (London).

Wedderburn, D. (1973) 'Working and Not Working' in D. Weir (ed.) *Men and Work in Modern Britain* (London).

Wedderburn, D. and Crompton, R. (1972) *Workers' Attitudes and Technology* (London).

Weindling, P. (ed.) (1985) *The Social History of Occupational Health* (Beckenham).

Weir, D. (ed.) (1973) *Men and Work in Modern Britain* (London).

Whiteside, N. (1996) 'Industrial Relations and Social Welfare, 1945–1979' in C. J. Wrigley (ed.) *A History of British Industrial Relations, 1939–1979*, (Brighton), pp. 120–41.

Wight, D. (1993) *Workers not Wasters: Masculine Respectability, Consumption and Employment in Central Scotland* (Edinburgh).

Williams, J. L. (1960) *Accidents and Ill-Health at Work* (London).

Willis, P. (1977) *Learning to Labour: How Working Class Kids get Working Class Jobs* (Aldershot).

Willis, P. (1979) 'Shop Floor Culture, Masculinity and the Wage Form' in J. Clarke, C. Critcher and R. Johnson (eds) *Working Class Culture* (London), pp. 185–98.

Wilton, T. (1999) 'Selling Sex, Giving Care: The Construction of AIDS as a Workplace Hazard' in N. Daykin and L. Doyal (eds) *Health and Work: Critical Perspectives* (Basingstoke), pp. 180–97.

Wilson, D. F. (1972) *Dockers* (London).

Wolkowitz, C. (2006) *Bodies at Work* (London).

Wolmar, C. (2001) *Broken Rails: How Privatisation Wrecked Britain's Railways* (London).

Wood, S. (ed.) (1982) *The Degradation of Work?: Skill, Deskilling and the Labour Process* (London).

Woolfson, C. and Beck, M. (2005) *Corporate Social Responsibility Failures in the Oil Industry*, Amityville (New York).

Wrench, J. (1987) 'Unequal Comrades: Trade Unions, Equal Opportunity and Racism' in R. Jenkins and J. Solomos *Racism and Equal Opportunity Policies in the 1980s* (Cambridge), pp. 160–86.

Wright, P. (1968) *The Coloured Worker in British Industry*, (London).

Wrigley, C. J. (ed.) (1996) *A History of British Industrial Relations, 1939–1979* (Brighton).

Wrigley, C. (2007) 'Industrial Relations' in N. Crafts, I. Gazeley and A. Newall (eds) *Work and Pay in Twentieth Century* Britain (Oxford), pp. 203–24.

Yankelovitch, D., Zetterberg, H., Strumpel, B. and Shanks, M. (1985) *A World at Work* (New York).

Yeo, E. (2004) 'Taking it Like a Man' in E. Yeo (ed.) *Working Class Masculinities in Britain, 1850 to the Present,* special edition, *Labour History Review*, 69(2), August, pp. 129–34.

Young, H. (2007) 'Hard Man, New Man: Re/composing Masculinities in Glasgow, c1950–2000', *Oral History*, 35(1), pp. 71–81.

Young, H. (2010) 'Being a Man: Everyday Masculinities' in L. Abrams and C. G. Brown (eds) *A History of Everyday Life in Twentieth Century Scotland* (Edinburgh), pp. 131–52.

Young, K. (1992) 'Class, Race and Opportunity' in R. Jowell et al. (eds) *British Social Attitudes: The 9th Report* (Aldershot), pp. 175–94.

Young, M. and Wilmott, P. (1973) *The Symmetrical Family: A Study of Work and Leisure in the London Region* (London).

Zeitlin, J. (2004) 'Americanising British Engineering? Strategic Debate, Selective Adaptation and Hybrid Innovation in Post-War Reconstruction, 1945–1960' in J. Zeitlin and G. Herrigel (eds) *Americanization and Its Limits: Reworking US Technology and Management in Post-war Europe and Japan* (Oxford), pp. 123–52.

Zimbalist, A. (ed.) (1979) *Case Studies on the Labor Process* (New York).

Zweig, F. (1948), *Men in the Pits* (London) Victor Gollancz.

Zweig, F. (1951), *Productivity and Trade Unions* (Oxford) Basil Blackwell.

Zweig, F. (1952a) *The British Worker* (Harmondsworth).

Zweig, F. (1952b) *Women's Life and Labour* (London).

Zweig, F. (1961) *The Worker in an Affluent Society: Family Life and Industry* (New York).

Index

Notes: **bold type** = extended discussion or term emphasized in text;
n = footnote; t = table.

309